LEGAL SOURCES AND BIBLIOGRAPHY OF EASTERN EUROPE
YUGOSLAVIA

LEGAL SOURCES
AND
BIBLIOGRAPHY OF
YUGOSLAVIA

BY FRAN GJUPANOVICH AND ALEXANDER ADAMOVITCH

VLADIMIR GSOVSKI, GENERAL EDITOR

Published for FREE EUROPE COMMITTEE, *Inc.*

by FREDERICK A. PRAEGER, *New York*

LEGAL SOURCES AND BIBLIOGRAPHY OF YUGOSLAVIA is a research study of the Mid-European Law Project at the Library of Congress. Preparation and publication was made possible by Free Europe Committee, Inc.

Number 21 of
Praeger Publications in Russian History and World Communism

196735

PREFACE

The present volume is one of the series of bibliographies prepared by the Mid-European Law Project and published by the Mid-European Studies Center. The Mid-European Law Project, part of the Law Library of the Library of Congress, was staffed by exiled lawyers from countries which are presently under communist domination. The Project was under the administration of Dr. L. Quincy Mumford, Librarian of Congress, and Dr. Lawrence Keitt, Law Librarian of Congress, and was under the direction of Dr. Vladimir Gsovski, Chief of the European Law Division. The Project was supported by funds supplied by the Free Europe Committee, Inc. and was terminated effective June 30, 1960.

The preparation and publication of studies of legal sources and bibliographies of this nature by the Project were encouraged for several reasons. There are no bibliographical tools in English for the study of the law of these countries. In a totalitarian state, laws and decrees by the government are potent channels of society and a mirror of life.

With the establishment of communist governments in Eastern and Central Europe, there was initiated a change of laws which was largely inspired by the Soviet legal system and resulted in the adoption of new codes and statutes. New legal collections, new legal writings, and new periodicals appeared.

The first aim of the series is to control this material bibliographically.

Moreover, the legal history of those countries is not widely known. In order to provide an essential tool for the study of the laws, both old and new, these bibliographical studies were prepared. A description of the main legal sources and their publication introduces the legal treatises, commentaries and other forms of legal writings. The bibliographical listing is preceded by an introduction giving the legal sources of each country in brief, the roots of the national legislative system, and the transition to the present system under the communist government.

The bibliography lists not only the material in the official languages of Yugoslavia but also the books and articles in English, French, German and Italian.

The studies are concluded by a list of the most important laws and decrees in force on January 1, 1962, which concern the major fields of law. They are arranged by subject.

Volumes on the Baltic States (Estonia, Latvia, Lithuania), Bulgaria, Czechoslovakia, Hungary, Poland and Romania were prepared in the same series.

FOREWORD

The present work was undertaken with the aim of offering a selective bibliographical tool for studying the present and past laws of Yugoslavia. It covers the works of legal writers as well as the primary legal sources, but it does not include Yugoslav translations of law books of other countries, nor does it cover original Yugoslav contributions on subject matter not directly connected with Yugoslav laws and decrees.

Six different jurisdictions formed the state of Yugoslavia. Their legal heritage made itself strongly felt for a considerable time and presented a special problem in the organization of the material included. A main grouping by topics or types of material was selected, and the separate subsections reserved for local material under these topics which warranted such subdivision. Thus, the general scheme of the book is the following:

Chapter 1 is in the nature of an introduction describing the formation of Yugoslavia, and outlines the stages of its legal development up to the present.

Chapters 2 to 7 list the publications containing the official sources of law, such as law journals, official gazettes (Chapter 2), departmental bulletins (Chapter 3), privately printed collections of laws (Chapter 4), parliamentary records (Chapter 5), court decisions (Chapter 6), and international treaties (Chapter 7).

Chapter 8 lists legal periodicals, while Chapter 9 surveys legal bibliographies.

Chapter 10 contains the main body of the bibliography. It lists books and articles in Serbo-Croatian, Slovenian and Macedonian. In the distribution of material by topics a compromise between systematic and alphabetic arrangements was reached. In Section A the broad traditional subjects, such as constitutional law, civil law, etc., are covered in a systematic arrangement. In Section B specific legal topics are arranged in alphabetical order. These topics are indicated in English but their Yugoslav equivalents are given in the subject index. Within the topics the alphabetical order of entries is not always followed. Where warranted by the material, the entries listing the texts of laws and decrees are placed before the treaties, which follow in alphabetical order. In some instances, material covering the same subject matter or a local jurisdiction is listed together.

Chapter 11 lists the works in other than the vernacular languages, Section A being reserved to publications in English. This material is distributed according to subject, the text of the laws always being listed before the other material. Sections B, C and D list the publications in French, German and Italian, each in alphabetical order.

The book is concluded by an index of individual laws of primary importance (Chapter 12). Sections A and B list the uniform laws enacted in Yugoslavia before World War II and Section C lists the laws and decrees in force on January 1, 1962, under 39 topics arranged alphabetically.

The present work does not follow the new structure of legal topics adopted by the Yugoslav socialist legal doctrine. The traditional pattern was preferred for this bibliography since it renders the material more easily accessible to any reader accustomed to the organizational structure of the legal systems of the West for whom it is primarily prepared.

All the bibliographical entries are made in the language of the publication. The titles in Cyrillic are transliterated into the Latin alphabet. Titles in the vernacular languages are followed in parentheses by an English translation seeking to convey the gist of the publication rather than to be a literal translation of the title. All bibliographical entries are numbered consecutively throughout the work, and references, if not otherwise indicated, are made to these numbers.

When the present work was begun there was no comprehensive legal bibliography of Yugoslavia in any language. The legal bibliography in French by the Yugoslav Professor Borislav T. Blagojević appeared in 1959 and was received when the work was practically finished but still in time to collate the information before sending the manuscript to the printer.

In contrast to Professor Blagojević's bibliography of legal writings, the present work covers also the publications containing primary legal sources for all six jurisdictions of which Yugoslavia was originally composed. It also contains an index of Yugoslav laws and decrees as well as an author, title, and subject index.

In the style of bibliographical entries, the rules of the Library of Congress were followed as stated in *Bibliographical Procedure and Style, a Manual for Bibliographers in the Library of Congress* (Washington, 1954), with departures warranted by the nature of the material.

Symbol (DLC) means that the publication is in the Library of Congress.

Acknowledgment is hereby expressed to Messrs. Božidar Maksimovich and Kiril Jaszenko for the preparatory work done on the bibliography. A special contribution was made by Mr. Maksimovich who drew on his experience and memory in the preparation of some entries. Further acknowledgment is expressed to Dr. Ivan Sipkov for the efficient assistance in editing the publication, Mr. Edmund Jann for his critical reading of the manuscript and valuable suggestions, and Mrs. Valentine Gianturco for her painstaking efforts in preparing the manuscript.

Dr. Fran Gjupanovich
Dr. Alexander Adamovitch

Vladimir Gsovski, Ph. D., Editor

CONTENTS

ABBREVIATIONS

AVNOJ   Antifašističko veće narodnog oslobodjenja Jugoslavije (Anti-Fascist Liberation Council of Yugoslavia)

DFJ   Demokratka Federativna Jugoslavija (Democratic Federal Yugoslavia)

DFY   Democratic Federative Yugoslavia

FLRJ   Federativna Ljudska Republika Jugoslavija (Federal People's Republic of Yugoslavia)

FNRJ   Federativna Narodna Republika Jugoslavija (Federal People's Republic of Yugoslavia)

FPRY   Federal People's Republic of Yugoslavia

LRS   Ljudska Republika Slovenija (People's Republic of Slovenia)

NR   Narodna Republika (People's Republic)

NRH   Narodna Republika Hrvatska (People's Republic of Croatia)

NRM   Nardona Republika Makedonija (People's Republic of Macedonia)

NRS   Narodna Republika Srbija (People's Republic of Serbia)

PRC   People's Republic of Croatia

PRM   People's Republic of Macedonia

PRS   People's Republic of Slovenia

PRS   People's Republic of Serbia

PTT   Poštanski, telegrafski i telefonski ([Bulletin for] Postal, Telegraph and Telephone Services)

SCS   Serbs, Croats and Slovenes

SHS   Srbi Hrvati i Slovenci (Serbs, Croats and Slovenes)

Sl.L.   *Službeni list Demokratske Federativne Jugoslavije* (Official Law Gazette). Continued as *Službeni list Federativne Narodne Republike Jugoslavije.*

Sl.N.   *Službene Novine Kraljevine Jugoslavije* (Official Law Gazette)

LEGAL SOURCES AND BIBLIOGRAPHY OF EASTERN EUROPE

YUGOSLAVIA

1

THE LEGAL SYSTEM IN YUGOSLAVIA
BEFORE AND AFTER WORLD WAR II

A   The Formation of Yugoslavia

Yugoslavia, the Kingdom of the Serbs, Croats, and Slovenes as it was called until 1929, came into being after World War I on December 1, 1918, through the union of the three branches of the South Slavs. This Kingdom was formed from the territories of the independent and sovereign Kingdoms of Serbia (population roughly four million); Montenegro (population 200,000); and several provinces of the Austro-Hungarian Empire: Slovenia (population one million), the Voyvodina (population 1.3 million), Bosnia and Herzegovina (population 1.9 million), Dalmatia (population 620,000), and Croatia-Slavonia (population 2.7 million) with two adjacent southwestern Hungarian counties.

The Serbs in Hungary did not enjoy national autonomy or the official use of their native language. Neither was there an organized Slovenian territory in Austria. Slovenia comprised the former province of Carniola with parts of Carinthia and Styria; the Voyvodina, parts of the former Hungarian provinces of *Bacs-Bodrogh* and *Torontal,* and shreds of the provinces of *Temes* and *Baranya.*

The former Ottoman provinces of Bosnia and Herzegovina were occupied by Austria-Hungary in 1878 and annexed in 1908. In 1910 Bosnia-Herzegovina was granted a provincial assembly and a local administration under the control of the joint Austro-Hungarian Ministry of Finance.

Dalmatia, assigned to Austria at the Peace of 1815, though nominally confirmed by the Croatian-Hungarian Compromise of 1868 as an integral part of the Kingdom of Croatia-Slavonia-Dalmatia, continued to be governed as an Austrian province. Croatia-Slavonia enjoyed a special status within the Hungarian Empire, with the official use of the Croatian language. It is described in greater detail *infra* p. 19.

Yugoslavia came into being by a series of acts which took place in November and December, 1918. On November 24, the National Council in Zagreb (capital of Croatia) proclaimed the formation of a new state uniting the Slovenes, Croats and Serbs within the Austro-Hungarian Empire with Serbia and Montenegro. The union of the Voyvodina and Montenegro with Serbia was proclaimed on November 25 and 26. Finally, the formation of the new state of Yugoslavia was announced on December 1, 1918, by a joint declaration of the representatives of the Zagreb National Council and Prince Alexander, Regent of Serbia. The union of the Serbs, Croats and Slovenes in a new state was proclaimed. The first government of the United Kingdom of the Serbs, Croats and Slovenes was formed on December 20, 1918, and a joint, provisional national assembly made up of eighty-four representatives for Serbia, sixty-two for Croatia, twelve for Dalmatia, thirty-two for Slovenia, forty-two for Bosnia-Herzegovina, twenty-four for South Serbia, and four for the Voyvodina, was convened on March 1, 1919.

B   Period of the Kingdom of the Serbs, Croats and Slovenes, 1918-1929

Since its inception in 1918 Yugoslavia has been essentially a country of written law and shared, with the exception of former Hungarian provinces, the system of codified statutes prevailing in continental Europe. In Yugoslavia, as in France, Germany, Italy and Spain, the major fields of law were based on enactments by the government called codes. Judicial decisions were not considered as being a law-creating source but served only for the interpretation of law. The exception was the former Hungarian provinces where there was no comprehensive civil code and civil law was governed by separate statutes, customary law and judicial precedent.

However, the codes in Yugoslavia were not uniform for the entire country. They were inherited from the countries from which Yugoslavia was made. Each component part of the country retained the law which had been in force prior to the formation of Yugoslavia, subject to repeal and amendment by the legislation of the new government. This principle was applied in Yugoslavia from the very beginning.

Six different jurisdictions and six different systems of civil and criminal law, substantive and procedural, as well as administrative law, existed in the Kingdom when it was created: Serbian law in what was formerly Serbia; Montenegrin law in what was formerly Montenegro; Hungarian law in the Voyvodina;[1] Austrian law, viz., the Civil Code *without* the last three amendments of 1914, 1915, and 1916, and local provincial law in Croatia and Slavonia; Austrian law, viz., the Civil Code *with* the 1914, 1915 and 1916 amendments in Slovenia and Dalmatia; and, finally, in Bosnia and Herzegovina, the Austrian Civil Code was not formally enacted but actually applied and combined with some laws enacted during the Turkish rule.

The following criminal codes were in force in the different

---

[1] The particular features of the Hungarian law are discussed in the Bibliography on Hungary. Hungarian law was also in force in two counties of Croatia, Čakovec and Prelog, and two counties of Slovenia, Donja Lendva and Morska Sobota.

jurisdictions: in Serbia, the Criminal Code for the Principality of Serbia of March 28, 1860; in Croatia and Slavonia, the Austrian Criminal Code of May 27, 1852; in Slovenia and Dalmatia, the same Criminal Code of May 27, 1852, with all supplementary laws which were in force in Austria; in the Voyvodina (Bačka, Banat, Baranja and Medjumurje), the Hungarian Criminal Code of 1878 and Code of Petty Offences of 1879; in Bosnia and Herzegovina, the Criminal Code of June 26, 1879; and in Montenegro, the Criminal Code for the Kingdom of Montenegro of February 23, 1906. The codes of criminal procedure were the following: the Serbian of 1865; the Croatian of 1875; the General Austrian of 1873; the Austrian for Bosnia and Herzegovina of 1891; the Hungarian of 1896; and the Montenegrin of 1910.

Accordingly, Austrian criminal law was in force in Croatia, Dalmatia and Slovenia and, with some trifling changes, also in Bosnia and Herzegovina. The Montenegrin criminal code was actually an exact copy of the Serbian criminal code which was based on the Prussian Criminal Code of 1851. The Hungarian criminal code, which was one of the most modern, in particular with regard to its amendment of 1908, was in effect in Voyvodina.

As soon as the government authorities of the Yugoslav state were organized, they started to work toward uniformity of the legal system. Some of the Serbian laws were extended to the remainder of the territory of Yugoslavia, by decrees with the force of law. They covered, however, a limited field.

The Constitution of June 28, 1921, *(Vidovdanski Ustav)* laid down the foundation of a constitutional and parliamentary central government and a local self-government. The Constitution created a Legislative Committee for the making of uniform laws for the country. With regard to the acts of the provisional government issued prior to the Constitution, it had full legislative authority but further unification of law required the approval of the National Assembly. Preparatory work on the uniform laws was soon under way, and the new laws were gradually enacted, superseding the old regional laws and the extended Serbian laws.

In brief, this period is characterized by the existence of six different jurisdictions, especially with respect to civil and criminal law; by the extension of some Serbian laws to the remainder of the territory of the Kingdom; and by the appearance of some uniform laws.

The most important laws extended to or enacted for all Yugoslavia during this period are listed *infra,* Chapter 12, A.

C   Period of the Kingdom of Yugoslavia, 1929-1941

On January 6, 1929, King Alexander suspended the 1921 Constitution and declared himself to be "the bearer of all the powers in the country" *(Sl. N.,* No. 9 of January 11, 1929, Sec. 2.) He emphasized, however, the temporary character of this assumption of power. Under the Constitution of September 3, 1931, which superseded the Act of 1929, the administration still was responsible only to the Monarch, but an elected National Assembly and a Senate composed partly of elected and partly of appointed members were introduced and, thereby, the way was paved for a return to parliamentary rule.

Thus began the period of the Kingdom of Yugoslavia, which lasted until the German invasion of 1941. During this period many uniform statutes were enacted, some of which were in preparation during the preceding period. By the end of this period (1941), practically all major fields of law were covered by nation-wide uniform laws. (For their list see *infra,* Chapter 12, B). Although no uniform laws were enacted to cover succession, domestic relations, real and personal property, torts, and the like, the draft of a civil code to cover these fields was prepared and was submitted for opinion to various institutions, law schools, and bar associations.

Unification of laws continued under the present regime which issued uniform laws for domestic relations and successions.

Another feature of the period was the substitution for the historical divisions of newly created administrative units, nine *banovinas,* named after rivers (Law of October 1, 1929, *Sl. L.,*

No. 233, October 5, 1929). However, a change in the powers of *banovinas* began to take place in August 1939, with regard to the former Croatian territory.

World War II, which began for Yugoslavia with the Axis' attack on April 6, 1941, halted any further progress in these directions.

D   Period of World War II, 1941-1945

After the German attack in April, 1941, Yugoslavia was divided up by the Axis Powers. The regime under which its individual parts were ruled was by no means uniform. The occupying powers agreed, however, on one point, that Yugoslavia as such had ceased to exist.

Some of its territories were directly incorporated by the Axis Powers into their own states. Germany annexed most of Slovenia and Italy took the southern part of Slovenia and the coastal territory with the Dalmatian Islands. Albania was assigned the territory of Kosovo, Debar and Struga, and Bulgaria received the rest of Yugoslavian Macedonia and a section of Eastern Serbia. Hungary reincorporated the territories of the former provinces of *Bacs-Bodrogh* and *Baranya,* two counties of Croatia and two of Slovenia. Montenegro was recreated under the Italian protectorate and Croatia, enlarged by Bosnia and Herzegovina, was proclaimed an independent state under the nominal government of Pavelich and his *Ustasha* movement. In reality it became an Italian protectorate under German economic and military control. Serbia had its own administration but was under the control of the German military authorities.

Thus, the legal continuity had been disrupted. Various parts of Yugoslavia, thus divided, had to live under laws and regulations controlled by occupying authorities.

To confuse the situation there were two resistance movements. One, that of General Mihailović, with his *četniks,* representing the Government-in-exile, and the other, that of Tito and his partisans. For the communist-led resistance under Tito there was established an Anti-Fascist Liberation Council of Yugoslavia (AVNOJ) which, on November 29, 1943, in Jajce (Bosnia), proclaimed itself the highest legislative and executive authority in Yugoslavia. The AVNOJ denied the authority of the government-in-exile.

E   The Present Yugoslav Political and Legal Order Since 1945

1   Origin

The present Yugoslav political, social and legal order originated by reason of several causes from the activities of the Anti-Fascist Council of National Liberation (AVNOJ).[2]

Prior to the adoption of the Constitution on January 31, 1946, the enacted laws had a provisional character. After the promulgation of the Constitution of 1946, all the laws previously enacted underwent reexamination (Sec. 136 of the Constitution); some of them were changed and others repealed. Thus the Constitution of January 31, 1946 opened a new phase in legislative activities. Still it is not the only source of the constitutional setup of Yugoslavia. In 1953 the Constitution was amended by the Constitutional Law which actually superseded the bulk of the Constitution of 1946. Thus, both of them simultaneously are the sources of constitutional law of Yugoslavia.

2   The Problem of the Continuity of Prewar Laws

On February 3, 1945, the Presidium of the Anti-Fascist Council of National Liberation of Yugoslavia (AVNOJ) had issued a decree dealing with the validity of the laws and regulations issued during the enemy occupation or prior to World War II

---

2 See K. Jaszenko and B. Maksimovich, "Yugoslavia," Chapter 12, in Gsovski and Grzybowski, editors, *Government, Law and Courts in the Soviet Union and Eastern Europe*, N.Y., 1959, 417 ff.

(*Sl. L.*, No. 4, 1945). On October 23, 1946, this decree was superseded by the Law of October 23, 1946 (*id.*, No. 86, 1946). Its provisions are by no means simple, and some of them are ambiguous. The law distinguishes several categories of laws which were enacted before the present regime came into power. Some of them, namely those enacted by the occupation authorities, were declared "non-existent" (Sec. 1), while those enacted before April 6, 1941, i.e., prewar laws, in general, were declared to have "lost their legal effect" (Sec. 2). However, the "principles of law" included in the prewar laws which have lost their effect were to continue to apply in cases not covered by the new legislation, provided that these principles were not inconsistent with the federal Yugoslav Constitution, the constitutions of the Yugoslav republics (states), and the laws and principles of the new "constitutional order" of present-day Yugoslavia (Sec. 4). But the government agencies could not "formally base their decisions and other acts upon such texts of law" (Sec. 4).

The law also made provisions regarding the validity of civil and criminal court decisions as well as administrative acts passed before 1945, and the application of new laws to old legal relations.

Thus, it may be stated that the Yugoslav legislation enacted before the German attack on Yugoslavia continued under the new regime as a source of law in the fields not covered by new laws and regulations.

3 *Federal Structure of Yugoslavia*

Since 1946 Yugoslavia, officially called the Federal People's Republic of Yugoslavia, has been organized as a federation of six federal units called, after the Soviet Russian pattern, republics. One of these units, Serbia, includes also two autonomous regions. The general idea behind the federal setup was a mixed one. The intention apparently was, as it is in the Soviet Union, to give a separate political entity, republic or autonomous region, to each of the major ethnic groups. Some units were based on their historic background. Thus, Serbia (population 6,989,000) is the state of the Serbs but it also includes the autonomous provinces of Voyvodina, with a mixed population of 1,712,000, and Kosovo-Metohia (population 809,000), which includes Albanians. Croatia is composed of 4,000,000 Croatians, with a fourteen percent Serbian minority, Slovenia of 1,500,000 Slovenians. With a population of 1,303,906, Macedonia is to provide a regional framework for a budding new nationality. Montenegro, with a population of 420,000, and Bosna and Herzegovina, with a population of 2,843,000, were set up with a view to their historical backgrounds.

The territories of the present republics do not quite coincide with the territories of the former units known under the same names. Thus, while the Republic of Bosnia and Herzegovina has remained within the old boundaries, the Republic of Slovenia was increased by territories acquired from Italy *(infra)* and the Republic of Serbia now embraces the Voyvodina. The Republic of Croatia has been increased by the addition of Dalmatia, Istria, and the counties of Beli Manastir and Darda. The Republic of Montenegro has been increased by the addition of the Kotor county; and the Republic of Macedonia was formed from Serbian Macedonia.

Moreover, pursuant to the Peace Treaty with Italy of February 10, 1947, and the Agreement between Yugoslavia, Italy, the United States of America and the United Kingdom of October 5, 1954, Yugoslavia received new territories which were formerly under Italian jurisdiction. These territories are now incorporated into their neighboring people's republics.

4 Government

The government of the present Yugoslavia (1962) operates under the doctrine of the dictatorship of the proletariat and under two constitutional acts, the Constitution of 1946 and the Constitutional Law of 1953. The Yugoslav jurists claim that the doctrine of the dictatorship of the proletariat is derived from Marxism-Leninism: "The teachings of Marx, Engels and Lenin regarding the state of the period of transition from capitalism to communism are consistently applied in our country."[3] "Our People's Democracy has a determined class character. It has all essential signs of the dictatorship of the proletariat."[4] This dictatorship is in fact exercised by the Communist Party of Yugoslavia. "The Communist Party of Yugoslavia is the leader of the entire state and social development in Yugoslavia."[5]

The federal government is a government of enumerated powers. But the enumeration is so broad that it covers all principal fields of political and economic activities (Art. 15, Constitutional Law of 1953). In the event of a conflict between a federal law and the law of a republic, the federal law prevails (ibid.). The most important feature in the relations between federal and state (republic) authorities is that the Constitution grants broad powers to federal authorities in repealing or modifying the decisions and resolutions of an agency of a republic. For example, the Federal Executive Council may withhold from execution acts of the people's republics if it deems that they contradict the federal acts (Art. 89, par. 1, Law of 1953).

The setup of the central government authorities under the 1946 Constitution of Yugoslavia resembled closely that of the Soviet Union. There was no president of the republic, the supreme power was exercised by an elected bicameral People's Assembly, one house representing the citizenry at large and the other, the individual Yugoslav States (republics) embraced in the federation. There was also a Presidium, a small committee elected by the assembly, a Cabinet and individual ministers, heads of government departments.

Since 1953 there is a President of the Republic elected by the National Assembly with some powers usually connected with this office. There is neither a Presidium nor a Cabinet but one Federal Executive Council, elected by the National Assembly. The Council performs in part some func-

3 "Neka nova pitanja naše teorije o socialističkoj državi i pravu" (Some New Problems of Our Theory of a Socialist State and Law). *Arhiv,* 1950, No. 3, p. 387.
4 Miloš Mimić, *Važnost organizacionog i vaspitnog rada u masama* (Importance of Organizational and Education Work Among the People). Beograd, 1950, pp. 29-30.
5 *Odluke V Kongresa Komunističke Partije Jugoslavije* (Decisions of the Vth Congress of the Communist Party of Yugoslavia). 1948, p. 55.

tions of the head of the State. "It orders a general mobilization and declares a state of war, appoints and dismisses state secretaries and under-secretaries, orders the dissolution of and elections for the People's Assembly and grants amnesties. It has also some of the functions of a Cabinet, takes care of the execution of the federal laws, submits bills and drafts of the federal economic plan and federal budget to the Assembly, handles government funds, attends to matters of international legal assistance and the like."[6] It has also inherited some functions of the Presidium, especially the power of issuing decrees (edicts), of directing the work of federal agencies and of issuing regulations in executing the laws.

The heads of individual departments are no longer called Ministers but Secretaries and Under-Secretaries. They no longer act as a body, as a cabinet, but individually and only two of them are members of the Executive Council. They are appointed by the Federal Executive Council.

5 People's Assembly

The Federal People's Assembly has very broad legislative power: it has the exclusive power of legislation in certain matters specifically enumerated, and in these fields the republics may legislate only if authorized directly by the federal assembly; it has, further, the power of basic legislation with respect to another category of affairs, also specifically enumerated, and the republic in such cases may enact only supplementary laws; finally, it has the power of enacting general law with respect to a third category in which it lays down principles for laws to be enacted by the republics in accordance therewith.

The republics are authorized to legislate independently only in fields outside the above three categories. However, in the event of a conflict between a federal and a republican law, the federal law would prevail, although the republic may institute proceedings before the Federal People's As-

---

6 "Yugoslavia" in Gsovski and Grzybowski, *Government, Law and Courts in the Soviet Union and Eastern Europe*, New York, 1959, Vol. I, pp. 446-447.

sembly for testing its conformity to the Federal Constitution. Generally, in such and similar cases, the Federal People's Assembly is the body which decides on the constitutionality of both federal and republican laws.

Since the constitutional reform of 1953, the structure of the National Assembly no longer follows the pattern of the Supreme Soviet of the Soviet Union. It has two chambers: the Federal Council and the Council of Producers. The Federal Council includes both representatives elected by the population at large and representatives of individual states of the Yugoslav Federation. The latter representatives now form a Council of Nationalities within the Federal Council and deliberate certain matters apart from it. The Council of Producers consists of representatives of industry and agriculture, but persons engaged in private business and farmers who are not members of collective farms are excluded from the electorate. The proportion of representatives of industry and agriculture is determined by the share of each group in the total national production (Sec. 27, Law of January 10, 1957). However, a rather arbitrary ratio was established in 1953, *viz.,* 202 for industry and 67 for agriculture. In other words, industrial workers elect two thirds and farmers one third of the representatives to the Federal Council of Producers, despite the fact that, according to official figures, the agricultural population forms more than one half of the total population. The new houses do not have equal powers as they did before, and certain kinds of law may be enacted by one house alone (Arts. 37 and 40, Law of 1953).

The structure of the federal government is followed in the structures of the individual republics. Each republic has an executive council, a national assembly and secretaries.

6 *Legal Sources*

Yugoslav legal theory and the Yugoslav Constitutional Law do away with the principle of the separation of powers. Their idea of the unity of power practically removes the distinction between legislative acts and administrative decrees. The settling of many problems and details connected with legislation was delegated to the administrative agencies for regulation. In this way many matters subject to legislation were regulated by administrative decrees which are more numerous than the legislative acts. E. Kardelj states that the administrative agencies became more important than the legislature.

As a matter of fact, the rules of law might be found in a variety of legislative and administrative acts without a settled hierarchy among them. The Constitution of 1946 and the Constitutional Law of 1953, as amended, do not necessarily prevail over ordinary legislation, since only the People's Assembly may declare the unconstitutionality of a law. The Law of 1953 sought to place the variety of legal rules in the following scheme: laws enacted by the National Assembly, edicts enacted by the Executive Council for the enforcement of laws, and finally, decrees, regulations, instructions, decisions, etc., issued by the state secretaries in implementation of the edicts of the Executive Council.

Another feature of the present Yugoslav law is that the interpretation of laws may be given not only by courts but also by higher government bodies. Such interpretation formed one of the functions of the Presidium under the 1946 Constitution and was not inherited by the Federal Executive Council which took the place of the Presidium to a certain extent.

Under the Constitutional Law of 1953 the task of the interpretation of laws is assigned to a standing Committee for the Interpretation of Laws *(Komisija za tumačenje zakona)*, which consists of nine members elected from the deputies of the Assembly and a number of officials trained in law. The Committee may also consult other legal experts when necessary *(Sl. L.,* No. 16, 1953). In carrying out its assignment the Committee may issue binding interpretations of Federal laws or submit its opinion on a law to the People's Assembly. It is noteworthy that some "binding interpretations" issued by the Committee have essentially changed the meaning of a legal provision which they aimed to interpret, e.g., "Binding Interpretation of the Law on the Agricultural Fund" and "Binding Interpretation of Sec. 2 of the Law on Nationalization" *(Sl. L.,* No. 27, 1953).

2

LAW JOURNALS, OFFICIAL GAZETTES, AND GENERAL COLLECTIONS OF LAWS AND TREATIES

A   Law Journals and Official Gazettes for the Whole of Yugoslavia

Yugoslav laws and decrees have been printed as a separate part of the official gazette which continued the official gazette of Serbia, *Srpske Novine* (*See* Nos. 22–24). The title varied: for the period of the Kingdom, 1918–1944, it was *Službene Novine* and from February 1, 1945 on, *Službeni List*. The subtitle also varied:

1   *Službene Novine Kraljevstva Srba, Hrvata i Slovenaca* (Official Gazette of the Kingdom of Serbs, Croats and Slovenes). Beograd, December 1918–January 1929. (DLC) *Službene Novine Kraljevine Jugoslavije* (Official Gazette of the Kingdom of Yugoslavia), from January 6, 1929 to April 6, 1941 (the last issue before the German invasion). (DLC) Under the same title the Yugoslav Government in Exile continued to publish its official gazette in London and Cairo, 1941 to 1944. (DLC)

2   *Službene Novine* (Official Gazette), without indicating the country, was printed in Beograd for the territory of Serbia during the period of the German occupation, 1941 to 1944. (DLC 1942–1943)

3   *Službeni List Demokratske Federativne Jugoslavije* (Official Gazette of Democratic Federal Yugoslavia). Beograd, February 1, 1945–November 29, 1945, (DLC), and thereafter *Službeni List Federativne Narodne Republike Jugoslavije* (Official Gazette

of the Federal People's Republic of Yugoslavia). Beograd, 1945–. Current. (DLC)

> After 1922, *Službene Novine* consisted of a main part, which was an official gazette carrying appointments, legal notices, and similar material, and a supplement for each year with the following subtitle:

4 *Zakoni, uredbe, pravilnici i t. d.* (Laws, Decrees, Regulations, etc.). Beograd, 1922–1944. (DLC)

> This was in fact a law journal containing laws, decrees and regulations. The issues of this part were appended to some but not all issues of the main part. Each issue of the part entitled *Zakoni, uredbe, pravilnici i t. d.* bore two numbers, one Arabic, indicating the number of the issue of the main part to which it was appended, and one Roman, the Roman numerals running consecutively for the issues of this part alone. The part *Zakoni, uredbe, pravilnici i t. d.* had separate consecutive pagination throughout the year. In addition to the above numbering of each issue, all the laws and decrees were numbered throughout each year and could be identified by this number alone.
>
> Since the title was changed to *Službeni List* in 1945, it has been continued also in two parts. But the former supplement, *Zakoni, uredbe, pravilnici i t. d.*, became the main part. Each issue is consecutively numbered and has consecutive pagination throughout the year. To some numbers of this part, which has no particular designation, issues are appended and designated as:

5 *Oglasni deo* (Official Advertisements). Beograd, 1945–. Current. (DLC)

> Each issue of this part is separately paged for each number. In content this part corresponds to the former main part. It also contains lists of nationalized and confiscated private enterprises. Each issue of *Oglasni deo* is not numbered separately but bears the number of the issue of the other part to which it is appended. The laws and decrees are separately and consecutively numbered as before.

B   Indices

Annual and semi-annual indices to the official gazette are rather
inadequate because they list the laws, for the most part, under the
ministry or other governing body to whose jurisdiction the law
pertains, and not under the subject. This caused the appearance
of privately and later officially published subject and chronological
indices:

6   *Registar-Indeks Službenih Novina* (Index of the Official Gazette) for the years 1919–1924 and 1926–28. Borivoje Frantlović,
editor. Beograd. (DLC)

7   *Zbirka zakona, naredaba, i svih propisa državne uprave* (Collection of Laws, Ordinances, and All Provisions of the Government Administration). Janko Bedeković, *editor.* Zagreb, 1926.
(DLC)

8   *Zakoni, uredbe i ostali propisi izdani od 1 Decembra 1918 do
Decembra 31, 1940* (Laws, Decrees and Other Legal Provisions
Enacted from December 1, 1918 until December 31, 1940). Nenad
Djordjević, *editor.* Beograd. 3 v.: v.1, 1918–1933 (1934); v.2,
1918–1936 (1937); v.3, 1937–1940 (1941). (DLC)

9   *Registar propisa objavljenih u Službenom Listu FNRJ* (Index
of Provisions Published in the Official Gazette of the FPRY).
Beograd, (1945–1949) 1950; (1945–1950) 1951; (1945–1953) 1954;
(1945–1955) 1956; (1945–1957) 1958; (1945–1959) 1960; (1945–
1961) 1962. (DLC)

C   Law Journals During the Enemy Occupation

During World War II Yugoslav territory was partly occupied and
partly incorporated into other countries. The laws, decrees and
orders issued during that period were printed as follows:

For occupied Serbia:

10   *Verordnungsblatt des Befehlshabers. List uredaba vojnog za-*

povednika u Srbiji (Collection of Orders of the Military Commander in Serbia); title varies. Beograd, 1941–1944, in the German and Serbian languages (DLC: 1941–1943), and also in the *Službene Novine* (*See* No. 2);

For the territory of the Independent State of Croatia—in the *Narodne Novine* (*See* No. 29 and also in the following):

11 *Sbornik zakona i naredaba Nezavisne Države Hrvatske, izdaje Ministarstvo Pravosudja i Bogoštovlja* (Collection of Laws and Regulations of the Independent State of Croatia, published by the Ministry of Justice and Religion). Zagreb, 1941–? (DLC: 1941, Sv. I–XII, br. 1–1258)

12 *Zakoni, zakonske odredbe i naredbi* (Laws, Decrees and Regulations). Promulgated from April 11 (11. *Travnja*), 1941 to March 7 (7. *Ožujka*), 1944. A. Mataić, editor. At the head of the title: *Nezavisna Država Hrvatska* (Independent State of Croatia). Knjiga 1–42 (svezak 1–42), 1941–1944 (DLC). *Stvarno Kazalo* (Subject-Index). (DLC: Vol. 3–4, to kn. 21–40, 1943–1944)

For the territories under Italian domination in the following Italian official gazettes:

13 *Gazzetta Ufficiale del Regno d'Italia.* Roma, 1941–1945.
14 *Il Giornale Ufficiale del Governo della Dalmazia* (Official Gazette of the Dalmatian Administration). Zara, 1941–1943.

For Slovenia in particular:

15 Regno d'Italia. *Bollettino Ufficiale per la provincia di Lubiana.* Kraljevina Italia. *Službeni list za Ljubljansko pokrajno* (Kingdom of Italy. Official Gazette for the Province of Ljubljana) 1941–December 30, 1944. In the Slovenian and Italian languages. Title varies: 1943–1944, *Službeni list šefa pokrajinske uprave v Ljubljani* (Official Gazette of the Chief of the Provincial Government in Ljubljana). (DLC)
16 *Reichsgesetzblatt,* the German law gazette, for the territory incorporated into Germany.
17 *Dŭrzhaven Vestnik,* the Bulgarian law gazette, for the territory incorporated into Bulgaria.
18 *Országos Törvénytár,* the Hungarian law gazette, for the territory incorporated into Hungary.

19   *Gazzetta Ufficiale del Regno d'Albania,* the Albanian law
gazette, for the territory under Albanian domination.

   A collection of English translations of the decrees issued during
   the occupation was printed in the following:

20   Mayer, Belle, *comp.* Preliminary Study of Certain Financial
Laws and Institutions. Yougoslavia. Washington, D. C., Treasury
Department, Office of the General Counsel, September 1, 1943.
563 p. Mimeographed. (DLC)
21   Lemkin, Rafaël. Axis Rule in Occupied Europe. Laws of Occupation. Washington, 1944. Yugoslavia, pp. 569–635. (DLC)

D   Law Journals and Official Gazettes of Component Parts of
     Yugoslavia

1 *Prior to 1945*

a Serbia

22   *Novine Srbske* (Serbian Gazette). Beograd, 1834–1837. Under
this title the first Serbian gazette began and had the appearance
of a general newspaper also carrying legal material. Continued
as No. 23.
23   *Srpske Novine.* 1837–1856; 1861–1918. For the gap in this
publication, *see* No. 24. During the enemy occupation of Serbia
in World War I, *Srpske Novine* was published (1916–1918) in
Corfu, Greece, the temporary seat of the Serbian Government
and Parliament.
24   *Zvanične Novine Knjažestva Srbie* (Official Gazette of the
Principality of Serbia), 1856–1860. Continued as No. 23.

During the Turkish administration which lasted until 1912,
two official gazettes were published in that part of South Serbia
which belongs today to the People's Republic of Serbia:

25   *Prizren.* Prizren since 1871–1877 weekly, in Turkish and
Serbian.

26 *Kosovo.* Priština, 1877–1912, in Turkish and Serbian.

27 *Zbornik zakona i uredaba* (Collection of Laws and Decrees), from Feb. 13, 1829 to Dec. 31, 1909. Beograd, 1–64, 1840–1912. Title varies: 1840–1908, *Sbornik.* Subtitle: 1840–1881, *u Kneževini Srbiji,* thereafter *Kraljevini Srbiji.* Other minor changes. (DLC) *Hronologijska i azbučna Tablica* (Chronological and Alphabetical Subject Index), to v. 1–31, 1835–July 1877, 1877 (DLC). Supplements: 1, to v. 32–44, August 5, 1877–December 1888 (1889). (DLC); 2, to v. 45–62, December 31, 1888–January 1, 1908 (1909). (DLC)

b Montenegro

28 *Glas Crnogorca* (Voice of the Montenegrin). Cetinje, 1873–1915. It began publication in 1873 as a private weekly newspaper. Soon thereafter it became the semi-official gazette and later the official gazette of Montenegro. It was published until the enemy occupation of Montenegro in World War I (1915).

c Croatia and Slavonia

As a part of the Austro-Hungarian Empire, Croatia (official name: Kingdom of Croatia, Slavonia and Dalmatia) enjoyed a special status, the scope of which was extended or restricted, depending upon the political situation.

According to the Croatian-Hungarian Compromise of 1868 between the Hungarian Parliament and the Croatian *Sabor* sanctioned by the monarch as fundamental law, the Croatian affairs were divided into three categories.

In joint Austro-Hungarian affairs, Croatia was one of the countries under the Hungarian crown. They were settled by the Delegation of the Austrian and Hungarian Parliament, Croatia being represented by five members in the Hungarian Delegation.

Joint Hungarian-Croatian affairs were within the jurisdiction of the Hungarian Parliament in Budapest. Croatia was represented by forty members having the right to use their own language.

Finally there were the autonomous affairs of Croatia organized under three branches: general administration, education and religious affairs, and justice. The chiefs of these services, appointed by the *Ban* of Croatia formed under his authority the equivalent of a Cabinet. The legislation in these fields was a joint responsibility of the *Sabor* and the King.

All of this complex setup was dissolved after the formation of Yugoslavia in 1918. In 1929 the greatest part of the territory of Croatia-Slavonia became one of the nine *banovinas* (*supra*). However, an agreement was reached on August 26, 1939 between Dragisha Tsvetkovitch, the President of the Yugoslav Government, and Dr. Vladko Maček, President of the Croatian Peasant Party and of the Peasant Democratic Coalition, subject to the approval of the Yugoslav Parliament. Broad fields of public life were assigned to the autonomous jurisdiction of the *Banovina* of Croatia such as internal administration, justice, agriculture, commerce, industry, forestry, mining, public works, social welfare, public health and education.

29   *Narodne Novine* (National Gazette). Zagreb, 1861–1944. This was the official gazette of the Croatian autonomous government after the Croatian-Hungarian Compromise. After the formation of Yugoslavia it continued to be the official gazette of government branches charged with the administration of Croatia. In August 1939, it became the official gazette of the territorial unit of Yugoslavia called *Banovina Hrvatska*. It also contained laws and decrees pertaining to Yugoslavia as a whole.

   During World War II, the territory of Croatia was declared the Independent State of Croatia, and *Narodne Novine* was resumed as its official gazette.

30   *Landesgesetze der Königreiche Kroatien, Slavonien und Dalmatien*, Zagreb, 1868–1910. Title varies: as *Gesetzartikel* (other slight changes). For Croatian edition, *see* No. 33. (DLC: 1868–1907)

31   *Sbornik Ugarsko-hrvatskih skupnih zakonah* (Collection of Joint Hungarian-Croatian Laws). Zagreb ?, 1871–1917.

32   *Sbornik zakonah i naredbi valjanih za Kraljevinu Hrvatsku i Slavoniju* (Collection of Laws and Decrees in Force in the Kingdom of Croatia and Slavonia). Title varies: 1868–1876; *Zakonski članci sabora* . . . (1868–1870 in one v.; 2d ed., 1871). Zagreb, 1863–1918. For the German edition, *see* No. 30. (DLC: 1868–1870, 1900, 1911–1913). Index 1863–1887.

33 *Uredovna sbirka naredaba pravosudne struke* (Official Collection of Decrees Important for the Administration of Justice), Zagreb, v. 1–7, (Nos. 1–960), 1885–1905. (DLC)

34 *Zbornik zakona, uredbi i naredbi* (Collection of Laws, Decrees and Regulations). L. Hönigsberg *and* S. Hirc, *editors.* Zagreb. Monthly. (DLC: 1927–1929)

35 *Zbirka zakona i uredaba* (Collection of Laws and Decrees which Contain Federal and Local Laws). V. Sredojević *and* T. Vojnović, *editors,* (in 1930–1931, S. Hirc; in 1935, Marčac). Monthly. Zagreb, v. 1–10?, 1927–1936? (DLC: 4–10, 1930–1936)

36 *List zemaljske uprave za hrvatsko-slavonsku vojnu Krajinu. Landes-Verwaltungsblatt für die Kroatisch-Slavonische Militärgrenze* (The Gazette of the Provincial Government of the Croatian-Slavonian Military Frontiers). In the Croatian and German languages. Zagreb, v. 1–10, 1872–1881. (DLC)

d Slovenia

Slovenia is not to be confused with Slavonia. It consists of the former Austrian provinces of Carniola (*Krain*) with parts of Carinthia (*Kärnten*) and Styria (*Steiermark*).

37 *Deželni zakonik za vojvodino Kranjsko. Landesgesetzblatt für das Herzogtum Krain* (Provincial Laws for the Duchy of Krain) in German and Slovenian. Ljubljana. 1849–1918. Title varies: 1849–1852 as *Deželni zakonik in vladni list za krajnsko kronovino;* 1853–1859, *Deželni vladni list;* 1860–1863, pt. 2, *Ukazi c. k. deželnih gospósk za vojvodstvo Krajnsko;* 1863, pt. 3–1869, *Zakonik in ukazni list.* German title also varies. (DLC: 1868–1917)

38 *Landesgesetzblatt für Kärnten,* 1850–1918, and thereafter continued for the Austrian part of the province. Title varies: 1850–1852 as *Landesgesetz und Regierungsblatt für das Kronland Kärnten;* 1853–1862 as *Landesregierungsblatt;* 1863–1918 as *Landesgesetz- und Verordnungsblatt für das Herzogtum Kärnten.* (DLC: 1863–1918)

39 *Državni zakonik za Kraljevine in Dežele zastopane v Državnem Zboru* (It is the Austrian *Reichsgesetzblatt* in Slovenian). (DLC: 1870–1917)

40 *Službeni list* (Official and Law Gazette). Ljubljana, v. 1–11,

November 4, 1918—November 10, 1929. Title varies: 1918–1922 as *Uradni List*. Continued as No. 41.

41 *Službeni list Kraljevske Banske Uprave Dravske Banovine* (Official and Law Gazette of the Royal Local Government of *Drava Banovina*). Ljubljana, 1–12, November 1929—April 17, 1941. Continued as No. 15 and No. 59.

e Dalmatia

42 *Bollettino provinciale delle leggi e delle ordinanze.* 1848–1917. Title varies, 1860–1864: *Ordinanze dell'autorità provinciale.* (DLC: 1848–1859)

43 *Landes-Gesetze- und Verordnungsblatt für das Königreich Dalmatien.* Title varies, Zara. 1848–1917. For Croatian edition, *see* No. 45. 1848–1859 printed together with No. 42. (DLC): 1848–1859; 1868–1900, 1904, 1906–1915)

44 *Objavitelj Dalmatinski, Avvisatore Dalmato* (Dalmatian Herald). In Italian and Croatian. 1849–1920. Title varies: 1849–1866, *Glasnik Dalmatinski.*

45 *Pokrajinski list zakona i naredaba za Dalmaciju* (Provincial Law Gazette for Dalmatia). 1848–1917. Title varies: 1848–1852 as *List Zakonah i Spisah Vlade;* 1853–1859 *Pokrajinski list;* 1848–1859 printed together with No. 42; 1860–1864 *Naredbe Pokrajinskih Vlastih za Dalmaciju;* 1865–1867 *List Zakonah i Naredba.* (DLC 1848–1859)

46 *Raccolta delle leggi ed ordinanze per la Dalmazia.* Zara, 1819–1848. Index. (DLC)

f Bosnia and Herzegovina

47 *Bosna* (The Official Gazette for the Turkish Province of Bosnia). Sarajevo, 1866—July 18, 1878. In Serbian (Cyrillic alphabet) and Turkish (Arabic script).

48 *Neretva* (Official Gazette for the Turkish Province of Herzegovina). Mostar, Nos. 1–30, 1876. In Serbian and Turkish.

49 *Gesetz- und Verordnungsblatt für Bosnien und die Herzegowina.* Sarajevo, 1881–1918. Title varies: 1881–1886 as *Sammlung der Gesetze- und Verordnungen für Bosnien und die Herzegowina.* Index 1878–1902. (DLC: 1881–1915, 1917)

50 *Sammlung der für Bosnien und die Herzegowina erlassenen Gesetze, Verordnungen und Normalweisungen.* Sarajevo, 1–3, 1878–1880. (DLC)

51 *Glasnik zakona i naredaba za Bosnu i Hercegovinu* (Herald of Laws and Decrees). Sarajevo, 1881?–1918. In Latin and Cyrillic alphabets. (DLC: 1887–1889, 1894–1895, 1897, 1901, 1903, 1909, 1915–1916, 1918)

52 *Zbornik zakona i naredaba za Bosnu i Hercegovinu* (Collection of Laws and Decrees for Bosnia and Herzegovina). Sarajevo, 1881–1922.

g Illyria

During Napoleon's Wars Ljubljana (Slovenia) was the capital of Illyria which under the French administration included a part of Slovenia, Croatia and Dalmatia.

These provinces were a part of Austria-Hungary from 1814 to 1918 when they were incorporated into the Kingdom of Serbs, Croats and Slovenes *(supra).*

53 *Sammlung der politischen Gesetze und Verordnungen für das Laibacher Gouvernementgebieth im Königreiche Illyrien.* 1–31, 1819–1849. Title varies: 1819–1824 as *Sammlung der politischen Gesetze und Verordnungen für das Herzogthum Krain und den Villacher Kreis Kärntens im Königreiche Illyrien.* Index 1819–1835. (DLC) Supplement 1–5, October 17, 1813, December 1818, 1 v. in 3 pts. (DLC)

54 *Recueil des lois, décrets et règlements à l'usage des provinces Illyriennes de l'Empire. Raccolta di leggi, decreti e regolamenti ad uso delle provincie Illiriche dell'Impero.* Paris, v. 1–14?, 1812. In French and Italian. (DLC: v. 9–10, 13–14)

2 *After 1945*

55 *Službeni Glasnik Narodne Republike Srbije* (Official Herald of the People's Republic of Serbia). Beograd, 1945– In the Latin and Cyrillic alphabets, interchangeably. (DLC)

56 *Narodne Novine, Službeni List Narodne Republike Hrvatske* (Official Gazette of the People's Republic of Croatia). Zagreb, 1945– In the Latin alphabet. (DLC)

57 *Službeni List Narodne Republike Bosne i Hercegovine* (Official Gazette of the People's Republic of Bosnia and Herzegovina). Sarajevo, 1945– In the Cyrillic alphabet. (DLC)

58 *Službeni List Narodne Republike Crne-Gore* (Official Gazette of the People's Republic of Montenegro). Cetinje, 1945– In the Cyrillic alphabet. (DLC)

59 *Uradni List Ljudske Republike Slovenije* (Official Gazette of the People's Republic of Slovenia). Ljubljana, March 23, 1944– In the Slovenian language and Latin alphabet. Subtitle varies: 1944, Nos. 1–4, *Slovenskega Oslobodilnega Sveta* (reprinted: *ponatis,* No. 5, June-December 1945, also *in narodne vlade Slovenije*). (DLC)

60 *Služben Vesnik na Narodna Republika Makedonija* (Official Gazette of the People's Republic of Macedonia). Skopje, 1945– In the Cyrillic alphabet. [DLC]

61 *Službeni List Autonomne Pokrajine Vojvodine* (Official Gazette of the Autonomous Province of Vojvodina). Novi Sad, 1945– In the Cyrillic alphabet. [DLC]

62 *Službeni List Autonomne Kosovsko-Metohijske Oblasti* (Official Gazette of the Autonomous Province of Kosovo-Metohia). Priština, 1945– [DLC]

63 *Fletorja Zyrtare e Krahinës Autonome të Kosovës e Metohis në Republikën Popullore të Sërbis.* Same as No. 62 in Albanian language.

In addition, many people's committees of cities, towns and counties publish their own official gazettes.

3

DEPARTMENTAL BULLETINS

Bulletins of ministries and other government agencies are a subsidiary legal source containing orders, instructions and decisions issued for the enforcement of laws.

A   Before 1918

1   Serbia

Note: Official publications in Serbia were in most cases discontinued in 1914 as a result of World War I.

64 *Finansijski pregled* (Financial Survey, Ministry of Finance). Beograd, v. 1–6, 1899–1904.

65 *Glasnik Ministarstva finansija* (Bulletin of the Ministry of Finance). Beograd, 1882–1887.

66 *Narodno Zdravlje* (Public Health, Ministry of the Interior, Division of Sanitation). Beograd, v. 1–19, 1881–1914 (?)

67 *Privredni Glasnik* (Economic Bulletin, Ministry of National Economy). Beograd, 1901–1914 (?)

68 *Prosvetni Glasnik* (Educational Bulletin, Ministry of Education). Beograd, 1880–1914 (?)

69 *Ratni Dnevnik* (War Journal, Ministry of War). Beograd, 1914–1918. (DLC: 1917–1918)

2 Croatia, Dalmatia, Slovenia

70 *Bericht*. Arbeiter-Unfallversicherungsanstalt. Triest, das Kuestenland, Krain und Dalmatien (Report. Workers' Social Security

Office [for] Trieste, Kuestenland, Slovenia and Dalmatia). 1889–1913.

71 *Supplementi per la Dalmazia al foglio delle ordinanze pei rami d'ammistrazione del Ministero delle Finanze austriaco,* Zara, Finanz-Landes-Direktion, 1854-1913. (DLC: 1856–94, 1905–08) During 1908–1911 also with the Croatian title: *Dodatak za Dalmaciju naredbenom listu za grane uprave Ministarstva Finansija.*

3 Montenegro

72 *Prosvjeta* (Education, Ministry of Education and Church Affairs). Cetinje (?), 1889–1910.

73 *Službeni List* (Official Gazette, Ministry of Post and Telegraph). Cetinje (?), 1911–1914.

B Yugoslavia, 1918-1941

Note: The majority, if not all, of the publications of this period were discontinued in 1941, as a result of World War II.

74 *Arhiv Ministarstva poljoprivrede* (Archive of the Ministry of Agriculture). Beograd, 1934–1941 (?).

75 *Belgrade Economic Review,* published by the Ministry of Finance. Beograd, 1926–1941 (?).

76 *Finansijska Služba* (Financial Service, the official organ of the Ministry of Finance). Irregular. Beograd, 1924–1941 (?).

77 *Finansijski Zbornik* (Collection of Financial Provisions, Ministry of Finance). Beograd, 1930–1940. (DLC)

78 *Glasnik* (Herald, Ministry of Agriculture and Waters). Beograd, 1923–1941 (?).

79 *Glasnik Direkcije za poljoprivredni kredit* (Herald of the Board for Agricultural Credit). Beograd, 1929–1941 (?).

80 *Glasnik, stručno-administrativni organ* (Herald, professional and administrative publication, Ministry of Social Welfare and Public Health). Beograd, 1919–1928. (DLC)

81 *Glasnik Uprave za zaštitu industrijske svojine* (Herald of the

Board for Protection of Industrial Property). Beograd, v. —15, 1921–1941. (DLC: [1921–1935])

82 *Glasnik Zavoda za unapredjenje spoljne trgovine* (Herald of the Board for Promotion of Foreign Trade). Beograd, 1930–1941 (?).

83 *Policijski Glasnik* (Police Bulletin, Ministry of the Interior). Beograd, 1905–1941 (?). (DLC: 1906–1913)

84 *Prosvetni Glasnik* (Education Bulletin, Ministry of Education). Beograd, 1920–1941 (?). (DLC: 1938)

85 *Ratnik* (Warrior, Ministry of the Army and Navy). Beograd, 1885–1941 (?). (DLC: 1909–1912; 1921–1925; 1927–1931)

86 *Službene Novine Državnih Saobraćajnih Ustanova Kraljevine Jugoslavije* (Official Gazette of the Government Transportation Agencies of the Kingdom of Yugoslavia). Semimonthly. Beograd, 1924–1941 (?).

87 *Socijalni Preporodjaj. Službeni organ Ministarstva Socijalne Politike* (Social Rebirth. Official organ of the Ministry of Social Affairs). Bimonthly. Beograd, 1921–1941 (?).

88 *Vesnik* (Herald, Ministry of Post and Telegraph). Beograd, 1889–1941 (?).

89 *Vojni List* (Military Gazette, Ministry of the Army and Navy). Beograd, 1890– (?). (DLC: 1890, 1927–1940)

C   Independent State of Croatia, 1941-1945

90 *Službeni Glasnik Ministarstva Narodne Prosvjete* (Official Bulletin of the Ministry of National Education). Zagreb, 1941–1945. (DLC: 1944–1945)

91 *Vjesnik Odjela za željeznički promet* (Bulletin of the Office for Railway Traffic). Monthly. Zagreb, 1941–1945 (?).

D   Since 1945

Note: For this period not only the publications of governmental agencies, but also those of semiofficial organizations and institutions are listed.

92 *Bilten. Službeno glasilo Ministrstva za socijalno skrbstvo LRS* (Bulletin, the Official Gazette of the Ministry of Social Welfare of the People's Republic of Slovenia). Ljubljana, 1950–

93 *Bilten Komiteta za zakonodavstvo i izgradnju narodne vlasti Vlade FNRJ* (Bulletin of the Committee on Legislation and Organization of the People's Authority of the Yugoslav Government). Monthly. Beograd, Službeni List FNRJ, 1948 (?)– (DLC: 1948; 1949 Nos. 1–3, 5–6)

94 *Bilten Sekretarijata za zakonodavstvo i organizaciju Izvršnog Veća N. R. Hrvatske* (Bulletin of the Secretariat for Legislation and Organization of the Executive Council of the People's Republic of Croatia). Monthly. Zagreb, 1952 (?)–

95 *Bilten za personalnu službu* (Bulletin for Personnel Service, Secretariat of the Government of the FPRY for Personnel Matters). Monthly. Beograd, 1949–

96 *Bilten Zavoda za socijalno osiguranje NR Bosne i Hercegovine* (Bulletin of the Office of Social Security of the People's Republic of Bosnia and Herzegovina). Irregular. Sarajevo, 1953–

97 *Glasnik* (Herald, Central Association of Cooperatives of the Republic of Macedonia). Monthly. Skopje, 1952–

98 *Glasnik Narodne Banke FNRJ* (Bulletin of the National Bank of Yugoslavia). Monthly. Beograd, 1947– (DLC: 1948; 1949; 1950; 1–11, 1955; 1956; 1–8, 10–12, 1957; 1–11, 1958)

99 *Informativni Bilten* (Information Bulletin, Federal Chamber of Industry). Monthly. Beograd, 1954– (DLC: 1950)

100 *Javna uprava.* Ljudska skupščina LRS. Izvršni svet, Sekretarijat za občo upravo (Public Administration. People's Assembly of the PRS, Executive Council, Secretariat for the General Administration). Ljubljana, 1948–. From 1948 to 1959, *Ljudska Uprava.* (DLC: 1948–)

101 *Narodna Milicija* (People's Militia, Administration of the

People's Militia, Ministry of the Interior). Monthly. Zagreb, 1948– (DLC: 1950; 1951; 1–5, 1952; 1–2, 1954; 1–2, 1955; 1–2, 1956; 1–8, 11–12, 1957; 1958; 1959; 1–2, 1960)

102 *Narodna Uprava* (People's Administration, Secretariat for Legislation and Organization of the Executive Council of the People's Republic of Bosnia and Herzegovina). Monthly. Sarajevo, 1950– (DLC: 1950; 1, 5–6, 1951; 1–6, 1952; 4–12, 1956; 8–9, 1958)

103 *Naše Gradjevinarstvo* (Our Construction, Ministry of Construction). Monthly. Beograd, 1945 (?)–

104 *Patentni Glasnik* (Bulletin of Patents and Trade Marks. Official Gazette for Patents and Trade Marks of the FPRY). Beograd, 1950– (DLC: 1958–59)

105 *Privredni List* (Economic Gazette, Chamber of Commerce of Bosnia and Herzegovina). Weekly. Sarajevo, 1954–

106 *Privredni Vjesnik* (Economic Bulletin, Chamber of Commerce of the Republic of Croatia). Semi-weekly. Zagreb, 1953–

107 *Pronalazaštvo* (Inventions, Federal Board of Patents). Quarterly. Beograd, 1951– (DLC: 2–5, 1951; 1953–57)

108 *Prosvetni Glasnik* (Educational Bulletin, Board of Education and Culture of the Republic of Serbia). Monthly. Beograd, 1951– (DLC: 1951; 1952; 10–11, 1954; 1, 12, 1955; 1–2, 9, 1957; 10–12, 1958; 1–12, 1959)

109 *Prosvjetni Vjesnik* (Educational Bulletin, Board of Education and Culture of the Republic of Croatia). Monthly. Zagreb, 1948– (DLC: 1950–1952; 1954; 1–7, 9–11, 1955; 1–7, 9, 1957; 1–7, 10, 1958; 1–3, 7–9, 1959)

110 *PTT Vesnik* (Bulletin for Postal Services, Telegraph and Telephone, the Ministry of the Post). Monthly. Beograd, 1949– (DLC: 1952; 1954; 1955–1959)

111 *Rad. List za pitanja sindikata i radničkog upravljanja* (Labor. The Gazette for Questions Concerning Trade Unions and Workers' Administration, Central Council of the Association of Trade Unions of Yugoslavia). Semi-monthly. Beograd, 1945–

112 *Samouprava Socijalnega Osiguranja* (Self-Administration of Social Security, Office of Social Security of the Republic of Slovenia). Monthly. Ljubljana, 1953–

113 *Službena Saopštenja Saveznog Ureda za Cene* (Official An-

nouncements of the Federal Board for Prices). Weekly. Službeni List FNRJ. Beograd, 1945–

114 *Službeni Glasnik Generalne Direkcije Jugoslovenskih Železnica* (Official Bulletin of the General Administration of the Yugoslav Railroads). Monthly. Beograd, 1945–

115 *Službeni Vesnik Ministarstva Gradjevina FNRJ* (Official Bulletin of the Yugoslav Ministry of Construction). Monthly. Published as supplement to the bulletin *Naše Gradjevinarstvo*. Beograd, 1950–

116 *Socijalna i zdravstvena politika* (Social and Health Policies, Board of People's Health and Social Welfare of the Republic of Serbia). Bimonthly. Beograd, 1948– (DLC: 1956)

117 *Socijalno Osiguranje* (Social Security, Federal Bureau for Social Security). Monthly. Beograd, 1955– (DLC: 11–12, 1956; 1958–1959; 1, 1960)

118 *Socijalno Osiguranje* (Social Security, Office of Social Security of the Republic of Croatia). Monthly. Zagreb, 1952– (DLC: 11, 1958; 6–7, 1959)

119 *Vesnik Direkcije železnica* (Bulletin of the Railway Department, in Ljubljana, Slovenia). Semi-monthly. Ljubljana, 1947–

120 *Vjesnik Rada* (Labor Bulletin, Yugoslav Ministry of Labor). Monthly. Beograd, 1946–

121 *Vojno-politički Glasnik* (Politico-military Bulletin, Political Administration of the Yugoslav Army). Monthly. Beograd, 1945 (?)– (DLC: 1950; [1951])

122 *Zadružni Glasnik* (Cooperatives' Herald, Central Association of Cooperatives of Yugoslavia). Monthly; since 1956, bimonthly. Beograd, 1952– (DLC: 1952; 1953; 1–10, 1954; 1, 1955; 1–12, 14–24, 1956; 1–2, 4–14, 17–24, 1957; 1958; 1–12, 18–21, 23, 1959)

123 *Zanatski Glasnik* (Artisans' Herald, Artisans' Chamber of Voyvodina). Monthly. Novi Sad, 1946–

4

COLLECTIONS OF LAWS

Prior to 1945, collections of laws, decrees and regulations were, as a rule, published in serials by private publishers. Some of them covered special topics and others were general in character. Nevertheless these collections were considered to be an authoritative source of law and were extensively used by the courts and the public at large.

Since 1945, laws and decrees have appeared in official and semi-official publications, and in addition have been printed by the Law Gazette in series reminiscent of the formerly privately printed series.

A   Prior to 1945

124   Biblioteka javnog prava (Library of Public Law). Mihailo Illić, editor. Beograd, v. 1–16?; 1929–1937?

125   Biblioteka za pravne i društvene nauke (Library for Legal and Social Science). Beograd, v. 1–30?; 1915–1934? (DLC: v. 2, 23, 24, 28–30 in 1934)

126   Crkveno zakonodavstvo (Legislation on the Serbian Orthodox Church). Beograd, Geca Kon, v. 1–3, 1926–1933.

127   Gradjansko zakonodavstvo (Civil Law Legislation). Agoston Franjo Agatonović, editor. Zagreb, v. 1, 1930. (DLC)

128   Hrvatski zakoni (Croatian Laws). Zagreb, Lav. Hartman (Kugli and Deutsch), v. 1–42?; 1885–1921? (v. 1 in 1899). Under this serial title individual volumes were printed containing annotated statutes also. (DLC: v. 1–9, 11–20, 22–24, 27–29, 31–33–34, 38, 42, 1918)

129   Novo sanitetsko zakonodavstvo (New Sanitary Legislation). Beograd, Geca Kon, v. 1–13, 1924–1935. (DLC)

130   Organizacijono zakonodavstvo (Legislation on the Organization of the Yugoslav Government). Agoston Franjo Agatonović, *editor*. Zagreb, v. 1–3?, 1929–1931? (DLC: v. 1–3)

131   Privredno zakonodavstvo (Economic Legislation). Beograd, Geca Kon, v. 1–8, 1923–1934 (v. 1, 1934).

132   Radničko zakonodavstvo (Labor Legislation). Beograd, Geca Kon, v. 1–4, 1928–1934 (v. 1, 1934).

133   Saobraćajno zakonodavstvo (Legislation on Transportation). Beograd, Geca Kon, v. 1–3, 1927. (DLC)

134   Šumarski zbornik (Collection of Provisions on Forestry). Beograd, Geca Kon, v. 1–2, 1934.

135   Upravno zakonodavstvo (Administrative Legislation). Themis Publications. V. J. Stefanović, *editor*. Zagreb, v. 1–4?, 1929?–1932?. (DLC: v. 2–4)

136   Zakoni in uredbe (Laws and Decrees). Tiskarna Merkur v Ljubljani, v. 1–12?; 19[–]–1931? (DLC: v. 12)

137   Zakoni Kraljevine Srba, Hrvata i Slovenaca (Laws of the Kingdom of the Serbs, Croats and Slovenes). Since 1930, Zakoni Kraljevine Jugoslavije. Zagreb, Jugoslovenska Štampa, D. D., v. 1–14?, 1928?–1931?. (DLC: 3–9, 11–14)

138   Zbirka Crkvenih zakona (Collection of Ecclesiastical Laws). Janić Vojislav *and* Milenko M. Janošević, *editors*. Beograd, v. 1, 1932.

139   Zbirka finansijskih zakona (Collection of Financial Laws). Živ. St. Devečerski, *editor*. Beograd, v. 1–50?; 19[–]–1936?. (DLC: v. 31–32, 38, 42, 43, 48)

140   Zbirka zadružnih zakona (Collection of Laws on Cooperatives). Josip K. Češljarević, *editor*. Beograd, v. 1–4?; 1933–1934? (DLC: v. 1–4)

141   Zbirka zakona (Collection of Laws). Beograd, Geca Kon, v. 1–56?, 1936–1941 (v. 1 in 1938). (DLC: v. 1–4, 6–7, 9–10, 16–20, 24–26, 28–30, 32–33, 36–44, 46–47, 49, 51, 53, 55–56 in 1941)

142   Zbirka zakona (Collection of Laws, Texts). Mihailo Ilić, *editor*. Beograd, v. 1–53?; 1920–1932? (v. 1 in 1927). (DLC: v. 1–9, 11–23, 25–32, 34–43, 46–51, 53)

143   Zbirka zakona protumačenih i objašnjenih sudskom i admi-

nistrativnom praksom (Collection of Laws Annotated and Explained by Judicial and Administrative Decisions). Gojko Niketić, *editor*. Beograd, v. 1–243?; 1922–1936? (Vol. 1 in 1927) (DLC: v. 1–9, 11–17, 19, 21–22, 25–30, 33, 36–37, 44–45, 49–51, 55, 57–59, 61, 65, 72–75, 77–82, 87–94, 97–99, 101–104, 106, 108–112, 114–118, 120–125, 127–129, 132–133, 135–137, 139–144, 147–155, 157–159, 161–165, 167–177, 179–181, 185–198, 200–202, 204–209, 211–219, 222–228, 230, 232–235, 237, 239–240, 242–243)

144 Zbirka zakona protumačenih i objašnjenih sudskom i administrativnom praksom (Collection of Laws Annotated and Explained by Judicial and Administrative Decisions). Nikolaj Pahorukov, *editor*. Beograd, v. 1–4, 1932–1938? (DLC: v. 1, 4)

145 Zbirka zakona, uredaba, pravila i uputa za vojsku, mornaricu. . . . (Collection of Laws, Decrees, Regulations and Instructions for the Army, Navy . . .). Konstantin B. Savatijević, *editor*. Beograd, v. 1–?, 1931–? (DLC: v. 1)

146 Zbirka zakona za upravnu službu (Collection of Laws for Administrative Service). Otomar Pirkmajer, *editor*. Beograd, v. 1–2?, 1928–1929?. (DLC: 1–2)

147 Zbirka zakonov (Collection of Laws). Delniška Tiskarna v Ljubljani, v. 1–45?, 19[–]–1930? (DLC: v. 33, 41, 45)

148 Žandarmerijski zbornik (Collection on the Constabulary). Beograd, Geca Kon, 1935. 4 v. (DLC)

B Since 1945

149 Biblioteka Novo zakonodavstvo (Library of New Legislation). Beograd, Savremena administracija, v. 1–3; 1955–? (DLC: 1–3)

150 Finansije (Finance). Beograd, v. 1–32?; 1945?–1956? (DLC: v. 20 in 1955, 24–25, 29, 32 in 1956)

151 Nova administracija (New Administration). Beograd, v. 1–87?, 1953–? (DLC: v. 1, 3, 9, 10, 13, 16, 19, 24–25, 27, 30, 34, 36, 39, 41, 45–46, 50–53, 58, 60–67, 70, 72–73, 80, 87 in 1958)

152 Priručna biblioteka za pravna i društvena pitanja (Library of Manuals for Legal and Social Problems). Beograd, Savremena

administracija, v. 1–16?, 1957?– (DLC: v. 2–10, 12–14, 16 in 1958)
153 Zbirka propisa iz oblasti financija (Collection of Provisions on Finance). Službeni List FNRJ. Beograd, v. 1–7?; 1947?–1951? (DLC: v. 2 in 1948, 7 in 1951)
154 Zbornik propisa Narodne Republike Srbije (A Systematic Arrangement of Federal and Serbian Laws and Decrees Covering up to December 31, 1956). Beograd, v. 1–6, 1955–1957. (DLC)
155 Zbirka propisa iz oblasti privrede (Collection of Laws on the Economy). Službeni List FNRJ. Beograd, v. 1–15?; 1947–1951? (DLC: 1, 3, 5–7, 9, 11–15 in 1951)
156 Zbirka propisa iz radnog prava (Collection of Provisions on Labor Laws). Beograd, v. 1–5?; 1947?–1950? (DLC: 2–5)
157 Zbirka zakona FNRJ (Collection of Laws of the FPRY). Beograd, v. 1–; 1947–; Since v. 111, 1954 title changed to Zbirka saveznih propisa (Collection of Federal Provisions) (DLC: v. 3, 8, 10–13, 16–21, 23–31, 48–53, 57, 59–64, 100, 102–103, 105, 111, 116–117, 119–120, 124–126, 129, 131–132, 136, 138–140, 144–145, 149, 152–155, 158, 160–161, 168 in 1959)
158 Zbirka zakonskih propisa (Collection of Laws of the Ministry of Railroads and Transportation). Beograd, v. 1–5?; 19[–]–1950? (DLC: v. 5)

5

PARLIAMENTARY RECORDS

159 Privremeno narodno predstavništvo, stenografske beleške (Provisional National Representation, Stenographic Records). Beograd, 1–5 (No. 1–137); March 1, 1919–October 22, 1920. (DLC)

160 Ustavotvorna skupština, stenografske beleške (Constituent Assembly, Stenographic Records). Beograd, No. 1–68; December 12, 1920–July 2, 1921. (DLC)

161 ———. Rad ustavnog odbora (Work of the Constituent Committee). Beograd, No. 1–65; February 1–June 27, 1921. (DLC)

162 Narodna skupština, stenografske beleške (National Assembly, Stenographic Records). Beograd, 1921/22–1928/29. (DLC)

163 ———. Zakonodavan odbor, stenografske beleške (Legislative Committee, Stenographic Records). Beograd, 1921/22–1928/29. (DLC: 1921/22)

164 ———. Stenografske beleške Narodne skupštine Kraljevine Jugoslavije od 7 decembra 1931 do 17 marta 1939 (Stenographic Records of the National Assembly of the Kingdom of Yugoslavia, December 7, 1931–March 17, 1939). Beograd, 1932–1939. (DLC)

165 ———. Senat. Stenografske beleške Senata Kraljevine Jugoslavije od 11 januara 1932 do 26 marta 1938 (Stenographic Records of the Senate of the Kingdom of Yugoslavia). Beograd, 1932–1938. (DLC)

166 Pijade, Moša, comp. Antifašističko veće narodnog oslobodjenja Jugoslavije. Prvo i drugo zasedanje veća, 26 i 27 novembra 1942, 29 i 30 novembra 1943 (Anti-Fascist Council of National Liberation of Yugoslavia. First and Second Session of

the Council, Nov. 26 and 27, 1942; Nov. 29 and 30, 1943, According to Stenographic Records and other Sources). Beograd, 1953. 331 p. (DLC)

167 Privremena Narodna Skupština. Treće zasedanje Antifašističkog veća narodnog oslobodjenja Jugoslavije i zasedanje Privremene Narodne Skupštine. Stenografske beleške od 7–26 augusta, 1945 (Provisional National Assembly. Third Session of the Anti-Fascist Council of National Liberation of Yugoslavia and the Temporary National Assembly. Stenographic Records, August 7–26, 1945). Beograd, 1945? 708 p. (DLC)

168 Nešović, Slobodan, *comp.* Zakonodavni rad pretsedništva Anti-fašističkog veća narodnog oslobodjenja Jugoslavije i Pretseddištva Privremene Narodne Skupštine DFJ, 19 nov. 1944–27 okt. 1945 (Legislative Work of the Presidency of the Anti-Fascist Council of National Liberation of Yugoslavia and the Presidency of the Provisional National Assembly of the DFY, November 19, 1944–October 27, 1945). Beograd, 1951. 1064 p. (DLC)

169 Ustavotvorna Skupština. Zasedanje Ustavotvorne Skupštine. Stenografske beleške (Constituent Assembly. Session of the Constituent Assembly. Stenographic Records). Beograd, 1945–1946. 992 p. (DLC)

170 ———. Ustavotvorni odbori Savezne Skupštine i Skupštine Naroda. Stenografske beleske od 10 decembra 1945–4 januara, 1946 (Committee to Prepare the Constitution of the Federal Council and Council of Nationalities. December 10, 1945–January 4, 1946). Beograd, 194– (?), 892 p. (DLC)

171 Savezna Narodna Skupština. Stenografske Beleške (Federal National Assembly. Stenographic Records). Beograd, v. 1, January 31, 1946– (DLC).

> Issued January 31, 1946-September 10, 1953 in two series, each numbered separately: Redovno zasedanje and Vanredno zasedanje. These volumes appeared under their earlier name: Narodna Skupština FNRJ.

6

COURT DECISIONS

A   Before 1945

Two types of supreme courts existed in Yugoslavia prior to World War II: (1) supreme courts for civil and criminal cases decided by the lower courts in various jurisdictions, and (2) a single supreme administrative tribunal, *Državni Savet* (State Council) having jurisdiction over administrative matters for the whole country.

The following supreme courts functioned for judicial cases originating in six separate jurisdictions:

Kasacioni Sud, in Belgrade, for the territory formerly under the jurisdiction of the Supreme Court of Serbia; *Odelenje B. Beogradskog Kasacionog Suda,* in Novi Sad, for Voyvodina, the territory formerly under the jurisdiction of the Hungarian *Curia; Veliki Sud,* in Podgorica, for the territory of the former Kingdom of Montenegro; *Vrhovni Sud,* in Sarajevo, for the territory of the former provinces of Bosnia and Herzegovina; *Stol Sedmorice,* in Zagreb, for the territory of Croatia and Slavonia; and *Odelenje B. Stola Sedmorice,* in Zagreb, for the territory of Slovenia and Dalmatia.

There was no official reporting system in Yugoslavia prior to 1945 except for one specific and very limited category of court decisions designated as *načelne odluke opšte sednice Kasacionog Suda* (authoritative decisions of the plenary sessions of the Supreme Court). These were binding upon lower courts and individual benches of the Supreme Court until overruled in another plenary session of the Supreme Court. Such decisions were usually, although not necessarily, published in the current official gazette. Other decisions occasionally appeared in legal periodicals or were published in selective collections by individual reporters.

1 All Jurisdictions

172 Odluke vrhovnih kao kasacionih sudova u krivičnim i disciplinskim stvarima (Decisions of the Supreme Courts Acting as Courts of the Last Resort in Criminal and Disciplinary Cases). Ljub. Milanović *and* Aleksa Vragović, *comp.* Zagreb, 1931–? (DLC: v. 1, 1931)

173 Krivični zakonik...343 rešenja svih apelacionih sudova i svih odelenja Kasacionog Suda godina 1930–1935 (Criminal Code... 343 Decisions of All Appellate Courts and All Divisions of the Supreme Court, 1930–1935). J. Vesel *and* V. Timoškin, *comp.* Sarajevo, 1935. 298 p. (DLC)

2 *Kasacioni Sud* in Belgrade

174 Zbirka sudskih rešenja i članaka o pravu (Collection of Court Decisions and Articles on Law). S. Maksimović, *comp.* Beograd, 1876, 1877, 1879. 3 v.

175 Nova zbirka načelnih odluka odelenja i opštih sednica Kasacionog Suda (New Collection of Authoritative Decisions of the Divisions and Plenary Sessions of the Supreme Court). St. Maksimović, *comp.* Požarevac, 1894–1899. 4 v. (DLC)

176 Odluke opšte sednice Kasacionog Suda (Decisions of the Plenary Session of the Supreme Court). Gojko Niketić, *comp.* Beograd, 1922–1924. 12 v. (DLC)

177 Pravosudje Kasacionog Suda za 1926 (Court Decisions of the Supreme Court for 1926). Gojok Niketić, *comp.* Beograd, 1928. 544 p. (DLC)

178 Vojno-sudska praksa: skupljene važnije odluke Velikog Vojnog i Kasacionog Suda u Beogradu od 1920 do 1930 (Court Decisions in Military Cases: Collected Important Decisions of the Highest Military Court and Supreme Court in Belgrade for the Period from 1920 to 1930). Dragutin Marinković, *comp.* Zagreb, 1930. 127 p. (DLC)

179 Sudska praksa u godini 1925–1928 (Judicial Practice for the

Years 1925–1928). Srbisav Kovačević, *comp.* Beograd, 1926–1929. 4 v. (DLC)

180   Sudska praksa u godini 1930[–1939] (Judicial Practice for the Years 1930[–1939]). Tihomir Ivanović, *comp.* Beograd. 3 v. (DLC: v. 2–3)

181   Odluke Kasacionog Suda u Beogradu u gradjanskim predmetima, 1940–1942 (Decisions of the Supreme Court in Belgrade in Civil Cases, 1940–1942). Beograd, Ministarstvo Pravde, 1943. xiv, 197 p. (DLC)

3   *Odelenje B. Beogradskog Kasacionog Suda* in Novi Sad

182   Zbirka viših sudskih odluka (Collection of Decisions of Higher Courts). N. Ignjatović, *comp.* Novi Sad, [v. 1–?], 1924–1941 (?). (DLC: v. 1–10)

183   Registar gradjansko-sudskih i krivično-sudskih odluka objavljenih u Pravničkom Glasniku za god. 1939–1940 (Index-Digest of Court Decisions in Civil and Criminal Matters published in *Pravnički Glasnik* for 1939–1940). (DLC)

4   *Stol Sedmorice* in Zagreb

184   Rješenja Stola Sedmorice u gradjansko-pravnim predmetima (Decisions of the Supreme Court in Civil Matters). E. Čimić, *comp.* Zagreb, 1913–1917. 2 v. (DLC)

185   Rješenja Kasacionog Suda u krivičnim i disciplinskim stvarima (Decisions of the Supreme Court in Criminal and Disciplinary Cases). L. Milanović *and* V. Strasser, *comp.* Zagreb, Obnova, 1920. 4 v. (DLC)

186   Rješenja Kasacionog Suda u gradjansko-pravnim stvarima (Decisions of the Supreme Court in Civil Cases). Ljuba Milanović *and* Vinko Strasser, *comp.* Zagreb, 1920–1926. 7 v. (DLC: v. 1–3, 6–7)

187   Vrhovne upravne i sudske rješidbe k zakonu od 9. V. 1889 o zadrugama (Supreme Administrative and Court Decisions Relating to the Law on Cooperatives of May 9, 1889). Dragutin Tončić, *comp.* Zagreb, 1925. 292 p. (DLC)

188   Zbirka rješidaba Stola Sedmorice (Collection of Decisions of the Supreme Court). Aleksa Vragović, *comp.* Zagreb, 1927–1930. 3 v. (DLC)

189 Zbirka rješidaba Stola Sedmorice u gradjansko-pravnim stvarima (Collection of Decisions of the Supreme Court in Civil Cases). Josip Rucner *and* Petar Strohal, *comp.* Zagreb, 1939–1941. 3 v. (DLC)

189[1] Zbirka rješidaba Stola Sedmorice u gradjanskim pravnim stvarima (Collection of Decisions of the Supreme Court in Civil Matters). Klement Puharić, *comp.* Zagreb, 1944–1945. 2 v. (DLC)

> It covers the period between the second part of 1940 through 1944.

5 *Odelenje B. Stola Sedmorice* in Zagreb (for Slovenia and Dalmatia)

190 Odločbe Stola Sedmorice odd B (a) v Kazenskih stvareh, 1920–1943 (Decisions of the Supreme Court, Division B, in Criminal Matters, 1920–1943). Ljubljana, Pravnik, n. d. 2 v. (DLC); (b) v civilnih stvareh [1920–1935] (in Civil Cases [1920–1935]). 2 v. (DLC)

191 Rješenja Stola Sedmorice i Stola Sedmorice (Odelenje B) u gradjanskim stvarima (Decisions of the Supreme Court and the Supreme Court, Division B, in Civil Cases). A. Vragović *and* Lj. Milanović, *comp.* Zagreb, Jugoštampa, v. 1, 1935–? (DLC: v. 1)

6 *Državni Savet* (State Council)

The State Council (supreme administrative tribunal) functioned as a single court for the whole territory.

192 Zbirka odluka Državnog Saveta (Collection of the Decisions of the State Council). M. Vukičević, *comp.* Beograd, 1908. xxxviii, 450, 246, 18, 28 p. (DLC)

193 Odluke Državnog Saveta od 1919–1936 (Decisions of the State Council, 1919–1936). Beograd. 1924-n. d. 6 v. (DLC)

194 Odluke opšte sednice i načelne odluke Državnog Saveta, 1923–1933 (Decisions of the Plenary Session and Authoritative Decisions of the State Council, 1923–1933). Aleksandar Davinić *and* Bogdan R. Majstorović, *comp.* Beograd, 1933. 525 p. (DLC)

195 Odluke Državnog Saveta (Decisions of the State Council). A. Dj. Agorić, *comp.* Beograd, 1928. 178 p. (DLC)

196   Upravno-sudska rješenja (Decisions of the Administrative Court). Jovan V. Stefanović, *comp.* Zagreb, 1927–1928. 2 v.

197   Odluke Državnog Saveta i upravnih sudova po zakonu o neposrednim porezima (Decisions of the State Council and Administrative Courts Based on the Law on Direct Taxation). B. Frantlović *and* B. R. Majstorović, *comp.* Beograd, Geza Kon, 1932. 2 v. (DLC)

198   Odluke opšte sednice Državnog Saveta u 1937, 1938, 1939 (Decisions of the Plenary Session of the State Council in 1937, 1938, 1939). Slavoljub Popović *and* Janko Tahović, *comp.* Beograd, 1940. 180 p. (DLC) For decisions prior to 1937, *see* Nos. 683–686.

B   Since 1945

See also No. 989b.

1 Regular Courts

After 1945 the court system of Yugoslavia underwent considerable change. Today there is a separate supreme court for each republic (state), a supreme court for the autonomous region of Voyvodina, and a federal supreme court for the whole territory. These courts exercise jurisdiction in criminal and civil matters and, since 1954, also in administrative matters.

Court decisions in postwar Yugoslavia are still published at irregular intervals, but the practice of publishing court decisions in the official gazette has been discontinued. Certain decisions are, however, from time to time discussed or published in an abbreviated form in current legal periodicals. Selective collections of court decisions have been issued.

199   Zbirka odluka vrhovnih sudova i upustava Vrhovnog Suda FNRJ 1945–1954 (Collection of Decisions of the Supreme Courts and Directives of the Federal Supreme Court 1945–1954). M.

Gajić, *joint editor*. Beograd, Arhiv za Pravne i Drustvene Nauke, 1952–1954. 2 v. (DLC)

200 Zbirka Sudskih Odluka (Collection of Court Decisions). Aleksandar Goldštajn, Vladimir Kalember, Vitomir Petrović, *comp*. Beograd, v. 1–, 1956– (DLC: 1956–1959)

2 Special Tribunals

In 1947 special tribunals were established in Yugoslavia to decide disputes arising among government enterprises. Such tribunals were called *državna arbitraža* (government arbitration boards), and the tribunal of last resort in this system was *Glavna Državna Arbitraža* (Supreme Government Arbitration Board).

201 Zbirka odluka Državne Arbitraže (Collection of Decisions of Government Arbitration Boards). Beograd, Službeni List FNRJ, 1949–1954. 7 v. (DLC: v. 1–4)

In 1954 government arbitration boards were abolished and their jurisdiction was transferred to the newly established economic courts (*privredni sudovi*).

202 Zbirka odluka privrednih sudova (Collection of Decisions of Economic Courts). Beograd, Savremena Administracija, 1956– (DLC: Book [*Sveska*] 1)

7

INTERNATIONAL TREATIES

Most treaties entered into by Yugoslavia were published in the current Yugoslav official gazettes. The texts of the international treaties are, of course, also available in the language of the other parties to each treaty. In addition, most treaties have been printed in Martens' *Recueil de Traités* (DLC), in the *League of Nations Treaty Series*, 1920–1946 (DLC), and in the *United Nations Treaty Series*, 1946–current. (DLC)

In seeking an international treaty involving Yugoslavia, the name of the Yugoslav territory at the given historical period and its various spellings should be borne in mind (for example: Serbia, Servia, Serbie; Crna Gora, Montenegro; SHS, Serbo-Croat-Slovenian State (Etat), Serbe-Croate-Slovene; Jugoslavija, Jugoslawien, Yugoslavia, Yougoslavie; Hrvatska, Kroatien, Croatia, etc.).

Aside from the official gazettes and the above-mentioned international sources, individual reprints or collections of international treaties were prepared privately or by various governmental departments.

A   Serbia Prior to 1918

203   Zbirka konvencija izmedju Srbije i drugih država zaključenih i ratifikovanih od 1. Marta 1880 do 25. Maja 1883 God. sa uputima i izvodima iz raznih ugovora potrebnih za sudske i policijske vlasti (Collection of Conventions Between Serbia and Other Countries, Entered Into and Ratified from March 1, 1880, to May 25, 1883, with Instructions and Excerpts from Various Treaties for the Use of Courts and Police Authorities). Beograd, Državna Štamparija, 1883. 156 p. (DLC)

204   Ugovori i konvencije izmedju Srbije i stranih država od pro-

glašenja nezavisnosti do 1. january 1887 (Treaties and Conventions between Serbia and Foreign Countries from the Declaration of Independence to January 1, 1887). Beograd, 1887. 398 p. (DLC)

205 Trgovinski ugovori izmedju Kraljevine Srbije i Kneževine Bugarske (Commercial Agreements between the Kingdom of Serbia and the Principality of Bulgaria). Beograd, 1889.

206 Zbirka zakona, ugovora i pogodaba o srpskim zajmovima (Collection of Laws, Treaties and Agreements on Serbian State Loans). Beograd, Uprava Državnih Dugova, 1897. 49 p.; 2nd ed. 1899, 660 p. (DLC: 1899)

207 Zbirka trgovinskih ugovora zaključenih izmedju Srbije i drugih država (Collection of Trade Agreements Concluded between Serbia and Other Countries). Beograd, 1908.

An exhaustive list of international treaties concluded by Serbia in the period from 1880 to 1918 is contained in

208 Pregled razvoja medjunarodno-pravnih odnosa jugoslaven-skih zemalja od 1800 do danas, I sveska:...od 1800 do 1918 go-dine (Survey of the Development of International and Legal Relations of the Yugoslav Countries from 1800 to Date, Part I [Serbia]...from 1800 to 1918). Beograd, Institut za Medjunarod-nu Politiku i Privredu, 1953. 242 p. (DLC)

209 Liste des traités et des engagements internationaux de la Serbie (1878–1914). *Annuaire,* v. 2, 1934: 307–343. (DLC)

B   Treaties Relating to the Formation of Yugoslavia

210 Allied and Associated Powers. Peace Treaties. Various Treaties and Agreements between the Allied and Associated Powers and the Serbo-Croat-Slovene State,...at the Peace Conference at Paris and Saint-Germain-en-Laye. Washington, Government Printing Office, 1921. (DLC)

211 Allied and Associated Powers. Treaty between the Principal Allied and Associated Powers and the Serbo-Croat-Slovene State

Signed at Saint-Germain-en-Laye, September 10, 1919. London, H. M. Stationery Office, 1919. 96 p. (DLC)

212 Allied and Associated Powers. Treaty between the Principal Allied and Associated Powers and... the Serbo-Croat-Slovene State... Signed at Sèvres, August 10, 1920. London, H. M. Stationery Office, 1921. (DLC)

213 Declaration of Accession by the Serbo-Croat-Slovene State to the Treaty of Peace with Austria, the Treaty between the Principal Allied and Associated Powers and the Serbo-Croat-Slovene State,... Signed in Paris, December 5, 1919. London, H. M. Stationery Office, 1920. (DLC)

214 Treaties, Conventions, International Acts, Protocols, and Agreements between the United States of America and Other Powers, 1910–23. Washington, Government Printing Office, 1923. (DLC)

> Contains, among others, the Peace Treaty of Serbia with Austria of July 16, 1920 (p. 3149); with Germany of June 28, 1919 (p. 3329); with Hungary of June 4, 1920 (p. 3539); and the Treaty between the Principal Allied and Associated Powers and the Serbo-Croat-Slovene State of September 10, 1919 (p. 3731).

C   Yugoslavia, Period of the Kingdom (1918-1941)

215 Zbirka medjunarodnih ugovora (Collection of International Treaties). Beograd, Ministarstvo Inostranih Poslova Kraljevine Jugoslavije, 1929–1940. 12 v. Text given in Serbian and French. (DLC)

216 Zakon o trgovinskom ugovoru izmedju Kraljevine Srba, Hrvata i Slovenaca i Republike Austrije (Law on the Trade Agreement between the Kingdom of the Serbs, Croats, and Slovenes and the Republic of Austria). Beograd, Geca Kon, 1927. 143 p.

217 Zakon o ugovorima i konvencijama sa Kraljevinom Italijom (Law Concerning the Treaties and Conventions with the Kingdom of Italy). Beograd, Geca Kon, 1929. 231 p. (DLC)

218 Zakonodavstvo o medjunarodno-pravnom saobraćaju (Legis-

lation Concerning International Relations). Beograd, Geca Kon, 1931. 2 v.

219 Zbirka ugovora i konvencija o pravnoj pomoći u krivičnim i gradjanskim stvarima (Collection of Treaties and Conventions on Legal Assistance in Criminal and Civil Cases). N. D. Pahorukov, *comp.* Beograd, Geca Kon, 1932. 518 p. (DLC)

220 Zbirka konkordata (Collection of Concordats). Beograd, Geza Kon, 1934. 156 p. (DLC)

221 Zbirka važnijih medjunarodnih konvencija iz pomorskog javnog prava (Collection of Important International Conventions Involving Public Maritime Law). D. A. Marinković, *comp.* Zemun, 1935.

222 Les affaires extérieures de la Yougoslavie (Dossier constitué par l'Europe Nouvelle, 1918–1928). *L'Europe Nouvelle* (Paris), 1929.

> Contains treaties concluded by Yugoslavia with the following countries: Albania, Czechoslovakia, France, Greece, Hungary, Italy, and Turkey.

223 Liste des traités et des engagements internationaux du Royaume de Yougoslavie (1919–1935). S. Tchirkovitch, *comp. Annuaire,* v. 1, 1931: 289–348; v. 2, 1934: 347–461. (DLC)

D   During World War II (1941-1944)

International treaties concluded by the Independent State of Croatia during World War II were published in the official gazette (*see* No. 29) and in the following collection:

224 Medjunarodni ugovori (International Treaties). Zagreb, Ministarstvo Vanjskih Poslova Nezavisne Države Hrvatske. [v. 1] (covers 1941), 1942; [v. 2] (covers 1942), 1943; [v. 3] (covers 1943), 1944.

E   Since 1944

International treaties and other agreements of Yugoslavia since
1944 were published 1945–1949 in No. 3. Since February 11, 1953,
the treaties have been published in the form of an appendix to
this as *Dodalak: Medjunarodni Ugovori i Drugi Sporazumi* (Appendix: International Treaties and Other Agreements).

In addition to the above, individual reprints of international
treaties are published by the Yugoslav Ministry of Foreign Affairs
under the title

225 Medjunarodni ugovori Federativne Narodne Republike Jugo-
     slavije (International Treaties of the Federal People's Republic
     of Yugoslavia). Beograd, Ministarstvo Inostranih Poslova, 1945–
     (DLC)

> List of the international treaties and agreements entered into
> by Yugoslavia since 1944 also began to appear in the periodical
> No. 245. The first four issues contain a list of the treaties con-
> cluded during the years 1944–1946.
>
> The publishing house of the Službeni List has announced the
> forthcoming publication of a collection of treaties:

226 Zbirka trgovinskih i platnih sporazuma izmedju FNRJ i dru-
     gih zemalja (Collection of Commercial and Payment Agree-
     ments Concluded between Yugoslavia and Other Countries).
     Ratko Filipović *and* Aleksandar Paštrović, *comp.* Beograd, 1956.
     379 p. (DLC)

8

LEGAL PERIODICALS

(The names referred to in this chapter are those of the editors)

227 *Anali Pravnog fakulteta u Beogradu* (Annals of the Law School of the Belgrade University). Beograd. Quarterly. 1953– (DLC)

228 *Annuaire de l'Association Yougoslave de droit international.* Belgrade. Irregular. 1931–1937. 3 v. (DLC)

229 *Arhiv za pravne i društvene nauke* (Archive for Law and Political Science). Beograd. February 25, 1906–May 25, 1914; August 25, 1920–. Published monthly by the Law School of the Belgrade University until 1953, and since 1953 as a quarterly by the Federation of the Lawyers' Association. (DLC 1906–1939, 1947–1950, 1952–)

230 *Diplomatski zbornik Kraljevine Hrvatske, Dalmacije i Slavonije* (Diplomatic Symposium of the Kingdom of Croatia, Dalmatia and Slavonia). Zagreb, Jugoslavenska akademija znanosti i umjetnosti, v. 1–15, 1903–1934. Monthly.

231 *Liga Naroda. Udruženje za promicanje ciljeva Lige Naroda* (League of Nations. An Association for the Promotion of the Aims of the League of Nations). Zagreb, v. 1–4, 1931–1934. Monthly.

232 *Branič. List za pravne i duštvene nauke* (Counsel for Defense. Periodical for Law and Political Science). Beograd, January 1, 1887–1889, October 1, 1897–1901, May 1, 1903–1906, January 31, 1925–. Fortnightly and monthly. From 1930 on an official publication of the Belgrade Chamber of Lawyers. (DLC [1887–88], 1898, 1900–01, 1906, 1925–1940–[1941])

233 *Glas prava, sudstva i administracije* (Voice of the Law, the Judiciary and the Administration). Beograd. Milan St. Marković, later Kosta D. Jezdić. Weekly and bimonthly. 1902–1905.

234 *Glasnik Advokatske komore u Novom Sadu* (Herald of the Novi Sad Chamber of Lawyers). Novi Sad. Nikola Nikolić. Monthly. 1928–1941.

235 *Glasnik Advokatske komore za A. P. Vojvodinu* (Herald of the Chamber of Lawyers of the Autonomous Province of Vojvodina). Novi Sad. Monthly. 1952–

236 *Godišnik na Pravniot fakultet vo Skopje* (Year-Book of the Law Faculty of Skoplje). Skopje. Annual. 1954–

237 *Godišnjak Društva za uporedno pravo* (Year-Book of the Society for Comparative Law). Beograd. Annual. 1938.

238 *Godišnjak Pravnog fakulteta Sveučilišta u Zagrebu* (Year-Book of the Law School of the Zagreb University). Zagreb. Annual. 1939/40.

239 *Godišnjak Pravnog fakulteta u Sarajevu* (Year-Book of the Faculty of Law of Sarajevo). Sarajevo. Annual. 1953– (DLC [1953], 1955–57)

240 *Govornica. List za politiku i pravo* (Tribune. Political and Law Periodical). Beograd. Stojan Živković. Weekly. January–June 1870, 26 issues.

241 *Hrvatski pravnik* (Croatian Jurist). Zagreb. Stjepan Ortner. 1905–1912.

242 *Istorisko-pravni zbornik. Organ opšteg seminara za istoriju države i državnog prava* (Historical–Legal Symposium. Publication of the Seminary for History of Government and Constitutional Law). Sarajevo. Irregular. 1949– (DLS 1949–50)

243 *Pravna misla* (Legal Thought). Organ of the Lawyers' Association of the P. R. of Macedonia. Skopje, 1950–.

244 *Jugoslovenska advokatura* (The Yugoslav Legal Profession). Beograd. Savez advokatskih Komora FNRJ. Quarterly. 1954– (DLC [1954–59])

245 *Jugoslovenska revija za medjunarodno pravo* (Yugoslav Review of International Law). Beograd. Jugoslovensko udruženje za medjunarodno pravo. Quarterly. 1954– (DLC [1954], [1956–57])

246 *Komuna. Časopis stalne konferencije gradova i gradskih opšti-*

na FNR Jugoslavije (The Commune. Periodical of the Permanent Conference of the Cities and Towns of the Federal People's Republic of Yugoslavia). Beograd. Bimonthly. 1954– (DLC [1954–55], [1958])

247 *Komunist* (The Communist). Beograd. Central Committee of the Federation of Yugoslav Communists. Monthly. 1949– (DLC [1954]–[1955]–[1956]–)

248 *Prikazi in Študije* (Surveys and Studies). Statistics of the People's Republic of Slovenia. Ljubljana, 1954–.

249 *Medjunarodni problemi* (International Problems). Beograd. Institut za medjunarodnu politiku i privredu. Ministarstvo Inostranih Poslova FNRJ. Bimonthly. 1949– (DLC [1949–52], 1955–58)

250 *Mesečnik* (Monthly Review). Beograd. Geca Kon. 1924–? Irregular.

251 *Mjesečnik. Glasilo Hrvatskog pravničkog društva* (Monthly Review. Organ of the Croatian Jurists' Association). Zagreb. [Title and imprint vary slightly]. Blaž Lorković, Josip Šilović, Ladislav Polić, Edo Lovrić, Ivo Politeo. 1875–1937. (DLC) Index, v. 1–13, by S. Kranjčić. Zagreb, 1888. 272 p. (DLC); Index, v. 1–25, by S. Posilović. Zagreb, 1925. 272 p.

252 *Razprave Akademije znanosti in umetnosti. Pravni razred* (Essays of the Academy of Science and Art. Legal Division). Akademija znanosti in umetnosti. Ljubljana, v. 1–3, 1941–1945. Irregular.

253 *Socialni arhiv* (Social Archive). Central Employment Office. Beograd, v. 1–7, 1935–1941. Monthly.

254 *Narodni odbor* (The People's Committee). Sarajevo. Sekretarijat za zakonodavstvo i organizaciju Izvršnog veća NR Bosne i Hercegovine. Bimonthly, later monthly. 1948– (DLC [1951–])

255 *Narodni pravnik* (The People's Lawyer). Beograd. Federation of the Employees of the Government-Administrative Agencies. Monthly, later bimonthly. 1946–50. (DLC) [1947], [1949]–1950

256 *Naša stvarnost* (Our Reality). Beograd. Central Committee of the Federation of the Yugoslav Communists. Monthly. 1947– (DLC [1947–], 1949–50–[1951]–1952–[1953], [1955–56], 1957–)

257 *Naša zakonitost* (Our Legality). Zagreb. Lawyers' Association

of the People's Republic of Croatia. Monthly. 1947—(DLC [1947—])

258 *New Yugoslav Law. Bulletin on Law and Legislation in the Federal People's Republic of Yugoslavia.* Beograd. Published in English by the Association of the Jurists of the Federal People's Republic of Yugoslavia. Quarterly. 1950—(DLC [1950—])

259 *Nouveau droit yougoslave. Bulletin sur le droit et la législation de la République Fédérale Populaire de Yugoslavie.* Published in French by the Association of Jurists of the Federal People's Republic of Yugoslavia. Quarterly. 1950—(DLC [1950–])

260 *Nova administracija. Bilten za pitanja državne uprave, društvene samouprave i organizaciju privrede* (New Administration. Local Government and Organization of the Economy). [Title varies: Narodna država (People's State), monthly, 1946–53]. Beograd. Since 1953 bimonthly. 1946—(DLC [1954–58])

261 *Novi pravnik* (New Jurist). Sisak, Croatia. Milan Makanec. Fortnightly. January 15, 1871—June 28, 1871.

262 *Odvjetnik. Buletin Društva odvjetnika u Hrvatskoj i Slavoniji* (The Lawyer. Bulletin of the Association of the Lawyers of Croatia and Slavonia). Zagreb. Monthly, irregular. 1927—(DLC [1927–30], [1932–38], [1951–52], [1956–59])

263 *Policija* (Police). Beograd. Dušan Dj. Alimpić, later Vasa Lazarević. Fortnightly. 1910–1914, 1919–41. (DLC 1923, 1927–28, 1934, 1937, 1940)

264 *Porota* (Jury). Beograd. Milan St. Marković. Published every ten days. January 10, 1880—December 31, 1888. (DLC [1880–88])

265 *Porotnik* (Juror). Beograd. Milan St. Marković. Monthly. 1898.

266 *Pravda* (Justice). Beograd. D. Novaković, S. Antić, U. Knežević. Monthly. 1869–72? (DLC [1870–72])

267 *Pravdonoša* (Bearer of Justice). Zadar, Dalmatia. The earliest Croatian, and, for that matter, Yugoslav legal periodical. Ante Kuzmanić, later Ivan Danilov. Weekly. March 1, 1851—September 18, 1852. (DLC 1851)

268 *Pravna misao. Časopis za pravo i sociologiju* (Legal Thinking). Beograd, 1935–41, 1945? (DLC [1935]–1936–41)

269 *Pravni pregled* (Law Review). Beograd. Udruženje pravnika Kraljevine SHS. Irregular. 1921–22.

270 *Pravni pregled* (Law Review). Sombor. Vinko Žganec. Monthly. 1935–41?

271 *Pravni savjetnik* (Legal Adviser). Zagreb. Monthly. 1919–24. (DLC 1919, 1921–24)

272 *Pravni vestnik* (Legal Herald). Trst. Društvo Pravnik v Trst. Monthly, irregular. 1921–1928. (DLC)

273 *Pravni Život* (Legal Life). Beograd, Stojan Jovanović. Monthly. 1936–1941. (DLC: 1937–1940)

274 *Savezni zavod za statistiku. Studije i analize* (Federal Institute of Statistics. Studies and Analyses). Beograd. Irregular. 1953– (DLC)

275 *Pravni život. Udruženje Pravnika NR Srbije i Bosne i Hercegovine* (Legal Life, Jurists Association of the People's Republics of Serbia and Bosnia and Herzegovina). Beograd. Irregular. 1952—(DLC [1952]–[1953]–[1954]–1956–[1957]–1958–[1959]).

276 *Pravni zbornik* (Legal Symposium). Podgorica, Montenegro. Božidar S. Tomović. Monthly. July 1, 1933–41.

277 *Pravnički glasnik* (Legal Herald). Novi Sad. Udruženje pravnika u Novom Sadu. Slavko Ćirić. Monthly. January 1937–March 1941. (DLC)

278 *Pravnički život* (Lawyers' Life). Novi Sad. A. F. Jesenski. Monthly. 1926.

279 *Pravnik. Časopis za pravne i državne znanosti* (The Jurist. Periodical for Law and Political Science). Rijeka, Croatia. Marijan Derenčin. October 4, 1862—September 5, 1863, 49 issues.

280 *Pravnik. Časopis za pravne i državne znanosti* (The Jurist. Periodical for Law and Political Science). Zagreb. Matija Mrazović. Weekly. 1853–1854

281 *Pravnik. Glasilo Kluba odvjetnika u Osijeku* (The Jurist. Bulletin of the Lawyers' Club in Osijek). Osijek, Croatia. Monthly. January 1, 1913 to the beginning of World War I.

282 *Pravnik. Glasilo za pravno teorijo in prakso* (The Jurist. Journal for Law Theory and Practice). Ljubljana. Društvo pravnikov LRS. Title varies. Monthly. 1946—(DLC 1946–[52], [1954–56])

283 *Pravnik. List za pravne i državne nauke* (The Jurist. A Review for Law and Political Science). Beograd. The Serbian Lawyers'

Society. Milenko R. Vesnić, Jovan Aćimović *and* Djordje B. Nestorović. Monthly. 1892–94. (DLC 1892)

284 *Pravnik slovenski. List za pravosodje, upravo in državoslovje* (Slovenian Jurist. Journal for Court Practice, Administration and Government). Ljubljana. The first Slovenian legal periodical. J. R. Razlog. Fortnightly and monthly, irregular. June 1, 1870– December 1872. (DLC)

285 *Pravo* (Law). Požarevac, later Beograd. St. Maksimović, later also Andra Djordjević *and* Milenko Vesnić. Monthly. 1885–1891. (DLC [1885–86], [1891])

286 *Pravo. Političko-upravni list* (Law. Political-Administrative Bulletin). Zara, later Split, Dalmatia. Antun Šimunić. Monthly. 1873–83. (DLC [1885–86], [1891])

287 *Pravosodni bilten.* Strokovno glasilo za pravosodno upravo in sodstvo LR Slovenije. Državni sekretariat za pravosodno upravo LRS. (Judicial Bulletin. Periodical for the Administration of the Judiciary Branch and Justice of the People's Republic of Slovenia. State Secretariat for Justice of the People's Republic of Slovenia). Ljubljana. Vlado Kraut. Mimeographed. Quarterly. 1953– (DLC [1954–] [1956]–1957)

288 *Pravosudje. Časopis za sudsku praksu* (Justice. Review of the Courts' Practice). Beograd. Stojan Jovanović, later Ivo Matijević. Monthly. January 1932–41. (DLC [1938])

289 *Pregled. Spisanie za ekonomski, pravni i drugi opštestveni prašanja* (Review. Periodical for Economic, Legal and Other Social Problems). Skopje. Združenie na ekonomistite na NR Makedonija. Quarterly. 1951–(DLC 1953)

290 *Zakonodavstvo* (Legislation). Aca Milovanović. Beograd, v. 1, 1903. Irregular.

291 *Radnička zaštita* (Protection of Labor). Zagreb. Monthly. 1919–41. (DLC [1926–32])

292 *Radno pravo. Obaveštajnik Centralnog sekretarijata radničkih komora* (Labor Law. Bulletin of the Central Secretariat of the Chambers of Workers). Beograd. Zarija Popović. Monthly. January 1940–March 1941. (DLC [1940])

293 *Slovenski pravnik* (Slovenian Jurist). Ljubljana. Društvo Pravnik. Alfonz Mosché, Danilo Majaron, Makso Pirc, Viktor Supan, Rudolf Sajovic. Monthly. 1881–83, 1888–1918, 1921–1944?

(DLC 1881–1883, 1888–1889, 1891–1894, 1897, 1900, 1903, 1906, 1913, 1925, 1927, 1929, 1938–1944)

294 *Spomenice Skupština Kongresa Pravnika Kraljevine S. H. S., Jugoslavije* (Collections of Articles Commemorating the Assemblies of the Lawyers' Federation of the Kingdom of the S. C. S., Yugoslavia). 1925, 1926, 1927, 1931, 1932, 1934, 1935, 1938. Dodaci (Supplements) 1928, 1932, 1934. Editors in various times: Metod Dolenc, Stojan Jovanovich, Ilija Pržić, *and* Josip Vesel. (DLC)

295 *Srpski pravnik* (Serbian Jurist). Beograd. Jovan Aćimović. Published every ten days. September 1, 1882—July 20, 1883.

296 *Sudnica. L'Aula, la gazzetta dei tribunali* (Court Room. Court Journal). Zara, Dalmatia, in Croatian and Italian. Bimonthly. 1868–69.

297 *Sudski list* (Court Journal). Beograd. The oldest Serbian law periodical. Djordje R. Pantelić. Published every ten days. January 1—July 30, 1869.

298 *Sudsko-administrativni glasnik. Organ Udruženja sudsko-administrativnog osoblja Kraljevine Jugoslavije* (Legal-Administrative Herald. Bulletin of the Association of the Administrative Personnel of the Courts of the Kingdom of Yugoslavia). Beograd. Monthly. 1937–41.

299 *Zbornik Pravnog Fakulteta u Zagrebu* (Symposium of the Zagreb Law School). Zagreb. Annual, and since 1954 quarterly. 1948—(DLC 1951, 1953–1954, [1957])

300 *Zbornik znanstvenih razprav. Ljubljana univerza. Juridična fakulteta v Ljubljani* (Symposium of Research Studies. University of Ljubljana. Ljubljana Law School). Ljubljana. Annual. 1, 1920—(DLC 1920–22, 1925–1948, 1954–58)

Some material on legal subjects also appears in the following non-legal periodicals:

301 *Godišnjak Srpske Akademije Nauka* (Yearbook of the Serbian Academy of Science). From 1886 to 1941? Srpska Kraljevska Akademija Nauka i Umetnosti. Beograd, 1887– (DLC)

302 *Ljetopis Jugoslavenske Akademije znanosti i umjetnosti* (Yearbook of the Yugoslav Academy of Science and Art). Zagreb, 1867– (DLC: 1867–1943, 1954–)

303   *Rad Jugoslavenske Akademije znanosti i umjetnosti.* Zagreb, 1867/68– (DLC)

304   *Ljetopis Slovenske Akademije znanosti in umetnosti* (Yearbook of the Slovenian Academy of Science and Art). Ljubljana, 1938– (DLC: 1938–)

305   *Letopis Matice Srpske* (Yearbook of the Serbian *Matica*). Title slightly varies. Novi Sad, 1824– (DLC: 1873–1940, 1947–)

9

LEGAL BIBLIOGRAPHIES

Until recently no comprehensive legal bibliography covering all jurisdictions of Yugoslavia in all its periods of legal development had been published in any language. However, in 1959 Prof. Blagojević of Belgrade prepared a comprehensive legal bibliography and published it in Serbo Croatian and French as follows:

306   Blagojević, Borislav T. (a) Pravna Bibliografija. Izbor knjiga i članaka iz Jugoslavenske pravne literature (Legal Bibliography, Selection of Books and Articles from the Yugoslav Legal Writings). Beograd, 1959. 262 p. Mimeographed. At head of title: Institut za Uporedno pravo, Monografie. (DLC); (b) *Bibliographie juridique yougoslave.* Beograd, 1959. lii, 262 p. Mimeographed. At head of title: Institut de Droit Comparé. (DLC)

The French edition contains an Introduction surveying in French the major fields of law into which the bibliography is divided. (p. I-LII). In both editions the Yugoslav titles are translated into French and the works are listed under 21 chapters, each devoted to a particular subject. Within the chapters the works are entered in alphabetical order, but there is no alphabetical or subject index to the whole book. The editions of codes and laws, even those which are profusely annotated, are not necessarily listed. Articles published in periodicals are listed in abundance. On the other hand, the author's primary attention was concentrated on the works published since 1945. In general, this is a bibliography of legal writings and not of sources of law. Therefore, it does not contain any index of laws and regulations.

A   Prior to 1918

1 Serbia

307   Maksimović, St. (a) Priložak našoj pravnoj književnosti (Contributions to Our Legal Literature). *Pravo,* v. 3, 1893; (b) Bibliografija pravničkih dela i časopisa (Bibliography of Legal Treatises and Periodicals). *Branič* (Beograd), v. 10, 1910.

308   Niketić, Gojko. Pravna bibliografija članaka i knjiga u srpskoj književnosti do kraja 1905 godine (Legal Bibliography of Articles and Books in Serbian Literature through 1905). Beograd, *Arhiv,* 1907. 234 p. (DLC)

> This is a comprehensive work for the period covered, containing 2,760 items. It includes also works in National Economy, Economic Policy, Finances, and Statistics. It also covers collections of laws and decrees, parliamentary records, statistical materials and a list of periodicals, newspapers and almanacs from which legal material was taken.

309   Biographic articles concerning individual legal writers, listing their works, published by the Serbian Royal Academy with respect to its members, as follows: Andra Djordjević, *Godišnjak,* v. 19, 1905: 426–427; Slobodan Jovanović, *id.,* v. 18, 1904: 371–372; v. 21, 1906: 429; Nikodim Milaš, *id.,* v. 15, 1901: 289–292; Živojin M. Perić, *id.,* v. 19, 1905: 377–381; v. 21, 1906: 429–431. (DLC)

310   Novaković, St. Srpska bibliografija za noviju književnost, 1841–1867 (Serbian Bibliography of Recent Literature, 1841–1867). Beograd, 1869. 644 p. Supplements by Rajković, Dj., *Letopis Serbske,* v. 113, 1870–1871; Djemakov, D., *id.,* v. 118, 1875; Mušicki, B., *id.,* v. 119, 1876; Krusić, V., *id.,* v. 120, 1879; Krecarević, M., *id.,* v. 165, 1891. (DLC)

2 Croatia

311   Šilović, Josip. (a) Gesetzgebung und Literatur Kroatiens. *Jahrbuch der Internationalen Vereinigung für vergleichende Rechtswissenschaft und Volkswirtschaftslehre* (Berlin), 1896–

1899, 1904, 1910. (DLC); (b) Gesetzgebung und Literatur in Kroatien. *Mitteilungen der Internationalen Kriminalistischen Vereinigung* (Berlin), v. 6, 1897. (DLC)

312 Bogišić, Valtazar. Pisani zakoni na slavenskom jugu, bibliografski nacrt (Written Laws of the Southern Slavs, a Bibliographic Outline). Zagreb, 1872. 201 p. (DLC)

313 Strohal, Ivan. Statuti primorskih gradova i općina, bibliografski nacrt (Statutes of the Littoral Cities and Municipalities, a Bibliographic Outline). Zagreb, 1911. 125 p. (DLC)

314 As in Serbia, there appeared in Croatia prior to 1918 articles concerning individual legal writers, which contained the lists of their works. The works of the following writers were thus described: Valtazar Bogišić, *Mjesečnik*, No. 31, 1905; Šandor Bresztyenszky, *id.*, No. 30, 1904: 469; Marijan Derečin, *id.*, No. 34, 1908: 167–175; Ivo Malina, *id.*, No. 33, 1907: 232, 257; Josip Pliverić, *id.*, No. 33, 1907: 553–560; Ivan Ružić, *id.*, No. 41, 1915: 122; Josip Šilović, *id.*, No. 39, 1913: 319–325; Hugo Štefanić, *id.*, No. 24, 1898: 632–634. (DLC) Ivan Strohal, *Ljetopis*, No. 33, 1918: 192–195; Fran Vrbanić, *id.*, No. 26, 1911: 154–227. (DLC); Fran Vrbanić, *Mjesečnik*, No. 39, 1913: 889–899. (DLC) Milovan Zoričić, *Ljetopis*, No. 27, 1912: 119–163. (DLC)

B Period from 1918 to 1941

315 Namysłowski, Władysław. Bibliografja prac historicznoprawnych Serbsko-chorwackich (Bibliography of Serbo-Croatian Legal History Works). Lwów, 1921.

316 Pržić, Ilija A. La bibliographie yougoslave de Droit International, 1918–1936. *Annuaire*, v. 1, 1931: 351–393; v. 3, 1937: 353–431. (DLC)

317 Sajovic, Rudolf. Rassegna di Letteratura Giuridica Yugoslava. *Annuario di Diritto Comparato e di Studi Legislativi* (Roma): years 1925–1928 in v. 4–5 (part 1), 1930: 545–560; year 1929 in v. 7 (part 2), 1932: 3–19; year 1930 in v. 8 (part 2), 1933: 218–236; year 1931 in v. 11 (part 1), 1940: 212–232. (DLC)

317[1] Štitić, Lina *and* Hamid Dizdar, *editors.* Bibliografija knjiga i periodičnih izdanja štampanih u Hercegovini, 1873–1941 (Bibliography of Books and Periodicals Published in Herzegovina, 1873–1941). Mostar, 1958. 132 p. (DLC)

318   J. A. Izložba jugoslovenske pravne literature (Exhibition of Yugoslav Legal Literature). *In* Dodatak Spomenici Kongresa Pravnika u Zagrebu 1934. Zagreb, 1935.

319   Bibliografija nastavnika i pomoćnoga osoblja Sveučilišta u Zagrebu školske godine 1933/1934—1938/1939, br. 5: za teološki i pravni fakultet (Bibliography of the works of the Instructors of the University in Zagreb for the School Years from 1933/1934 to 1938/1939, No. 5: for the Theological Department and the Law School). Zagreb, n.d.

Additional legal bibliographical material was published in periodicals, particularly in *Arhiv, Branič, Mjesečnik,* and *Slovenski Pravnik.*

320   Nikić, F. Politika, pravo i sociologija u Letopisu Matice srpske od 1826 do 1926 (Politics, Law and Sociology in the Yearbook of the Serbian *Matica,* 1826–1926). Novi Sad, 1929. 20 p.

321   Subotić (Soubbotitch), Ivan V., *joint author.* Bibliographie des ouvrages ... en langue allemande, 1919–1929, concernant le droit yougoslave. *Annuaire,* v. 1, 1931: 407–418, v. 3; 1937: 305–313. Same for publication: in England by G. Bloch, *id.* v. 3: 317–319; in the United States by L. Pitamic, *id.* v. 1: 419; in French by Subotić, Korenić and Stojković, v. 1: 395–405, v. 3: 323–332; in Polish by E. Muszalski and I. A. Pržić, v. 1: 425–426; in Italian by G. Avakumović, v. 3: 335–338; in Czechoslovak by I. V. Subotić and Markov, v. 3: 341–350. (DLC)

322   The bibliographies of the works of the individual members of the *Srpska Kraljevska Akademija* (Serbian Royal Academy) in Belgrade appeared in the Academy's *Godišnjak:* v. 30, 1921: 331–333 (Toma Živanović); v. 35, 1926: 214–215 (Slobodan Jovanović); v. ? (Živojin M Perić); v. 44, 1935: 211–235; (Teodor Taranovski). (DLC)

323   Bibliographies of the works of the members of the Yugoslav Academy in Zagreb appeared in *Ljetopis,* organ of the Academy: v. 35, 1920: 37–38; v. 36, 1921: 55–57 (Marko Kostrenčić); v. 41, 1927–1928: 94 (Metod Dolenc); v. 41, 1927–1928, p. 96 (Leonid

Pitamic); v. 42, 1928–1929: 78, (Hugo Werk); v. 42, 1928–1929; 133 (Ladislav Polić); v. 42, 1928–1929: 146 (Ernest Miler); v. 53, 1939–1940: 130 (Gregor Krek). (DLC)

324 Bibliographic data on individual writers also appeared in *Mjesečnik*: v. 53, 1927: 94 (Dragutin Čupović); *ibid.*, 466–467 (Ladislav Polić); v. 54, 1928: 210–212 (Aleksandar Badaj); *ibid.*, 214–215 (Nikola Ogorelica); *ibid.*, 503–505 (Ernest Miler); v. 55, 1929: 46 (Mihailo Zobkow); *ibid.*, 453–454 (Hinko Hinković); *ibid.*, 555 (Juraj Vrbanić); v. 55, 1929: 135–137 (Stjepan Posilović); v. 56, 1930: 367–368 (Ante Verona); v. 56, 1930: 554–555 (Nikola Ogorelica); v. 62, 1936: 572–573 (Dragutin Tončić). (DLC) Similar bibliographies appeared also on Valtazar Bogišić in *Glasnik Etnografskog Muzeja* (Beograd), 1934. (DLC); on Dušan M. Subotić in *Pravosudje*, 1934; on Slobodan Jovanović in Sabrana dela Slobodana Jovanovića, Beograd, 1935, v. 16: 441–463; on Živojin M. Perić in *Arhiv*, v. 53, 1938: 245–270. (DLC); and on Valtazar Bogišić in Spomenica Valtazara Bogišića, Dubrovnik, 1940: 21–23.

C   Period Since 1941

325 Spisak izdanja novinarsko-izdavačkog preduzeća Službeni List FNRJ (List of Publications of the Journalistic-Publishing House, the Official Gazette of Yugoslavia). Beograd, 1950.

326 Auly, J. M. *and* Y. Marx. (sous la direction de Marc Ancel). Bibliographie méthodique des études de langue française consacrées au Droit slave. Yougoslavie. *Sociologie et droit slaves* (Paris), v. 1, No. 1, December 1945: 58–59; v. 2, No. 2, March-May, 1946: 180–182. (DLC)

327 Szladits, Charles. A bibliography on foreign and comparative law. New York, 1955–1962. 2 v. (DLC)

328 Knežević, Milivoje V. Bibliografija radova o Dušanovom Zakoniku (Bibliography of the Works on Tsar Dushan's Code). *Bibliotekar* (Beograd), 1948–1949: 473–482. (DLC)

329 Vošnjak, Bogumil. Yugoslav bibliography: political science, law, economics, foreign politics, Yugoslavia and the Balkans, 1915–1941. Washington, D. C., 1951. Mimeographed. (DLC)

330 Bibliographies of the works of L. Pitamic in *Letopis Slovenske Akademije Znanosti in umetnosti* (Ljubljana), v. 1, 1938–1942: 80–83; Janko Polec, *ibid.*: 98–101; Milan Škerlj, *ibid.*: 128–130; v. 2, 1943–1947: 106–125; Rado Kušej, *ibid.*: v. 1, 1938–1942: 185–190; Metod Dolenc, *ibid.*: 195–197; Gregor Krek, *ibid.*: 226–227; Edvard Kardelj, *ibid.*, v. 3, 1948–1949: 120–132; Janko Šlebinger, *ibid.*, v. 4, 1950–1951: 111–124). (DLC)

331 *Bibliografija Jugoslavije* (Bibliography of Yugoslavia). Bibliographic Institute of FPRY. Beograd, 1950– . It is published in two series. The first series lists new books, pamphlets, and musical works published in Yugoslavia as a monthly, later becoming a semimonthly. The second series lists the contents (treatises and articles) of Yugoslav periodicals, newspapers and collections of works; it is published in three subdivisions: social science, literature and art. This series started with *Bibliografija Yugoslavije, članci i književni prilozi u časopisima za 1950–1952* (Bibliography of Yugoslavia, articles and literary works published in periodicals, 1950–1952). Since 1953 as a monthly. (DLC)

332 Andrassy, J. Pravo (Law Bibliography). Zagreb, 1943. 18 p.

333 Smirnov, S. Mihailo. Jugoslovenska bibliografija vazduhoplovnog prava (Yugoslav Bibliography on Air Navigation Law). Beograd, 1959. 129 p. Mimeographed. (DLC)

10

BIBLIOGRAPHY OF BOOKS AND ARTICLES IN THE VERNACULAR

A Comprehensive Topics

1 History of Law

See also Nos.: 542; 549; 573; 587; 598; 1070; 1078; 1414; 2266; 2268; 2269; 2364; 2369; 2388; 2393; 2400; 2427; 2431; 2459; 2463.

334 Adamović, Jova. Privilegije Srpskog naroda u Ugarskoj (Privileges of the Serbian People in Hungary). Zagreb, 1902.

335 Alimpić, Dušan Dj. Upravne vlasti u staroj Srpskoj Carevini (Administrative Authorities of the Old Serbian Empire). Beograd, 1921. 135 p. (DLC)

336 Antonijević, T. Hrvatski ustavni program u Državi Srba, Hrvata i Slovenaca (The Croatian Constitutional Program in the State of the Serbs, Croats and Slovenes). Beograd, 1940. 160 p. (DLC)

337 Avakumović, J. Dj. Engeleska, francuska i srpska porota (The English, French and Serbian Juries). Reprint from *Glasnik srpskog učenog društva*, Beograd, 1885. 160 p. (DLC)

338 Babnik, J. Sledovi slovenskega prava (Traces of Slovenian Law). *Letopis Matice slovenske*, 1882–1883: 64–95.

339 Bakotić, Lujo. (a) Državno-pravni položaj Dalmacije prema Hrvatskoj i Austriji (Constitutional Status of Dalmatia with Respect to Croatia and Austria). *Arhiv*, 1910: 251–270, 365–385. (DLC); (b) Ženidba i udadba u sjevernoj Dalmaciji (Marriage

in Northern Dalmatia). *Id.*, 1909: 114–120, 185–192, 286–294. (DLC)

340 Barbalić, Fran. Prvi istarski sabori, 1861–1877 (The First Diets of Istria, 1861–1877). Zagreb, 1954. 148 p.

341 Bayer, V. Prestanak prava azila u Hrvatskoj (Extinction of the Right of Asylum in Croatia). Zagreb, 1957. 96 p. (DLC)

342 Begović, M. Tragovi našeg srednjevekovnog krivičnog prava u turskim zakonskim spomenicima (Traces of Our Mediaeval Criminal Law in the Ottoman Legal Sources). *Istoriski časopis Srpske akademije nauka* (Beograd), 1951–52: 67–84, 1956: 1–11. (DLC)

343 Beuc, I. Statut zadarske komune iz 1305 godine (Statute of the Municipality of Zara of 1305). *Vjesnik Državnog arhiva* (Rijeka), 1954: 493–781. (DLC)

344 Blagojevlć, B. I. Zakonik Cara Dušana, osnov zakonitosti srednjevekovne srpske države (The Code of Emperor Dushan and Legality in the Mediaeval Serbian State). Skoplje, 1939. 106 p.

345 Bogišić, Valtazar (Baltazar). (a) Desetina sudskih zapisa iz Paštrovića (Notes on Some Legal Records of the Region of Paštrovići). *Arhiv,* 1906: 393–408, 489–504. (DLC); (b) Glavnije crte obiteljskog pisanog prava u starom Dubrovniku (Main Features of the Written Law on Domestic Relations in Old Ragusa). *Rad Jugoslavenske akademije,* 1868: 123–149; (c) Gradja u odgovorima iz različnih krajeva Slovenskog Juga (Material on the Life and Customs of the Various Regions of the Slavic South). Zagreb, 1874. 74, 714 p. (DLC); (d) Liber statutorum civitatis Ragusii compositus anno 1272. *In* No. 395. Vol. 9, 1904, lxix p., il., 466 p., il., (DLC); (e) Na ocienu zbornika sadašnjih pravnih običaja u južnih slovena uvrštenu u XXXII Radu Jugoslavenske akademije (Comments on the Criticism of the Current Customary Law of the South Slavs, inserted in the *Rad Jugoslavenske akademije,* Vol. 32). Spljet, 1877. 35 p. (DLC); *See also:* Hanel; (f) Naputak za opisivanje pravnijeh običaja, koji živu u narodu (Instructions for the Description of Legal Customs among the People). Vienna, 1867. 16 p.; (g) O sabiranju pravnih običaja (On the Collecting of Customary Law Material). *Branič,* 1901: 549–554. (DLC); (h) O važnosti sakupljanja narodnijeh pravnijeh običaja kod Slovena (On the Importance of the Col-

lecting of Slavic Customary Law Material). *Književnik* (Zagreb), 1866: 1–47, 161–241, 408–476; (i) Stanak po dubrovačkom zakoniku od 1272 godine (*Stanak* under the Statute of Ragusa of 1272). *Glasnik Srpskog učenog društva*, 1877: 197–231. (DLC)

346 Bresztyenszky, Š. Pravno-povjestni podatci o Turopolju (Some Data on the History of Law of Turopolje). *Mjesečnik*, 1892. (DLC)

347 Codex diplomaticus regni Croatiae, Dalmatiae et Slavoniae. Zagreb. Compiled by T. Smičiklas, M. Kostrenčić and E. Laszowski. Zagreb, 1904–1916. 14 v. Vol. 1 published as Vol. 7 of Monumenta spectantia historiam Slavorum meridionalium. (DLC: v. 2–14)

348 Čulinović, Ferdo. (a) Državnopravna historija jugoslovenskih zemalja XIX i XX vijeka (History of Government of the South Slav Territories in the XIXth and XXth centuries). Zagreb. 1953–1954. 2 v.; 2nd ed. 1956–1959. 2 v. (DLC); (b) Dušanov zakonik (The Code of Emperor Dushan). Beograd, 1931. 68 p.

349 Dabinović, Antun. Hrvatska Država i Pravna Povijest, s reprodukcijama najvažnijih dokumentata i slikama (Croatian State and History of Law). Zagreb, 1940. 563 p. (DLC)

350 Djurdjev, Branislav. (a) Sremska Kanun-nama iz 1588/89 godine (The Code for Srem of 1588/89). Reprint from *Glasnik Zemaljskog muzeja* (Sarajevo), 1950; (b) Kanuni i Kanun-Name za Bosanski, Hercegovački, Zvornički, Kliški, Crnogorski i Skadarski Sandžak (The Code for the Sandzaks of Bosnia, Herzegovina, Zvornik, Klis, Montenegro and Skadar). Sarajevo, 1957. 212 p. (DLC); (c) Požeška Kanun-nama iz 1545 godine (The Code for Požega of the Year 1545). Reprint from *Glasnik Zemaljskog muzeja u Sarajevu*, 1946; (d) Kanun-nama Bosanskog Sandžaka 1530 godine (Code for the Bosnian Sandžak of 1530). *Ibid.* 1948; (e) Kanum-nama za Bosanski, Hercegovački i Zvornički Sandžak iz 1539 godine (Code for the Sandzaks of Bosnia, Herzegovina and Zvornik of the Year 1539). Reprint from *Istorisko-pravni zbornik* 1950.

351 Dolenc, Metod. (a) Dušanov zakonik (Institutions of the Code of Emperor Dushan). Ljubljana, 1925. 214 p. (DLC); (b) *Gorske bukve* v izvirniku, prevodih in priredbah (*Gorske bukve*

in the original with a translation and adaptation). Ljubljana, 1940. 276 p.; (c) Kmečko dedno nasledstvo za časa veljavnosti gorskih bukev (Inheritance Law of the Peasants under the Regime of *Gorske bukve*). *Časopis za zgodovino in narodopisje* (Maribor), 1927: 105–149. (DLC); (d) Kolektivna odgovornost za kazniva dejanja pa naše narodno pravo (Collective Responsibility for criminal acts and the Criminal Law of Our People). *Pravni vestnik* (Trst), 1923: 184–191, 206–212. (DLC); (e) Kultura in kazensko pravo v luči pravne zgodovine (The Civilization and the Criminal Law in the Light of the History of Law). *Ibid.*, 1924: 129–135, 145–150, 164–167. (DLC); (f) Osebno in rodbinsko-pravna vprašanja v pravosodstvu slovenskih ljudskih sodnikov (Questions of Personal Status and Domestic Relations in the Decisions of the Slovenian Laymen's Courts). *Zbornik znanstvenih razprav*, 1933/34: 1–28. (DLC); (g) Pravna zgodovina za slovensko ozemlje (History of Law of the Slovenian Territories) Ljubljana, 1935. XV, 559 p. (DLC); (h) Pravne razmere v Brežicah od 1. 1585 do 1. 1651 (Legal Life in Brežice from 1585 to 1651). *Zbornik zranstvennih razprav*, 1935/36: 26–67; (i) Pravnozgodovinska studija o prisegi pri Slovencih (The Oath in Slovenian Law, a Study in the History of Law). *Ibid.*, 1939/40: 44–86. (DLC); (j) Pravnozgodovinski prikaz dokaznega postopanja pri sodiščih slovenskega ozemlja (Evidence Before the Courts of the Slovenian Territory, a Study in the History of Law). *Ibid.*, 1937/38: 35–84. (DLC); (k) Pravosodstvo cistersienske opatije v Kostanjevici in jezuitske rezidence v Pleterju od konca 16. do konca 18. stoletja (Jurisdiction of the Cistercian Abbey of Kostanjevica and of the Priory of the Jesuits of Pleterje from the End of the 16th to the Beginning of the 18th Century). *Ibid.*, 1923/24: 1–118. (DLC); (l) Pravosodstvo klevevške in boštanjske graščine od konca 17. do začetka 19. stoletja (Justice of the Feudal Courts of Klevevž and Boštanj from the End of the XVIIth to the Beginning of the XIXth Century). *Ibid.*, 1925/26: 153–247. (DLC); (m) Prispevek k zgodovini zelenaštva med Slovani (Contribtion to the History of Usury among the Slavs). Zagreb, 1929; (n) Simbolična pravna dejanja in izražanja med

Slovenci (Symbolic Acts and Statements in the Law of the Slovenes). *Slovenski pravnik* (Ljubljana), 1938: 241–258, 323–336. (DLC); (o) Značaj zakonika Cara Dušana za Našu državu (Significance of Emperor Dushan's Code from the Yugoslav Viewpoint). Spomenica Kongresa pravnika, 1931: 29–36. (DLC); (p) Slovenska ljudska sodišča v dobi od 16 do 18 stoletja (Slovenian Laymen's Courts from the 16th to the 18th century). Reprint from *Rad Jugoslavenske akademije,* v. 239. 1930. 55 p.; (q) Sorodni odmevi črnogorskih pravnih zgodbic in slovenskega običajnega prava (Similarity of Features of the Montenegrin Institutions and the Slovenian Customary Law). *Časopis za zgodovino in narodopis* (Maribor), 1932: 137–171.

352   Filipović, Milenko S. Svojina Voćaka po narodnim pravnim običajima (Ownership of Fruit-Trees in the Customary Law). *In* Istorisko-pravni zbornik (Sarajevo), 1949: 69–99.

353   Florinskii, Timofei. Pamiatniki zakonodatel'noi Dieiatel'nosti Dushana, Tsaria Serbov i Grekov (Monuments of the Legislative Activities of Dushan, Emperor of the Serbs and Greeks). Kiev, 1888. 490, 222 p. (DLC)

354   Gerasimović, Jevrem. Staro srpsko pravo (The Old Serbian Law). Beograd, 1925. 161 p. (DLC)

355   Goršić, France. Župani in knezi v jugoslovenski pravni zgodovini (The Provincial Governors and Princes in the Yugoslav History of Law). Reprint from *Časopis za zgodovino in narodopisje* (Maribor), 1929. 34 p.

356   Grekov, Boris D. Politsa (Study on Public Relations in *Politsa,* 15th–17th Centuries with the Translation of Its Statute into Russian). Moscow, 1951. 318 p. (DLC)

357   Gremošnik, Gregor. (a) Bosanske i humske povelje srednjega vijeka (Mediaeval Charters of Bosnia and Hum). Reprint from *Glasnik Zemaljskog muzeja* (Sarajevo), 1948. (DLC); (b) Pravni položaj našega roblja u srednjem vijeku (Condition of Our Serfs in the Middle Ages). Reprint from *Glasnik Zemaljskog muzeja* (Sarajevo), 1947.

358   Grujić, Radoslav M. (a) Eparhiska vlastelinstva u srednjevekovnoj Srbiji (Diocesan Benefices in Mediaeval Serbia). Beograd, 1932; (b) Tri hilandarske povelje (Three Charters of Hilandar). *In* Zbornik za istoriju Južne Srbije (Skoplje), 1936.

359 Guzina, R. (a) Knežina i postanak srpske buržoaske države (The Serbian Principality and the Origin of the Serbian bourgeois state). Beograd, 1955. XVI, 270 p. (DLC); (b) Uslovi postanka država kod Južnih Slovena (Statehood among the South Slavs). *Anali Pravnog fakulteta u Beogradu*, 1956: 290–312. (DLC)

360 Hadžibegović, Hamid. (a) Bosanska kanun-hama iz 1565 godine (The Code for Bosnia of the Year 1565). Reprint from *Glasnik Zemaljskog muzeja* (Sarajevo), 1948; (b) Kanun-nama Sulejmana Zakonodavca (Code of Suleyman, the Legislator). Reprint from *ibid.*, 1950.

361 Hanel, Jaromir J. (a) Kritički pogled na djela o slovenskom pravu. I. Zbornik sadašnjih pravnih običaja o južnih slavena od V. Bogišića (Critical Evaluation of Writings on Slavic Law. I. Collection of Current South Slav Customs by V. Bogišić). *Rad Jugoslavenske akademije*, v. 32; (b) Pravni život u splijetskoj obćini (Legal Relations in the Municipality of Split). *Ibid.*, v. 54, 1880: 178–212; (c) Statuta et Leges Civitatis Spalati. In No. 395, Part I. Vol. 2. 1878. 336 p. (DLC); (d) Statuti i zakoni grada i otoka Korčule 1214–1558. Statuta et leges Civitatis et insulae Curzolae, 1214–1558. In No. 395, Part I. Vol. 1, 1877. 306 p. (DLC)

362 Herkov, Zlatko, *editor*. Statut grada Rijeke iz godine 1530 (Statute of the City of Fiume of 1530). Zagreb, 1948. 609 p. (DLC)

363 Hristov, A. Odluke Rilskog kongresa /1905/ o organizaciji i radu revolucionarnih sudova u Makedoniji (Resolutions of the Congress of Rilo /1905/ on the Organization and Operation of the Revolutionary Tribunals in Macedonia). *Arhiv*, 1952: 235–241. (DLC)

364 Hrvatski spomenici (Croatian Monuments). In No. 395, v. 6, 1899. (DLC)

365 Janković, D. (a) Bogišićevi komentari Dušanovog zakonika (Bogišić's Comments on Emperor Dushan's Code). *Anali Pravnog fakulteta u Beogradu*, 1953: 393–409. (DLC); (b) Istorija države i prava feudalne Srbije /XII–XV vek/ (History of the Feudal Serbian State and Its Law). Beograd, 1953. 128 p. (DLC); (c) Istorija država i prava naroda F.N.R.J. I. Ranofeudalne države jugoslovenskih naroda do XII veka (History of the States of the

Federal People's Republic of Yugoslavia and of the Law of Their Peoples. I. The Early Feudal States of the South Slav Peoples up to the XII Century). Beograd, 1st ed.?; 2d ed. 1950. 107 p.; 3d ed. 1952. 123 p. (DLC); 5th ed. 1960. 113 p. (DLC); (d) Istorija države i prava Srbije /XII–XV vek I (History of the Serbian State and Law /XIIth–XVth centuries/). Beograd, 1953. 128 p. (DLC); 1956. 168 p.; (e) Istorija države i prava Srbije u XIX veku (History of the Serbian State and Law in the XIXth Century). Beograd, 1952. 240 p. (DLC); 1956, 173 p.; 3d ed. 1959, 157 p. (DLC)

366 Jantolek, Stevan. (a) Istorija države i prava Hrvatske od XIV do XIX veka (History of the Croatian State and Law from the XIVth to the XIXth century). Beograd, 1952. 64 p.; (b) Istorija države i prava naroda F.N.R.J. Feudalni period (History of the FPR, of Yugoslavia and the Law of Its People. The Feudal Period). Beograd, 1951. 242 p. (DLC); (c) Istorija na državata i pravoto na narodite na FNRJ (History of the State and Law of the People of the FPRY). Skopje, 1960. 170 p. (DLC)

367 Jasinski, Mihail. (a) Iz istorije Kastavskog statuta (A Study on the Statute of Kastav). Zbornik znanstvenih razprav, 1927/28: 52–72. (DLC); (b) Prehod od ustnega običajnega prava k pisanemu zakonu (Transition from the Oral Customary to Written Law). Ibid., 1924/25: 1–18.

368 Jelić, Ilija M. (a) Krvna osveta i umir u Crnoj Gori i Severnoj Albaniji (Feud and Conciliation in Montenegro and Northern Albania). Beograd, 1926. 154 p. (DLC); (b) Vasojevićki zakon od dvanaest točaka, s komentarom (The Law of the Vasojevići Tribe in Twelve Points, with a Commentary). Beograd, 1929.

369 Jireček, Hermengild. Svod zákonův Slovanských (Compilation of Slavic Laws). Prague, 1880. 596. (DLC)

370 Jovanović, Aleksa S. (a) Istorijski razvitak srpske zadruge (History of the Serbian Family Community). Beograd, 1896. 188 p. (DLC); (b) Logoteti u crkvi i državi srpskog (The Logotets in the Serbian Church and State). Reprint from Videlo (Beograd), 1886. 42 p.; (c) Nasledno pravo u starih Srba (Old Serbian Inheritance Law). Reprint from Otadžbina (Beograd), 1888. 33 p.; (d) O pravu nasledstva kod Srba (Serbian Inheritance Law). Beograd, 1888; (e) Prinosci na istoriju starog srpskog prava

(Contributions to the History of the Old Serbian Law). Beograd, 1900. 156 p.

371 Jovanović, Jovan M. Zakonodavstvo u XVIII i XIX veku u Crnoj Gori (Montenegrin Legislation of the XVIIIth and XIXth Centuries). *Arhiv,* 1910: 349–364. (DLC)

372 Jovanović, Milenko. Porota srednjevekovne Srbije (Jury in Medieval Serbia). Beograd, 1959. 59 p. (DLC)

373 Kadlec, Karel. (a) Dějiny veřejného práva ve střední Evropě. Část VI, Státy jihoslovanské (History of Public Law in Central Europe. Part IV, the State of South Slavs). Prague, 1st ed. 1920; 2nd ed.?; 3rd ed. 1923; 4th ed. 1928. (DLC: 3rd ed., 514 p.); (b) Prvobitno slovensko pravo pre X veka. (The Pre-Tenth Century Original Slavic Law. Translated by F. Taranovski). Beograd, 1924. 130 p. (DLC)

374 Kapidžić, Hamdija. Postupak s dužnicima u Dubrovniku. Primjer iz XVIII stoleća (Treatment of Debtors in Dubrovnik. An Example from the XVIIth Century). *In* Istorisko-pravni zbornik (Sarajevo), 1949.

375 Karano-Tvrtković, Pavleh. Srpski Spomenici, ili Stare Risovulje, Diplome, Povelje, i Spomenici Bosanski, Serbski, Hercegovački, Dalmatinski i Dubrovački Kraljeva, Careva, Banova, Despota, Knezova, Vojvoda i vlastelina (Serbian, Bosnian, Herzegovinian, Dalmatian and Dubrovnik Documents of Kings, Emperors, Princes and Overlords). Beograd, 1840. 336 p. (DLC)

376 Kercselich de Corbavia, Balthasar Adam. De Regnis Dalmatiae, Croatiae Sclavoniae Notitiae Preliminares Periodis IV Distincti. Zagabriae, n. d., 522 p. (DLC)

377 Klaić, Vjekoslav. Statut grada Zagreba od god. 1609 i Reforma njegova god. 1618 (Statute of the City of Zagreb of 1609 and Its Amendment of 1618). Zagreb, 1912. 135 p. (DLC)

378 Kostrenčić, Marko. (a) Fides publica /javna vera/ u pravnoj istoriji Srba i Hrvata do kraja XV veka (Public Trust in the History of Law of the Serbs and Croats to the End of the XVth Century). Beograd, 1930. 159 p.; (b) Hrvatska pravna povijest (History of Croatian Law). Zagreb, 1919. 223 p.; 1933, 328 p. (DLC); (c) Nacrt historije hrvatske države i hrvatskog prava (An Outline of the History of Croatian Government and Croatian Law). Zagreb, 1956. 235 p. (DLC); (d) O Dušanovom zakonu

(On the Code of Emperor Dushan). *Arhiv,* 1949: 557–570; (e) Običajno pravo (Customary Law). *Zbornik Pravnog fakulteta u Zagrebu,* 1948: 177–187; (f) Pomorsko pravo u statutima primorskih naših gradova i otoka (The Maritime Law in the Statutes of Our Coastal Cities and Islands). *Mjesečnik,* 1914: 885–892, 960–967, 1001–1005; 1915: 285–296, 336–347. (DLC); (g) Slobode dalmatinskih gradova po tipu trogirskom (Franchises of the Dalmatian Cities after the Pattern of those of Trogir). Zagreb, *Rad Jugoslavenske akademije,* v. 239, 1930: 56–150. (DLC); (h) Vinodolski zakon (The Statute of Vinodol). *Ibid.,* v. 227, 1923: 110–230. (DLC)

379   Krmčija moračka (*Kormchaia* of Morach). Description of the Manuscript. City Statute. N. Dučić, *editor.* Beograd, 1877. 134 p. (DLC)

380   Krstajić, P. Zakonodavstvo u NR Crnoj Gori, 1942–1946 (Legislation of the People's Republic of Montenegro, 1942–1946). *Istoriski zapisi* (Cetinje), 1954: 43–64. (DLC)

381   Kukuljević-Sakčinski, Joannes, *editor.* Jura regni Croatiae, Dalmatiae & Slavoniae. Zagreb, 1861–1862. 3 v. (DLC)

382   Kušević. De municipalibus juribus et statutis regnorum Dalmatiae, Croatiae, et Slavoniae. Zagabriae, 1830. 88 p.

383   Lanović, Mihajlo. Lukno u Hrvatskoj (The Parochial Contribution in Croatia). Zagreb, 1914. 227 p. (DLC)

384   Leontovich, Fedor Ivanovich. Drevnee Horvato-dalmatskoe zakono'datel'stvo (The Old Croatian-Dalmatian Legislation). *Zapiski Imperatorskago Novorosiiskago universiteta,* Odessa, v. 1, No. 34, 1868: 1–12, 1–155. (DLC)

385   Liebald-Ljubojević, J. Prisega u našem narodu (The Oath among our People). *Rad Jugoslavenske akademije,* v. 16, 1871: 22–58. (DLC)

386   Maciejowski, Wacław. Istorija slovenskih prava. Preveo i sa svojim primjetbama, koje se na srpsko pravo odnose, popunio Nikola Krstić (History of Slavic Law. Serbian Translation by Nikola Krstić, with the Translator's Remarks Referring to Serbian Law). Buda, 1856. 366 p.

387   Milović, Jevto M. Zbornik dokumenata iz istorije Crne Gore, 1685–1782 (Collection of Documents on the History of Montenegro, 1685–1782). Cetinje, 1956. 458 p. (DLC)

388 Marković, Laza. Jugoslovenska država i Hrvatsko pitanje /1914–1929/ (The Yugoslav State and the Croatian Question, 1914–1929). Beograd, 1935. 372 p. (DLC)

389 Barada, Miho. Hrvatski vlastelinski feudalism (Croatian Feudalism). Zagreb, 1952. 133 p. (DLC)

390 Maurović, M. Opća pravna povijest (General History of Law). Zagreb, 1923. 256 p.

391 Mažuranić, Antun. Zakon Vinodolski od lěta 1280. S priloženim izgledom glagolskog pisma u rukopisu (The Statute of Vinodol of the Year 1280. With a Facsimile of the Statute in Glagoletic Alphabet appended). Zagreb, 1843.

392 Mažuranić, Vladimir. Prinosi za hrvatski pravno-povjesni rječnik (Contributions toward a Croatian Dictionary of History of Law). Zagreb, 1908–1922. 10 v. Dodatci (Supplements), 1923. 76 p. (DLC)

393 Mijušković, D. Sistem Dušanova zakonika (The System of Emperor Dushan's Code). Srpski pregled (Beograd), 1895: 115–122, 145–151, 176–181.

394 Mitrović, A. Feudalno pravo u Dalmaciji (Dalmatian Feudal Law). Mjesečnik, 1908: 401–412. (DLC)

395 Monumenta historico-juridica Slavorum meridionalium. Zagreb, 1877–1926. 11 v. (DLC)

396 Monumenta spectantia historiam Slavorum meridionalium. Zagreb. S. Ljubić, F. Rački, R. Lopašić, S. Nodilo, E. Fermendzin, B. Bogišić, C. Horvat, F. Šišić, E. Laszowski, D. Körbler, V. Klaić and M. Barada, comp. 1868–1919. 44 v. (DLC)

397 Nedeljković, B. (a) Istorija baštinske svojine u novoj Srbiji od kraja 18 veka do 1931 (History of the Land Tenure in Serbia from the End of the XVIIIth Century to 1931). Beograd, 1936. XV, 348 p.; (b) Postanak Zadruge (Origin of the Family Communities). Pravna Misao, 3, 1937: 595–604. (DLC); (c) Sarajevski sidžil iz godine 1555–59 (The Code of Sarajevo of 1555–59). Arhiv, v. 69, 1954: 189–199, 419–434. (DLC); (d) Sok i sočbina u starom srpskom pravu (Sok and Sočbina in the Old Serbian Law). Istoriski časopis Srpske akademije nauka, 1957: 53–81. (DLC)

398 Nikčević, T. Organizacija i nadležnost sudova u Srbiji 1804–1813 godine (Organization and Jurisdiction of the Courts in

Serbia during the Years 1804–1813). *Istoriski zapisi* (Cetinje), 1954: 382–406.

399 Nikić, Fedor. Lokalna uprava Srbije u XIX i XX veku (Local Government in Serbia in the XIXth and XXth Centuries). Beograd, 1927. 396 p. (DLC)

400 Ninčić, Momčilo. (a) Istorija agrarno-pravnih odnosa srpskih težaka pod Turcima. I deo: Ranije doba (History of the Land Tenure System of the Serbian Serfs under the Turks. Part I: The Early Period). Beograd, 1920. 133 p. (DLC); (b) Pitanje o svojini zemlje u Srba pod Turcima (Serbian Landowners under Turkish Rule). Beograd, 1913. 25 p.

401 Novaković, Stojan. (a) *Baština* i *Boljar* u jugoslovenskoj terminologiji srednjega veka (*Baština* and *Boljar* in the Yugoslav Mediaeval Terminology). Beograd, 1913; (b) Die Wiedergeburt des Serbischen Staates. 1804–1813. Sarajevo, 1912. VII, 185 p. (DLC); (c) *Pronijari* i *baštinici* (*Pronoia and Baštinici*). Beograd, 1888. 102 p.; (d) Rimsko-vizantijsko pravo i narodni pravni običaji. Pravo prvenstva rodjaka ili suseda pri kupovini zemlje (Roman-Byzantine Law and the Customary Law of the People. The Right of Preemption of the Relatives and Neighbors). *Godišnjica Nikole Čupića* (Beograd), v. 9, 1887: 214–234; (e) Srednjevekovna Srbija i rimsko pravo (Mediaeval Serbia and Roman Law). *Arhiv*, 1906: 209–226. (DLC); (f) Srpska baština u starijim turskim zakonima (The Serbian *baština* in the Early Turkish Laws). *Pravnik* (Beograd), v. 2, 1892: 21–37, 135–142; (g) Udava ili samovlasno apšenje za dug u starome srpskom zakonodavstvu i u narodnim običajima (*Udava,* or Capture of the Debtor by the Creditor under the Old Serbian Law and the People's Customary Law). *Pravnik* (Beograd), v. 1, 1892: 13–21, 97–107. (DLC); (h) Ustavno pitanje i zakoni Karadjordjeva vremena (The Constitutional Problem and the Laws under Karadjordje). Beograd, 1907. IV, 131 p. (DLC); (i) Vaskrs države srpske. Politička istorijska studija o prvom srpskom ustanku 1804–1813 (Resurrection of the Serbian State. A Political-Historical Study on the First Serbian Uprising 1804–1813). Beograd, 1914. XIV, 236. (DLC); (j) Zakonik Stefana Dušana Cara srpskog, 1349 i 1354 (Code of the Serbian Emperor Dushan, 1349 and 1354). Beograd, 1st ed. 1870; 2nd ed. 1898. cliii, 312 p. (DLC 2nd ed.); (k) Zakonski

spomenici srpskih država srednjega veka (Legal Sources of the Mediaeval Serbian States). Beograd, 1912. 912 p.; (l) *editor*. Matije Vlastara sintagmat, Slovenski prevod vremena Dušanova (Matija Vlastar's Sintagma. Slavic Translation of the Time of Emperor Dushan). Beograd, 87 p. Added title page: Srpska Kraljevska Akademija. Zbornik za Istoriju Jezik i Književnost Srpskog Naroda, Part 1, Book 4. (DLC)

402 Ortner, Stjepan. Repetitorij iz pravne povjesti Germana i Slavena (Synopsis of the History of Law of the Germans and Slavs). Zagreb, 1898. 272 p. (DLC)

403 Ostrogorski, G. Pronija (The *Pronia* System). Beograd, 1951. 200 p.

404 Palacký, F. (a) Srownání zákona cara Stefana Dušana srbského s nejstaršjimi řády zemskými w Čechách (The Code of the Serbian Emperor Dushan as Compared with the Oldest Statutes of the Czech Land). Piague, 1937; (b) Translated into Serbian by Milash Popović: Zakonik Cara Srbskog Stefana Dušana Silnog, sravnjen sa starim zemaljskim uredbama u Českoj. Reprint from *Glasnik Društva srpske slovesnosti*, Beograd, 1949. 67 p.

405 Drinković, M. Hrvatska i državna politika (Croatia and the State Policy). Zagreb, 1928. 125 p. (DLC)

406 Pappafava, V. O kmetstvu s osobitim obzirom na Dalmaciju (On Serfdom, with Special Reference to Dalmatia). *Mjesečnik,* 1886: 410–425, 475–489, 528–543, 590–595. (DLC)

407 Pavich, A., T. Matić *and* M. Rešetar. Statut der Poljica. Vienna, 1912. 81 p.

408 Pavičević, Bronko. Stvaranje crnogorske države (Origin of the Montenegrin State). Beograd, 1955. 428 p. (DLC)

409 Pavlov, A. S. Soobshchenie o serbskom zakoniku Stefana Dushana, 1349–1355 (Report on the Serbian Code of Stephan Dushan, 1349–1355. Studies of the Imperial Society of History and Russian Antiquities. Book IV). Moscow, 1885.

410 Pellegrini, C. (a) Kmetstvo u dubrovačkom kotaru (Serfdom in the Territory of Ragusa). *Mjesečnik,* 1909, No. 11; 1910, Nos. 5, 8–9. (DLC); (b) Običaji (Customs). *Ibid.,* 1906, Nos. 7, 9, 11; 1911, No. 2. (DLC); (c) Sulla colonia dalmata. Zadar, 1896. 52 p.

411 Perić, Živojin M. Medjunarodno običajno /nepisano/ pravo

(International Customary /Unwritten/ Law). *Branič*, 1932: 517–529. (DLC)

412 Petranović, Božidar. (a) O osveti, mirenju i vraždi po negdašnjem srbsko hrvatskome pravnom običaju (Retaliation, Reconciliation and Blood Money in the Serbo-Croatian Ancient Customary Law). *Rad Jugoslavenske akademije,* 1867/68. (DLC); (b) O pravu nasljedstva kod Srba na osnovu pravnih običaja i pisanih spomenika (Serbian Inheritance Law as Based on Custom and Written Sources of Law). Beograd, 1923. 30 p. (DLC); (c) O robstvu o srbskim spomenicima i statutima primorskih dalmatinskih gradova (On Serfdom Pursuant to Serbian Sources and Statutes of the Dalmatian Cities). *Rad Jugoslavenske akademije,* 1872.

413 Petrović, Njegoš Stevo. Zakonik Petra I (The Code of Peter I). Cetinje, 1903. 34 p.

414 Petrović, Radmila S. (a) Doba postanka Grbaljskog zakonika (Historical Background of the Code of Grbalj). Reprint from *Zapisi,* Cetinje, 1929; (b) Čl. 16 Grbaljskog zakonika; kamen o vratu (Art. 16 of the Code of Grbalj; Stone around the Neck). Reprint from *Policija,* Beograd, 1930, Nos. 9 and 10; (c) Kazne u Grbaljskom zakoniku (Punishments Provided by the Code of Grbalj). Reprint from *Ibid.,* 1930, No. 4; (d) Zakonik Petra I, vladike crnogorskog, 1798 i 1803 (Code of Peter I, Bishop of Montenegro, 1798 and 1803). Reprint from *Godišnjica Nikole Čupića,* v. 39, 1930. (DLC)

415 Polec, J. (a) Kraljestvo Ilirija (Kingdom of Illyria). Ljubljana, 1925. 337. (DLC); (b) Razpored sodnih instanc v slovenskih deželeh od 16. do 18 stoletja (Courts in the Slovenian Territories from the XVIth to the XVIIIth century). *Zbornik znanstvenih razprav,* 1927/28: 116–142. (DLC)

416 Polić, L. Povijest modernoga izbornoga zakonodavstva hrvatskoga (History of Modern Croatian Election Legislation). *Mjesečnik,* 1908: 641–691, 745–789. (DLC)

417 Poličević, M. Ustrojstvo pravosudja u staroj srpskoj državi u XIII i XIV veku (Organization of the Administration of Justice in Serbia in the XIIIth and XIVth centuries). *Arhiv,* v. 23, 1923. (DLC)

418 Pop-Georgiev, D. Sopstvenosta voz čifličite čifligarskite agrar-
no-pravni odnosi vo Makedonija do Balkanskata vojna 1912
(Ownership of the Tchifliks and the Status of the Tchifligars in
Macedonia up to the Balkan War of 1912). Skopje, 1956. 188 p.

419 Pucić, Medo. Spomenici srbski od 1395 do 1423 to est pisma
pisana od Republike Dubrovačke Kraljevima, Despotima, Vojvo-
dama, i Knezovima Srbskiem, Bosanskiem, i Primorskiem (Serbian Documents of the Period 1395–1423, i.e., Notes Addressed
by the Republic of Ragusa to the Serbian, Bosnian and Coastal
Kings, Despots, Vojvods and Princes). Beograd, 1858–1862. 2 v.

420 Rački, Franjo. Odlomci iz državnoga prava hrvatskoga za
narodne dinastije (Contributions to the Study of Croatia's Government under Its National Dynasty). Vienna, 1861. 162 p.

421 Radić, Frano, editor. Knjiga o uredbama i običajima skup-
štine i obćine otoka Lastova (Code of the Regulations and
Customs of the Assembly and Commune of the Island of Lastovo).
Zagreb, 1901.

422 Radičević, Stefan. Projekt Ustava za Vojvodinu srbsku, sa
državoslovnim primjetbama (Draft of the Constitution for the
Serbian Voyvodina, annotated). Zemun, 1949.

423 Radojčić, Nikola. (a) Dušanov zakonik. Preveo, Nikola Radojčić (Emperor Dushan's Code. Translated by Nikola Radojčić).
Novi Sad, 1950. 70 p. (DLC); (b) Sudije i zakon u srednjevekovnoj Srbiji i u Ugarskoj (The Judges and the Law in Mediaeval Serbia and Hungary). *Letopis Matice Srpske,* 1925: 53–68;
(c) Vizantisko pravo u Dušanovom Zakoniku (Byzantine Law in
the Dushan Code). Beograd, 1951. 18 p. (DLC); (d) Zakonik
Cara Stefana Dušana (The Code of Emperor Dushan). *Arhiv,*
1949: 542–556. (DLC); (e) Zbornik u čast šeste stogodišnjice
Zakonika Cara Dušana (Commemorative Volume on the Occa-
sion of the Six Hundredth Anniversary of Emperor Dushan's
Code). Beograd, 1951. 268 p. (DLC)

424 Radonić, Jovan, editor. Dubrovačka akta i povelje (Records
and Charters of Ragusa). Beograd, Book I: v. 1, 1934, 496 p.;
v. 2, 1934, 497 p.; Book II: v. 1, 1935, 536 p.; v. 2, 1938, 670 p.;
Book III: v. 1, 1939, 544 p.; v. 2, 1939, p. 545–1098; Book IV:
v. 1, 1941, 787 p.; v. 2, 1942, 859 p.

425 Radosavljević, M. Baština i svojina ili kolektivizam i indivi-

dualizam kod Srba (Land Property and Private Ownership, or Collectivism and Individualism Among the Serbs). *Branič,* 1887: 517–524; 1888: 85–107. (DLC)

426 Regulamentum seu Constitutiones Mariae Theresiae pro Illyrica natione. Vienna, 1771. Lat. et Illyr.

427 Ribnikar, V. Oblici svojine u našoj istoriji srednjega veka (Forms of Preperty among the Serbs in the Middle Ages). Beograd, 1891. 79 p.

428 Ristić, Siniša J. Razvitak vladalačke vlasti u srpskom narodu (Development of the Ruler's Power among the Serbs). Beograd, 1902.

429 Roganovich, Jovan P. Chernogorskiĭ teokratizm (Montenegrin Theocracy, 1496–1851). Kazan, 1899. 96 p.

430 Safarik, P. I. Kratko izvestje o ustanovi poljičkoj (Short report on the Statute of Poljica). Transl. from Czech by Antun Berčić. Zadar, 1857. 16 p.

431 Sindik, I. Dušanovo zakonodavstvo u Paštrovićima i Grblju (The Code of Emperor Dushan in Paštrović and Grbalj). Beograd, 1951. 64 p.

432 Škaberne, F. Slovenski advokati in javni notarji v književnosti (Slovenian Attorneys and Notaries Public in Literature, Science and Politics). Ljubljana, 1936. 60 p.

433 Škarić, V. Staro rudarsko pravo i tehnika u Srbiji i Bosni (The Old Mining Law and Techniques in Serbia and Bosnia). Beograd, 1939.

434 Solovjev, Aleksandar. (a) Dušanov Zakonik g. 1349 i 1354 (Code of Emperor Dushan of 1349 and 1354). Beograd, 1929. 54 p. (DLC); (b) Dušanov Zakonik kod Paštrovića (Emperor Dushan's Code among the Paštrovići). *Arhiv,* 1933: 17–26. (DLC); (c) Grčke povelje srpskih vladara (Charters of the Serbian Kings in Greek). Beograd, 1936. 537 p. (DLC); (d) Knjiga privilegija Grbaljske župe, 1647–1767 (Collection of the Privileges of the Province of Grbalj). Beograd, 1938. 78 p.; (e) Manastirske povelje starih srpskih vladara (Charters of Privileges Granted to the Monasteries by the Old Serbian Rulers). Skoplje, 1938; (f) O Karadjordjevom Zakoniku (The Code of Karadjordje). *Arhiv,* 1932: 373–382. (DLC) ; (g) Odabrani spomenici srpskog prava od XII do kraja XV veka (Selective Collections of Sources of

Serbian law from the XIIth to the XVth Century). Beograd, 1926. 234 p. (DLC); (h) Paštrovske isprave XVI–XVIII veka (The Paštrovići Records of the XVI-XVIII Centuries). Beograd, 1936; (i) Pojam države u srednjevekovnoj Srbiji (The State Concept in Mediaeval Serbia). *Godišnjica Nikole Čupića* (Beograd), v. 42, 1933: 64–92. (DLC); (j) Postanak i značaj Dušanovog Zakonika (Origin and Significance of Emperor Dushan's Code). Beograd, 1st ed.? 2nd ed. 1931: 31 p. (DLC); (k) Povelje Cara Uroša u Hilandarskom Arhivu (The Charters of Emperor Urosh in the Archives of the Monastery of Hilandar). *Bogoslovlje* (Beograd), 1927: 281–293; (l) Sebrov zbor (Assemblies of Free Peasants). *Arhiv*, 1928: 170–177. (DLC); (m) Seljaci plemići u istoriji jugoslovenskog prava (Peasant Nobility in the History of Yugoslav Law). *Arhiv*, 1935: 455–464. (DLC); (n) Srbi i vizantijsko pravo u Skoplju početkom XIII veka (The Serbs and Byzantine Law in Skoplje in the XIIIth Century). Reprint from *Glasnik Skopskog naučnog društva*, Skoplje, v. 11–16, 1936; (o) Srpska crkvena pravila iz XIV veka (Serbian Church Rules of the XIVth Century). Reprint from *Ibid.*, v. 14, 1935; (p) Srpske zakonske kompilacije XVII veka (Compilation of XVIIth Century Serbian Laws). Beograd, 1933. 63 p.; (q) Stonske odredbe. Ordines Stagni. Izvori za istoriju Južnih Slovena (The Ordinances of Ston. Sources of the History of the South Slavs). Beograd, 1936. 383 p.; (r) Studije iz istorije našega narodnog prava iz XVIII vijeka (Studies on the History of Our National Law in the XVIII Century). Reprint from *Glasnik Zemaljskog muzeja,* Sarajevo, 1939; (s) Ugovor o kupovini i prodaji u srednjevekovnoj Srbiji (Purchase and Sale Contracts in Mediaeval Serbia). *Arhiv*, 1927: 429–448; (t) Zakonodavstvo Stefana Dušana Cara Srba i Grka (Legislation of Stephan Dushan, Emperor of the Serbs and Greeks). Skoplje. 1928. VIII, 248 p.; (u) Značaj vizantijskog prava na Balkanu (The Significance of the Byzantine Law in the Balkans). Reprint from *Godišjica Nikole Čupića* (Beograd), v. 37, 1928.

435   Spaić, V. (a) Nasljedno pravo u srednjevekovnoj Bosni (Inheritance Law in Mediaeval Bosnia). *Godišnjak Pravnog fakulteta* (Sarajevo), 1953: 103–120; (b) O baštinskom sistemu u srednjevekovnoj Bosni (Land Tenure in Mediaeval Bosnia) . *Is-*

toriskopravni Zbornik (Sarajevo), 1949: 107-115. (DLC); (c) Pravni režim u Bosni i Hercegovini za vrijeme Turaka (Law in Bosnia and Herzegovina under the Turks). *Ibid.,* 1949: 101-115. (DLC); (d) Zemljišno-knjižni sistem u Bosni i Hercegovini za vrijeme Turaka (The Land Title System in Bosnia and Herzegovina under Turkish Rule). *Ibid.,* 1950: 15–37. (DLC)

436 Spevec, F. (a) Oporuka po statutu korčulanskom i spljetskom (The Testament under the Statutes of Curzola and Spalato). *Mjesečnik,* 1889: 297–307, 339–349. (DLC); (b) Pravo bliže rodbine glede odsvoja nekretnina po starom germanskom i staroslovenskom pravu (The Right of Preemption of the Next of Kin under Germanic and Old-Slavic Law). Zagreb, 1883. 167 p.

437 Stanojević, St. Car Dušan (Emperor Dushan). Reprint from *Bratstvo.* Beograd, 1922.

438 Statut grada Zagreba od godine 1732 i Zbornik Statuta grada Zagreba od godine 1773 (Statute of the City of Zagreb of 1732 and Collection of the Statutes of the City of Zagreb 1773). Zagreb, 1952. 69. (DLC)

439 Strohal, Ivan. (a) Bratstva /bratovština/ u starom Trogiru (Brotherhoods in Old Trogir). *Rad Jugoslavenske akademije,* v. 201, 1914: 47-66. (DLC); (b) Osnova za sabiranje gradje o pravu koje u narodu živi (Basic Plan for the Collecting of Data on Customary Law). *Mjesečnik,* v. 36, 1910. (DLC) ; (c) Otkupno pravo u starih Hrvata (The Right of Preemption in Early Croatian Law). *Rad Jugoslavenske akademije,* v. 189, 1911: 1-115. DLC); (d) Pravna poviest dalmatinskih gradova (Legal History of the Dalmatian Cities) . Zagreb, 1913. 375 p. (DLC); (e) Razvitak vlasnosti (Evolution of the Concept of Ownership). *Rad Jugoslavenske akademije,* v. 164, 1906: 37-156. (DLC); (f) *Sprega* kao argument prvotne zajednice dobara kod starih Slovena (*Sprega,* an Argument in Evidence of Collective Ownership in the Primitive Slavic Societies). *Mjesečnik,* 1904: 188–197, 256–268. (DLC); (g) Statut i reformacije grada Trogira (Statute of the City of Trogir and its Changes) . Zagreb, 1915. 371 p. (DLC); (h) Statut veprinački (The Statute of Veprinac). *Mjesečnik,* 1910: 899–910. (DLC); (i) Sudovanje u Veprincu u 16. vijeku (Administration of Justice in Veprinac in the 16th Century). *Mjesečnik,* 1910: 1037–1076. (DLC); (j) Ustanovljenje prava

koje u narodu živi (Legal Institutions Alive Among the People). Zagreb, 1909. 54 p.; (k) Zakon vinodolski (The Statute of Vinodol). *Mjesečnik,* 1912: 240–243, 343–352, 882–888. (DLC)

440 Taranovski, Fedor. (a) Dušanov Zakonik i Dušanovo Carstvo (Dushan's Code and Dushan's Empire). Novi Sad, 1926; (b) Istorija srpskog prava u nemanjićkoj državi (History of Serbian Law under the Dynasty of the Namanjići), I deo, Istorija državnog prava (History of Constitutional Law). Beograd, 1931, 262 p.; II deo, Istorija krivičnog prava (History of Criminal Law), 1931, 144 p.; III deo, Istorija gradjanskog prava; IV deo, Istorija sudskog uredjenja i postupka (History of Civil Law and History of the Judiciary and the Court Procedure Parts 1-4), 1935. 232 p. (DLC)

441 Tomanović, Lazar. Nasljedno pravo po Danilovom zakoniku (Inheritance Law under the Code of Prince Danilo). *Arhiv,* 1906: 1-18. (DLC)

442 Tomašić, Nikola. Temelji državnoga prava Hrvatskoga Kraljevstva. Pacta conventa /Fundamenta juris publici Regni Croatiae/. Zagreb, 1910. 175 p.

443 Tončić, D. Plemićke Zadruge (Nobiliary Family Communities). *Mjesečnik,* 1923: 26-32, 49-70. (DLC)

444 Troicki, S. Ktitorsko pravo u Vizantiji i u Nemanjićkoj Srbiji (Patronage in Byzantium and in Serbia under the Dynasty of the Nemanjići). Beograd, 1935. 54 p.

445 Truhelka, Ćiro. Državno i sudbeno ustrojstvo Bosne u doba prije Turka (Government and Organization of the Judiciary in Bosnia Prior to Turkish Rule). *Glasnik Zemaljskog Muzeja,* Sarajevo, 1910: 71–112. (DLC)

446 Urošević, Laz. Pravosudje i pisano pravo u srednjevekovnoj Srbiji u svetlosti današnjeg pisanog prava (Administration of Justice and Written Law in Mediaeval Serbia in the Light of the Written Law of Our Days). Beograd, 1939. 246 p. (DLC)

447 Vilfan, S. Slovenska pravna zgodovina in njene zveze s prakso (History of Slovenian Law in Connection with the Current Law Practice). *Pravnik* (Ljubljana), 1954: 15–29. (DLC)

448 Vladisavljević, Milan. Državnopravni položaj Hrvatske u okviru Habsburške monarhije (The Constitutional Status of Croatia

within the Framework of the Hapsburg Monarchy). Beograd, 1937. 78 p.

449 Vojnović, K. (a) Crkva i država u dubrovačkoj republici (Church and State in the Republic of Ragusa). *Rad Jugoslavenske akademije,* 1894: 32–142, 1895: 1–91. (DLC); (b) O državnom ustrojstvu republike dubrovačke (Government in the Republic of Ragusa). *Ibid.,* 1891: 24–67. (DLC)

450 Vošnjak, Bogumil. Ustava in uprava Ilirskih dežel (Constitution and Administration of the Illyrian Provinces, 1809–1813). Ljubljana, 1910. 285. (DLC)

451 Vukosavljević, Sreten V. (a) Istorija seljačkog društva. I. Organaizovanje seljačke zemljišne svojine (History of the Peasant Society. I. Origin of the Peasant Land Property). Beograd, 1953. 336 p.; (b) O zemljišnoj svojini na selu (Peasant Land Ownership). *In* Istoriskopravni zbornik (Sarajevo), 1949: 37–77; (c) Seoske uredbe o vodama (Water Regulations in Villages). Beograd, 1847. 147 p. (DLC)

452 Zakon Vinodol'skii (Law of Vinodol). Preface by A. M. Evreinova. St. Petersburg, 1878. 16 p. (DLC)

453 Zigel', F. Zakonik Stefana Dušana (The Code of Emperor Stephan Dushan). Sankt Petersburg, 1872. 149 p. (DLC)

454 Živanović, T. Izvršenje smrtne kazne po Dušanovom Zakoniku i u obnovljenoj srpskoj državi pre i posle izdanja kaznenog zakonika /1860/ (The Death Penalty under the Code of Emperor Dushan, and in the Restored Serbian State Prior to and after the Promulgation of the Criminal Code in 1860). *Branič,* 1906: 371-392. (DLC)

455 Zobkow, M. Pravo preče kupnje u otomansko-bosanskom zakonodavstvu (The Right of Preemption in the Bosnian-Ottoman Law). *Mjesečnik,* 1926: 207–238, 249–309. (DLC)

456 Zontar, J. (a) Kastavščina in njeni statuti do konca 16. stoletja (The Region of Kastav and Its Statutes up to the End of the XVIth Century). *Zbornik znanstvenih razprav,* 1945/46: 154-200. (DLC); (b) Skupna podlaga zgodovine slovenskega prava (A General Outline of the Slovenian History of Law). *Slovenski pravnik,* 1933: 162-171.

2 Jurisprudence

See also Nos.: 2465; 2466.

457 Arandjelović, Drag. Erencvajgova gledišta o tumačenju i popunjavanju zakona (Ehrenzweig's Views on the Question of Interpreting and Amending Laws). *Branič*, 1935: 1-14.

458 Arnautović, Dobrivoje. O pojmu prava (The Concept of Law). *Srpski Književni Glasnik* (Beograd), 1901.

459 Blagojević, Borislav T. Pojam prava u sistemu dr. Djordja Tasića (The Concept of Law in the System of Dr. Dj. Tasić). *Branič*, 1935. (DLC)

459¹ Čuković, Milan. Princip zakonitosti u Jugoslaviji (Rule of Law in Yugoslavia). 1959. 358 p.

460 Čulinović, Ferdo. Narodno pravo (The Law of the People). Beograd, 1938. 495 p. (DLC)

461 Demčenko, G. Slobodno i strogo pravo (Strict and Free Interpretation of Law). Ljubljana, 1936. 15 p.

462 Denisov, Andrej I. Osnovi marksističko-lenjinističke teorije države i prava (Elements of the Marxist-Leninist Theory of the State). Beograd, 1949. 478 p. (DLC)

463 Djordjević, Jovan. (a) Neka pitanja o problemu birokratije i birokratizma (Problems of Bureaucracy). *Narodni pravnik,* 1950: 116–137. (DLC); (b) Osnovni principi i organizacioni oblici socijalističke demokratije (Basic Principles and Organizational Forms of Socialist Democracy). *Vojno-politički glasnik,* 1952: 8–40; (c) Politika i društvena tehnika u socijalističkoj demokratiji (Politics and Techniques of Society Organization in Social Democracies). *Arhiv,* 1957: 23–42. (DLC); (d) Prilog pitanju sistema socijalističkog prava FNRJ (Contribution to the Problem of Yugoslav Socialist Law). Beograd, 1951. 44 p. (DLC); (e) Ustavni Zakon i elementi nove deklaracije prava (The Constitutional Law and the Elements of a New Declaration of Human Rights). *Arhiv,* 1953: 23-54. (DLC)

464 Filipović, Jovan. Filosofija prava (Philosophy of Law). Beograd, 1st ed. 1839. 132 p.; 2nd ed. 1863. 266 p. (DLC)

465 Geršković, L. O socijalističkoj demokratiji (Socialist Democracy). Beograd, 1953. 30 p.

466 Institut za uporedno pravo [Publikacije]. Beograd, 1956.

Serija A-G. (Institute for Comparative Law [Publications]. Series A-G.) Series A. Survey of Foreign Legal Publications Available in the Libraries of the FPRY. No. 1, 1956- (DLC: Nos 2, 3, 1957, 1958) ; Series B. Survey of Legal Provisions Published in *Sl. L.* of the FPRY; Series C. Recent Legal Publications; Series D. Foreign Law (Theory, Legislation, Court Decisions. Reviews of Publications and Bibliography.) (DLC: 3-8, 10-20, 1956-1959); Series E. Foreign Legislation (DLC: Nos. 1–21, 1957–1960); Series F. Comparative Law; Series G. Survey of Legislation in Foreign Countries. (DLC: Nos. 2-4, 1958-1959).

467 Jovanović, Slobodan. (a) Osnovi pravne teorije o državi (Elements of a Legal Theory on the State). Beograd, 1st ed. 1906, 256 p.; 2nd ed. 1914. 321 p.; 3rd ed. under title: O državi, osnovi jedne pravne teorije, 1922. 448 p. (DLC); (b) Političke i pravne rasprave (Political and Legal Essays). Beograd, 1st ed. 1908. 278 p. (DLC); 2nd ed. 1932–33. 3 v. (DLC)

468 Jovanović, Vladimir. Politički rečnik (Political Dictionary). 2 v. v. 1, Novi Sad, 1870; v. 2, Beograd, 1871–1878. (DLC)

469 Krbek, I. (a) Odumiranje države (Withering Away of the State). Zagreb, 1951. 24 p.; (b) Prilog teoriji o pojmu prava (Contribution to the Theory of the Concept of Law). Zagreb, 1952. 93 p.

470 Krikner, Jovan. Uticaj pravnih škola na ekonomske koncepije (Influence of Schools of Legal Thought on Economic Concepts). Beograd, 1909. 40 p.

471 Lanović, Mihajlo. Uvod u pravne nauke (Introduction to Legal Sciences). Zagreb, 1st ed. 1934. 435 p.; 2nd ed. 1942. 435 p. (DCL)

472 Lukić, Radomir. (a) Istorija Političkih i pravnih teorija (History of Political and Legal Theories). Beograd, 1956. 343 p.; (b) Teorija države i prava (Theory on State and Law). Beograd, 1st ed. 1953–1954; 2nd ed. 1956–1957. 2 v.; 3rd ed. 1958– (DLC); (c) Osnovi nauke o državi i pravu (Basic Principles of State and Law). Beograd, 1958. 183 p.; 2nd ed. 1959. 183 p. (DLC); (d) Materijal za izučavanje teorije države i prava (Material on the Theory of Law and State). Beograd, Part 1 (?); Part 2. 1952. 213 p. (DLC); (e) Uvod u pravne nauke (Introduction to Legal Studies). Beograd, 1960. 430 p. (DLC)

473 Marković, Božidar S. Pravičnost kao izvor prava (Equity, Source of Law). *Arhiv* (Beograd), 1939. (DLC)

474 Marković, Čed. Pravna svest (Legal Consciousness). Beograd, 1921. 56 p. (DLC)

475 Marković, Milivoje Č. Pravna država (Rule of Law). Beograd, 1939. 56 p.

476 Legradić, Rudolf. Opća teorija prava. Uvod u pravo (General Theory of Law. Introduction to Law). 2nd ed. Zagreb, 1960. 96 p.

477 Martinac, Borivoje, M. Pravo i država u normativnoj doktrini Feliksa Šomla (Law and Government in the Normative Theory of Felix Somló). Beograd, 1938. 581 p. (DLC)

478 Matić, Dimitrije. Načela umnog državnog prava (Principles of Constitutional Law). Beograd, 1851. 193 p. (DLC)

479 Mikulčić, M. Encyclopaedija prava i državoslovnih znanosti (Legal and Political Encyclopedia). Zagreb, 1886. 140, 40 p.

480 Perić, Ž. (a) O školama u pravu (The Schools of Legal Thought). Beograd, 1921. 42 p.; (b) Princip stečenih prava i socijalizacija dobara (Vested Rights and Nationalization). Reprint from *Društveni Život,* Beograd, 1920. 20 p.

481 Rajović, Radošin. Pravo. Osnovni pojmovi o državi i pravu. Društveno i državno uredjenje Jugoslavije (Law. Basic Principles on State and Law. Social and Constitutional Setup). 3rd ed. Beograd, 1960. 135 p.

482 Pitamic, Leonid. Pravo i revolucija (Law and Revolution). Ljubljana, 1920.

483 Rašić, Vojislav V. Deoba nauke o pravu (Division of the Science of Law). Beograd, 1904. 51 p.

484 Spalajković, Miroslav. O racionalnosti u pravu (Rationalistic School of Thought in Law). Reprint from *Godišnjak,* 1938, 1939. 88 p. (DLC)

485 Spektorskii, E. Država i njen život (The State and Its Life). Beograd, 1933. 222 p.

486 Spevec, Fr. I. O pravu i pravednosti (Law and Justice). *Mjesečnik,* 1896: 385–410. (DLC)

487 Taranovski, Feodor. Enciklopedija Prava (Jurisprudence). Beograd, 1923. 534 p. (DLC)

488 Tasić, Djordje. (a) Uvod u pravne nauke (Introduction to

the Science of Law). Beograd, 1941. 234 p. (DLC); (b) Da li običaj može ukinuti zakon (Superseding of Statutes by Customary Law). *Arhiv,* 1937. (DLC); (c) Problem opravdanja države (Justification of the State). Beograd, 1920. 90 p.; (d) Savremeni politički sistemi i shvatanja o državi (Contemporary Political Systems and State Concepts). Beograd, 1936. 82 p.; (e) Socijalizam i država (Socialism and the State). Beograd, 1946. 82 p.

489 Tucaković, M. Škola egzegeze i njena kritika (The Exegetic School and' its Criticism). Beograd, 1940. 22 p.

490 Vukotić, M. Interpretacija pravnih propisa (Interpretation of Legal Provisions). Zagreb, 1953. 144 p.

491 Vuksanović, V. O pojmu pravnog poretka (The Concept of Rule of Law). Beograd, 1931. 107 p. (DLC)

492 Živanović, T. Sistem sintetičke pravne filozofije (A System of Synthetic Philosophy of Law). Beograd, 1959. 939 p. (DLC)

3 Constitutional Law

See also: Ch. 11, A, 2c; Specific Topics: Aliens; Church and State; Elections; Nationality Law; The Press.

a Yugoslav Law and General Works

See also Nos.: 2243; 2281; 2282; 2285; 2286; 2287; 2293a; 2295; 2319aa; 2341; 2356; 2388; 2366; 2392; 2398a; 2428; 2454; 2460; 2461; 2462.

493 Ustav (Constitution). 3rd ed. Zagreb, 1948. 44 p. (DLC)

494 Ustav Federativne Narodne Republike Jugoslavije (Constitution of the Federal People's Republic of Yugoslavia). Beograd, 1950. 50 p. (DLC)

495 Ustav FNRJ i Ustavi Narodnih Republika (Constitution of the FPRJ and Constitutions of the People's Republics). Beograd, 1950. 355 p. (DLC)

496 Osnutek Ustave (Draft of the Constitution). Ljubljana (?), 1946. 16 p. (DLC)

497 Ústava Federativní Lidové Republiky Jugoslavie (Constitution of the People's Republic of Yugoslavia). Translated by Otokar Kolman. Praha, Svoboda, 1946. 38 p. (DLC)

498 Ustav na Federativna Narodna Republika Jugoslavija (Constitution of the Federal People's Republic of Yugoslavia). Beograd, 1950. 54 p. (DLC)

499 Novi Ustav Federativne Narodne Republike Jugoslavije (The New Constitution of the Federal People's Republic of Yugoslavia). Beograd, 1953. 125 p. (DLC)

500 Ustavni Zakon o Osnovama Društvenog i Političkog uredenja Federativne Narodne Republike Jugoslavije i Saveznim Organima Vlasti (Constitutional Law of 1953). Govor Maršala Tita, 14. I. 1953. Ekspose Eduarda Kardelja. Zagreb, 1953. 141 p. (DLC)

501 Ustav Kraljevine Jugoslavije (Constitution of the Kingdom of Yugoslavia). Beograd, 1931. 39 p. (DLC); 51 p. (DLC); 57 p. (DLC)

502 Ustav Kraljevine Jugoslavije od 3 Septembra 1931 God. sa Zakonom o Kraljevskoj Vlasti, Porodičnim Pravilnikom za Članove Kraljevskog Doma i Zakonom o Zemaljskoj Odbrani (Constitution of the Kingdom of Yugoslavia of September 3, 1931, Law on the Power of the King, Family Regulation for the Members of the Royal Family and Law on National Defense). 2nd ed. Beograd, 1932. 63 p.; 3rd ed. 1933. 78 p. (DLC)

503 Zakon o Kraljevskoj Vlasti i o Vrhovnoj Državnoj Upravi (Law on the Power of the King and the Organization of the Executive Branch of the Government). Beograd, 1929. (DLC); 2nd ed. 1929. 14 p. (Zbirka Zakona, Sveska 116.) (DLC)

504 Andrassy, Juraj. Kritički pogledi na teoriju o narodnoj suverenosti (Criticism of the Theory on National Sovereignty). Zagreb, 1947. 80 p.

505 Bastaić, Konstantin. Nova Jugoslavija. Pregled državno-pravnog razvitka povodom desetgodišnjice drugog zasjedanja AVNOJ-a (New Yugoslavia. Survey of the Constitutional Development on the Tenth Anniversary of the AVNOJ). Zagreb, 1954. 420 p. (DLC)

506 Biankini, Juraj. O upravi Dalmacije. Govori izrečeni na Dalmatinskom saboru u zasjedanjima 1892 (The Government of Dalmatia). Zadar, 1892. 235 p. (DLC)

507 Čulinović, Ferdo. (a) Prestanak Kraljevine Jugoslavije i postanak Demokratske Federativne Jugoslavije (The End of the

Kingdom of Yugoslavia and the Creation of a Democratic Federal Yugoslavia). *Rad Jugoslavenske Akademije znanosti i umjetnosti,* 311, 1957; 239-299; (b) Nacionalno pitanje u jugoslovenskim zemljama (The National Problem in the South Slav Territories). Zagreb, 1955. 158 p. (DLC)

508 Dimitrijević, Pavle. Ustav na FNRJ i trudovo zakonodavstvo (Constitution of the FPRY and Labor Law). Beograd, 1950. 196 p. (DLC)

509 Djisalović, Radivoj. Namesništvo. Studija iz uporednog ustavnog prava (Regency. A Study on Comparative Constitutional Law). Novi Sad, 1940. 240 p.

510 Djordević, Jovan. (a) Elementi ustavnog prava Federativne Narodne Republike Jugoslavije (Principles of Constitutional Law of the FPRY). Beograd, 1951. 303 p. (DLC); (b) Ustavno pravo Federativne Narodne Republike Jugoslavije (Constitutional Law of the FPRY). Beograd, 1947. v. 1, 131 p. (DLC); Beograd, 1st ed. 1953. 436 p. (DLC); 2nd ed. 1958. 510 p. (DLC); 1961. 787 p. (DLC); (c) Političko i državno uredjenje Jugoslavije (Political and Constitutional Setup of Yugoslavia). Beograd, 1956. 212 p.; (d) Osnovna pitanja federalne države (Basic Principles of a Federative State). Beograd, 1939, 191 p.; (e) Jugoslovenski ustav i odvojenost crkve od države (Yugoslav Constitution and Separation of Church and State). *Medjunarodni problemi,* 1953: 3–10; (f) Društveno uredjenje FNRJ (Governmental Setup of the FPRY). Beograd, 1954. 131 p.; 1956. 211 p.; 1959. 350 p. (DLC) Title varies slightly.

511 Dolenc, Metod. Kriminalnopolitična presoja zadnjega dostavka člena 12 Vidovdanske Ustave (Criminal and Political Meaning of Article 12, Last Paragraph, of the Constitution of 1921).Ljubljana, 1923.

512 Gaber, Stevan. Osnovi na teorija na državata i pravoto (Elements of Constitutional Law). Part I. Skopje, 1954. 124 p.

513 Geršković, Leon. (a) Dokumenti o razvoju narodne vlasti (Documents on the Development of the People's Power). Beograd, 1946. 320 p.; (b) Historija narodne vlasti (History of the People's Power). Beograd, 1950–1951. 2 v.; 1954–1955. 2 v.; rev. ed. 1957. 300 p. (DLC); (c) Material za izučavanje historije narodne vlasti (Study of the History of the People's Power). Mime-

ographed. Beograd, 1951. 65 p. (DLC); (d) Državna uprava Jugoslavije (Governmental Administration of Yugoslavia). Beograd, 1956. 120 p. (DLC)

514 Jovanović, Dragoslav. (a) Donošenje zakona (Legislative Procedure). Beograd, 1923. 194 p. (DLC); (b) Pojam zakona (Concept of Statute). Beograd, 1923. 79 p. (DCL)

515 Jovanović, Slobodan. Ustavno pravo Kraljevine Srba, Hrvata i Slovenaca (Constitutional Law of the Kingdom of Serbs, Croats and Slovenes). Beograd, 1924. 472 .

516 Jovičić, Miodrag. Referendum. Pokušaj uporednopravnog izučavanja (Referendum. A Comparative Study). Beograd, 1957. 48 p. (DLC)

517 Kardelj, Edward. (a) Glavne karakteristike Ustava (Main Features of the Constitution of the FPRY). Sarajevo, 1945. 22 p.; (b) O osnovama društvenog i političkog uredjenja FNRJ (Principles of the Social and Political Setup of the FPRY). Beograd, 1953. 172 p.

518 Kojić, Dragutin. Političke i pravne rasprave (Political and Legal Essays). Beograd, 1926. 89 p. (DLC)

519 Kostić, Laza. (a) Komentar Ustava Kraljevine Jugoslavije (Jugoslovensko Ustavno Pravo). (Commentary on the Constitution of the Kingdom of Yugoslavia). Beograd, 1934. 298 p. (DLC) ; (b) Odlikovanja. Pravna priroda akta o odlikovanju (Decorations. Legal Nature of the Act of Awarding Decorations). Subotica, 1937. 19 p.

520 Krišković, Vinko. Uprava i sudstvo (Administration and Judiciary). Zagreb, 1900. 95 p. (DLC)

521 Kapor, Vladimir and Slavoljub Popović. Pravni priručnik o pravima i dužnostima gradjana (Manual of the Rights and Duties of Citizens). 2nd ed. Beograd, 1961. 746 p.

522 Kušej, Gorazd. Materijal za studij predmeta primerjalno ustavno pravo (Material for the Study of Comparative Constitutional Law). Ljubljana, 1960. 317 p.

523 Lukić, Rad. D. (a) Načelo jedinstva vlasti u Saveznom ustavnom zakonu (Principle of Unity of Power in Federal Constitutional Law). *Arhiv* (Beograd), 1953: 55–65; (b) O datumu nastanka Nove Jugoslavije (Date of the Creation of New Yugoslavia). *Ibid.* 1953: 308–314). (DLC)

524   Miladinović, Žarko. Parlamentarno pravo interpelacije (Parliamentary Right of Interpellation). Subotica, 1929. 88 p.

525   Mojić, Sava. Privredni parlament. Političko-pravna studija (Economic Parliament. A Politico-Legal Study). Beograd, 1929. 126 p.

526   Nadvornik, Branislav. Osnovi državnog privrednog i radnog prava; društveno uredjenje FNRJ (Principles of Constitutional, Economic and Labor). Zagreb, 1954. 140 p. (DLC)

527   Narodni Odbor Grada Zagreba. Ustavno uredjenje FNRJ i Radno Zakonodavstvo (Constitutional Setup of the FPRY and Labor Law). Zagreb, 1951. 238 p. (DLC)

528   Nedeljković, Milorad. Ekonomsko-finansijska studija o državi teorija činilaca proizvodnje, teorija poreza) (An Economic and Financial Study on the State). Beograd, 1923. 50 p.

529   Novo zakonodavstvo o centralnom državnom uredjenju (New Legislation on the Organization of the Central Government). Beograd, 1929. (Zbirka Zakona, sv. 136). (DLC)

530   Odluka o saglašavanju saveznih zakona sa promenama izvršenim u državnoj upravi i u sistemu upravljanja privredom (Decree on the Adjustment of Federal Laws with the Changes Made in the Government Administration and in the System of National Economy). Beograd, 1950. 11 p. (DLC)

531   Pavlović, Danilo B. Izborni sistem po Vidovdanskom ustavu. Doktorska rasprava (Electoral System under the Constitution of 1921. Doctoral thesis). Beograd, 1939, 137 p.

532   Perić, Živojin. (a) Jugoslovenska Savezna Država. (Yugoslav Federal State). 2nd ed. Beograd, 1940. 10 p.; (b) Federativna Evropa in federativna Jugoslavija (Federal Europe and Federal Yugoslavia). Ljubljana, 1940. 6 p.

533   Petrović, Milivoje J. O decentralizaciji uprave (Decentralization of the Administration). Beograd, 1920. 71 p.

534   Pijade, Moša. O nacrtu Ustava FNRJ (Draft of the Constitution of the FPRY). Zagreb, 1946. 50 p.

535   Pitamic, Leonid. Država (The State). Prevalje, 1927. 480 p. English translation: A Treatise on the State. Baltimore, 1934. 301 p. (DLC)

536   Polić, Ladislav. (a) O nacrtima ustava (Drafts of the Consti-

tution). Zagreb, 1921; (b) Zakoni i sankcije (Laws and Sanctions). Zagreb, 1923; (c) Opće državno pravo (Constitutional Law). Zagreb, 1925.

537 Propisi o Narodnoj Skupštini FNRJ i o Presidijumu Narodne Skupštine FNRJ (Provisions on the National Assembly of the FPRY and the Presidium of the National Assembly of the FPRY). Beograd, 1948. 128 p. (DLC)

538 Dakić, Krsta. Osnovi državnog i društvenog uredjenja FNRJ (Principles of the Government and Social Setup of the FPRY). Beograd, 1961. 120 p.

539 Protić, Stojan M. (a) Nekoliko misli o novom ustavu (Some Thoughts on the New Constitution). Beograd, 1919. 40 p.; (b) Nacrt Ustava po predlogu Stojana M. Protića, Ministra pripreme za Ustavotvornu skupštinu (Draft of the 1921 Constitution). Definitivni tekst, posle diskusije sa komisijom. Sa dodatkom: Nacrt Ustava izradjen od Ustavne komisije (Gradja za Ustav i osnovne zakone, 1). Beograd, 1920. 127 p. (DLC); (c) Uoči Ustavotvorne Skupštine (On the Eve of the Constitutional Assembly). Beograd, 1920. 85 p.; (d) Oko ustava. Kritika i polemika (The Constitution, Criticism and Polemics). Beograd, 1921. 93 p.; (e) Vladin predlog ustava (Government Draft of the Constitution). Beograd, 1921. 120 p.; (f) Privremeni poslovnik za Ustavotvornu Skupštinu (Temporary Rules of Procedure of the Constitutional Assembly). Beograd, 1921. 32 p.

540 Pržić, Ilija A. (a) Poslovnik Narodne Skupštine Kraljevine SHS, sa objašnjenjima iz parlamentarne prakse i zakonskim odredbama (Rules of Procedure of the National Assembly of the Kingdom of the S. C. S.). Beograd, 1924. 276 p. (DLC); (b) Državno i medjunarodno pravo (Constitutional and International Law). Beograd, 1934. 34 p.

541 Radovanović, Ljubomir. Narodna Skupština i izborni zakon (National Assembly and the Electoral Law). Beograd, 1937. 37 p.

542 Režek, Borut. Razvoj poslanskega mandata v najvišjih predstavniških organih fevdalne in buržoazne države. Doktorska disertacija (Development of the Representative's Mandate in the Highest Representative Organs of the Feudal and Bourgeois State). Ljubljana, 1955. 98 p. (DLC)

543 Ristić,Milovan. Narodne skupštine u Prvom srpskom ustanku

(National Assemblies in the First Serbian Uprising). Beograd, Prosveta, 1955.

544   Sagadin, Stefan. Naš sadašnji ustavni položaj (Our Present Constitutional Situation). Ljubljana, 1920. 77 p. (DLC)

545   Simić, Nikola Dj. Smendova integraciona teorija o državi i pravu. Doktorska rasprava (Smend's Integration Theory on the State and Law. Doctoral Thesis). Beograd, 1937. 142 p. (DLC)

546   Smodlaka, J. Nacrt Jugoslovenskog Ustava (Draft of the Yugoslav Constitution). Zagreb, 1920. 119 p.

547   Sokić, Miloje M. Statistika izbora narodnih poslanika za Prvu Jugoslovensku Narodnu Skupštinu održanih 8 novembra 1931 (Statistics of the Election of People's Representatives for the First Yugoslav National Assembly on November 8, 1931). Zemun-Beograd, 1935. 320 p.

548   Stefanović, Jovan. (a) Ustavo Pravo FNRJ i Komparativno (Constitutional Law of the FPRY). Zagreb, 1950, 701 p. (DLC) ; 2nd ed., 1956. 2 v. (DLC); (b) Odnos izmedju crkve i države (Relation Between Church and State). Zagreb, 1953. 146 p.; (c) Zamjenjivanje šefa države (Substitution for the Chief of State). Zagreb, 1935. 36 p.; (d) Širenje federalizma i njegovo uporedno slabljenje po sadržaju (The Spreading of Federalism and Its Concurrent Weakening). Sarajevo, 1954. 144 p.; (e) Krivična Odgovornost ministara i šefa izvršne vlasti *Spomenica Dolencu, Kreku, Kušeju, i Škerlju* (Criminal Liability of Cabinet Ministers and the Chief of the Executive Department). Ljubljana, 1936. 78 p.

549   Šišić, Ferdo. Dokumenti o postanku Kraljevine SHS, 1914-1919 (Documents Concerning the Creation of the Kingdom of the SCS, 1914-1919). Zagreb, 1920. 329 p.

550   Šnuderl, Makso. (a) Ustavno Pravo FLRJ (Constitutional Law of the FPRY). Ljubljana, 1956-1957. 2 v. (DLC); (b) Vprašanje Delegirane Zakonodaje v FLRJ in Pravni Značaj Ukaza (Delegation of Legislative Power). Ljubljana, 1951. 47 p. (DLC); (c) Dve Deklarativni Normi Naše Ustave (Two Declaratory Provisions of Our Constitution). Ljubljana, 1950. 214 p. (DLC)

551   Štambuk, Milko. Osnovi društvenog uredjenja FNRJ. Ustav

i zakonodavstvo (Basis of the Social Setup of the FPRY. Constitution and Legislation). Zagreb, 1955. 86 p.

552 Tasić, Djordje. (a) Odgovornost države po principu jednakosti tereta (Responsibility of the State under the Principle of Equal Sharing of Burdens). Beograd, 1921. 245 p. (DLC); (b) Pravne razprave. Naš sadašnji ustavni položaj. Sindikati i štrajk činovnika. Pravne granice u radu Parlamenta i odgovornost države za zakonodavne radnje. O konzervativnom i demokratskom nacionalizmu (Essays. Our Present Constitutional Setup. Syndicates and Strike of Employees. Liability of the State for Legislative Acts. Conservative and Democratic Nationalism). Belgrad, 1921. 88 p.; (c) Jedan pokušaj podele državnih funkcija u formalnom i materijalnom smislu (An Attempt to Separate Governmental Functions). Ljubljana, 1926. 82 p.; (d) Tri rasprave iz javnog prava (Three Essays on Public Law). Beograd, 1931. 71 p.; (e) Prava i dužnosti gradjana (Rights and Duties of Citizens). Novi Sad, 1925. 38 p.

553 Trumbić, Ante. Govor u sednici Ustavotvorne Skupštine 23 i 25 aprila 1921 povodom generalnog pretresa o Ustavu (Speech Delivered at the Meeting of the Constitutional Assembly on April 23, 25, 1921 in the General Discussion on the Constitution). Beograd, 1921. 58 p.

554 Vladisavljević, Milan. Problem jedinstva javnog prava. Država i medjunarodna zajednica (Unity of Public Law, State and International Community). Beograd, 1934. 174 p.

555 Vošnjak, Bogumil. Kriza suvereniteta i državna vlast u savremenoj državi (Crisis of Sovereignty and State Power in a Contemporary State). Zagreb, 1926. 8 p.

556 Domaćina, Stjepan. Državno i društveno uredjenje FNRJ. Skripta (Government and Social Setup of the FPRY. Lectures). Zagreb, 1960. 149 p.

557 Vulović, Ljubomir. Naš samoupravni problem (Our Self-Government). Beograd, 1925. 151 p.

558 Zakoni o Državnoj Upravi sa Uredbom o Organizaciji i Radu Saveznog Izvršsnog Veća. Komentar od Milorada Vučkovića. Preface by J. Djordjević (Laws Establishing the Executive Branch of the Government; Decree on the Organization of the Federal Executive Council). Beograd, 1956. 273 p. (DLC)

559　Zakon o Uredjenju Vrhovne državne uprave, sa Zakonom o Ustrojstvu državne uprave, Uredbom o Podeli na odeljenja Pretsedništva ministarskog saveta i Ministarstava i Zakonom o uredjenju Protsedništva ministarskog saveta (Law on the Organization of the Executive Branch of the Government). Beograd, 1929. 62 p. (Zbirka Zakona, sv. 22). (DLC)

560　Zakonodavstvo o Centralnom Državnom Uredjenju (Legislation on the Organization of the Central Government). Beograd, 1928. (Zbirka Zakona, sv. 82). (DLC)

561　Zakon o Ministarskoj odgovornosti (Law on Cabinet Minister's Responsibility). Beograd, 1922. 16 p. (DLC)

562　Zakon o Poslovnom Redu u Senatu i Narodnoj Skupštini (Rules of Procedure for the Senate and the National Assembly). Beograd, 1932. 91 p. (DLC)

563　Zakon o Poslovnom Redu u Narodnoj Skupštini i Zakon o Poslovnom Redu u Senatu (Rules of Procedure for the National Assembly and Senate). Beograd, 1932. 128 p. (DLC)

564　Zakon o Javnim Zborovima i Udruženjima (Law on Public Meetings and Assemblies). Beograd, 1926. 18 p. (DLC)

565　Zakon o Udruženjima, Zborovima i Dogovorima od 18 Septembra 1931 (Law on Associations, Meetings and Assemblies). Beograd, 1931. 28 p. (DLC)

566　Živančević, Mihailo M. (a) Jugoslavija i federacija (Yugoslavia and Federation). Beograd, 1918. 423 p.; (b)Federalizam i unitarizam (Federalism and Unitarianism). Beograd, 1936. 179 p.

b　Component Parts of Yugoslavia

　　aa　Serbia
　　　　See also Nos.: 401h; 2319a; 2346; 2349a; 2359; 2361; 2410; 2425h; 2449.

567　Ustav Knjažestva Serbie (Constitution of the Principality of Serbia) Sultanskij hatišerif, istekšij okolo polovine Ševala 1254 (od 10/22 do 12/24 Dekemvrija 1838), sodržavajućij Ustav, darovanij Njegovim Visočestvom žiteljima Něgove provincije Serbije. Beograd, n. d.

568 Ustav Knjažestva Serbie (Constitution of the Principality of Serbia). Proglašen U Kragujevcu 1869. Beograd, 1869. 51 p. (DLC)

569 Ustav Kraljevine Srbije (Constitution of the Kingdom of Serbia). Beograd, 1888. 65 p. (DLC); 1894. 135 p. (DLC); 1901. 36 p. (DLC); 1903. 56 p. (DLC); 1911. 58 p. (DLC); 1911. 203 p. (DLC)

570 Čulinović, Ferdo. Neki državnopravni problemi Prvog srpskog ustanka (Some Constitutional Problems of the First Serbian Uprising). Zbornik Pravnog fakulteta u Zagrebu, 1954: 111–129. (DLC)

571 Djordjević, Jovan. (a) Novi Ustav NRS (New Constitution of the PRS). Beograd, 1954. 133 p. (DLC); (b) Ustavni zakon o osnovama društvenog i političkog uredjenja i organima vlasti NR Srbije, sa predgovorom i Komentarom (Constitutional Law of the People's Republic of Serbia). Beograd, 1956.

572 Grebenac, Svetolik M. Vrhovna uprava i političke borbe u Karadjordjevoj Srbiji (Executive Branch of the Government and Political Struggle of Karadjordjevich's Serbia). Beograd, 1940. 129 p.

573 Istorija Srbskog Ustava (History of the Serbian Constitution). Novi Sad, 1861. 119 p.

574 Janković, Dragoslav. O političkim strankama u Srbiji XIX veka. Doktorska disertacija (Political Parties in Serbia in the Nineteenth Century. Doctoral Thesis). Beograd, 1951. 284 p.

575 Jovanović, Slobodan. Naše Ustavno pitanje u XIX veku (Our Constitutional Problems in the Nineteenth Century). Beograd, 1908.

576 Jovanović, Slobodan and Kosta Kumanudi. Osnovi javnog prava Kraljevine Srbije (Principles of Public Law of the Kingdom of Serbia). Beograd, 1907–1909. 2 v. (DLC).

577 Kasanović, Josif. Ministarska odgovornost u srpskom javnom pravu (Cabinet Ministers' Responsibilities in Serbian Public Law). Beograd, 1911. 219 p.

578 Lončarić, J. Državni savet po Ustavu od 1838 godine (The Council of State under the Constitution of 1838). Beograd, 1907. 81 p.

579 Matić, Dimitrije. Javno pravo knjažestva Srbije (Public Law of the Principality of Serbia). Beograd, 1851. 164 p. (DLC)

580 Milanović, A. Ustavi i ustavnost u Srbiji (Constitutions and Constitutionality in Serbia). Beograd, 1903.

581 Milanović, Milovan Dj. (a) Jedan ili dva doma (One or Two Houses). Beograd, 1901; (b) Udaljenje Kraljice Natalije iz Srbije izvršeno autoritetom državne vlasti nije protivno Ustavu (Queen Natalie's Removal from Serbia not an Unconstitutional Act). Beograd, 1891.

582 Nenadović, Jaša M. O zadatku države (The Task of the Government). Beograd, 1893.

583 Miličević, Milan Djuro. Školica za gradjanska prava i dužnosti (Manual for Civil Rights and Duties). 2nd ed. Beograd, 1889. 133 p. (DLC)

584 Perić, Živojin. (a) Političke studije (Political Studies on Various Problems of the Constitution). Beograd, 1908; (b) Državni budžet i Državni Savet (The Budget and the State Council). Beograd, 1910. 31 p.

585 Popović, Milivoje. (a) Poreklo i postanak Ustava od 1888 (Origin of the Constitution of 1888). Beograd, 1939. 166 p. (DLC); (b) Borba za parlamentarni režim u Srbiji (Struggle for a Parliamentary Regime in Serbia). Beograd, 1939. 111 p.

586 Prodanović, Jaša. Ustavni razvitak i ustavne borbe u Srbiji (Constitutional Development and Constitutional Struggles in Serbia). Beograd, 1936. 436 p. (DLC)

587 Radojčić, Nikola. Srpski državni sabori u srednjem veku (The Serbian Parliaments of the Middle Ages). Beograd, 1940. 318.

588 Rašić, Voj. Ustavno uporedno pravo. O Ustavu u Srbiji i u stranim državama, Opšti deo (Constitutional Comparative Law on the Constitution in Serbia and in Foreign Countries, General Part). Beograd, 1897. 176 p.

589 Vladisavljević, M. Razvoj ustavnosti u Srbiji (Constitutional Development in Serbia). Beograd, 1938. 77 p.

590 Vojnović, Lazar. Nastavlenije prava deržavnoga (Constitutional Law) Beogradska Velika Škola 1808–1813, od Andre Gavrilovića. Beograd, 1902.

bb   Montenegro

See also No. 2265.

591   Ustav za Knjaževinu Crnu Goru (Constitution of the Principality of Montenegro). 2d ed., Cetinje, 1907. 55 p. (DLC)
592   Zakon o javnim zborovima i udruženjima (Law on the
Right of Assembly and Association). Cetinje, 1907. 19 p. (DLC)
593   Zakon o ministarskoj odgovornosti (Law on Liability of
Cabinet Ministers). Cetinje, 1906. 16 p. (DLC)
594   Zakon o uredjenju privrednog saveta (Law on the Organization of the Economic Council). Cetinje, 1906. 9 p. (DLC)

cc   Croatia, Slavonia, Dalmatia

See also Nos.: 336; 378g; 448; 449b; 506; 2255.

595   Uredba o Banovini Hrvatskoj sa ostalim uredbama o prenosu poslova od 26 Augusta 1939 (Decree of August 26, 1939,
Creating the Croatian *Banovina* and Delegating some Constitutional Powers to it). Beograd, 1940. 245 p. (Zbirka Zakona, sv.
51) . (DLC)
596   Nagodba. Svi zakoni o nagodbi koju s jedne strane kraljevina Ugarska, sjedinjena s Erdeljom, s druge strane Kraljevina
Hrvatska, Slavonija i Dalmacija sklopiše za izravnanje postojav-
ših izmedju njih državnih i financijskih pitanja (Compromise.
Laws Pertaining thereto between Hungary and Croatia, Slavonia
and Dalmatia). Zagreb, 1906. 62 p. (DLC)
597   Andrović, Ivan. Habsburški dom i hrvatsko državno pravo
(The Hapsburg Dynasty and Croatian Constitutional Law).
Sarajevo, 1907.
598   Čulić, Djordje. Državnopravni karakter Hrvatske za domaće
dinastije (Constitutional Character of Croatia under the Ruling
Croatian Dynasty). *Zbornik pravnog fakulteta* (Zagreb), 1957:
67–81. (DLC)
599   Bjelanović, Sava. O Hrvatskom državnom pravu (Croatian
Constitutional Law). 2d ed. Zadar, 1893. 28 p.
600   Bojničić Kninski, Ivan. Zakoni o ugarsko-hrvatskoj nagodi
(The Hungarian-Croatian Agreement). Zagreb, 1907. 80 p.

601 Ćulinović, Ferdo. (a) Statut grada Senja (Statute of the City of Senj). Beograd, 1934. 80 p.; (b) Rijeka u državnopravnom pogledu (Constitutional Status of Fiume). *In* Rijeka — zbornik (Rijeka), 1953: 253–276. (DLC)

602 Dabinović, A. Prilozi za proučavanje ugovora god. 1102 (pacta conventa) i trogirske diplome (Contributions to the Study of the Treaty of 1102 (Pacta Conventa) and the Charter of Trogir). *Mjesečnik*, 1937: 38–58; 120–139. (DLC)

603 Lanović, Mihailo. Ustavno pravo Hrvatske narodne države (Constitutional Law of Croatia). Reprint from *Rad Jugoslavenske akademija.* Zagreb, 1939.

604 Pliveritsch, Josip. (a) Realna i osobna unija (Real and Personal Union). Zagreb, 1887; (b) Spomenica o državopravnih pitanjih hrvatsko-ugarskih (Survey of Constitutional Problems between Croatia and Hungary). Zagreb, 1907. 63 p.

605 Polić, L. Parlamentarna povijest Kraljevine Hrvatske, Slavonije i Dalmacije 1860–1880 (Constitutional History of the Kingdom of Croatia, Slavonia and Dalmatia, 1860–1880). Zagreb, 1899–1900. 2 v. (DLC)

606 Radić, Stjean. Savremena ustavnost. Svezak 1. Temelji i načela ustavnosti (Contemporary Constitutionality. Book 1. Principles of Constitutionality). Zagreb, 1911. 329 p. (DLC)

607 Smrekar, Milan. Ustavno zakonoslovlje (Collection of Constitutional Laws). Zagreb, L. Hartman, 1888. 213 p.

608 Statutarno pravo grada Zagreba (Statute of the City of Zagreb). *Mjesečnik*, 1943: 1–14.

609 Subotić, Jovan. Punktovi poravnanja izmedju trojedne kraljevine i Ungarske (The Croatian-Hungarian Compromise). Novi Sad, 1852.

610 Šulek, Bogoslav. (a) Hrvatski ustav ili Konstitucija godine 1882 (The Croatian Constitution of 1882). Zagreb, 1883. 318 p.; (b) Hrvatsko-Ugarski Ustav ili Konstitucija (The Croatian and Hungarian Constitution). Zagreb, 1861. 122 p. (DLC); (c) Naše pravice (Our Customs). Zagreb, 1868. 496 p. (DLC); (d) Austrijski državni ustav (The Austrian Constitution). Zagreb, 1850. 60 p.

611 Tomašić, Nikola. Hrvatsko-Ugarsko državno pravo (Croatian-Hungarian Constitutional Law). Zagreb, n.d. 142 p. (DLC)

612 Vladisavljević, Milan. Hrvatska autonomija pod Austro-Ugarskom (Croatian Self-Government under Austria-Hungary). Beograd, 1939. 106 p. (DLC)

613 Žigrović Pretočki, Fr. X. O samosvojnih pravih i pravih Kraljevina Dalmacije, Hrvatske, i Slavonije (Constitutional Privileges of the Kingdoms of Dalmatia, Croatia and Slavonia). Zagreb, 1883. 40 p.

dd Slovenia

614 Predlog ustavnega zakona o temeljih družbene in politične ureditve in o republiških organih oblasti L.R.S. (Draft of the Constitutional Law of the P.R.S.). Ljubljana, 1953. 11 p. (DLC)

615 Predlog poslovnika Ljudske skupščine L.R.S. (Draft of the Rules of Procedure for the Assembly of the P.R.S.). Ljubljana, 1953? 16 p. (DLC)

616 Uredba o organizaciji in delu Izvršnega sveta (Decree Concerning the Organization and Operation of the Executive Council of the P.R.S.). Ljubljana, 1958. 62 p. (DLC)

617 Lapajne, Štefan. Državni osnovni zakoni in drugi ustavni in upravni zakoni z odločbami najvišjih sodnih dvorov, ter spremenjeni deželni redi in deželni volilni redi slovenskih dežel (Constitutional and Administrative Law). V Ljubljani, Pravnik, 1910. 432 p. (Zbirka avstrijskih zakonov v slovenskem jeziku, zv. 7). (DLC)

ee Bosnia and Herzegovina

See also Nos.: 2271; 2376; 2379.

618 Zemaljski ustav za Bosnu i Hercegovinu. Previšnje riješenje od 17 februara 1910 o uvodenju ustavnih uredaba (Constitution of Bosnia and Herzegovina). Sarajevo, 1910. 134 p.

619 Čaldarević, Vladimir, *joint editor.* Zakon o teritorijalnoj podjeli Federalne Bosne i Hercegovine na okruge, srezove i područja mijesnih narodnih odbora (Law on the Territorial Division of Bosnia and Herzegovina). Sarajevo, 1945. 131 p. (DLC)

620 Čemerlić, H. Razvoj organa pravosudja u Bosni i Hercegovini u toku narodno-oslobodilačke borbe (Organization of the Judiciary in Bosnia and Herzegovina during the War of Liberation). *Godišnjak Pravnog fakulteta u Sarajevu*, 1955: 281–303. (DLC)

621 Geršić, Gl. Pogled na medjunarodni i državno-pravni položaj Bosne i Hercegovine i ostrva Kipra (The International and Constitutional Status of Bosnia and Herzegovina and of the Island of Cyprus). Beograd, 1893. 86 p.

622 Radić, Stjepan. Živo hrvatsko pravo na Bosnu i Hercegovinu (Croatian [Constitutional] Law Applicable to Bosnia and Herzegovina). Zagreb, 1908. 60 p. (DLC)

623 Škarić, Vladislav. Bosna i Hercegovina pod Austro-ugarskom upravom (Bosnia and Herzegovina under the Austrian-Hungarian Administration). Beograd, 1938. 166 p. (DLC)

ff Macedonia

624 Ustav na N.R.M. (Constitution of the P.R.M.). Skopje, 1947. 35 p. (DLC)

625 Noviot ustav na N.R.M. Ustavniot zakon od 2.II.1953 i Ustavot od 31.XII.1946 (The New Constitution of the P.R.M.). Skopje, 1953. 91 p. (DLC)

626 Dokumenti od sozdavanjeto i razvitokot na N.R.M., 1944–46 (Documents on Constitutional Development of P.R.M., 1944–1946). Skopje, 1949. 112. (DLC)

gg Voyvodina

627 Patent tsarskii za Voivodstvo Serbie i Temeshkii Banat', 18 ga (6 ga) noembria 1849 proistekshii (Imperial Patent for Serbian Voyvodina and Temishvar Banat of the 18th 6th) of November, 1849). Beč, 1849. 30 p. (DLC)

628 Statut Autonomne Pokrajine Vojvodine od 20 Marta 1953 i odluka o sprovodjenju Statuta Autonomne Pokrajine Vojvodine (Statute of the Autonomous Province of Voyvodina of March 20, 1953 and Enforcing Decree). Novi Sad, 1953. 36 p. (DLC)

629 Statut (Statute of the Autonomous Province of Voyvodina). Subotica, 1956 (?). 55 p. (DLC)

hh Kosovo-Metohija

630 Statut (Statute of the Autonomous Region of Kosovo-Metohija). Priština, 1953. 25 p. (DLC)

631 Statuti i Krahinës Autonome të Kosovë-Metohis. Prishtinë, 1953. 28 p. (DLC)

632 Ligji për këshillat popullore të rretheve, qyteteve, komuneve të qytetit dhc për komunet. Prishtinë, 1953. 277 p. (DLC)

4 Administrative Law and Procedure

See also: Comprehensive Topics: Constitutional Law; Specific Topics: Civil Service; Public Health; Nos.: 2279; 2336; 2341; 2355b.

a General, Pre-Yugoslavia

633 Zakon o uredjenju Državnog Saveta (Law on the Organization of the State Council of Montenegro). Cetinje, 1906. 7 p. (DLC)

634 Zakon o Kotarskim Vijećima za Bosnu i Hercegovinu (Law on District Councils for Bosnia and Herzegovina). Sarajevo, 1910 (?). 24 p. (DLC)

635 Zbirka upravnih zakona i naredaba (Collection of Administrative Laws and Ordinances). Osijek, 1906. 248 p. (DLC)

636 Zakon o opštinama (Law on Municipalities). Josif K. Stojanović *and* Aleksandar D. Bodi, *editors*. Preface by Kosta Kumanudi. Beograd, 1914. 244 p. (DLC)

637 Lazarević, Vasa. Prijavljivanje stanovništva kod policijskih i opštinskih vlasti i njegov značaj s naročitim pogledom na Beogradsku Policiju (Reporting of Inhabitants to Police and Municipal Authorities in Particular with Respect to the Belgrade Police). Beograd, 1908. 151 p. (DLC)

638 Levstik, Fr. Nauk slovenskim županom, kako jim je delati, kadar opravljajo domačega in izročênega podróčja dolžnósti (Instructions for Slovenian Mayors). Ljubljana, 1880. 207 p. (DLC)

639 Marković, Stojan. Administracija Kraljevine Srbije (Administration of the Kingdom of Serbia). Beograd, 1893. 586 p.

640 Milošević, R. Organizacija sreza na načelu samouprave i izbornog prava (Organization of a District on the Basis of Self-Government and Electoral Rights). Beograd, 1883. 102 p.

641 Petrovič, Simeon. Policaj po izloženiju G. Sonnenfelsa, serbskim ezikom darovanij (The Constable). Budim, 1813. 86 p. (DLC)

642 Raić, Jovan. Načalni osnovi umopravoslovne položitelne policije (The Police). Beograd, 1841. 141 p. (DLC)

643 Sladović, Eugen. Upravna nauka i upravno pravo Bosne i Hercegovine (Administrative Law of Bosnia and Herzegovina). Sarajevo, 1916. 415 p. (DLC)

644 Smrekar, Milan. Priručnik za političku upravnu službu u kraljevinah Hrvatskoj i Slavoniji (Handbook for the Police Service in the Kingdom of Croatia and Slavonia). Zagreb, 1899–1905. 5 v. (DLC)

645 Štefanić, Hugo. Upravno sudovanje (Administration of Justice by Administrative Agencies). Zagreb, 1894. 95 p. (DLC)

646 Veljković, Vojislav. Odnos izmedju sudske i administrativne vlasti u državi (Relation between the Judicial and Administrative Power). Beograd, 1895.

647 Vežić, Milivoj. Pomoćnik za javnu upravu. Zbirka najvažnijih zakonah i naredabah (Manual for Public Service. Collection of Most Important Laws and Ordinances). Zagreb, 1884. 820 p. (DLC)

648 Vrbanić, Fran. Rad Hrvatskog zakonodavstva na polju uprave od 1861 do najnovijeg vremena (Work of the Croatian Legislation in the Field of Administration from 1861 to Recent Times). Zagreb, 1893. 232 p.; also in *Rad Jugoslovenske akademije,* 1889, 1890 and 1893.

649 Škerović, Nikola. Zapisnici sednica Ministarskog saveta Srbije, 1862–1898 (Records of the Meetings of the Council of Ministers of Serbia, 1862–1898). Beograd, 1952. 539 p. (DLC)

650 Žigrović-Pretočki, I. (a) Upravno pravo Kraljevine Hrvatske i Slavonije (Administrative Law of the Kingdom of Croatia and Slavonia). Zagreb, 1911. 640 p. (DLC); (b) Upravna nauka i Hrvatsko upravno pravo u kratkim crtama (Administrative Teachings and Croatian Administrative Law). Zagreb, 1917. 128 p. (DLC); (c) Zakoni i naredbe tičuće u Kraljevinah Hrvatskoj

i Slavoniji (Laws and Ordinances Pertaining to Rural Municipalities in the Kingdoms of Croatia and Slavonia). 2d ed. Zagreb, 1897. 512, 194 p. (DLC)

b Yugoslavia

aa Lowest Administrative Divisions

651 Nacrt Statuta opštine, sreza (Draft of the Statute for Municipalities and Districts). Beograd, 1955. 79 p. (DLC)

652 Zakon o podeli teritorije NRS na opštine, gradove i srezove, sa registrom opština NRS (Law Concerning the Partition of the Territory of the PRS into Municipalities, Cities, and Districts). Beograd, 1952. 235 p. (DLC)

653 Jović, Milan, editor. Zbirka propisa o novom uredjenju opština i srezova u NRS (Collection of Provisions on the New Organization of Municipalities and Districts in the PRS). Beograd, 1955. 264 p. (DLC)

654 Vučković, Milorad, editor. Savezni zakon o uredjenju i nadležnosti novih opština srezova (Federal Laws on the Organization and Jurisdiction of New Municipalities and Districts). Beograd, 1955. 552 p. (DLC)

655 Uredba grada Zagreba (Statute of the City of Zagreb). Zagreb, 1937. 119 p. (DLC)

656 Statut slob. i kralj. Glavnog grada Zagreba o uredjenju gradske uprave od 8 travnja 1896 (Statute of the City of Zagreb of April 8, 1896). Zagreb, 1938.

657 Zakon o gradskim opštinama od 22 jula 1934 (Law on City Municipalities of July 22, 1934). Beograd, 1940. 123 p. (DLC); Commentary by Stanko Majcen, Beograd 1935. 335 p. (DLC)

658 Zakon o opštinama (Law on Municipalities). Beograd, 1933. 55 p. Commentary by Stanko Majcen, 1933. 307 p.; 1936. 374 p. (DLC)

659 Zakoni o izmenama i dopunama u zakonima o opštinama i sreskim i oblasnim samoupravama (Laws Amending the Laws on Municipalities and District and Regional Self-Government). 2d ed. Beograd, 1930. 93 p. (DLC)

660   Geršković, Leon. O izgradnji komuna (The Buildup of Communes). Beograd, 1955. 68 p. (DLC)

661   Prijedlog zakona o administrativno — teritorijalnoj podjeli NRH (Draft of the Law Concerning the Territorial Partition of the PRC). Zagreb, 1950. 15 p. (DLC)

662   Predlog zakona o razdelitvi LRS na okraje, mesta in občine (Draft of the Law Concerning the Partition of the PRS into Districts, Towns and Municipalities). Ljubljana, 1952. 37 p. (DLC)

663   Bajović, Vojin. Novi propisi o nadležnosti opština i srezova u NRS (New Provisions on the Jurisdiction of Municipalities and Districts in the PRS). Beograd, 1958. 110 p. (DLC)

664   Hristov, Aleksandar T. Saveti narodnih odbora (Councils of Peoples' Committees). Beograd, 1960. 80 p.

665   Opći zakon o narodnim odborima (General Law on People's Committees). Beograd, 1953. 35; 46 p. (Zbirka zakona FNRJ, br. 105, 112). (DLC)

666   Predlog zakona o ljudskih odborih mest in mestnih občin (Draft of the Law on People's Local Committees and Town Municipalities). Ljubljana, 1952. 67 p. (DLC)

667   Savezni i republički zakoni o narodnim odborima (Federal and Republican Laws on People's Committees). Zagreb, 1953. 283 p. (DLC)

668   Splošni zakon o ljudskih odborih (General Law on People's Committees). Beograd, 1949. 96 p. (DLC)

669   Zakon o občinskih ljudskih odborih (Law on People's Committees of Municipalities). Ljubljana, 1954. 55 p. (DLC)

670   Zbirka odluka narodnog odbora grada Beograda, 1947–1949 (Collection of Decisions of the People's Committee of the City of Belgrade, 1947–1949). Beograd, 1949. 179 p. (DLC)

671   Zbirka zakoni za narodnite odbori (Collection of Laws on People's Committees). Skopje, 1952. 253 p. (DLC)

672   Zakoni o narodnim odborima. (Laws on People's Committees). 2d ed. Zagreb, 1952 [cover 1953]. 191 p. (DLC)

673   Zakoni o narodnim odborima srezova, gradova i gradskih opština i opština (Laws on People's Committees of Districts, Cities and Town Municipalities and of Municipalities). 2d ed. Beograd, 1954. 169 p. (DLC)

674 Zakoni o narodnim odborima srezova, opština i gradova i gradskih opština (Laws on People's Committees of District Municipalities, Cities, and Town Municipalities). Sarajevo, 1952. 180 p. (DLC)

675 Djordjević, Jovan. (a) Sistem lokalne samonprave u Jugoslaviji (System of Local Self-Government in Yugoslavia). Beograd, 1957. 250 p. (DLC); (b) Naši narodni odbori-lokalni organi državne vlasti socijalističke države (NRS) (Our People's Committees, Local Organs of the Government of the PRS). Beograd, 1949. 79 p. (DLC)

676 Globevnik, Josip. (a) Ljudski odbori — organi ljudske samouprave (People's Committees, Organs of People's Self-Government). Ljubljana, 1952. 250 p. (DLC); (b) Krajevni odbori v komunalni ureditvi (Local Committees in the Municipal System). Ljubljana, 1956. 105 p. (DLC)

677 Hristov, A. Sovetite i upravnite organi na narodnite odbori (Executive Organs of People's Committees). Skopje, 1956. 166 p.

678 Kardelj, Edvard. Ekspoze o novom Zakonu o narodnim odborima održan u narodnoj skupštini FNRJ 1. aprila 1952 (Report on the New Law on People's Committees of April 1, 1952). Beograd, 1952. 32 p. (DLC)

679 Petrović, Svetomir and Viden Andrejević. Mesni odbori i mesne kancelarije u novom komunalnom sistemu (Local Committees and Local Offices in the New Municipal System). Beograd, 1956. 131 p. (DLC)

680 Polić, Ladislav. O samoupravi i upravi gradskih općina (On Self-Government and Administration of City Municipalities). Mjesečnik, 1924: 177–205. (DLC)

681 Živanović, Dragomir, editor. Zbirka saveznih propisa o uredjenju i nadležnosti narodnih odbora (Collection of Federal Provisions on the Organization and Jurisdiction of People's Committees). Beograd, 1958. 311 p. (DLC)

682 Čaldarević, Vladimir, joint autor. Propisi o organima državne vlasti u Bosni i Herzegovini (Provisions on Government Agencies in Bosnia and Herzegovina). Sarajevo, 1946. 161 p. (Zbirka zakona i uredaba, 2). (DLC)

bb   *Državni Savet*

See also: Chapter 6, Court Decisions, A6, *Državni Savet* (State Council).

683   Zakon o državnom savetu i upravnim sudovima (Law on the State Council and Administrative Tribunals). Beograd, 1930. 42 p.; 1932. 188 p.; 1935. 141 p. (DLC)

684   Cavalieri, Celso. Komentar Zakonu od 17. maja 1922 o Državnom savjetu i upravnim sudovima (Commentary on the Law of May 17, 1922 on the State Council and Administrative Tribunals). Zagreb, 1925. 194 p. (DLC)

685   Sagadin, Stevan. Upravno sudstvo. Povodom stogodišnjice rada Državnog Saveta [1839–1939] (Quasi Judicial Function of Administrative Agencies). Beograd, 1940. 234 p. (DLC)

686   Stefanović, Jovan, *editor*. Priručnik za zakone: o opštoj upravi, o državnom savetu i upravnim sudovima (Manual for Laws: on the Executive Branch of the Government, the State Council and Administrative Tribunals). Zagreb, 1925. 188 p. (DLC)

cc   Regional and Central Administration

687   Uredba o podeli zemlje na oblasti. Zakon o opštoj upravi. Zakon o oblasnoj i sreskoj samoupravi, s uputstvima za predlagače kandidatskih lista i pretsednike biračkih odbora (Decree on the Administrative Partition of the Country into Regions with Pertinent Provisions). Beograd, 1925. 206 p. (DLC); 2d ed. 1927. 214 p. (Zbirka zakona, sv. 1).

688   Jovanović, Aleksandar. Komunalno uredjenje Jugoslavije (Local Self-Government Organization in Yugoslavia). Beograd, Savremena administracija, 1962. 462 p.

689   Urošević, Slobodan. Zbirka propisa o organizaciji državne uprave u NR Srbiji (A Collection of Provisions on the Organization of the Governmental Administration in the PR of Serbia). Beograd, 1960. 264 p.

690   Zakon o nazivu i podeli Kraljevine na upravna područja (Law on the Name and Partition of the Kingdom into Adminis-

trative Units). Beograd, 1929. 29 p. (DLC); 1930, 99 p. (Zbirka zakona sv. 25, 141). (DLC)

691 Zakon o banskoj upravi, sa uredbom o utvrdjenju imovine, načinu uprave i budžetiranju banovina (Law on the Government of Banovina with Pertinent Provisions). Beograd, 1930. 111 p. (Zbirka zakona, sv. 27) (DLC) Commentary by J. V. Stefanović. Zagreb, 1930. 491 p. (DLC)

692 Zakon o unutrašnjoj upravi od 19. juna 1929 sa izmenama i dopunama od 19. jula 1929 i 9 octobra 1929 (Law on the Internal Administration of June 19, 1929, as Amended). Beograd, 1929. 107 p. (Zbirka zakona, sv. 21); 2d ed. Beograd, 1930. 183 p. (Zbirka zakona, sv. 137) (DLC); 1938. 354 p. (Zbirka zakona, sv. 20) (DLC). Commentary by Franja Goršić. Beograd, 1936. 490 p. (DLC)

dd   Administrative Procedure

See also No. 721.

693 Zakon o općem upravnom postupku (Code of General Administrative Procedure). Zagreb, 1957. 136 p. (DLC)

694 Zakon o splošnem upravnem postopku (Code of General Administrative Procedure). Ljubljana, 1957. 153 p. (DLC)

695 Zakon o opštem upravnom postupku od 9 novembra 1930 (Code of General Administrative Procedure of Nov. 9, 1930). Beograd, 1931. 76, 163 p. (DLC) (Zbirka Zakona, sv. 40., 174).

696 Poslovnik za opšte upravne vlasti (Rules of Procedure for General Administrative Agencies). Beograd, 1931. 64 p. (DLC); 1932. 99, 90 p. (DLC)

697 Davinić, Aleksandar *and* Bogdan Majstorović, *editors.* Zbirka propisa za sprovodjenje zakona o opštem upravnom postupku (Collection of Provisions for the Enforcement of the Law on Administrative Procedure). Beograd, 1958. 102 p. (DLC)

698 Firšt, Božidar. Sistem upravnog postupanja po Zakonu o općem upravnom postupku (System of Administrative Proceedings under the Code of Administrative Procedure). Zagreb, 1957. 387 p. (DLC)

699   Glavne značilnosti splošnega postopka (Main Characteristics of Administrative Procedure). Ljubljana, 1957. 279 p. (DLC)

700   Goršić, Franja. Komentar Zakona o Opštem Upravnom Postupku od 9 novembra 1930 (Commentary on the Code of Administrative Procedure of November 9, 1930). Beograd, 1931. 21, 354 p. (DLC)

701   Hristov, A. Priručnik za Osnovite Principi na Upravnata Postupka (Basic Principles of Administrative Procedure). Skopje, 1954. 94 p.

701¹   Jevtić, Ljubomir *and* Radomir Šramek. Upravni postupak i upravni spor (Administrative Procedure and Administrative Controversies). 2nd ed. Beograd, 1961. 384 p. (DLC)

702   Jović, Sreten R. Upravni postupak i osnovi opšte administracije (Administrative Procedure and General Principles of Administration). Beograd, 1951. 99 p. (DLC)

703   Krbek, Ivo. (a) Opći upravni postupak (General Administrative Procedure). Zagreb, 1957. 479 p. (DLC); (b) Zakon o opštem upravnom postupku (Code of General Administrative Procedure). Zagreb, 1931. 219 p. (DLC) ; 2d ed. 1938. 342 p. (Zakoni Kr. Jugoslavije Knj. 13) (DLC); (c) Stranka u upravnom postupku (Parties in Administrative Procedure). Zagreb, 1928. 132 p. (DLC)

704   Radovanović, Ljubomib V. *and* Božidar Protić. Iz upravnosudskog postupka (Administrative Judicial Procedure). Beograd, 1928. 132 p. (DLC)

705   Stefanović, V. J. (a) Zakon o opštem upravnom postupku . . . Zakon o Glavnoj kontroli, pravilnik za izvršenje zakona o glavnoj kontruli (Code of General Administrative Procedure). Zagreb, 1931. 394 p. (Upravno zakonodavstvo, knj. 3) (DLC); (b) Poslovnik za opšte upravne vlasti (Rules of Procedure for Administrative Agencies). Zagreb, 1932. 463 p. (Upravno zakonodavstvo knj. 4) (DLC); (c) Komentar Zakona o opštem Upravnom Postupku od 9 novembra 1930 (Commentary on the Code of Administrative Procedure of Nov. 9, 1930). Beograd, 1930. 394 p.; 2d ed. Beograd, 1933. 416 p. (DLC); (d) Zakon o Općem Upravnom Postupku, sa komentarom (Code on General Administrative Procedure). Zagreb, 1931. 394 p. (DLC)

706 Stjepanović, Nikola S. Položaj gradjana i organizacija u upravnom postupku (Status of Citizens and Organizations under Administrative Procedure). Beograd, 1957. 204 p. (DLC)

707 Vavpetič, L. O posebnosti splošnega upravnega postopka v naši družbni ureditvi (Some Problems Concerning General Administrative Procedure). Ljubljana, 1955. 116 p.

708 Ivančević, Velimir, *joint editor.* Zakon o upravnim sporovima s komentarom i sudskom praksom (Law on Administrative Controversies with Commentary and Court Reports). Zagreb, 1958. 323 p. (DLC)

709 Majstorović, Bogdan. (a) Komentar Zakona o upravnim sporovima (Commentary on the Law on Administrative Controversies). Beograd, 1952. 134 p. (DLC); 1957, 169 p.; (b) Komentar Zakona o opštem upravnom postupku (Commentary on the Law on General Administrative Procedure). Beograd, 1957. 322 p. (DLC)

710 Perović, Mirko. Problemi upravnog spora (Problems of Administrative Controversy). Beograd, 1959. 153 p. (DLC)

711 Popović, Slavoljub. O upravnom sporu (Administrative Controversy). Beograd, 1955. 235 p. (DLC)

ee General and Specific Problems of Administration

712 Alimpić, Dušan Dj. (a) Policijski Rečnik (Police Dictionary). Beograd, 1924–1927. 3 v. (DLC); (b) Policijska Uredba (Decree on Police). 2d ed. Beograd, 1920. 90 p.

713 Alimpić, Dušan Dj., *joint editor.* Policijski zbornik zakona i zakonskih propisa po struci upravno-policijskoj i samoupravnoj, izdatih od 1 decembra 1918 do 15 jua 1924 (Collection of Laws Concerning the Police from December 1, 1918 to June 15, 1924). Beograd, 1924. 524 p. (DLC)

714 Bedeković, Janko. Zbirka zakona, naredaba, i svih propisa državne uprave (Collection of Laws, Ordinances and Provisions Pertaining to Government Administration). Zagreb, 1926. 408 p.

715 Danić, Danilo. Razvitak administrativnog sudstva u Srbiji (Development of the Administration of Justice by Administrative Agencies in Serbia). Beograd, 1926. 174 p. (DLC)

716 Dimitrijević, P. Nauka o administraciji (Teachings on Administration). Beograd, 1951. 130 p. (DLC)

717 Geršković, Leon. (a) Društveno upravljanje u Jugoslaviji (Corporate Management in Yugoslavia). Beograd, 1957. 202 p. 2nd ed. 1959. 230 p. (DLC); (b) Državna uprava Jugoslavije (Government Administration of Yugoslavia). Beograd, 1956. 120 p.; (c) Nauka o administraciji; o organizaciji administracije u socijalistickoj državi (Teachings on Administration). Edited by P. Dimitrijević. Beograd, 1951. 132 p. (DLC)

718 Jagedić, Jovan. Administrativni pregled za sva pravna područja kraljevine Jugoslavije (Administrative Survey of All Jurisdictions of the Kingdom of Yugoslavia). Novi Sad, 1930. 339 p. (DLC)

719 Jakovljević, Atanasije J. Služba javne bezbednosti (Public Safety Service). Skoplje, 1938.

720 Kostić, Lazo M. Administrativno Pravo Kraljevine Jugoslavije (Administrative Law of the Kingdom of Yugoslavia). Beograd, 1933–1939. 3 v.

721 Krbek, Ivo. (a) Upravno pravo (Administrative Law). Zagreb, 1929–1932. 2 v. (DLC); 1955–1957. 2 v. (DLC); (b) Osnovi upravnog prava FNRJ (Principles of Administrative Law of the FPRY). Zagreb, 1950. 610 p. (DLC); (c) Sudska kontrola naredbe (Judicial Supervision of Ordinances). Zagreb, 1939. 254 p. (DLC); (d) Diskreciona ocjena (Discretionary Power). Zagreb, 1937. 530 p. (DLC); (e) Zakonitost uprave (Legality of the Administration). Zagreb, 1936. 50 p.; (f) Pravo javne uprave FNRJ. I. Osnovna pitanja i prava gradjana (Administrative Law of the FPRY. I. Basic Problems and Rights of Citizens). Zagreb, 1960. 278 p. (DLC)

722 Krstić, Mih. A. Političko upravni zbornik zakona, uredaba i pravilnika (Collection of Administrative Laws, Decrees and Regulations). Beograd, 1935– (DLC)

723 Kumanudi, Kosta. Administrativno pravo (Administrative Law). Beograd, 1912. 192 p.; 2d ed. 1921. 279 p. (DLC)

724 Matić, Djordje. Pouke i obaveštenja (Police Instruction and Information). Beograd. Reprint from Časopis Policija. Beograd, 1930. 695 p. (DLC)

725 Niketić, G. O pravnom karakteru eksproprijacije (The Legal Meaning of Eminent Domain). Beograd, 1922. 49 p.

726 Izveštaj Saveznog izvršnog veća za 1959 godinu (A Report of the Federal Executive Council for 1959). Beograd, 1959. 332 p.; 1960. 132 p. The same for 1960. Beograd, 1961. 142 p.

727 Pirkmajer, Otomar, *editor*. Zakon o držanju i nošenju oružja s odnosnim pravilnikom i tumačenjem i zakon o zaštiti javne bezbednosti (Law Concerning the Possession and Carrying of Firearms and Law for the Protection of Public Safety). Beograd, 1928. 203 p. (DLC)

728 Popović, Slavoljub. (a) Sudska kontrola zakonitosti upravnih akata u FNRJ (Judicial Supervision of the Legality of Administrative Acts in the FPRY. Administrative Controversies in the FPRY). Beograd, 1955. 36 p. (DLC); (b) Upravno pravo (Administrative Law). 2nd ed. Beograd, 1959. 288 p. (DLC)

729 Popović, Slavoljub *and* P. Dimitrijević. Organizacija i funkcionisanje državne uprave (Organization and Function of the Government Administration). Beograd, 1951. 206 p. (DLC)

730 Ranković, Aleksandar. Zakon o organima unutrašnjih poslova (Law on Agencies of Internal Affairs). Beograd, 1956. 76 p. (DLC)

731 Stefanović, J. V. Poremećaj nadležnosti u korist izvršne vlasti usled stanja nužde (Change of Jurisdiction in Favor of the Executive Branch of Government Due to Emergency). Beograd, 1934. 44 p.

732 Stjepanović, Nikola. (a) Administrativno pravo (Administrative Law). Beograd, 1948; 1954, 504 p. (DLC); (b) Upravno pravo FNRJ (Administrative Law of the FPRY). 2d ed. 1958. 728 p. (DLC)

733 Strobl, M. Razlastitev v pravnem sistemu FLRJ (Expropriation in the Legal System of the FPRY). Ljubljana, 1954. 96 p.

734 Zbirka propisa o organizaciji državne uprave u NRS (A Collection of Provisions on the Organization of Governmental Administration in the PR of Serbia). Beograd, 1960. 263 p.

735 Vasiljević, Tihomir, *joint editor*. Zbornik propisa NRS. Propisi o organizaciji republičkih organa vlasti (Collection of Provisions of the PRS. Provisions Concerning the Organization of

Republican Government Agencies). Beograd, 1955. 398 p. (DLC)

736 Vavpetič, L. Pravna narava odločb v upravi (Legal Nature of a Decision Issued by the Administration). Ljubljana, 1952. 51 p. (DLC)

ff Police

737 Zakon o narodnoj miliciji (Law on the People's Militia). 3d ed. Beograd, 1949. 91 p. (DLC)

738 Zakon o organima unutrašnjih poslova sa predgovorom Aleksandra Rankovića (Law Governing Officials of Internal Affairs. Preface by Alexander Ranković). Beograd, 1956. 76 p. (DLC)

739 Alimpić, Dušan Dj. Policijski potsetnik za žandarme i ostale policijske organe (Police Survey Used by Constables and Other Police Officers). 2d ed. Beograd, 1904. 203 p. (DLC)

740 Trumić, Aleksandar. Priručnik za upravno-policijsku službu (Manual for the Police). Sarajevo, 1927. 239 p. (DLC)

741 Walka, Artur. Priručnik za redarstvenu službu (Manual for the Police). Zagreb, 1923. 840 p. (DLC)

5 Civil Law

See also: Ch. 11, A, 2e; Special Topics: Contracts and Torts; Cooperatives; Corporations and Partnership; Domestic Relations; Inheritance; Patents, Trade Marks, Copyright; Property Law; Roman Law; No. 2114.

a Yugoslav Law and General Works

See also Nos. 1260b; 2318; 2373d; 2373e.

742 Bajalović, Ljubomir. Osnovi gradjanskog prava (Elements of Civil Law). Beograd, 1951–1954. 2 v. (DLC)

743 Čubinski, A. O zastarelosti u gradjanskom pravu (Statute of Limitations in Civil Law). Beograd, 1927. 158 p. (DLC)

744 Djordjević, Živomir S. Osnovi imovinskog i porodičnog prava (Elements of Property and Domestic Relations Law). Beograd, 1959. 2 v. (DLC)

745   Eisner, B. *and* M. Pliverić. Mišljenja o Predosnovi gradjanskog zakonika za Kraljevinu Jugoslaviju (Criticism on the Draft of the Yugoslav Civil Code). Zagreb, 1937. 629 p. (DLC)

746   Gams, A. Uvod u grandjansko pravo (Introduction to Civil Law). 1st ed. Beograd, 1952. 340 p. (DLC); 2d ed. 1956. 384 p. (DLC); 4th ed. 1961. 278 p.

747   Marković, B. S. Reforma našega gradjanskog zakonodavstva (Reform of the Yugoslav Civil Legislation). Beograd, 1939. 48 p.

748   Marković, Čedomir. Predosnova gradjanskog zakonika za Kraljevinu Jugoslaviju (Draft of a Yugoslav Civil Code). Ljubljana, 1936. 153 p.

749   Maurović, I. Naše opće privatno pravo i nastojanja oko njegove reforme (Yugoslav Private Law and Its Reform). Zagreb, 1941–1945. 4 v.

750   Miladinović, Ž. Stečena prava (Vested Rights) . Beograd, 1926. 71 p.

751   Loza, Bogdan Dj. Pitanja osnova odgovornosti u gradjanskom pravu (Problems of Liability in Civil Law). *In* Godišnjak Pravnog Fakulteta (Sarajevo), 1955: 139–156. (DLC)

752   Perić, Ninko. Teorija zloupotrebe prava i gradjansko zakonodavstvo (Theory of the Abuse of Rights and the Civil Legislation). Beograd, 1912. 150 p.

753   Perić, Živojin M. Obrazloženje, §§ -a 1–319 Predosnove gradjanskoga zakonika za Kraljevinu Jugoslaviju, (Draft of Secs. 1–319 of the Civil Code of the Kingdom of Yugoslavia). Beograd, 1939. 346 p. (DLC)

754   Spaić, Vojislav. (a) Uvod u gradjansko pravo s naročitim obzirom na pravo FNRJ (Introduction to the Civil Law with Reference to the Law of FPRY). Sarajevo, 1950. 196 p. (DLC); (b) Osnovi gradjanskog prava (Principles of Civil Law) . Sarajevo, 1957–1960. 2 v. (DLC); 3rd ed. General Part, 1961. 356 p.

755   Štempihar, J. Civilno pravo (Civil Law). Ljubljana, 1951–1952. 3 v. (DLC: v. 1)

756   Stražnicki, M. Misao socijalizacije Privatnoga Prava (The Idea of Socialization of Private Law) . *Mjesečnik,* 1908: 81–89, 175–184.

757   Vuković, Mihajlo. (a) Opći dio gradjanskog prava (Civil Law. General Part). Zagreb, 1951. 127 p. (DLC); (b) Obći dio

Gradjanskog Prava (General Part of Civil Law). Zagreb, 1959–1960. 2 v. (DLC)

b Serbia

See also Nos.: 1203; 1314e.

758 Zakonik gradjanski za Knjaževstvo Srbsko obnarodovan na Blagovesti 25 marta 1844 godine (Civil Code of the Principality of Serbia promulgated on March 25, 1844). Beograd, 1844. 159 p. (DLC); 2d ed. 1873. 286 p. (DLC); 3d rev. ed. 1922. 464; 111 p. (DLC)

759 Grazhdanskoe i Torgovoe Ulozhenia Kniazhestva Serbii — 1844 i 1860 g. (Civil and Commercial Codes of Serbia of 1844 and 1860). St. Peterburg, 1887. 337 p. (DLC)

760 Gradjanski zakonik sa zakonom trgovačkim . . . za kraljevinu Srbiju. Službeno izdanje (The Civil and Commercial Codes . . . of the Kingdom of Serbia. Official edition). Corfu, 1918. 386 p. (DLC)

761 Gradjanski zakonik Kraljevine Srbije. (a) Protumačen odlukama . . . Kasacionog suda (Serbian Civil Code Annotated by Decisions of the Supreme Court), prepared by Gojko Niketić, preface by Ž. M. Perić and D. Arandjelović. Beograd, 1st ed. 1909, 484 p. (Zbirka zakona . . . Kr. Srbije.) (DLC); 2d ed. 1912, 468 p.; 3d ed. 1922, 464 p. (DLC); (b) — objašnjen odlukama Kasacionog suda (Serbian Civil Code Annotated by Decisions of the Supreme Court). Prepared by I. Petković. Beograd, 1939. 479 p. (c) — Gojko Niketić, comp. Beograd, 1927. 379 p. (Zbirka zakona). (DLC)

762 Arandjelović, D. Rasprave iz privatnog prava (Essays in Civil Law). Beograd, 1913. 160 p. (DLC)

763 Bartoš, M. Osnovi privatnog prava (Principles of Private Law). Beograd, 1934. 391 p.

764 Stupar, Mihailo. Gradjansko pravo. Opšti deo (Civil Law. General Part). Beograd, 1962. 182 p.

765 Janković, Dragutin. Problemi gradjanskog prava (Problems of Civil Law). Beograd, 1926. 121 p. (DLC)

766 Marković, Čedomir. Gradjansko pravo (Civil Law). Beograd, 1928. 156 p. (DLC)

767 Marković, Lazar. Gradjansko pravo (Civil Law). Beograd, 1920. 2 v.; 1927–28. 2 v. (DLC)

768 Matić, Dimitrije. Objašnenje gradjanskog zakonika za Knjažestvo Srbsko (Commentary on the Civil Code of the Serbian Principality). Beograd, 1850–51. 3 v. in 4. (DLC)

769 Narodni uputnik u gradjanskim, meničnim i stečajnim stvarima (Handbook on Questions of Civil Law, Bills and Notes, and Bankruptcy). Beograd, 1886.

770 Perić, Ninko. (a) Osnovi gradjanskog prava. Opšti deo (Principles of Civil Law; General Part). Beograd, 1922, 176 p. (DLC); (b) Teorija zloupotrebe prava i gradjansko zakonodavstvo (Abuse of Law). Beograd, 1912. 123 p. (DLC)

771 Perić, Živojin. Specialni deo gradjanskog prava; stvarno pravo, nasledno pravo, obligaciono pravo, porodično pravo (Special Part of the Civil Law; Property, Inheritance, Obligations, Domestic Relations). Beograd, 1920. 5 v.; 1922–1923. 4 v. (DLC)

772 Šeroglić, Pavel. Replika na odgovor Miloša Svetića u utuku jezikoslovnome, ili Pregled Zakonika gradjanskog za Serbiju (Review of the Serbian Civil Code Exposed in an Answer to Miloš Svetić). Novi Sad, 1847. 105 p. (DLC)

773 Urošević, Laza, editor. Sudski trebnik; Gradjanski zakonik za Kraljevinu Srbiju, sa komentarom; Trgovački zakonik; Zakonik o akcionarskim društvima; Zakon o zaštiti industrijske svojine (Lawyers' Manual; Serbian Civil Code with a Commentary; Commercial Code; Corporation Law; Patent Law). Beograd, 1917. 983 p. (DLC)

c Montenegro

See also Nos.: 2247a; 2259; 2263; 2266; 2270; 2367; 2377; 2378; 2455; 2467a; 2467c; 2467d.

774 Medaković, Milorad G. Zakonik obšti Crnogorski i Brdski, ustanovljen 1798 oktobra 18 na Cetinje (Civil Code of Montenegro of 1798). Zemun, 1850.

775 Marković, Momčilo. Odgovornost za povredu radnika na poslu (Liability for Injury Caused to a Worker in the Performance of his Duty). Pravni Zbornik (Titograd), No. 3, 1961: 175–188. (DLC)

776 Obshchiii imushchestvennyi zakonnik dlia kniazhestva Chernogorskago po 2-mu izdanie 1898 g. (General Civil Code of Montenegro,/ Translated from the 2nd ed. 1898/). Translated by M. P. Kusakov, V. D. Spasovich, *editor*. St. Peterburg, 1901. 239 p. (DLC)

777 Opšti imovinski zakonik za Knjaževinu Crnu Goru (General Civil Code of Montenegro). Cetinje, 1898. 362 p. (DLC); Beograd, 1927. 312 p. (DLC)

778 Vesnić, M. Imovinski zakonik za Crnu Goru u novim prevodima (New Translations of the Civil Code of Montenegro). *Branič*, 1901: 887–894.

779 Vojnović, K. Opšti imovinski zakonik za Crnu Goru obzirom na ostalo crnogorsko zakonodavstvo (The Civil Code of Montenegro and the Montenegrin Legislation). Zagreb, 1889. 111 p.

780 Bogišić, B. Povodom Crnogorskog gradjanskog zakonika. O načelima i metodu usvojenim pri izradi (The Montenegrin Civil Code. Principles and Methods Applied Therein). Beograd, 1888. 20 p. (DLC) Translated from the French by N. Dučić.

781 Zakon o zauzimanju privatnih dobara za javnu potrebu (Law on Expropriation). Cetinje, 1906. 28 p. (DLC)

d Croatia and Slavonia, Slovenia, Dalmatia, Bosnia and Herzegovina

See also No. 2428.

782 Sveopći gradjanski zakonik za sve nemačke nasledne zemlje Austrijske monarhije (Civil Code for the German Lands of the Austrian Monarchy). Vienna, 1849. 3 v. (DLC)

783 Cesarski patent od 29, novembra 1852, krepostan za kraljevine, Ugarsku, Hrvatsku, Slavoniu, Voivodinu Srbsku i Tamiški Banat, koim se za ove krunovine, uvodi . . . Opći gradjanski Zakonik od 1. junia 1811 . . . s dodatkom potonjih naredaba . . . (Imperial Patent of November 1852, Effective in the Territories of the Kingdoms of Hungary, Croatia, Slavonia, the Serbian Voyvodina, and the Banat of Temešvar Introducing into these Territories the Austrian Civil Code of June 1, 1811). Vienna, 1853. 122 p. (DLC)

784 Opći austrijanski gradjanski zakonik proglašen Patentom od 29. studenoga 1852 u Kraljevinama Hrvatskoj i Slavoniji (General Civil Code of Austria as Introduced into the Kingdoms of Croatia and Slavonia by the Imperial Patent of November 29, 1852). F. J. Spcvec *and* A. Rušnov, *comp.* 1st ed. ?; 2d rev. ed. Zagreb, 1899, 21, 534, 11 p. (DLC); 3d ed. ?; 4th ed. with title slightly changed. Stjepan Posilović, *comp.* Zagreb, 1918. 676 p. (DLC)

785 Arandjelović, D., *editor.* Austrijski gradjanski zakonik (Austrian Civil Code). Translated by Dragoljub Arandjelović. Beograd. 1st ed. 1906, p. ?; 2d ed. 1921. 498 p. (DLC)

786 Ćepulić, I. Sistem općeg privatnog prava (Civil Law). Zagreb, 1925. 814 p.

787 Derenčin, M. Tumač k Občemu austrijanskomu gradjanskomu zakoniku (Commentary on the Austrian Civil Code). Zagreb, 1880–1883. 2 v.

788 Krainz, Joseph. Sistem austrijskoga općega privatnoga prava. Opći dio obveza (System of the Austrian Civil Law. General Part on Obligations). Translated from the 4th German ed. and amended by Ivan Maurović. Zagreb, 1911. 250 p. (DLC)

789 Krek, G. Anton Randa, 1834–1914. Ljubljana, 1934. 35 p.

790 Maurović, I. Nacrt predavanja o općem privatnom pravu (General Civil Law Course), Zagreb, 1919–1927. 5 v.

791 Petranović, B. O austriskom gradjanskom zakoniku i o srpskom prevodu istoga (The Austrian Civil Code and Its Translation into Serbian). Beč, 1850. 47 p. (DLC)

792 Posilović, Stjepan. Pučki pravnik; ili, Pravni katekizam. (Practical Manual of Civil Law) Zagreb Editions 1–3?; 4th ed. 1889?. 424 p. (DLC)

793 Rastovčan, P. Moral, dobri običaji i zloporaba prava u Gradjanskom zakoniku (Morals, Good Faith and Abuse of Law in the Civil Code). Zagreb, 1927. 96 p.

794 Rušnov, A. *and* S. Posilović. Tumač Obćemu austrijskom gradjanskomu zakoniku (Commentary on the Austrian Civil Code). Zagreb, 1910. 2 v.

795 Spevec, F. Volja i očitovanje volje u njemačkom i u našem gradjanskom zakoniku (Free Will and Its Manifestation in the German and Austrian Civil Codes). Zagreb, 1900. 46 p.

796 Finžgar, Alojzij. Osebe civilnega prava (Persons in Civil Law). Ljubljana, 1961. 116 p. (DLC) Mimeographed.

797 Vuković, Mihailo, Martin Vedriš *and* Djuro Vuković, *editors*. Opći gradjanski zakonik s novelama i ostalim naknadnim propisima (General Civil Code with Amendments). Zagreb, 1955. 615 p. (DLC)

e Voyvodina

See also No. 1661.

798 Domin Imbrih. Navučanje vu pravicah samosvojneh vugerskeh (Introduction to the Hungarian Civil Law). Zagreb, 1821–1830. 5 v.

799 Bogdanfi, G. *and* N. Nikolić. Opšte privatno pravo koje važi u Vojvodini (General Private Law in Force in Voyvodina). Pančevo, 1925. 379 p.

800 Jesensky, A. *and* P. Protić. Privatno pravo u Vojvodini (Civil Law of Voyvodina). Sombor, 1922. 333 p.

801 Milić, I. Pregled madžarskog privatnog prava u poredjenju sa austrijskim gradjanskim zakonikom (Survey of the Hungarian Private Law Compared with the Austrian Civil Code). Subotica, 1921. 76 p.

802 Piškulić, Zvonimir. Osnovi privatnoga prava u Vojvodini (Fundamentals of the Civil Law of the Voyvodina). Beograd, 1924. 284 p. (DLC)

6 Civil Procedure

See also: Special Topics: Judicial System; Nos.: 1022; 2114; 2363; 2373c; 2381b; 2398b; 2399; 2401b; 2405a; 2425b; 2446; 2452.

803 Arandjelović, Drag. (a) Gradjansko procesno pravo Kraljevine Jugoslavije (Civil Procedure of the Kingdom of Yugoslavia). Beograd, 1932–34. 3 v.; (b) šta se ne može uzeti u popis za izvršenje sudskih odluka (Property Exempted from Execution). Beograd, 1909. 49 p.

804 Bačmedjeji, Aleksije *and* Stevan Branković. Komentar Jugoslovenskog izvršnog postupnika (Commentary on Execution of Judgments). Novi Bečej, 1932. 752 p. (DLC)

804¹ Bazala, Branko. Priručnik obrazaca za praktičnu primjenu

Zakona o parničnom postupku (A Manual of Forms for the Practical Application of the Code of Civil Procedure). 2nd ed. Zagreb, 1960. 433 p.

805 Blagojević, Borislav T. (a) Načela privatnoga procesnoga prava (Basic Principles of Yugoslav Civil Procedure). Beograd, 1936. 430 p. (DLC); (b) Zakon o izvršenju i obezbedjenju od 9 jula 1930 (Law on the Execution of Judgments of July 9, 1930). Beograd, 1938. 588 p. (DLC); (c) Sistem izvršnoga postupka (Yugoslav System of Execution of Judgments). Beograd, 1936. 640 p. (DLC); (d) Egzekvatura stranih presuda po Zakonu o izvršenju i obezbedjenju (Execution of Foreign Judgments). Beograd, 1934. 23 p. (DLC); (e) Samopomoć kao oblik pravne zaštite (Self-help as a Means of Legal Protection). *Mjesečnik*, 1941: 64–75; (f) Socijalne težnje novoga izvršnoga prava (Social Aims of the New System of Execution of Judgments). *Arhiv*, 1937: 146–157. (DLC)

806 Blagojević, Vidan O. (a) Izmena propisa Gradjanskog parničnog postupka o presudi usled izostanka i propuštanja (Amending the Provisions of the Code of Civil Procedure Governing Judgments by Default). Reprint from Spomenica Kongresa pravnika. Beograd, 1937. 19 p. (DLC); (b) Istraživanje materjalne istine u gradjanskom parničnom i vanparničnom postupku (Finding of Substantive Truth in Civil and Non-Adversary Proceedings). Beograd, 1938. 77 p.

807 Branković, S. O posebnom ovlašćenju za vodjenje parnice (Power of Attorney under the Code of Civil Procedure). Petrovgrad, 1937. 71 p.

808 Juhart, Jože. (a) Civilno procesno pravo FLRJ (Civil Procedure). Ljubljana, 1961. 654 p.; 1962. 211 p.; (b) Civilno izvršilno pravo (Execution of Civil Judgments). Ljubljana, 1962. 140 p.

809 Culja, Srećko. (a) Gradjansko procesno pravo Kraljevine Jugoslavije (Civil Procedure of the Kingdom of Yugoslavia). Beograd, 1926. 2 v. (DLC); (b) Gradjanski parnični postupak FNRJ (Civil Procedure of the Federal People's Republic of Yugoslavia). Zagreb, 1957. 656; (c) Gradjanski parnični postupak u Hrvatskoj i Slavonji (Croatian-Slavonian Civil Procedure). Zagreb, 1928. 258 p. (DLC); (d) Vanparnični postupak u osta-

vinskim, porodičnim, zemljišno-knjižnim, ekspropriacijonim i drugim stvarima (Non-Adversary Proceedings in Matters of Succession, Domestic Relations, Land Register, Expropriation by Right of Eminent Domain, and Other Proceedings). Zagreb, 1956. 220 p.; (e) Dispozicione parnične radnje i njihova primena u parničnom postupku (Court Rulings in Civil Procedure). *Zbornik Pravnog fakulteta* u Zagrebu. 1951: 331–376; (f) O izgradnji gradjanskog parničkog postupka nove Jugoslavije (Drafting the Code of Civil Procedure in New Yugoslavia). *Nova Jugoslavija,* 1954: 336–361; (g) Studija za reformu gradjanskog pravosudja (A Study on the Reform of the Administration of Justice in Civil Affairs). *Godišnjak Pravnog Fakulteta Sveučilišta u Zagrebu,* 1941: 13–60.

810   Derenčin, Marjan. (a) Ovršni postupak (Procedure for the Execution of Civil Judgments). Zagreb, 1877. 265 p. (DLC); (b) Tumač Zakona o maličnom postupku (Commentary on Small Claims Procedure). Zagreb, 1877.

811   Djordjević, Andra. Teorija gradjanskog sudskog postupka s pogledom na zakonik o postupku sudskom u grajanskim parnicama (Theoretical Foundations of the Serbian Civil Procedure). 1st ed. Beograd, 1891. 520 p. (DLC); 2d ed. 1924. 2 v. Title varies slightly. (DLC)

812   Godina, Dionis. (a) Praktični prikaz osnovnih ustanova novog postupka u gradjanskim parnicama (Synopsis of the Elements of the New Civil Procedure). Beograd, 1932. 147 p.; (b) Teoretsko-praktični komentar zakona o sudskon vanparničnom postupku za Kraljevinu Jugoslaviju (Commentary on the Law Providing for Non-Adversary Proceedings of the Kingdom of Yugoslavia). Beograd, 1934. 582 p.; (c) Praksa Jugoslovenskog gradjanskog parničnog postupka (The Yugoslav Code of Civil Procedure as Applied by the Courts). Beograd, 1934. 207 p. (DLC); (d) Priručnik novog zakona o izvršenju i obezbedjenju sa obrascima sudskih podnesaka, predloga, zaključaka, tužbi, itd. (Handbook on the New Law on the Execution of Judgments, with Forms of Applications, Motions, Decisions, etc.). Beograd, 1932. 267 p. (DLC).

813   Goldštajn, A. Izvršenje na opčenarodnoj imovini (Execution on Property Owned by the People). *Arhiv,* 1949: 314–326. (DLC)

814 Goršić, Franja. (a) Komentar Gradjanskog parničnog postupka (Commentary on the Code of Civil Procedure). Beograd, 1933. 2 v.; (b) Komentar Vanparničnog postupka (Commentary on the Code of Non-Adversary Proceedings). Beograd, 1935. 846 p.; (c) Tumač zakona o izvršenju i obezbedjenju (Commentary on the Law on the Execution of Civil Judgments). Zagreb, 1933. 621 p.; (d) Dodatak tumaču zakona o izvršenju i obezbedjenju (Supplement to the Commentary on the Execution of Civil Judgments). Zagreb, 1937. 77 p.

815 Grujić, Jefrem. Pravni pretres propasti velikog suda u Srbiji 1864 godine (Discussion of the Failure of Serbia's High Court in 1864). Novi Sad, 1867. 114 p.

816 Hinković, H. Izlučna parnica (Action for Exemption from Attachment). Sušak, 1881. 33 p. (DLC)

817 Janjić, Sv. Gradjanski sudski postupak, protumačen načelnim odlukama opšte sednice Kasacijonog suda i odelenja, i odlukama upravnih vlasti (The Code of Civil Procedure as annotated by Decisions of the Supreme Court and Administrative Agencies). Policijski Glasnik, 1904.

818 Jovanović, Aleksa S. Predlozi o reorganizaciji sudovodstva (Plans for the Reorganization of the Judiciary). Beograd, 1874.

819 Kamhi, Samuel. Gradjanski Sudski Postupak (Code of Civil Procedure). Sarajevo, 1st ed. 1951, 270 p.; 2d ed. 1957, 453 p. (DLC); 3rd ed. 1961. 506 p.

820 Kisel, Franjo. Zakon o sudskom postupku u gradjanskim parnicama na teritoriji Apelacionog Suda u Novom Sadu: Zakonski članak I, 1911 (Code of Civil Procedure Effective in the Territory under the Jurisdiction of the Court of Appeals of Novi Sad: Law I of 1911). Senta, 1927. 526 p.

821 Kovačević, Dobrosav M. Zakletva u našim sudovima (Oath in our Courts). Beograd, 1902. 14 p.

822 Kruszelnicki, Franciszek. Gradjanski parnički postupnik za Bosnu i Hercegovinu s novelom Gr.p.p i drugim naredbama i uputstvima (Code of Civil Procedure for Bosnia and Herzegovina, as Amended by Ordinances and Instructions). Sarajevo, 1918. 296 p. (DLC)

823 Kugler, Milan. Tumač maličnom postupku (Commentary on Small Claims Procedure). Zagerb, 1917. 96 p. (DLC)

824   Lazarević, Adam P. (a) Osnovi izvršnog Postupka, sa stečaj-
nim postupkom i prinudnom likvidacijom preduzeća (The Basic
Principles of the Code of Execution with the Bankruptcy and
Composition Proceedings). Skopje, 1956. 358 p. (DLC); (b)
Poravnanje po novom Gradjanskom parničnom postupku (Com-
promise under the New Code of Civil Procedure). Reprint from
Branič, 1934.

825   Marković, Milan St. Knjiga za opštinske sudove. Uputstvo za
sudjenje gradjanskih sporova kod opštinskih sudova (Handbook
on Municipal Courts). Beograd, 1883. 64 p.

826   Marković, Milivoje Č. (a) Teorija Gradjanskog parničnog
postupka (Theoretic Foundations of the Civil Procedure). Beograd, 1948– (DLC v. 1); (b) Gradjansko procesno pravo (Civil
Procedure). Beograd, 1957– (DLC v. 1)

827   Mataić, Adam. Zakon o sudskom vanparničnom postupku od
24 jula 1934 sa uvodnim zakonom od 26 jula 1934 (Law on
Non-Adversary Proceedings of July 24, 1934 with the Enacting
Law of July 26, 1934). Zagreb, 1934. 209 p. (DLC)

828   Matijević, Ivo *and* Ferdo Čulinović. Komentar Zakona o izvršenju i obezbedjenju (Commentary on the Law on the Execution of Judgments and Attachment). Beograd, 1937–40. 5 v.
(DLC)

829   Meichsner, Eugen. Zakon o izvršenju (Law on Execution).
Beograd, 1938. 772 p.

830   Milić, Ivan. Gradjanski sudski postupak (Code of Civil Procedure). Zagreb, 1951. 140 p. (DLC)

831   Muha, M. (a) Presuda zbog izostanka ili propuštanja (Judgment by Default). *Mjesečnik*, 1935: 372–384; (b) Izvršba proti
državi (Enforcement of Court Decisions against the Government).
Slovenski pravnik, 1922: 168–172.

832   Najman (Neuman), Georg. Komentar gradjanskog parničnog postupka od 13 jula 1929 (Commentary on the Code of
Civil Procedure of July 13, 1929). Beograd, 1935. 2 v. (DLC)

833   Nestorović, Dj. B. Pravne rasprave i članci, I. Gradjanski Postupak (Legal Studies and Articles. I. Civil Procedure). Beograd,
1905. 164 p.

834   Pajnić, Edvard *and* Franja Goršić. Novi gradjanski parnični

postupak u praksi, sa obrascima (The New Code of Civil Procedure in Practice). Beograd, 1935. 423 p. (DLC)

835 Petrović, Vitomir. O dokazu (Burden of Proof). Niš, 1959. 48 p.

836 Perić, Živojin M. (a) Svedoci kao dokazno sredstvo u novom jugoslovenskom gradjanskom postupku (Witnesses in the New Yugoslav Civil Procedure). Beograd, 1934. 64 p.; (b) O intervenciji u privatnom pravu (Intervention in Civil Proceedings). Reprint from *Mjesečnik*, 1902. 21 p.; (c) O popisu za izvršenje odluka sudskih (Attachment). Beograd, 1902. 157 p.

837 Perić, Ž. *and* D. Arandjelović. Gradjanski sudski postupak. Predavanja (Civil Procedure. Lectures). Beograd, 1920-? 2 v. (DLC: v. 1)

838 Petraš, Marijan. Teorija suda (Court Decisions. Theory). Zagreb, 1935. 160.

839 Poznić, B. (a) Zakon o parničnom postupku (Code of Civil Procedure). Beograd, 1957. 460 p.; (b) Mirovanje postupka de lege ferenda (Discussion on the Suspension of Court Proceedings). *Arhiv*, 1954: 169–175. (DLC); (c) O uticaju krivične presude na gradjanski spor (Dependence of Civil Suits on Decisions in Criminal Proceedings). *Arhiv*, 1952: 30–39. (DLC)

840 Rušnov, Adolf. Zakon o postupku u slučajevih smetanja posjeda od 8. svibnja 1890 (Trespass under the Law of May 8, 1890). Zagreb, 1891. 104 p.; 2nd ed. 1904. 108 p. (DLC)

841 Rušnov, Adolf *and* J. Šilović. Tumač gradjanskome parbenome postupku (Commentary on the Code of Civil Procedure). Zagreb, 189- . 936 p. (DLC)

842 Sajovic, R. Civilni pravdni postopnik (Civil procedure). Ljubljana, 1939. 757 p. (DLC)

843 Urošević, L. (a) Sudski trebnik, III deo. Zakonik o postupku sudskom u gradjanskim parnicama, sa komentarom; Pravilnik o ubaštinjenju na nepokretnim dobrima u Južnoj Srbiji; Zakon o stecišnom postupku, Zakon o ustrojstvu sudova; Zakon o postavljanju sudija za vanparnična (nesporna) dela; Zakon o sudijama; Zakon o sreskim i gradskim sudovima; Uredba o ubrzanju rada kod sudskih i islednih vlasti; Zakon o konvenciji zaključenoj sa Kraljevinom Bugarskom o sudskoj pomoći; Zakon o ugovoru zaključenom sa Čehoslovačkom Republikom radi ured-

jenja uzajamnih pravnih odnosa (Court Manual, Part III, Code of Civil Procedure [Serbian] with a Commentary; Regulation Governing the Transfer of Real Property in South Serbia; Bankruptcy Law; Law on the Organization of the Courts; Law on the Appointment of Judges for Non-Adversary Proceedings; Law on Judges; Law on County and Municipal Courts; Decree Providing for Means to Speed up the Operation of the Courts; Law Ratifying the Convention on Legal Assistance with Bulgaria; Law Ratifying the Convention with the Republic of Czechoslovakia on Outstanding Legal Questions). Beograd, 1927. 613 p.; (b) Sudski Trebnik, III deo, Zakon o sudskom postupku u gradjanskim parnicama (od 13 jula 1929), sa komentarom i uvodnim zakonom (Judicial Manual, Part III, Yugoslav Code of Civil Procedure (of July 13, 1929) with a Commentary and the Introductory Law). Beograd, 1934. 720 p. (DLC)

844   Veljković, Stojan. Nešto o zadatku Kasacionog Suda (The Role of the Supreme Court). Reprint from *Srbske Novine*, 1865. 41 p.

845   Verona, Ante *and* Srećko Zuglia. Zakonik o sudskom postupku u gradjanskim parnicama (Code of Civil Procedure). Zagreb, 1930. 1028 p. (DLC)

846   Vujanac, Voj. M. Porabni sporovi, skraćen postupak, 655–671 Gradjanskog parničnog postupka (Landlord and Tenant Proceedings). Beograd, 1934. 40 p.

847   Werk, Hugo. (a) O izjednačenju sudskog gradjanskog izvršnog prava u slovenskim zemljama: Bugarskoj, Čehoslovačkoj, Jugoslaviji, i Poljskoj (A Unified Procedure for the Excution of Judgments for Bulgaria, Czechoslovakia, Yugoslavia and Poland). Reprint from *Mjesečnik*, 1933. 23 p.; (b) Teoretsko-praktični priručnik jugoslavenskog gradjanskog parničnog prava (Handbook on the Theory and Practice of Civil Procedure). Zagreb, 1932. 2 v. (DLC)

848   Pompe, Leon *and* Ciril Kržišnik. Izvršilni, nepravdni in zemljiško knjižni postopek (Execution, Non-Adversary Proceedings, and Land Title Recording). 2nd ed. Ljubljana, 1959. 96 p.

849   Zakonik o postupku sudskom u gradjanskim parnicama (20 februara 1865) sa svima izmenama i dopunama, i zakon o postupku stecišnom sa zakonom o ustrojstvu prvostepenih i viših

sudova i zakonom o postavljanju sudija za nesporna dela (Code of Civil Procedure of February 20, 1865, as Amended, with the Laws on Bankruptcy, the Organization of the Courts, and the Appointment of Judges for Non-Adversary Proceedings). Beograd, 1917.

850 Zakonik o sudskom postupku u gradjanskim parnicama za Knjaževinu Crnu Goru (Code of Civil Procedure of the Principality of Montenegro). Cetinje, 1905. 92 p. (DLC)

851 Zakonik o postupku sudejskom u gradjanskim parnicama za Knjažestvo Srbiju (Code of Civil Procedure for the Principality of Serbia). Beograd, 1860. 96 p. (DLC)

852 Žilić, Franjo *and* Miroslav Šantek. Zakon o sudskom vanparničnom postupku i Uvodni zakon . . . s tumačem i sudskim rešidbama . . . (Law on Non-Adversary Proceedings). Zagreb, 1934. 801 p (DLC)

7   Commercial Law

See also: Special Topics: Banking, Foreign Exchange and Currency; Bankruptcy; Corporations and Partnership; Negotiable Instruments; Unfair Competition; Nos.: 226; 759; 760; 773; 1888; 2294; 2373a; 2383; 2404; 2414; 2436; 2449.

853   Bajalović, Ljubomir. Trgovačko pravo (Commercial Law). Beograd, 1950. 125 p. (DLC)

854   Danić, Danilo J. Osnovi trgovačkog prava (Elements of Commercial Law). Beograd, 1921. 79 p.

855   Djordjević, Andra. Trgovačke knjige i njihova dokazna vrednost (The Account Books and their Probative Value). *Pravo* (Beograd), 1891. (DLC)

856   Djordjević, Djor. Z. (a) O podnašanju i pokazivanju trgovačkih knjiga sudu, članovi 18. i 19. Trg. Zakona (Account Books as Evidence in Court). *Pravo* (Beograd), 1891. (DLC); (b) O udatoj ženi trgovkinji (The Married Woman as Merchant). *Pravo* (Požarevac), 1886. 85 p.

857   Godina, Dionis. Trgovački zakon za Kraljevinu Jugoslaviju s obrazloženjem Ministarstva Pravde (The Yugoslav Commercial Code, with the Official Message of the Ministry of Justice). Beograd, 1937. 485 p.

858 Kapor, Vladimir. Osnovni elementi trgovinskog prava sa osvrtom na inostrana zakonodavstva (Elements of the Yugoslav Commercial Law with Reference to Foreign Legislations). Beograd, 1956. 154 p. (DLC)

859 Konferencija privrednih komora Kraljevine Jugoslavije, Split, 1927. Obrtni Zakon; izveštaj o konferenciji privrednih Komora (Conference of the Chambers of Commerce, Industry, Trade and Agriculture of Yugoslavia, Split, 1927. Report on the Trade Law). Split, 1927. 145 p. (DLC)

860 Marković, Lazar. Trgovački Zakonik, Zakon o akcionarskim društvima i Zakon o radnjama (The Commercial Code, the Laws on Corporations and Retail Stores). Beograd, 1914. 301 p.

861 Milovanović, Jov. S. Pravo trgovinsko (Commercial Law). Beograd, 1899. 596 p.

862 Mirković, Djordje Ž. O zamerkama koje se čine Predlogu jugoslovenskog trgovačkog zakonika (On the Objections Against the Draft Commercial Code). Reprint from *Pravosudje,* 1937. (DLC)

863 Mitrović, Velizar J. Obim radnje kao uslov za pravni kvalitet trgovca (The Size of the Enterprise as a Criterion of its Owner's Commercial Status). *Branič,* 1926. (DLC)

864 Nestorović, Dj. B. Maloletnik trgovac (Commercial Status of a Minor as Merchant). *Branič,* 1888. (DLC)

865 O razumevanju zakonskih propisa za ženin miraz kod trgovaca (Interpretation of the Legal Provisions Governing the Dowry of a Businessman's Wife). *Srpske Novine,* 1875.

866 Pahorukov, Nikolaj. Trgovački zakon za Kraljevinu Jugoslaviju od 20 oktobra 1937 (The Yugoslav Commercial Code). Beograd, 1938. 699 p.

867 Petrović, Petar J. Trgovačko pravo (Commercial Law). Beograd, 1933. 70 p.

868 Pirnat, A. Ugovor o skladištenju, prevozu i špediciji (Storage, Transport, and Shipping Contracts). Beograd, 1956. 100 p.

869 Popović, Radomir. Problemi trgovačkog prava (Problems of Commercial Law). Beograd, 1932. 267 p. (DLC)

870 Pretnar, Stojan. Oris primerjalnega trgovinskega prava (Outline of Comparative Commercial Law). Ljubljana, 1953–1955. 2 v. (DLC)

871 Prica, B. Kupoprodajni ugovori u spoljnoj trgovini (Purchase and Sales Contracts in Foreign Trade). Beograd, 1956. 145 p. (DLC)

872 Radojičić, Spasoje. Osnovi trgovačkog prava Kraljevine Srbije (Elements of Commercial Law of the Kingdom of Serbia). Beograd, 1899; 2nd ed. 1912. 368 p.; 3rd ed. 1920. 368 p.; 4th ed, 1922. 368 p.; 5th ed. 1926. 315 p. (DLC 1926)

873 Radovanović, Ljub., editor. Trgovački Zakon za Kraljevinu Jugoslaviju (Yugoslav Commercial Code). Beograd, 1937. 431 p. (DLC)

874 Rastovčan, Pavao. (a) Komparativno trgovačko pravo (Comparative Commercial Law). Zagreb, 1954. 104 p. (DLC); (b) Osnovi trgovačkog [Privrednog] prava. Opći deo (Elements of Commercial [Economic] Law. General Part). Zagreb, 1957. 142 p.

875 Rušnov, Adolfo. Trgovački i mjenbeni zakon, sravnan sa Trgovačkim zakonom i mjenbenim redom, krijepostnim za zemlje zastupane u Carevinskom vijeću (A Comparison of the Croatian Commercial and Bills and Notes Law with the Commercial and Bills and Notes Law Effective in the Lands Represented in the Imperial Diet). Zagreb, 1898. 354 p. (DLC)

876 Stojković, Slavko. Kupoprodajni ugovor u spoljnoj trgovini (Purchase and Sale Contracts in Foreign Trade). Beograd, 1959. 86 p. (DLC)

877 Stražnicki, M. (a) Predavanja iz Trgovačkog prava (Lectures in Commercial Law). Zagreb, 1st ed. 1924. 128 p.; 2nd. ed. 1926.; (b) Tumač trgovačkog zakona (Commentary on the Commercial Code). Zagreb, 1939. 673 p.; (c) editor. Trgovački Zakon valjan za Hrvatsku i Slavoniju (The Commercial Code Effective in Croatia and Slavonia). Zagreb, 1918. 631 p. (DLC)

878 Mrkušić, Žarko, editor. Zbirka propisa o spoljnoj trgovini i deviznom poslovanju (A Collection of Provisions on Foreign Trade and Foreign Exchange). 4th ed. Beograd, 1956. 403 p. (DLC)

879 Tauber, L. (a) Trgovačko pravo (Commercial Law). Beograd, 1939. 311 p.; (b) Udžbenik Trgovačkog Prava (Textbook on Commercial Law). Beograd, 1935. 204 p.

880 Tomić, Jovan. Trgovačko pravo (Commercial Law). Beograd, 1885.

881 Veljković, Stojan Jov. Objašnjenje trgovačkog zakonika za

Knjažestvo Srbiju (Commentary on the Commercial Code of the Serbian Principality). Beograd, 1866. 544 p. (DLC)

882 Vrbanić, Fran. Trgovački zakon. Tumač zakonskomu članku XXXVII: 1875 zajedničkoga Hrvatsko-Ugarskoga Sabora uz obzir na Austrijski i Bosansko-Hercegovački trgovački zakon (The Commercial Code. Commentary on the Law XXXVII of 1875 of the Joint Croatian-Hungarian Parliament with Reference to the Commercial Code for Austria and Bosnia and Herzegovina). Zagreb, 1892. 528 p. (DLC)

883 Vrbanić, Juraj. Trgovačko zakonoslovlje (Commercial Law Science). Zagreb. 1st ed.?; 2nd ed. 1909.

884 Vuković, M. Pravo trgovačke retencije (Right of Retention in Commercial Law). In Spomenica Mauroviću, 1934: 221–249.

885 Winter, Vilim. Trgovački zakon. Tumuč zakonskomu članku XXXVII: 1875, i Bosansko-Hercegovačkom trgovačkom zakonu, s obzirom na Austrijski trgovački zakon (Commercial Law, Commentary on the Law XXXVII of 1875, and on the Commercial Law for Bosnia and Herzegovina, with Reference to the Austrian Commercial Code). Osijek, 1912. 766 p. (DLC)

886 Zakonik trgovački za Knjažestvo Srbiju (Commercial Code of the Principality of Serbia). Beograd, 1860. 37 p. (DLC)

887 Zbirka propisa o trgovini, sa objašnjenjima (Annotated Collection of Commercial Rules and Regulations). Beograd, 1952. 139 p.; 1955. 127 p. (DLC)

887[1] Zbirka propisa o trgovini (A Collection of Commercial Rules and Regulations). Beograd, 1957. 335 p.; 2nd ed. 1960. 399 p. (DLC)

8 Criminal Law

See also: Ch. 11, A, 2d; Special Topics: Forensic Medecine; Military Penal Law; Trials.

a Prior to the Code of 1929

See also Nos.: 454; 933c; 965; 1009f; 2319g; 2370; 2419; 2425i; 2425j; 2441b; 2453.

888 Avakumović, Jovan Dj. (a) Teorija kaznenog prava, I-III deo, 1–10 sveska (Theory of Criminal Law v. 1–3; Parts 1–10). Beog-

rad, 1887–97. (DLC); (b) Kradja (Larceny). Beograd, 1887; (c) Nužna odbrana i istorija nužne odbrane (Self-Defense and History of Self-Defense). Beograd, 1883. 170 p.; (d) Pokušaj (Attempt). Beograd, 1884. 220 p.; (e) Produženi zločin (Continuing Crime). Beograd, 1883. 70 p.; (f) Saučešće (Parties to the Crime). Beograd, 1885. 235 p.; (g) Sticaj zločina (Plurality of Crimes and Compound Crimes). Beograd, 1883. 200 p.; (h) Važnost Kaznenog zakona (Importance of the Criminal Law). Beograd, 1882. 150 p.

889 Cenić, Dj. D. Objašnjenje kaznitelnog zakona za knjažestvo Srbiju (Commentary on the Criminal Code for the Principality of Serbia). Beograd, 1866. 2 v. (DLC)

890 Djuričić, Marko S. (a) Posebni deo Kaznenog Zakonika. Projekat i motivi Kaznenog Zakonika za Kraljevinu Srbiju (Criminal Code, Special Part, Draft of the Criminal Code of the Kingdom of Serbia). Beograd, 1910. 747 p.; (b) Krivično-pravni članci (Articles on Criminal Law). Beograd, 1910. 78 p.; (c) O krivokletstvu (Perjury). Beograd, 1906. 80 p.

891 Jelić, Illija. O brakolomstvu. . . s naročitim osvrtom na srpsko običajno pravo (On Adultery . . . with Special Reference to the Serbian Customary Law). Beograd, 1928. 88 p.

892 Kazneni zakonik i kazneni postupak (Criminal Code and Criminal Procedure for Serbia). Beograd, 1880. 695 p. (DLC); 2d ed. 1882. 711 p. (DLC); 3d rev. ed. 1887. 685 p. (DLC); 4th ed.?; 5th ed. 1900. 501 p. (DLC); Solun, 1916. 224, 172 p. (DLC)

893 Kaznitelni zakonik za Knjažestvo Srbiju (Criminal Code of the Principality of Serbia). Beograd, 1860. 168 p. (DLC); 1864. 195 p. (DLC)

894 Kriminalni (Kaznitelni) Zakonik za Kraljevinu Srbiju (Criminal Code of the Kingdom of Serbia). Beograd, 1908. 186 p.

895 Kostić, Milan. (a) Alkohol, kriminalitet, i pravo, (Alcohol, Crimes and Law). Beograd, 1914, 242 p.; (b) Statistika kriminaliteta u Kralj. zemaljskoj kaznioni u Mitrovici (Criminal Statistics of the Penitentiary in Mitrovica). Zagreb, 1909. 30 p.

896 Kriminalna statistika za 1922 i 1923 godinu (Criminal Statistics for the Years 1922 and 1923). Beograd, 1932. 212 p. (DLC)

897 Krivični zakonik za Knjaževinu Crnu Goru (Criminal Code of the Principality of Montenegro). Cetinje, 1906. 187 p. (DLC)

898 Lončarić, Jovan. (a) Krivična dela po carinskom zakonu (Crimes under The Customs Law). Beograd, 1908. 175 p.; (b) O pojmu carinskog krivičnog dela (The Concept of Customs Law Offenses). Beograd, 1907. 41 p.

899 Marinković, Mih. O uslovnoj osudi (Suspended Sentence). Beograd, 1906. 375 p.

900 Marinković, S. Kriminološke slike kod srpskih sudova (Trials before Serbian Courts). Beograd, 1906. 145 p.

901 Marković, Božidar. (a) Krivično pravo (Criminal Law). Beograd, 1909. 629 p. (DLC); (b) Opšti deo Kaznenog Zakonika. Projekat i motivi (General Part of the Criminal Code. Draft). Beograd, 1910. 747 p.; (c) Sedmi Medjunarodni Kongres za kaznene zavode (The Seventh International Penitentiary Congress). Beograd, 1906. 109 p.

902 Makanec, M. Kazan smrti (Death Penalty). Zagreb, 1880. 23 p.

903 Maširević, Branko and Miša Kupusarević. Tabelaran iskaz i registar dela kažnjivih. . . u celoj Kr. S.H.S. i . . . u Vojvodini i Medjumurju (Table Index of Offenses Punishable under the Laws of Yugoslavia Including those in Force in the Vojvodina and the Medjumurje). Sombor, 1926. 391 p. (DLC)

904 Miler, E. Pokušaj delikta s naročitim obzirom na t.zv. nepodaban pokušaj (Criminal Attempt by Using Inadequate Means). Zagreb, 1902. 91 p.

905 Miljković, Milutin. Posebni deo Kaznenog Zakonika, glava XIII, XVI, XXV, XXVI, XXVIII, XXIX, XXXIII, XXXIV, i prestupi. Projekat i motivi Kaznenog Zakonika za Kraljevinu Srbiju (Special Part of the Criminal Code, Chapters 13, 16, 25, 26, 28, 29, 33, 34, and Minor Crimes. Draft of the Serbian Criminal Code). Beograd, 1910. 747 p.

906 Milovanović, Milovan Dj. Krivično pravo (Criminal Law). 1889. 92 p. (DLC)

907 Niketić, Gojko. Kazneni zakonik i krivični postupak, protumačen (Criminal Code and Code of Criminal Procedure for Serbia, annotated). 3d rev. ed. Beograd, 1924. 508 p. (Zbirka zakona Kr. Srbije II). (DLC)

908 Obchinska naredba od zločinstvâ i njihovih pedepsâ (General Law on Crimes). Transl. by Ivan Matković. Budim, 1788. 144 p.

909 Obščij zakon (Iosifa II) na prestuplenija i njiova nakazanija (General Law on Crimes). Vienna, 1788. 128 p.

910 Osnova novoga kaznenoga zakona o zločinstvih i prestupcih za Kraljevinu Hrvatsku i Slavoniju uz obrazloženje (Draft of the Code on Crimes and Petty Offenses for the Kingdom of Croatia and Slovenia with Motives). Zagreb, 1879. 424 p. (DLC)

911 Pantelić, Dj. R. O pravnim sredstvima u krivičnim delima i našoj Kasacionoj vlasti (Legal Remedies in Criminal Matters and Authority of the Supreme Court). Beograd, 1867. 78 p.

912 Papazoglu, Dimitrije. Krivično pravo i pravosudje u Srbiji 1804–1813 (Criminal Law and Justice in Serbia 1804–1813). Beograd, 1954. 177 p. (DLC)

913 Pavlović, Gojko. (a) Krivično Pravo. Opšti deo (Criminal Law. General Part). Beograd, 1905. 204 p.; (b) O dvoboju (On Duels). Beograd, 1903.

914 Pekić, Petar. Rasprava o smrtnoj kazni (The Capital Punishment). Subotica, 1928. 27 p.

915 Perić, Živojin M. O amnestiji u srpskom krivičnom pravu (Amnesty in the Serbian Criminal Law). Beograd, 1909. 59 p. (DLC)

916 Petković, K. Komentar kaznenog zakonika (Commentary on the Criminal Code). Beograd, 1903. 331 p.

917 Projekat i motivi kaznenog zakona za Kraljevinu Srbiju (Draft of the Criminal Code for Serbia. Official Edition). Beograd, 1910. 747 p. (DLC)

918 Protić, Dimitrije. Krivično-pravni položaj maloletnika i kriminalno-političke mere za suzbijanje maloletničkog kriminaliteta (Status of the Minors in Criminal Law and the Criminal Policy in Fighting Juvenile Delinquency). Beograd, 1925. 84 p.

919 Stevanović, Aleksa. O istupnim delima po kaznenom zakoniku i njihovom izvidjanju i sudjenju (Petty Offenses under the Criminal Code; their Investigation and Trial). Beograd, 1910. 123 p.

920 Subotić, Dušan. (a) Posebni deo Kaznenog Zakonika. Projekat i motivi Kaznenog Zakonika za Kraljevinu Srbiju (Special Part of the Criminal Code. Draft of the Criminal Code for the Kingdom of Serbia). Beograd, 1910. 747 p.; (b) Zločini i prestupi zbog lažnog novca (Counterfeiting of Bank Notes and Coins).

Beograd, 1907; (c) O krivokletstvu i lažnom svedočenju (Perjury and False Testimony). Reprint from *Branič*. Beograd, 1907. 99 p.; (d) Kazna i njen cilj (The Punishment and its Purpose). Beograd, 1909; (e) Otpust bez kazne (Release without Punishment). Reprint from *Arhiv*. Beograd, 1941. 28 p.

921 Šilović, Josip. (a) Kazneni zakon o zločinstvih, prestupcih i prekršajih od 27. svibnja 1852 sa zakoni od 17. svibnja 1875 . . . preinačenimi zakonom 14 svibnja god 1907 . . . sa rešitbami (Criminal Code of 1852 Supplemented by the Laws of 1875 and 1907 and Court Decisions). 1st, 2d, and 3d ed.? 4th ed. Zagreb, 1921. 494 p. (DLC); (b) Čedomorstvo (Infanticide). Zagreb, 1907. 15 p. (DLC); (c) O razvoju krivnje u hrvatskom kaznenom pravu (The Concept of Guilt in Croatian Criminal Law). Reprint from Rad Jugoslavenske akademije, 1912; (d) Nuždna obrana (Self-Defense). Zagreb, 1910. 104 p.; (e) Pokušaj u hrvatskom kaznenom pravu (Attempt in Croatian Criminal Law). Rad Jugoslavenke Akademije, 1915; (f) Sloboda volje i Kazneno Pravo (Free Will and Criminal Law). Zagreb, 1898. 25 p.; (g) Uzroci zločina (The Motives of Crime). Zagreb, 1913.

922 Urošević, Lazar. Kazneni zakonik sa komentarom (Criminal Code with a Commentary). Beograd, 1911. 430.

923 Vesnić, Mil. R. Krivična odgovornost u svetlosti današnje nauke (Criminal Responsibility in the Light of Contemporary Science). Beograd, 1890. 275 p. (DLC)

924 Virovac, Petar. Pervi osnovi glavnokrivnog Madjarskog prava; Elementa juris criminalis Hungarici (Principles of Hungarian Criminal Law). Budim, 1831. 110 p.

925 Vujanac, Vojislav M. Pred sudom i zakonom; plediranja o mitu, krivokletstvu, falsifikatu (Pleadings). Beograd, 1936.

926 Vulović, Svetislav. Problem smrtne kazne (The Problem of Capital Punishment). Beograd, 1925. 51 p. (DLC)

927 Jovanović, Mih. P. Retroaktivnost krivičnih zakona (Ex-Post Facto Laws). *Arhiv*, 1921: 1–13. (DLC)

928 Petrović, Andre. O bosanskom preljubu (Adultery in Bosnia). *Mjesečnik* (Zagreb), 1914: 1005–1014. (DLC)

929 Živanović, Toma. (a) Položaj dragovoljnog odustanka od pokušaja u krivično-pravnom sistemu (Voluntary Giving Up an Attempt in the Criminal Law System). *Arhiv*, 1923: 321–329.

(DLC); (b) Istupi iz Krivičnog zakonika (Minor Crimes in the Criminal Code). Beograd, 1914. 206 p. Reprint from *Policijski Glasnik*. (DLC); 2d ed. 1925. 167 p. (DLC); rev. ed. 1926. 356 p.; (c) Zbirka Krivičnih zakona, uredaba, pravila, uputstava, i raspisa, dopunjujućih kazneni zakonik i krivični sudski postupak Srbije (Collection of Criminal Laws, Decrees, Regulations and Instructions Amending the Serbian Criminal Code and the Code of Criminal Procedure). Beograd, 1921. 475 p.; (d) Krivični (Kazneni) Zakonik i Zakonik o Postupku Sudskom u krivičnim delima Kraljevine Srbije, s kratkim objašnjenjem, s obzirom na odluke Kasacionog Suda (Criminal Code and Code of Criminal Procedure of the Kingdom of Serbia, Annotated). Beograd, 1913. 247, 184 p.; (e) O uvredi i kleveti (Libel and Slander). Beograd, 1937. 125 p. (DLC); (f) Dualitet krivičnih sankcija, kazne i mere bezbednosti (Dual System of Criminal Sanctions, Punishments, and Security Measures). Beograd, 1928. 61 p

930 Zuglia, Srećko. Stanje nužde (Necessity). Veliki Bečkerek, 1920. 52 p.

b From the Code of 1929 to the End of World War II

See also Nos.: 929; 2374; 2409b; 2409d; 2409f.

931 Aćimović, Miodrag. Krivično pravo (Criminal Law). Subotica, 1937–1940. 2 v.

932 Breberina, Stevan *and* Ivan Ilić. Krivični Zakonik za Kraljevinu Jugoslaviju od 27 januara 1929, sa . . . rešidbama Stola Sedmorice . . . i Apelacionog suda u Zagrebu (Criminal Code for the Kingdom of Yugoslavia, January 27, 1929, as amended, with the Supreme Court's Decisions). Zagreb, 1934. 329 p. (DLC)

933 Čubinski, Mih. (a) Naučni i praktični komentar Krivičnog zakonika Kraljevine Jugoslavije (Theoretical and Practical Commentary on the Criminal Code of the Kingdom of Yugoslavia). Beograd, 1930. 598 p. (DLC); ———. Posebni deo (Special Part). 1930. 390 p.; 2d rev. ed. 1934. 746 p.; (b) Kriminalna politika. Pojam, sadržaj, i odnos prema nauci Krivičnog prava (Criminal Policy. Concept, Contents and Relationship to the Theory of Criminal Law). Beograd, 1937. 297 p. (DLC); (c) Opšta karakteristika novih škola u krivičnom pravu (General Characteristics

of the New Schools in Criminal Law). Beograd, 1925. 45 p. (DLC); (d) Problemi izjednačenja prava u ujedinjenom Kraljevstvu SHS, i osnovne odredbe projekta Srpskog kaznenog zakonika (Problems of the Unification of Laws in the United Kingdom of the Serbs, Croats and Slovenes). Beograd, 1921. 108 p. (DLC)

934 Čulinović, F. (a) O slobodi volje (Freedom of Will). Bečkerek, 1930. 143 p.; (b) Žena u našem krivičnom pravu (Woman in our Criminal Law). Beograd, 1934. 119 p.

935 Dolenc, Metod *and* A. Maklecov. (a) Sistem celokupnog krivičnog prava Kraljevine Jugoslavije (Principles of the Yugoslav Criminal Law). Beograd, 1935. 320 p. (DLC); (b) Same in Slovenian. Sistem celokupnega Kazenskega prava (System of the Entire Criminal Law of Yugoslavia). 1934. 414 p. (DLC); (c) Tumač Krivičnog zakonika Kr. Jugoslavije (Commentary on the Yugoslav Criminal Code). Zagreb, 1930. 510; 43 p. (DLC); Dodatak (Supplement), 1931. (DLC); (d) same in Slovenian: Tolmač k kazenskemu zakoniku Kraljevine Jugoslavije (Commentary on the Yugoslav Criminal Code). Ljubljana, 1929. 608 p. (DLC); (e) Sadašnji položaj kaznenopravnog zakonodavstva Kraljevine Srba, Hrvata i Slovenaca (Yugoslav Criminal Legislation in its Present State). Ljubljana, 1923.

See also articles in *Zbornik znanstvenih razprav* v. 4, 1924/25; v. 6, 1 Apr. '28; v. 9, 1932/33; v. 11, 1934/35; v. 13, 1932/33; v. 18, 1940/41, also *Arhiv* v. 31, no. 1, 1927; v. 32, no. 5, 1927; v. 25, no. 4, 1924; v. 41, no. 5, 1928; v. 50, no. 1, 1936 (DLC).

936 Dolenc, Metod *and* Rudolf Sajovic. Novelirani kazenski zakonik za Kraljevino Jugoslavijo, s kratkimi pojasnili (Amended Criminal Code of the Kingdom of Yugoslavia, Annotated). Ljubljana, 1932. 207 p.

937 Dravić, V. O nehatu (Negligence). Beograd, 1935. 35 p.

938 Dolenc, Metod. O povratu i ponavljanju u našem krivičnom zakoniku (Habitual Criminals under Our Criminal Code). *Mjesečnik* (Zagreb), 1933: 170–188. (DLC)

939 Karajovanović, Djoka. Komentar opšteg Krivičnog zakonika (Commentary on the Criminal Code). Beograd, 1930. 399 p. (DLC)

940 Koštunica, J. Psihoanaliza i novo krivično zakonodavstvo

(Psychoanalysis and the Modern Criminal Legislation). Beograd, 1937. 23 p.

941 Krivični zakonik. Zakon o sudskom krivičnom postupku (Criminal Code—Code of Criminal Procedure). Beograd, 1929. 498 p.; 1929. 546 p. (DLC)

942 Krivični zakonik za Kraljevinu Srba, Hrvata i Slovenaca (Criminal Code of Yugoslavia of 1929). Beograd, 1929. 109 p. (DLC); 1929. 156 p. (DLC); 1932, prepared by N. Pahorukov, 175 p. (DLC); 8th ed. 1932. 202 p. (DLC)

943 Kulaš, I. Problem pravnih lekova u krivičnom pravu (Legal Remedies in Criminal Law). Beograd, 1939. 222 p.

944 Lazić, Dragoslav M. Krivični zakonik od 27 januara 1929. sa izmenama . . . od 8 oktobra 1931 god. (Criminal Code of 1929, as Amended on October 8, 1931). Beograd, 1932. 173 p. (DLC)

945 Maklecov, A. (a) Očuvalne odredbe v sistemu modernega prava (Temporary Measures for the Protection of Property Interests in Modern Law). Ljubljana, 1932. 103 p.; (b) Osebnost zločinca v modernem kazenskem pravu s posebnim ozirom na zakonik Kraljevine Jugoslavije (The Criminal in Modern Criminal Law and Especially in the Yugoslav Criminal Code). Ljubljana, 1930. 40 p.

See also articles in *Zbornik znanstvenih razprav*, v. 7, 1929; v. 9, 1932/33; v. 10–13, 1933–37; v. 15–17, 1938–41; v. 20–22, 1943-1948, *also Arhiv*, v. 42, 1932; v. 45, 1934; v. 56, 1939. (DLC).

946 Marjanović, Čed. O položaju maloletnika u materijalnom krivičnom pravu (The Status of Juveniles under Substantive Criminal Law). Beograd, 1935. 184 p.

947 Marković, Čedomir. Zabrana ili sloboda voljnog pobačaja (Prohibition or Freedom of Voluntary Abortion). Subotica, 1925. 32 p.

948 Mijušković, Mirko B. *and* Milaš K. Vojvodić. Priručnik za rad po carinsko-krivičnim predmetima (Handbook on Offenses under Customs Laws and Regulations). Ljubljana, 1934. 172 p. (DLC)

949 Niketić, Gojko. Krivični Zakonik (Criminal Code, Annotated, with Court Decisions and Supplementary Rules and Regulations). Beograd, 1939. 778 p.

950 Opšti krivični zbornik (General Collection of Criminal Laws). Beograd, 1929. 546 p. (Zbirka zakona, sv. 124). (DLC)

951 Petrović, Borivoje D. (a) Problem akcesorne prirode saučešća . . . (Nature of the Relationship Between Parties to a Crime). Beograd, 1935. 132 p. (DLC); (b) Krivična odgovornost pravnih lica (Criminal Responsibility of Legal Entities). Beograd, 1938; (c) Savremeni problemi krivičnog prava (Present Problems of Criminal Law). Beograd, 1938. 304 p.

952 Politeo, Ivo. Politički delikt (Political Offenses). Zagreb, 1921.

953 Subotić, Dušan M. Šest osnovnih problema krivičnog prava (Six Basic Problems of Criminal Law). Beograd, 1933. 147 p. (DLC)

954 Szanto, Dragutin. Krivični zakonik i zakonik o sudskom krivičnom postupku (Criminal Code and Code of Criminal Procedure, Annotated). Zagreb, 1939. 700 p. (DLC)

955 Šil, Andrija O. O pokušaju krivičnog dela u krivičnom pravu i Jugoslovenskom krivičnom zakoniku (Attempt in Criminal Law and the Yugoslav Criminal Code). Novi Sad, 1939. 193 p. (DLC)

956 Šilović, Josip and Stanko Frank. (a) Kazneno pravo prema Krivičnom zakonu od 27 januara 1929 (Criminal Law According to the Code of January 27, 1929). Zagreb, 1929–34. 2 v. (DLC); (b) Krivični zakonik za Kraljevinu Srba, Hrvata i Slovenaca od 27 januara 1929 (Criminal Code of January 27, 1929). Zagreb, 1929. 276 p. (DLC); (c) Zakon o izmenama i dopunama o Krivičnom zakoniku od 9 oktobra 1931 godine (Amendments to the Criminal Code of October 9, 1931). Zagreb, 1932. 68 p. (DLC)

957 Timoškin, Vladimir. Nužna odbrana (Self-Defense). Sarajevo, 1939. 66 p.

958 Tregubov, Sergije and Aleksandar Andonović. Kriminalna tehnika. Naučno-tehničko istraživanje krivičnih dela (Criminal Techniques. Scientific Detection of Crimes). Beograd, 1935. 480 p.

959 Uredbe za izvršavanje krivičnog zakonika i zakona o sudskom krivičnom postupku (Provisions Concerning the Enforcement of the Criminal Code and the Code of Criminal Procedure). Beograd, 1930. 2 v. (DLC)

960 Urošević, Laz. Sudski Trebnik, II deo, Krivični zakonik

(Judicial Handbook, Part II, Criminal Code). Beograd, 1929. 859 p. (DLC)

961 Vasiljević, Tihomir. Uslovna osuda (Suspended Sentence). Beograd, 1935. 280 p. (DLC)

962 Subotić, Strahinja M. Motiv i njegov značaj u krivičnom pravu i jugoslovenskom krivičnom zakoniku (The Motive and Its Significance in Criminal Law and Especially in the Yugoslav Criminal Code). Novi Sad, 1938. 266 p. (DLC)

963 Vragović, Aleksa. Sporedni krivični zakoni (uredbe, pravilnici, konvencije) (Special Criminal Statutes, Decrees, Regulations, International Treaties). Zagreb, 1930. 790 p. (DLC)

964 Zakon o zaštiti javne bezbednosti (Law on the Protection of Public Safety). 2d ed. Beograd, 1929. 48 p. (Zbirka zakona, sv. 117) (DLC); (Zbirka zakona br. 7) 32 p. (DLC); 1938 (Zbirka zakona, sv. 17) 144 p. (DLC); 1938, 350 p. (*idem*, sv. 53) (DLC)

965 Živanović, Toma. (a) Osnovi Krivičnog Prava. Opšti i Posebni deo (Principles of Criminal Law. General and Special Parts). Beograd, 1912; (b) ———. Opšti deo (General Part). Beograd, 1910. 176 p.; 2d ed. 1922. 380 p.; 1930. 92, 48 p.; 1934. 144 p.; 1935. 388 p. (DLC); 1937. 472 p.; 1941. 47 p. (DLC); (c) ———. Posebni deo (Special Part). Beograd, 1911. 191 p.; 1912. ?; 2d rev. ed. 1923. 2 v. (DLC); 1931. v. 2, sv. 2. 80 p.; 1933. v. 2, sv: 1: 232 p. (DLC); 1936. 208 p.; 3d ed. 1938. 164 p. (DLC); 1939. v. 1, sv. 2. 200 p. (DLC); v. 2, sv. 3. 100 p. (DLC); (d) Krivični zakonik u postupku sudskom u krivičnim delima (Criminal Code and Code of Criminal Procedure). 3d ed. Beograd, 1922, 486 p.; 4th ed. 1930. 565 p. (DLC); (e) Osnovni problemi Krivičnog prava (Basic Problems of Criminal Law). Beograd, 1910. 64 p.; 1930, 219 p. (DLC); Same in French: Les problèmes fondamentals du droit criminel. Paris, 1929. 227 p.; (f) Krivično pravo (Criminal Law). Beograd, 1933–1939. 2 v. in 5.

c Since World War II

See also Nos.: 2339b; 2418; 2456.

966 Krivični zakonik; opći dio (Criminal Code; General Part). 3d ed. Beograd, 1950. 46 p.; *id.*, 52 p. (Zbirka zakona FNRJ, br. 20) (DLC)

967 Krivični zakonik sa uvodnim zakonom (Criminal Code).
Beograd, 1951. 215 p. (DLC); 1954. 216 p.; Zagreb, 1954. 259 p.
(DLC); 4th ed. Beograd, 1957. 240 p.; 5th ed. 1961. 272 p.
(DLC)

968 Objašnjenja uz nacrt krivičnog zakonika FNRJ; Osnovna problematika (Criticism on the Draft of the Criminal Code of the
F.P.R.Y. Basic Principles). Beograd, 1951. 411 p. (DLC)

969 Zakoni o krivičnim delima protiv službene dužnosti i o zaštiti
opštenarodne imovine (Laws on Offenses Constituting Breach
of Official Duty and on the Protection of National Property).
Beograd, 1948. 30 p. (Zbirka Zakona FNRJ, br. 24) (DLC)

970 Kazne u privredi (Punishments in the National Economy).
Zagreb, 1955. 224 p. (DLC)

971 O krivičnoj odgovornosti i kazni (Criminal Responsibility
and Punishment). Beograd, 1954. 74 p. (DLC); ed. in Macedonian "Za krivičnata," 1950. 79 p. (DLC)

972 Zbirka krivičnih zakona (Collection of Criminal Laws, annotated). Beograd, 1946. 170 p. (DLC); 4th ed. 1948. 166 p.
(Zbirka zakona FNRJ, br. 10). (DLC)

973 Zbirka propisa o prekršajima i privrednim prestupima . . . NR
Bosne i Hercegovine (Collection of Provisions on Petty Offenses
and Economic Crimes in Bosnia and Herzegovina). 1956. 82 p.
(DLC)

974 Vojvodina A. P. Glavni izvršni odbor. Pokrajinska komisija
za utvrdjivanje zločina okupatora. Saopštenje o zločinima okupatora i njihovih pomagača u Vojvodini, 1941–1944. Knj. 1,
Bačka i Baranja (Report of the Commission for the Investigation of the Crimes of the Occupiers and their Collaborators, Book
1-Bačka and Baranja). Novi Sad, 1946. 335 p. (DLC)

975 Bavcon, Ljubo. (a) Kriminalna politika in njene tendence v
socialistični družbi (Criminal Policy and its Trends in a Socialist
Society with a Summary in English). Ljubljana, 1958. 163 p.
(DLC); (b) coauthor. Kazenski zakonik. Prečiščeno besedilo (The
Criminal Code. Unified Text). Ljubljana, 1960. 570 p. (DLC)

976 Jevremović, Branko T. Pregled najvažnijih izmena i dopuna
krivičnog zakonika (A Survey of the Most Important Amendments to the Criminal Code). Arhiv, 1959: 396–412. (DLC)

977 Crnogorčević, Jovo. Osnovi kaznenopravnog sistema FNRJ

(Basic Principles of the System of Criminal Law of the F.P.R.Y.). Beograd, 1958. 120 p. (DLC)

978 Dimitrijević, Dragoljub. Osnovi Krivičnog Prava FNRJ. Opšti deo (Principles of the Criminal Law of the F.P.R.Y. General Part). Sarajevo, 1953. 98 p. (DLC)

979 Dokić, Milan *and* Vladimir Mikić. O privrednim prestupima (Economic Offenses). 1957. 168 p. (DLC)

980 Dolničar, Matej *and* Heli Modic. Komentar splošnega dela Kazenskega zakonika (Commentary on the General Part of the Criminal Code). Ljubljana, 1948. 304 p.

981 Frank, Stanko. (a) Teorija kaznenog prava po Krivičnom zakoniku od godine 1951. Opći deo (Theory of Criminal Law and the Criminal Code of 1951. General Part). Zagreb, 1955. 299 p. (DLC); (b) Kazneno pravo (Criminal Law). Zagreb, 1950. 213 p. (DLC)

982 Gelfer, Miron Abramovich. Osnovnye cherty ugolovnogo prava FNRIu (Outline of the Criminal Law of Yugoslavia). Moskva, 1956. 53 p. (DLC)

983 Hrnčević, Josip. O predlogu Krivičnog Zakonika, opšti deo (Draft of the Criminal Code, General Part). n.p. 1947.

984 Jevtić, Dušan. O uračunljivosti sa sudsko-psihijatriskog gledišta (Ability to be Held Responsible from the Psychiatric Forensic Point of View). Beograd, 1953. 104 p.

985 Kirichenko, V.F. F.N.R.IU, Ugolovnyi Kodeks (Criminal Code of the FPRY). Moskva, 1957. 81 p. (Ugolovnoe zakonodatel'stvo zarubezhnykh sotsialisticheskikh gosudarstv) (DLC)

986 Maklecov, Aleksandar. Naše novo kazensko pravo in njegove vodilne ideje (Our New Criminal Law and its Main Principles). Ljubljana, 1948. 31 p. (DLC)

987 Miličević, Spasoje. Osnovi krivičnog prava i krivičnog postupka (Principles of Criminal Law and Procedure). Beograd, 1958. 219 p.; 2nd ed. 1959. 210 p. (DLC)

988 Munda, August. (a) Uvod v kriminalistiko (Introduction to Criminology). Ljubljana, Državna založba Slovenije, 1951. 284 p.; (b) Sistematika kaznivih dejanj zoper življenje in telo (Systematic Classification of Punishable Acts against Life and Bodily Injuries). Ljubljana, 1951. 42 p. (DLC)

988¹ Obrenović, Živko. Osnovi prekršajnog prava FNRJ (Principles of the Law on Petty Offenses of the FPRY). Beograd, 1960. 199 p.

989 Pavić, Dragutin. (a) Neki problemi iz krivičnog prava FNRJ (Some Problems of Criminal Law of the F.P.R. of Yugoslavia). Zagreb, 1957. 226 p. (DLC); (b) coauthor. Pregled osnovne literature i judikaturc uz krivični zakonik i zakonik o krivičnom postupku od 1. januara 1957 do 31. marta 1959. Knjiga druga (A Survey of Basic Literature and Court Decisions Relating to the Criminal Code and the Code of Criminal Procedure, January 1, 1957—March 31, 1959. Second Book). Zagreb, 1959. 450 p. Mimeographed. (DLC)

990 Pijade, Moša, joint editor. (a) Komentar Splošnega dela Kazenskega zakonika (Commentary on the General Part of the Criminal Code). Translated into Slovenian by Matej Dolničar and others. Ljubljana, 1948. 304 p. (DLC); (b) Komentar općeg dijela Krivičnog zakonika (Commentary on the General Part of the Criminal Code). Beograd, 1948. 288 p. (DLC)

991 Radovanović, Miloš V. Zloupotreba službenog položaja (Abuse of Official Position). Beograd, 1958. 260 p. (DLC)

992 Radovanović, Bora. Kriminal u privredi (Criminology in the National Economy). Beograd, 1954. 126 p.

993 Srzentić, Nikola. (a) Problemi privrednih delikata (Economic Offenses). Arhiv, 1954: 336–363. (DLC); (b) Obrazloženje izmena i dopuna krivičnog zakonika (A Commentary on the Amendments to the Criminal Code). Arhiv, 1960: 84–131. (DLC)

994 Srzentić, Nikola and Aleksandar Stajić. Krivično pravo FNRJ. Opšti deo (Criminal Law of the FPR of Yugoslavia. General Part). Beograd, 1953. 555 p. (DLC); 1954. 552 p. (DLC); 2d ed. 1957. 551 p. (DLC); 3rd ed. 1961. 431 p.

995 Szanto, Dragutin, editor. Zakoni o krivičnim djelima protiv službene dužnosti i o zaštiti općenarodne imovine (Laws against Crimes Constituting Breach of Official Duty and the Protection of National Property). Beograd, 1948. 30 p. (DLC)

996 Tahović, Janko. (a) Krivično pravo. Posebni deo (Criminal Law. Special Part). Beograd, 1947–1953. 2 v.; 2nd ed. 1955. 526 p. (DLC); (b) Komentar krivičnog zakonika (Commentary on the Criminal Code). Beograd, 1956. 695 p. (DLC)

997 Stajić, Aleksandar. (a) Pojave i uzroci saobraćajnih delikata

(Features and Causes of Traffic Violations). *Godišnjak pravnog fakulteta* (Sarajevo), 1960: 59–81. (DLC); (b) Pravni i stvarni osnovi odmjeravanja kazne (Legal and Actual Basis for Imposing Punishment). *Ibid.*, 1959: 31–50. (DLC)

998 Zbirka odredaba o prekršajima sadržanih u saveznim i republičkom propisima (A Collection of Provisions on Petty Offenses, Both Federal and Republican). Beograd, 1959. 2 v. (DLC)

999 Vučković, Milorad *and* Njegoslav Ocokoljić, *editors.* Osnovni zakon o prekršajima, sa komentarom (Basic Law on Petty Offenses, annotated). Beograd, 1952. 286 p. (DLC); 2d ed. Beograd, 1953. 307 p. (DLC); 3d rev. ed. 1954. 351 p. (DLC); 4th ed. 1956. 400 p.; 5th ed. 1959. 430 p. (DLC)

1000 Zlatarić, Bogdan. Krivični zakonik u praktičnoj primjeni; kritički pregled judikature (Criminal Code as Applied in Practice; a Critical Survey of Court Decisions). Zagreb. 1956–1958. 2 v. (DLC)

9 Criminal Procedure

See also: Ch. 11, A, 2d; Special Topics: Judicial System; Trials.

a Prior to 1929

See also Nos.: 907; 929d; 2351b; 2405b; 2440.

1001 Zakonik o postupku sudskom u krivičnim delima za knjažestvo Srbiju od 10 aprila 1865 (Code of Criminal Procedure for Serbia of April 10, 1865). Beograd, 1865. 166 p. (DLC)

1002 Zakon od 17. svibnja 1875 ob uvedbi kaznenoga postupnika (Introductory Law of May 17, 1875 to the Code of Criminal Procedure, Law on the Press, Law on Jurors' Lists, and Law Concerning Procedure in Press Cases). Zagreb, 1875. 192, 52 p. (DLC)

1003 Kazneni postupak za Bosnu i Hercegovina (Criminal Procedure for Bosnia and Herzegovina). Sarajevo, 1891. 137 p. (DLC)

1004 Zakon o istražnim vlastima (Law on Investigating Authorities). Beograd, 1895. 3 p. (DLC)

1005 Zakon o poroti (Law on the Jury). Beograd, 1892. 16 p. (DLC)

1006 Hönigsberg, Lavoslav. Osnova zakona o krivičnom postupku (A Draft of the Code of Criminal Procedure). *Mjesečnik* (Zagreb), 1922: 145–161. (DLC)

1007 Dolenc, Metod. Zgodovina porote v Srbiji (History of the Jury in Serbia). Ljubljana, 1922.

1008 Lazarević, V. Daktiloskopija (Fingerprinting). Beograd, 1907. 52 p. (DLC)

1009 Marković, Božidar V. (a) Udžbenik srpskog krivičnog postupka (Textbook on Serbian Criminal Procedure). Beograd, 1926. 540 p.; (b) Rasprave iz krivičnog postupka (Treatise on Criminal Procedure). Beograd, 1914. 147 p. (DLC); (c) O dokazima u krivičnom postupku (Evidence in Criminal Procedure). Beograd, 1908. 385 p.; 2d ed. 1921. 213 p. (DLC); (d) Ponovno sudjenje u krivičnom postupku (Reopening of Criminal Cases). Beograd, 1902. 32 p.; (e) Postupak protivu odsutnih i odbeglih krivaca (Proceedings Against Unaccounted-for or Fugitive Criminals). Beograd, 1902. 37 p.; (f) Sredstva za zamenu kratkovremene kazne lišenja slobode s naročitim obzirom na uslovnu osudu (Means for Substituting Short Term Imprisonment with Particular Respect to Suspended Sentences). Beograd, 1909. 164 p. (DLC); (g) Treba li porotu ukinuti ili reformisati? (Should the Jury be Abolished or Reorganized?). Beograd, 1906. 74 p.

1010 Milosavljević, Živko M. Novi zakonik o Krivičnom postupku za Bosnu i Hercegovinu (New Code of Criminal Procedure for Bosnia and Herzegovina). Reprint from *Pravnik*. Beograd, 1893. 33 p.

1011 Namyslowski, Vladislav *and* Šutej Zdravko, *editors.* Kazneni postupnik za Bosnu i Hercegovinu (Code of Criminal Procedure for Bosnia and Herzegovina). Sarajevo, 1919. 488 p. (DLC)

1012 Maroević, Ivo. Za ili protiv porote (For or Against the Jury). *Mjesečnik* (Zagreb), 1924: 418–422. (DLC)

1013 Ogorelica, Nikola. Kazneno procesualno pravo, s osobitim obzirom na judikaturu Stola Sedmorice i Kasacionog suda Bečkoga (Criminal Procedural Law with Respect to the Judicial Practice of the Supreme Courts of Zagreb and Vienna). Zagreb, 1899. 867 p. (DLC)

1014 Seifert, Franjo. Istražni zatvor i nastup kazne (Arrest Pending Judicial Investigation and Serving of Sentence). *Mjesečnik* (Zagreb), 1906: 760–763. (DLC)

1015 Radović, Dim. G. Teorija kaznenog postupka, s pogledom na zakonik o postupku sudskom u kriv. delima za Knjažestvo

Srbiju, od 10 april 1865 (Theory on Criminal Procedure with Respect to the Code of Criminal Procedure of the Principality of Serbia, April 10, 1865). Beograd, 1870. 355 p. (DLC)

1016 Rojc, Antun. Austrijanski kazneni postupnik od dana 29. Srpnja 1853 (Austrian Code of Criminal Procedure of July 29, 1853). Zagreb, 1855. 216 p. (DLC)

1017 Rušnov, Adolfo. Kazneni postupnik, sa novelom od g. 1888 (Code of Criminal Procedure with Amendments of 1888). Zagreb, 1888. 292 p. (Hrvatski zakoni, xii) (DLC)

1018 Savić, Panta J. Teorija sudskih dokaza u krivičnim delima (Theory on Evidence in Crimes). Beograd, 1886. 482 p. (DLC)

1019 Šilović, Josip. Kazneni postupnik od 17 svibna 1875 (Code of Criminal Procedure of May 17, 1875). 2d ed. Zagreb, 1898. 386 p. (DLC); 3d ed. 1909. 498 p. (DLC)

1020 Ugrić, Jevrem. Sudska praksa. Presuda prvostepenog suda po krivičnim delima (Judicial Practice. Judgment of the Court of Original Jurisdiction in Criminal Matters). Beograd, 1923. 93 p. (DLC)

1021 Veljković, Stojan J. (a) O kaznitelnom postupku sudskom na osnovu usmenosti i javnosti (Criminal Procedure on the Basis of an Oral Judicial Examination and Public Trial). Beograd, 1860. 51, 78 p. (DLC); (b) O poroti (The Jury). Beograd, 1880. 24 p.

1022 Živanović, Toma. Osnovni problemi Krivičnog i Gradjanskog procesnog prava (Basic Problems of Criminal and Civil Procedural Law). Beograd, 1940–1941. 2 v.

1023 Žujović, Milenko M. (a) Prilozi za reformu kaznenih zavoda (Studies for the Reform of Penitentiaries). Beograd, 1887. 194 p. (DLC); (b) O kaznenim zavodima (Penitentiaries). Beograd, 1884. 134 p.

b   After 1929

See also Nos.: 941; 959; 987; 989; 2342.

1024 Zakonik o krivičnom postupku od 30 septembra 1953 (Code of Criminal Procedure of September 30, 1953). Beograd, 1953. 204 p. (Zbirka zakona FNRJ, br. 110). (DLC); Beograd, 1953. 357 p. (DLC)

1025   Zakon o krivičnom postupku (Code of Criminal Procedure). Beograd, 1948. 207 p. (DLC)

1026   Prednacrt zakona o krivičnom postupku, za discusiju (Preliminary Draft of a Code on Criminal Procedure, for Discussion). Beograd, 1951. 111 p. (DLC)

1027   Izveštaj Zakonodavnog odbora Veća Naroda o Predlogu Zakonika o Krivičnom Postupku (Report of the Legislative Committee of the Council of Nationality on the Code of Criminal Procedure). Beograd, 1953. 54 p. (DLC)

1028   Zakon o izvršenju kazni (Law on Execution of Punishments). Beograd, 1948. 37 p. (DLC); 1951, 72 p. (Zbirka Zakona FNRJ, No. 103) (DLC); 2d ed. 1953. 186 p. (Zbirka zakona FNRJ, No. 107). (DLC)

1029   Zakonik o kazenskem postopku. Prečiščeno besedilo (Code of Criminal Procedure. Unified Text). Ljubljana, 1960. 282 p. (DLC)

1030   Zakonik o sudskom Krivičnom postupku (Code of Criminal Procedure for Yugoslavia). Beograd, 1929. 274 p. (DLC); 1929, 283 p. (Zbirka zakona, sv. 12). (DLC); 2d ed. 1930; 3d ed. 1931. 396 p. (DLC) (Zbirka zakona, br. 121). (DLC)

1031   Zakonik o sodnem kazenskem postopanju za Kraljevino Srbov, Hrvatov in Slovencev. Zakon o izvrševanju kazni na prostosti (Code of Criminal Procedure for the Kingdom of Serbs, Croats and Slovenes . . .). Ljubljana, 1929. 325 p. (DLC)

1032   Zakon o izvršivanju kazni lišenja slobode (Law on Execution of Punishments by Confinement). Beograd, 1929. 64 p. (DLC); 2d ed. 1931. 48 p. (DLC)

1033   Uredba o poslovnom redu za redovne krivične sudove od 21 novembra 1929 god., sa uredbom o poslovnom redu za krivična tužioštva (Decree on Rules of Procedure for Ordinary Criminal Courts of Nov. 21, 1929, and Decree on Rules of Procedure for the District Attorney's Office). Beograd, 1930. 150 p. (DLC); 1930. 136 p. (Zbirka zakona . . . sv. 143) (DLC)

1034   Bauer, H. Veštačenje pismenih isprava (Expert Testimony on Documents). Beograd, 1940. 235 p. (DLC)

1035   Bayer, Vladimir. (a) Teorija Krivičnog postupka FNRJ (Theory of Criminal Procedure in Yugoslavia). Zagreb, 1950. 315 p. (DLC); (b) Kazneno postupovno pravo (Criminal Procedure). Zagreb, 1943. 415 p.; (c) Jugoslovensko krivično procesno pravo. Knjiga prva (Yugoslav Criminal Procedural Law. First Book). Zagreb, 1960. 195 p. (DLC)

1036 Čubinski, Mih. Naučni i praktični komentar Zakonika o sudskom krivičnom postupku Kraljevine Jugoslavije od 16 februara 1929 (Theoretical and Practical Commentary on the Yugoslav Code of Criminal Procedure, February 16, 1929). Beograd, 1933. 831 p. (DLC)

1037 Dolenc, Metod. (a) Sodni kazenski postopnik Kraljevine Jugoslavije (Code of Criminal Procedure of the Kingdom of Yugoslavia). Ljubljana, 1932. 472 p. (DLC); (b) Teorija sudskog krivičnog postupka za Kraljevinu Jugoslaviju (Theory of the Code of Criminal Procedure for the Kingdom of Yugoslavia). Beograd, 1933. 378 p. (DLC)

1038 Dolenc, Metod and Aleksander Maklecov, editors. Zakonik o sudnem kazenskem postopanju, s kratkim pojasnili (Code of Criminal Procedure with Brief Survey). Ljubljana, 1938. 400 p. (DLC)

1039 Frank, S. Saradjivanje suca i psihijatra u utvrdjivanju smanjenja ubrojivosti (Cooperation between Judge and Psychiatrist in Establishing Limited Liability). Zagreb, 1929. 36 p.

1040 Henigsberg, Lav. (a) Zakonik o sudskom krivičnom postupku (Code of Criminal Procedure). Zagreb, 1930. 386 p. (DLC); 2d ed. Zagreb, 1930. 646 p. (DLC); (b) Osnovni propisi sudsko krivičnog postupka (Basic Provisions of the Code of Criminal Procedure). Zagreb, 1934. 409 p. (DLC); (c) Krivični postupak o pravnim lekovima (Legal Remedies in the Code of Criminal Procedure). Beograd, 1933. 136 p. (DLC)

1041 Henigsberg, Lavoslav and Marko Ružić. Obrazci za primenu zakonika o sudskom krivičnom postupku od 16. februara 1929 (Forms for Application of Code of Criminal Procedure of February 16, 1929). Zagreb, 1931. 448 p. (DLC)

1041[1] Jovanović, Ljubiša. Lekarska tajna (Physician and Patient Privilege). Beograd, 1959. 74 p. (DLC)

1042 Jovanović, Stojan. Potsetnik za primenu sudskog krivičnog postupka od 16. februara 1929 (Manual for the Application of the Code of Criminal Procedure). Beograd, 1931. 198 p. (DLC)

1043 Pauković, Milan. Vještačenje kod privrednih delikata (An Expert Witness in Economic Crimes). Zagreb, 1961. 206 p.

1044 Marina, Panta. Teorija na krivičnata postapka (Theory on Criminal Procedure). Skopje, 1958. 203 p. Mimeographed. (DLC)

1045 Marković, Božidar V. Udžbenik sudskog krivičnog postupka Kraljevine Jugoslavije (Textbook on Criminal Procedure of the Kingdom of Yugoslavia). Beograd, 1930. 695 p. (DLC); 1937. 615 p.

1046 Maširević, Branko. Krivični obrasci uz novi Krivični zakonik, Postupnik i Pravilnik (Forms Attached to the New Criminal Code, the Code of Criminal Procedure and Regulations). Sombor, 1930. 120 p.

1047 Munda, A. (a) Učbenik kazenskega postopka FLRJ (Textbook on Criminal Procedure of the FPRY). Ljubljana, 1957– v. 2. (DLC); (b) Naš zakon o kaznenom postupku i njegove vodilne ideje (Yugoslav Code of Criminal Procedure and its Fundamental Ideas). Ljubljana, 1950. 52 p.; (c) Obdolženec v pripravljalnem postopku (The Defendant in Pretrial Procedure). *Pravnik*, v. 11, No. 1–2, 1959; 35–51.

1048 Niketić, Gojko, *editor*. Zakonik o sudskom krivičnom postupku za kraljevinu Jugoslaviju od 16. februara 1929, sa izmenama (Code of Criminal Procedure for the Kingdom of Yugoslavia of February 16, 1929, as amended). 4th ed. Beograd, 1936. 314 p. (DLC)

1049 Ogorelica, Nikola. (a) Zakonik o sudskom krivičnom postupku (Code of Criminal Procedure). Zagreb, 1929. 308 p. (DLC); (b) Zakon o izmenama (Amending Law). Zagreb, 1932, 48 p. (DLC)

1050 Pajnić. E. *and* A. Munda. Sistematičen pregled pritožb v sodnem kazenskem postopniku (Systematic Survey of Appeals in Criminal Procedure). Ljubljana, 1933. 60 p.

1051 Peić, Dušan. Praktična primena Zakonika o sudskom krivičnom postupku Kraljevine Jugoslavije od 16 februara 1929 (Practical Application of the Code of Criminal Procedure of the Kingdom of Yugoslavia, February 16, 1929). Beograd, 1935. 53 p.

1052 Petrović, B. Izvršenje kazne lišenjem slobode (Execution of Punishments). Beograd, 1932. 100 p.

1053 Petrović, Vitomir. Predavanja iz Krivičnog sudskog postupka

(Lectures on Criminal Procedure). Beograd, 1951. 344 p. (DLC)

1054 Pijade, Moša *and* Josip Hrnčević. Zakonik o krivičnom postupku i organi pravosudja (Code of Criminal Procedure and Organs of the Administration of Justice). Beograd, 1953. 23 p.

1055 Simović, Lj. Kriminalističko veštačenje dokumenata (Expert Testimony on Documents in Criminal Proceedings). Beograd, 1956. 375 p.

1056 Stepanović, Velimir *and* Branko Petrić, *editors.* Zbirka obrazaca za primenu Zakonika o krivičnom postupku (Collection of Forms for the Application of the Code of Criminal Procedure). Beograd, 1957. 233 p. (Biblioteka stručnih izdanja). (DLC)

1057 Umićević, Dušan. Sistemi izvršivanja kazni lišenja slobode (Systems of Execution of Imprisonment). Sarajevo, 1938. 264 p. (DLC)

1058 Vasiljević, Tihomir. Komentar zakonika o krivičnom postupku (Commentary on the Code of Criminal Procedure). Beograd, 1957. 488 p. (DLC)

10   International Law, Public

See also: Special Topics: Maritime Law; Nos.: 2244; 2245; 2246; 2272; 2277; 2278; 2284; 2286; 2287; 2301; 2310; 2311; 2313; 2317; 2323; 2324; 2329; 2343b; 2345b; 2345c; 2351a.

1059 Adžija, Božidar. Medjunarodna organizacija rada (The International Labor Organization). Zagreb, 1926. 46 p.

1059[1] Andrassy, Juraj. (a) Medjunarodno pravo (International Law). Zagreb, 1949. 304 p.; 2nd ed. 1954. 351 p.; 3rd ed. 1958. 397 p. (DLC); (b) Epikontinental pojas (Continental Shelf). Zagreb, 1951. 102 p. (DLC); (c) Medjunarodno pravosudje (International Administration of Justice). Zagreb, 1948. 227 p. (DLC); (d) Liga naroda (League of Nations). Zagreb, 1931. 232 p. (DLC)

1060 Anonymus. Privatna svojina u pomorskom ratu (Private Property in Maritime War Law). *Branič*, 1898: 500–561. (DLC)

1061 Avakumović, Mirko G. Kratak pogled na Medjunarodnu organizaciju rada (A View on the International Labor Organization). Beograd, 1929. 24 p.

1062 Bartoš, Milan. (a) Osnovni pojmovi o Ujedinjenim Nacijama (Basic Notions on the United Nations). Beograd, 1953. 89 p.; (b) Medjunarodno javno pravo (International Law). Beograd, 1954–1958. 3 v. (DLC); (c) Savremeni medjunarodni problemi (Present International Problems). Sarajevo, 1955. 180 p. (DLC)

1063 Besarabić, Vojin L. Neutralnost i njena savremena shvatanja (Neutrality and its Contemporary Concepts). Beograd, 1939. 259 p.

1064 Blagojević, B. I. Medjunarodno uredjivanje radnih odnosa (International Settlement of Labor Relations). Beograd, 1940. 235 p.

1065 Bulajić, M. K. (a) Revizionizam u Sovjetkoj teoriji medjunarodnog Prava (Revisionism in the Soviet Theory of International Law). Beograd, 1950. 45 p.; (b) Pitanje Trsta u svjetlosti novih dogadjaja (The Question of Trieste in the Light of New Events). Beograd, 1950. 46 p. (DLC)

1066 Ćirić, Slavko M. Društvo Naroda (League of Nations). Novi Sad, 1928. 43 p.

1067 Ćirković, Stevan. Jedan pravni pogled na krizu Društva Naroda (Crisis of the United Nations from a Legal Point of View). Beograd, 1934. 28 p.

1068 Digović, Petar. Temelji Medjunarodnog javnog zračnog prava (Principles of the International Public Air Law). Zagreb, 1938. 95 p.

1069 Dimitrijević, Predrag J. Radio i televizija u Medjunarodnom javnom pravu (Radio and Television in International Public Law). Beograd, 1939. 271 p.

1070 Djetvaj, D. Razvoj medjunarodnog ugovornog kapaciteta Srbije u XIX veku (Serbia as Party to International Agreements in the Course of the XIXth Century). Novi Sad, 1939. 426 p.

1071 Geršić, Gl. (a) Današnje diplomatsko i konzularno pravo. I: Uvod. Diplomatsko pravo (Contemporary Diplomatic and Consular Law. I: Introduction. Diplomatic Law). Beograd, 1898. 650 p.; (b) Današnje ratno pravo (Contemporary War Law). Beograd, 1882. 223 p.; (c) Jedno interesantno, praktički važno pitanje iz današnjeg medjunarodnog prava (An Interesting Practical Problem of Contemporary International Law). Novi Sad,

1894. 68 p.; (d) Medjunarodna nauka o azilu, i pitanje o smrtnoj kazni (International Teachings on the Right of Asylum and
the Problem of the Death Penalty). Beograd, 1881. 148 p.; (e)
Medjunarodno-pravni bilans u poslednjoj Balkanskoj Krizi sa
gledišta medjunarodnog prava (International Legal Account of
the Last Balkan Crisis from the Point of View of International
Law). Beograd, 1909; (f) Pogled na neke novije pojave na polju
ratnog prava (Survey of Some New Features of the War Law).
Beograd, 1894. 64 p.

1072 Ilić, Mihailo. Pred Konkordatom (On the Eve of the Concordat). Beograd, 1937. 38 p.

1073 Patrnogić, Jovica. Medjunarodnopravni položaj saniteta u
oružanom sukobu (International Legal Status of the Medical
Corps in an Armed Conflict). Beograd, 1961. 136 p.

1074 Janićijević, Dušan. Medjunarodna zaštita prava čoveka (International Protection of Human Rights). Beograd, 1953. 78 p.

1075 Janković, Branimir M. (a) Savremene medjunarodnopravne
teme (Contemporary International Legal Topics). Sarajevo, 1953.
150 p.; (b) Uvod u savremeno Medjunarodno javno pravo (Introduction to the Contemporary International Public Law). Sarajevo, 1953. 158 p.; (c) Pitanja medjunarodnog prava (Problems of International Law). Sarajevo, 1957. 201 p.; (d) Načelo
jednakosti prema paktu Društva Naroda (The Principle of Un-
animity under the Charter of the League of Nations). Godišnjak
pravnog fakulteta (Sarajevo), 1956: 117–138; (e) Osnivanje medjunarodnog krivičnog suda (The Creation of an International
Criminal Court). Ibid., 1957: 47–64. (DLC)

1076 Janković, Velizar. Ugovor o miru i naša ošteta (The Peace
Treaty and Our War Damages Claim). Beograd, 1920.

1077 Jeremić, Dušan M. O problemu emigracije i imirgracije i o
medjunarodnim sporazumima za njegovo uredjenje (On Emigration and Immigration and International Agreements for their
Settlement). Zagreb, 1928.

1078 Jovanović, Jovan M. Diplomatska istorija nove Evrope 1918–
1938 (Diplomatic History of Contemporary Europe 1918–1938).
Beograd, 1938. 560 p.

1079 Jovanović, Vojislav M. Rapalski ugovor od 12. novembra

1920 (The Treaty of Rapallo of November 12, 1920). Zagreb, 1950. 70 p.

1080 Jugoslovenski institut medjunarodnih studija. Dokumenti o denacionalizaciji Jugoslovanov v Julijski Krajni (Yugoslav Institute of International Studies. Documents on the Denationalization of Yugoslavs in the Julian March). Beograd, 1946. 139 p.

1081 Katičić, Natko. More i vlast obalne države (The Sea and the Sovereign Authority of Coastal States). Zagreb, 1954. 375 p.

1082 Krizman, Bogdan. Diplomati i konzuli u starom Dubrovniku (Diplomats and Consuls in the Old Dubrovnik). Zagreb, 1957. 349 p. (DLC)

1083 Milić, Milenko K. Pakt o odricanju na rat (The Treaty Renouncing War as an Instrument of National Policy). Beograd, 1929. 22 p.

1084 Milojković, Borislav A. Medjunarodni terorizam i njegovo suzbijanje (International Terrorism and its Prevention). Beograd, 1937. 16 p.

1085 Moye, Marcel. Osnovni pojmovi medjunarodnog javnog prava (Basic Principles of International Public Law). Beograd, 1925. 336 p.

1086 Novaković, Mileta St. (a) Druga Haška konferencija mira (The Second Peace Conference of the Hague). Reprint from Arhiv. Beograd, 1911. 182 p.; (b) Osnovi Medjunarodnog javnog prava (Principles of International Public Law). Beograd, 1936–1938. 2 v.; (c) Srbija i Dunavska obalska komisija (Serbia and the Danube Commission). Reprint from Arhiv. Beograd, 1913. 72 p.

1087 Novković, Bogdan. Kratak pogled na razvitak i oblike medjunarodne pravde (Review of the Development and Features of International Justice). Beograd, 1929.

1088 Obradović, Sava. Najveće povlašćenje u trgovinskim ugovorima (The Most Favored Nation Clause). Beograd, 1933. 202 p.

1089 Ostojić, Despot. Medjunarodna organizacija rada (The International Labor Organization). Beograd, 1937. 137 p.

1090 Vesel, Josip. O sjedinjenim državama Evrope (The United States of Europe). Mjesečnik (Zagreb), 1926: 346–353. (DLC)

1091 Piroćanac, Milan S. Medjunarodni položaj Srbije (Serbia's International Status). Beograd, 1893. 55 p.

1092 Polit-Desančić, Mihailo. Narodnost i njen državni osnov (Nationality and Its Political Foundation). Novi Sad, 1862.

1093 Popović, Djura. (a) Klasici medjunarodno-pravne doktrine (Classic International Law Doctrines). Beograd, 1933. 132 p.; (b) Medunarodno-pravni položaj Papstva i Lateranski ugovori od 11 februara 1929 (International Status of the Papal State and the Lateran Conventions of February 11, 1929). Beograd, 1930. 32 p.; (c) Liga Naroda (The League of Nations). Beograd, 1931. 296 p.

1094 Protić, Stojan M. Tajna konvencija izmedju Srbije i Austro-Ugarske (The Secret Convention Between Serbia and Austria-Hungary). Beograd, 1911.

1095 Pržić, Ilija. (a) Novo medjunarodno pravo (New International Law). Beograd, 1934. 290 p.; (b) Zaštita manjina (Protection of the Ethnic Minorities). Beograd, 1933. 328 p.; (c) Zaštita manjina prema odredbama ugovora o miru 1919–1920 i suverena prava država (Protection of the Ethnic Minorities under the Peace Treaty of 1919–1920 and the Sovereignty of the State). Beograd, 1922. 40 p.

1096 Radojković, Miloš M. Srbija i medjunarodni položaj Djerdapa od Pariskog Kongresa do Svetskog Rata (Serbia and the International Status of the Iron Gates from the Congress of Paris to World War I). Beograd, 1935. 68 p.

1097 Schneller, Hans. Državno-pravni položaj Bosne i Hercegovine (Political and Legal Status of Bosnia and Herzegovina). Beograd, 1893. 159 p.

1098 Spasić, Aleksa N. Narodni predstavnici (diplomati) u inostranstvu (Foreign Service Representatives Abroad). Reprint from *Srpske Novine*. Beograd, 1874. 348 p.

1099 Srpsko-Austrijski i Evropski rat. Diplomatski dokumenti (The Serbian-Austrian and European War. Diplomatic Documents). Niš, 1914.

1100 Subotić, Ivan V. Analiza sistema klauzula o državljanstvu u ugovorima o miru sa Austrijom i sa Ugarskom (The Provisions of the Peace Treaties with Austria and Hungary on Citizenship). Beograd, 1920.

1100[1] Sukijasović, Miodrag. Pravne karakteristike dvostranih trgovinskih ugovora FNRJ (The Legal Aspects of the Bilateral

Trade Agreements). Preface by Borislav T. Blagojević. Beograd, 1959. 224 p.

1101 Todorović, Milan A. Medjunarodni položaj Dunava (The International Status of the Danube). Beograd, 1910. 44 p. (DLC)

1102 Tomašić, Ljubomir, comp. Zbirka konkordata (Collection of Concordats). Beograd, 1934. 156 p.

1103 Ujedinjene Nacije. Zbirka dokumenata 1941–1945 (United Nations. Collection of Documents, 1941–1945). Beograd, 1947. 144 p.

1104 Vesnić, Milenko R. Društvo Naroda (The League of Nations). Beograd, 1920. 43 p.

1105 Vošnjak, Bogumil. Problemi splošnega državnega nauka (Problems of International Law). Gorica, 1912.

1106 Zoričić, Milovan. Teritorijalno More, s osvrtom na otvoreno i unutarnje more, vanjski pojas i pitanja kontinentalne ravnine (Territorial Waters, High Sea, Internal Sea, Outer Belt and Continental Shelf). Zagreb, 1953. 270 p.

11 International Law, Private

See also Nos.: 2069[1]; 2144; 2252; 2256a; 2256c; 2262; 2288; 2289; 2291; 2319b; 2319e; 2319m; 2319r; 2319s; 2395d; 2396.

1107 Alagić, D. Problem apatridije (Problem of Statelessness). Godišnjak pravnog fakulteta u Sarajevu, 1954: 9–32.

1108 Bartoš, M. (a) Idealistička i teritorijalistička koncepcija dva antipoda ili dva dopunjujuća pojma u medjunarodnom privatnom pravu (Idealistic and Territorialist Concepts in Conflict of Laws). Arhiv, 1932: 33–50. (DLC); (b) Iz medjunarodnog privatnog prava (Private International Law Problems. Studies and Articles). Beograd, 1931. 207 p.; (c) Sukob privatnih zakona u krivičnom pravu (Conflict of Laws in Criminal Matters). Arhiv, 1931: 68–92. (DLC)

1108[1] Besarović, Mirko. Priznanje i izvršenje inostranih arbitažnih odluka (Full Faith and Credit and Enforcement of Foreign Arbitration Awards). Preface by Aleksandar Goldštajn. Beograd, 1959. 270 p. (DLC)

1109 Blagojević, B. T. Medjunarodno privatno pravo (Private International Law). Beograd, 1950. 398 p.

1110 Cigoj, S. (a) Kolizijska pravila kupne pogodbe (Conflict of Laws on Purchase and Sale). Ljubljana, 1951. 46 p. (DLC); (b) Zakonska zveza v mednarodnem zasebnem pravu (Marriage in Private International Law). Ljubljana, 1953. 95 p.

1111 Djordjević, Andra. Sistem privatnog prava Kraljevine Srbije u vezi sa medjunarodnim privatnim pravom (Serbian Civil Law System and Private International Law). Beograd, 1910. 136 p. (DLC)

1112 Eisner, Bertold. (a) Judikatura sudova na pojedinim pravnim područjima naše države o pitanjima medjunarodnog i medjupokrajinskog privatnog prava (Court Practice on International and Interregional Conflict of Laws under the Various Yugoslav Jurisdictions). Zagreb, 1941. 68 p.; (b) Medjunarodna plaćanja u materjalnom i medjunarodnom privatnom pravu kapitalističkih država (Payments in the Domestic and International Private Law). *Zbornik Pravnog Fakulteta u Zagrebu,* 1951: 55–96; (c) Medjunarodna zaštita autorskog prava i naše zakonodavstvo o autorskom pravu (Copyright in International Law and Our Legislation). *Arhiv,* 1953: 341–356; (d) Madjunarodno privatno pravo (Private International Law). 1953. 406 p. (DLC); (e) Medjunarodno, medjupokrajinsko i medjuversko bračno pravo (Domestic Relations in International, Interregional, and Interconfessional Conflicts of Laws). Zagreb, 1935. 189 p.; (f) O općim uzansama za promet robom sa gledišta medjunarodnog privatnog prava (Usages in the Trade of Goods in Private International Law). *Jugoslovenska revija,* 1955: 210–224.

1113 Jakšić, S. O ustanovi *renvoi* u jugoslovenskom medjunarodnom privatnom pravu (The Problem of *renvoi* in Yugoslav Private International Law). *Jugoslovenska revija,* 1954: 59–69.

1114 Jezdić, Mihailo. Medjunarodno privatno pravo (Private International Law). Beograd, 1952–1960. 2 v. (DLC v. 1)

1115 Jezdić, M. *and* B. Nikolajević. Tekstovi iz medjunarodnog privatnog prava (Textbook on Conflicts of Laws). Beograd, 1951. 235 p. (DLC)

1116 Lapajne. Mednarodno in medpokrajinsko zasebno pravo (International and Interregional Conflicts of Laws). Ljubljana, 1929. 398 p. (DLC)

1117 Lissitzyn, Oliver J. Judicial Decisions. Continuity of States.

Treaty of Extradition with Serbia. Ivančevic v. Artuković. *The American Journal of International Law,* 1954: 660–662. (DLC)

1118   Nikolajević, B. Nadležnost za tužbu za razvod braka državljana FNRJ (Jurisdiction in Divorce Suits of Yugoslav Citizens). *Arhiv,* 1952: 61–71.

1119   Nol'de, Boris Emmanuilovich. Osnovi medjunarodnog privatnog prava (Elements of Conflicts of Laws). Beograd, 1928. 158 p. (DLC)

1120   Perić, Ninko. (a) Medjunarodno privatno pravo (Private International Law). Beograd, 1926. 214 p. (DLC); (b) Teritorijalni sukob zakona (Conflict of Laws and the Principle of Territoriality). Beograd, 1922. 24 p. (DLC).

1121   Perić, Ž. O sukobu zakona u medjunarodnom privatnom pravu (Conflicts of Laws). 1st ed. ?; 2d rev. ed. 1926. 119 p. (DLC)

1122   Petković, I. Egzekvatura italijanskih presuda (Execution of Italian Court Decisions). *Arhiv,* 1936: 145–157; 259–269. (DLC)

1123   Štempihar, J. (a) Kolizijska pravila zakona o dedovanju (Rules Governing Conflict of Laws in Yugoslav Inheritance Law). *Zbornik znanstvenih razprav,* 1956: 183–201; (b) Uvod v mednarodno zasebno pravo (Introduction to Private International Law). Ljubljana, 1953. 96 p. (DLC)

1124   Stojković, Slavko. Obligacioni odnosi sa elementom inostranosti (Contracts in International Law). Beograd, 1956. 93 p. (DLC)

B   Special Topics

1   Air Law

See also Nos.: 1068; 2302; 2335.

1125   Tarife za osiguranje letača i putnika u vazdahoplovstvu od posledica nesrećnog slučaja (Tariffs for Insurance Against Accidents for the Crew and Passengers of Aircraft). Beograd, 1952. 15 p. (DLC)

1126 Zakon o vazdušnoj plovidbi . . . (Air Navigation Law). Beograd, 1928. 143 p. (Zbirka zakona, sv. 103) (DLC)

1127 Drakulić, Stevan S. Kratak uvod u vazduhoplovno pravo (Introduction to Air Law). Reprint from *Vazduhoplovni Glasnik*. Novi Sad, 1936. 36 p.

1128 Miklijan, Stevan. Vazduhoplovno pravno (Air Law). Novi Sad, 1929. 231 p.

1128[1] Nikolajević, Borko. Nova zakonodavstva o vazduhoplovstvu (New Legislation on Air Law). *Arhiv*, 1959: 341–349. (DLC)

1129 Pržić, Ilija. Osnovi vazduhoplovnog prava (Principles of Aviation Law). Beograd, 1926. 99 p. (DLC)

1129[1] Smirnov, M. Nekoliko ideja o našem budućem zakonodavstvu o civilnom vazduhoplovstvu (Some Ideas Concerning Our Future Legislation on Civil Aviation). *Arhiv*, 1959: 471–478. (DLC)

1130 Voršić, Josip. O pravni naravi ozračja (Legal Nature of Air Space). Ljubljana, 1932. 32 p.

2 Aliens

See also Nos.: 2314a; 2381a; 2389a.

1131 Bartoš, Milan *and* Borko D. Nikolajević. Pravni položaj stranaca (Legal Status of Aliens). Beograd, 1951. 226 p. (DLC)

1132 Blagojević, Borislav T. (a) Pojam lica bez državljanstva (Concept of the Stateless Person). Reprint from *Arhiv*, 1937. 16 p.; (b) Pravni položaj lica bez državljanstva (Legal Status of Stateless Persons). *Arhiv*, 1937: 507–527.

1133 Pavlović, Vladislav, *comp.* Zaposlenje stranaca u Jugoslaviji. Zbornik zakonskih propisa kojima se reguliše zaposlenje stranih državljana (Employment of Aliens in Yugoslavia). Beograd, 1936. 287 p.

1134 Perić, Ilija P. Stranci u jugoslovenskoj privredi (Aliens in the Yugoslav Economy). Beograd, 1936. 125 p.

1135 Ristić, Andrija M. Pravni položaj stranaca (Legal Status of Aliens). Beograd, 1934. 133 p.

3   Armed Forces

1136   Dimitrijević, Ljubiša, *editor*. Zbirka zakona o Jugoslavenskoj narodnoj armiji . . . (Collection of Laws on the Yugoslav Army . . .). Beograd, 1955. 332 p. (Zbirka saveznih propisa, br. 131) (DLC)

1137   Zbirka propisa o jugoslovenskoj armiji (Collection of Provisions on the Yugoslav Army). 2nd ed. Beograd, 1948. 263 p. (DLC); 3d ed. 1952. 199 p. (Zbirka zakona FNRJ, br. 51, 106) (DLC)

1138   Perunović Radosav I. *and* Ljubomir Kovijanić, *editors.* Zbirka vojnih propisa (Collection of Military Provisions). Beograd, 1956. 504, 40 p. (DLC)

1139   Zakoni o vojnoj obavezi i popuni oružane sile jahaćom, teglećom i tovarnom stokom (Laws on Supplying the Armed Forces with Horses, Cattle and Beasts of Burden). Beograd, 1946. 41 p. (Zbirka zakona FNRJ, 51). (DLC)

1140   Farkaš, S. Zakon o ustrojstvu vojske i mornarice (Law on the Organization of the Army and Navy, as Amended). Ljubljana, 1940. 233 p. (DLC)

1141   Zakon o ustrojstvu vojske i mornarice od 6. septembra 1929 (Law on the Organization of the Army and Navy of September 6, 1929, as Amended). 2d ed. Beograd, 1932, 264 p. (Zbirka zakona, sv. 151). (DLC)

1142   Zakon o ustrojstvu vojske in mornarice. Vojaški kazenski zakonik Kraljevine Jugoslavije (Law on the Organization of the Army and Navy. Military Criminal Code). Ljubljana, 1930. 268 p. (DLC)

1143   Zakon o ustrojstvu vojske (Law on the Organization of the Army). Beograd, 1901. 72 p. (DLC)

1144   Propisi o dodeljivanju pomoći porodicama čiji se hranioci nalaze na otsluženju vojnog roka u Jugoslovenskoj armiji (Provisions Concerning the Giving of Aid to Families Whose Supporters Are in the Jugoslav Army). Beograd, 1947. 26 p. (DLC)

1145   Zakon o administraciji vojske i mronarice (Law on the Administration of the Army and Navy). Beograd, 1930. 92 p. (Zbirka zakona sv. 29) (DLC); 1940. 108 p. (Zbirka zakona, sv. 55). (DLC)

1146 Zakon o vojnoj administraciji (Law on Military Administration). Beograd, 1921. 18 p. (DLC)

1147 Zakon o graničnoj trupi (Law on the Frontier Guard). Beograd, 1932. 75 p. (Zbirka zakona, sv. 53). (DLC); 67 p. (Zbirka zakona, sv. 198). (DLC)

1148 Tóth, Teodor, editor. Obranbeni zakoni i provedbeni naputak (National Defense Laws and Instructions for Making Them Effective. Parts One, Two, Three and Four). Budimpešta, 1908. 292 p.; 246 p. (DLC)

1149 Obrambeni zakon (National Defense Law. First Part). Budimpešta, 1889. 519 p. (DLC)

1150 Naputak za provedbu Zakonskoga članka vi od 1889 ob obranbenoj sili (Instructions for the Execution of Law No. VI of 1889 on National Defense. Part Two). U Budimpešti, 1889. 157 p. (DLC)

1151 Naputak za provedbu Ugarskoga zak. članka XL. 1868 ob obranbenoj sili (Instruction for the Execution of Hungarian Law No. XL of 1868 on Defense Force). Zagreb, 1876. 352 p. (DLC)

1152 Pravilo o vojnoj disciplini (Regulations on Military Discipline). Beograd, 1951. 49 p. (DLC)

1153 Jakovljević, Maleš J. (a) Komentar Uredbe o vojnoj disciplini (Commentary on the Decree on Military Discipline). Beograd, 1934; (b) Rang u našoj vojsci i mornarici (Ranks in our Army and Navy). Beograd, 1932. 146 p.; (c) Komentar Uredbe o ženidbi oficira, vojnih činovnika, podoficira, kaplara, i redoav (mornara) vojske mornarice, granične trupe i žandarmerije (Commentary on the Decree on Marriages of Officers, Military Employees, Noncommissioned Officers, Soldiers and Sailors). Beograd, 1936. 200 p.

1154 Lazarević, Milutin D., editor. (a) Privremena pravila službe (Temporary Service Regulations). Beograd, 1928. 2 v. (Zbirka vojničkih pravila, sv. 4–5) (DLC); (b) Uredba o vojnoj disciplini od 9 jula 1923 (Decree on Military Discipline of July 9, 1923, as amended). Beograd, 1933. 52 p. (Zbirka vojničkih pravila, sv. 9); (c) Pravilo o regrutovanju i prevodjenju, sa izmenama i dopunama (Regulations on Conscription as Amended). Beograd, 1927. 161 p. (Zbirka vojničkih pravila, sv. 3); (d) Pravilo za naplatu vojnice. Uredba o oceni sposobnosti za vojnu službu

(Regulation Concerning Fees Chargeable in Connection with Exemptions from Military Service). Beograd, 1928. 126 p. (Zbirka vojničkih pravila, sv. 7); (e) Pravilo za službenu prepisku u vojsci (Regulations Concerning Official Correspondence in the Army). Beograd, 1927. 198 p. (Zbirka vojničkih pravila, sv. 2).

1155 Marinković, Drag, A. O zaštiti oficirske vojničke časti (Protection of Officers' Honor). Beograd, n.d. 79 p.

1156 Niketić, Gojko, *editor.* Uredba o pravima, dužnostima, i odgovornosti vojno-administrativnih lica (Decree on Rights, Duties, and Responsibilities of Administrative Military Personnel). Beograd, 1927. 35 p.

1157 Vojna sanitetska pravila (Military Sanitary Regulations). Beograd, 1932. 432 p.

1158 Jović, Milan V. Vojno disciplinsko pravo (Military Disciplinary Law). 2d ed. Beograd, 1928. 93 p. (DLC)

1159 Sbornik zakonskih izmena i dopuna, propisa, rešenja, i objašnjenja, izdanih iz sviju odelenja Vojenog ministarstva u 1875 godini (Collection of Amendments of Laws, Decrees and Directions Concerning all the Departments of the Ministry of War in 1875). Beograd, 1878. 343 p.

1160 Pravilo o popunjavanju vojne sile popisnom stokom i prenosnim sredstvima (Regulations for Supplying the Armed Forces with Cattle and Means of Transportation). Beograd, 1932. 79 p. (DLC)

1161 Zakon o nabavkama vojnih potreba (Law on Military Supplies). Beograd, 1921. 26 p. (DLC)

4   Banking, Foreign Exchange, and Currency

See also Nos.: 878; 1352; 1358c; 1451; 2118; 2257; 2276; 2327.

1162 Pravila o organizaciji i poslovanju deviznih obračunskih mesta (Regulations on the Organization and Operation of Foreign Exchange Clearing Houses). Beograd, 1952. 10 p.; 1956. 10 p. (DLC)

1163 Devizno-valutni propisi Kraljevine Jugoslavije (Foreign Exchange Regulations of the Kingdom of Yugoslavia). Beograd, 1937. 217 p. (DLC)

1164 Zakon o uredjenju Uprave Fondova (Law on the Organiza-

tion of the Government Deposit, Mortgage and Credit Bank).
Beograd, 1898. 37 p. (DLC)

1165 Zbirka zakona i naredjenja o metalnom novcu (Collection
of Coinage Regulations). Beograd, 1925. 50 p. (DLC)

1166 Adamović, Stevan. Krivičnopravna odgovornost organa i činovnika novčanih zavoda (Criminal Responsibility of the Officers and Employees of Banks). *In* Spomenica Kongresa pravnika
u Beogradu 1935: 156–163. (DLC)

1167 Fuks, Rikard. Devizni propisi Jugoslavije sa komentarom.
(Foreign Exchange Regulations, Annotated). Zagreb, 1938. 561 p.
(DLC)

1168 Glomazić, Momir. Istorija Državne Hipotekarne Banke
1862–1932 (History of the State Mortgage Bank, 1862–1932).
Beograd, 1933. 223 p.

1169 Ilić, Aleksandar P. Zbornik najnovijih uredaba o novčanim
zavodima i kreditnim zadrugama (Collection of the Most Recent
Banking Regulations). Beograd, 1934. 86 p.

1170 Janković, Rista, *joint editor.* Zbirka propisa o bankarstvu
i o poslovanju sa bankom (Collection of Banking Regulations).
Beograd, 1957. 520 p. (DLC)

1171 Ljubisavljević, Kosta M. Devizni propisi Kraljevine Jugoslavije sa komentarom (Foreign Exchange Regulations of the Kingdom of Yugoslavia Annotated). Beograd, 1935. 168 p. (DLC);
Beograd, 1936. 87 p. (DLC)

1172 Nedeljković, Milorad. Ekonomsko-pravni problem uloga na
štednju (The Economic–Legal Problem of Savings Accounts).
Beograd, 1938. 71 p.

1173 Petković, Ivan D. O obavezi banke kao izdavaoca garantnog
pisma (Extent of the Banks' Liabilities in Connection with Issuing Letters of Credit). *Arhiv*, 1935: 67–72. (DLC)

1174 Pretner, L. Dokumentarni akreditivi sa inostransvom (Letters of Credit in Foreign Trade). Beograd, 1951. 108 p.; 1960.
174 p. (DLC)

1175 Rip, L., *joint author.* Komentar izmena i dopuna u deviznom sistemu (Commentary on the Amended Foreign Exchange
Regulations). Beograd, 1955. 234 p. (DLC)

1176 Sofrenović, Miloš R. Sistematizovana zbirka devizno-valutnih
propisa Kraljevine Jugoslavije (Systematic Collection of Yugo-

slav Foreign Exchange Regulations). Beograd, 1938–1941. Loose-leaf.

1177   Sofrenović, Miloš R. *and* Miodrag Matejić. Devizno poslovanje (Foreign Exchange). Beograd, 1955. 403 p. (DLC)

1178   Vukčević, Radoje. Krivična odgovornost organa novčanih zavoda (Criminal Responsibility of Officers of Banks). *In* Spomenica Kongresa pravnika u Beogradu, 1935: 164–199. (DLC)

1178[1]   Zakoni o bankama i o kreditnim i drugim bankarskim poslovima (Laws on Banks, Credit and Other Bank Transactions). Beograd, 1961. 100 p.

5   Bankruptcy

See also Nos.: 769; 2252.

1179   Culja, S. (a) Prinudna likvidacija [stečaj] privrednih orga-|nizacija (Compulsory Liquidation [Bankruptcy] of Government Economic Enterprises). Zagreb, 1956. 66 p. (DLC); (b) Stečaj nad imovinom pravnih subjekata koji nemaju značaj privredne organizacije (Bankruptcy of Legal Entities Not Having the Status of Economic Organizations). *Zbornik Pravnog fakulteta* (Zagreb), 1955: 206–214. (DLC)

1179[1]   Eisner, Bertold. O načelima novog stečajnog zakona (Principles of the New Bankruptcy Law). *Arhiv,* 1930: 346–359. (DLC)

1180   Goršić, Franja. Komentar stečajnog zakona, zakona o prinudnom poravnanju van stečaja, zakona o uvodjenju u život oba zakona, zakona o pobijanju pravnih dela van stečaja (Commentary on the Laws on Bankruptcy, Composition, their Introductory Laws, and on the Law Providing for Invalidation of Debtors' Transactions outside Bankruptcy). Beograd, 1934. 583 p. (DLC)

1181   Gospavić, Obrad. Stečajno pravo Kraljevine Jugoslavije (Yugoslav Bankruptcy Law). Beograd, 1930. 134 p.

1182   Hinković Dr., *editor.* Stečajni red od 18 srpnja 1859 (Bankruptcy Procedure of July 18, 1859). Zagreb, 1884. 135 p. (DLC)

1183   Hiršl, Jakov. O osiguranju imovine dužnika u postupku prinudnog poravnanja van stečaja te o otvaranju stečaja (Safeguard of a Debtor's Property in the Composition Procedure and Bankruptcy). Zagreb, 19–?. 63 p. (DLC)

1184 Ilić, A. Materjalno-pravne pretpostavke za pokretanje prinudne likvidacije (Conditions Required for the Compulsory Liquidation of Economic Enterprises). *Godišnjak Pravnog Fakulteta u Sarajevu*, 1954: 41–62. (DLC)

1185 Kruszelnicki, Franciszck, *editor*. Komentar zakona od 2. marta 1887 za Bosnu i Hercegovinu o pobijanju pravnih djela glede imovine insolventna dužnika (Commentary on the Bosnian-Herzegovinian Law on the Invalidation of an Insolvent Debtor's Transactions of March 2, 1887). Sarajevo, 1912. 128 p. (DLC)

1186 Marković, B. S. Pravo pobijanja izvan stečaja (Right of Creditors to Challenge Individual Transactions of their Debtors). Beograd, 1935. 189 p.

1187 Nedeljković, B. Pobijanje u stečaju (Invalidation of Transactions of a Debtor prior to his Bankruptcy). *Pravna misao*, 1935: 258–273. (DLC)

1188 Mitrović, Velizar. Stečajno pravo s naročitim osvrtom na srpsko zakonodavstvo (Bankruptcy Law with Special Reference to Serbian Legislation). Beograd, 1926. 258 p. (DLC)

1189 Mudrovčić, Josip, *editor*. Stečajni zakon od 28 ožujka 1897 (Bankruptcy Law of March 28, 1897). Zagreb, 1897?. 264 p. (DLC)

1190 Podgradski, M. Stečajno pravo i prinudno poravnanje van stečaja (Bankruptcy and Composition). Beograd, 1930. 142 p.

1191 Politeo, Ivo. (a) Stečajni Zakon za Kraljevinu Jugoslaviju, Zakon o Prinudnom Poravnanju van Stečaja (Yugoslav Bankruptcy and Composition Laws, Annotated). Zagreb, 1929. 322 p.; (b) Zakon o pobijanju pravnih djela izvan stečaja (Law on the Invalidation of Individual Transactions of Debtors by their Creditors outside Bankruptcy). Zagreb, 1931. 83 p.; (c) Vanstečajna prinudna nagoda (Composition outside Bankruptcy). Zagreb, 1923. 96 p.

1192 Radojičić, Spasoje. Prinudno poravnanje u stečaju (Composition). Beograd, 1908. 91 p. (DLC)

1193 Rušnov, Adolf, *editor*. Zakon o pobijanju i Stečajni zakon (Law on Invalidation of Individual Transactions of Debtors by their Creditors Outside Bankruptcy and Bankruptcy Law, Annotated). Zagreb, 1897. 382 p.

1194 Spevec, Franjo Josip. Tumač zakonu od 24 ožujka 1897 o pobijanju pravnih djela glede imovine insolventna dužnika

(Commentary on the Law on Invalidation of Transactions of Insolvent Debtors). Zagreb, 1898. 127 p. (DLC)

1195 Stečajni zakon za Kraljevinu Jugoslaviju i zakon o prinudnom poravnanju van stečaja (Laws on Bankruptcy and Composition Outside Bankruptcy). Beograd, 1930. 219 p. (DLC); 1932. 188 p. (DLC)

1196 Verona, A. *and* S. Culja. (a) Stečajni zakon (Bankruptcy Law). Zagreb, 1930. 628 p.; (b) Zakon o prinudnom poravnanju . . . s komentarom (Laws on Bankruptcy and Composition . . . Annotated). Zagreb, 1930. 628 p. (DLC)

1197 Zakon o pobijanju pravnih dela izvan stečaja (Law on Invalidation of Individual Transactions of Debtors by their Creditors Outside Bankruptcy). Beograd, 1933. 51 p. (DLC)

6 Church and State; Ecclesiastic Law

See also Nos.: 2119; 2120; 2319d; 2319k; 2334; 2380; 2391; and Sheriat Law.

a General

1198 Zakon o pravnom položaju verskih zajednica (Law on the Legal Status of Religious Denominations). Beograd, 1953. 28 p. (Zbirka zakona FNRJ, br. 112). (DLC)

1199 Vlachich, Ljubo, *editor.* Projekat osnovnog zakona o verama i medjuverskim odnosima (Draft of the Basic Law on Religious Denominations and Interconfessional Relations). Sarajevo, 1934. 28 p. (DLC)

1200 Beogradac, Jovan. Crkva i država (Church and State). Novi Sad, 1861. 45 p.

1201 Djurić, K. Crkva i država (Church and State). Beograd, 1925.

1202 Kušej, Gorazd. O razmerju med državo in veroizpovedjo po jugoslovenski verski zakonodaji (State and Church under Yugoslav Ecclesiastical Laws). Reprint from *Zbornik znanstvenih razprav pravne fakultete.* Ljubljana, 1937. 34 p. (DLC)

1203 Perić, Živojin. Religija u srpskom gradjanskom zakoniku (Religion in the Serbian Civil Code). Beograd, 1919. 26 p. (DLC)

1204 Ruvarac, Dimitrije. O odnošaju uzakonjenih hrišćanskih

veroispovesti (Relations Among Christian Churches Recognized by the State). Zemun, 1890.

1205 Valenčić, Ignjat, *editor*. Zakon od 17. siječnja 1906 o vjeroispovjednim odnosima (Law of January 17, 1906 on Relations Among Religious Denominations). Zagreb, 1908. 175 p. (DLC)

1206 Nikčević, Tomica. Običaji, religija i nauka (Customs, Religion and Science). Cetinje, 1953. 71 p. (DLC)

b   Serbian Orthodox Church

See also Nos.: 1416; 1421; 1432; 1433; 1442; 2388; 2319o; 2425c; 2425d.

1207 Andjelković, Miodrag. Nezavisnost Srpske Crkve (Independence of the Serbian Orthodox Church Proclaimed in 1879). Beograd, 1880. 37 p. (DLC)

1208 Ustav Srpske Pravoslavne Crkve (Constitution of the Serbian Orthodox Church). Beograd, 1947. 120 p. (DLC)

1209 Uredba o Srpskim pravoslavnim bogoslovijama (Decree on Serbian Orthodox Theological Schools). Beograd, 1952. 27 p. (DLC)

1210 Socijalno Osiguranje Sveštenika Srpske Pravoslavne Crkve (Social Security of Priests of the Serbian Orthodox Church). Beograd, 1952. 32 p. (DLC)

1211 Pravila za izvršenje zakona o uredjenju svešteničkog stanja (Regulation for the Enforcement of the Law on the Organization of Priests' Status). Beograd, 1909. 16 p. (DLC)

1212 Uredba crkveno-prosvjetne uprave srpskih pravoslavnih eparhija u Bosni i Hercegovini (Decree on the Church and Educational Administration under the Jurisdiction of Serbian Orthodox Bishops in Bosnia and Herzegovina). Sarajevo, 1905. 160 p. (DLC)

1213 Zakon o crkvenim vlastima istočno-pravoslavne Crkve u Kraljevini Srbiji (Law on Church Authorities of the Serbian Orthodox Church in the Kingdom of Serbia). Beograd, 1890. 92 p. (DLC)

1214 Zbornik pravila, uredaba i naredaba Arhijerejskog sabora Pravoslavne srpske crkve u Kraljevini Srbiji (Collection of Regulations, Decrees, and Ordinances of the Episcopal Council of the Serbian Orthodox Church in the Kingdom of Serbia). Beograd, 1900. 411 p. (DLC)

1215　Sinodalni Ustav Pravoslavne Bukovinsko-Dalmatinske Mitropolije (Synodic Constitution of the Eastern Orthodox Metropolis for Bukovina and Dalmatia). Zadar, 1884. 8 p.

1216　Nenadovič, Pavel. Privilegii črez Imperatora Leopolda, Josifa, i Karola Šestago, takožde ninje Carstv. Veličestvo Mariji Tereziji slavnomu narodu illiriko-rassianskomu darovania i pr., preveo Pavel Nenadovič (Privileges Granted to the Illyrian-Rascian People by Emperors Leopold, Joseph, Charles VI, and Empress Maria Theresa). Vienna, 1745. 17 p.

1217　Pravila monašeskaja, poveljeniem Vikentija Ioannoviča arhiepiskopa i mitropolita Karolvačkago (Monastic Rules by Bishop Vicente of Karlovci of 1733). Vienna, pis. Ios. Kurzbeka, 1777. 113 p.

1218　Rad Srpskog narodnocrkvenog sabora (Records of the Council of the Serbian Orthodox Church). Sremski Karlovci, 1911.

1219　Zapisnik svečane sednice prilikom otvaranja srpskog narodnog sabora na dan 16. (29) maja 1910 u Sremskim Karlovcima (Record of the Opening of the Serbian National Council on May 16 (29), 1910). U Sremskim Karlovcima, 1910. (DLC)

1220　Akta Sabora naroda srbskog u Temišvaru godine 1790 držanog . . . (Documents of the Council of Serbs Held at Temišvar in 1790). Zemun, 1861. 48 p.

1221　Narodna Srbska Skupština 1-ga i 3-ga maja 1848 u Karlovci držana (Serbian National Council of May 1–3, 1848 Held at Karlovci). Beograd, 1848. 60 p.

1222　Boljarić, Gavrilo. Ugarsko-državni zakonik, Ministarske naredbe od 1867 do 1873, odnoseće se na sve zakonom pripoznate crkve i crkv. opštine, s osobitim obzirom na srpsku narodnu crkvu (Hungarian Code, Ordinances from 1867 to 1873 Relating to all Churches Recognized by Law and in Particular to the Serbian Orthodox Church). Pančevo, 1874. 75 p. (DLC)

1223　Bukvić, S. Sveštenikova administracija (Priests' Administration). Skoplje, 1919.

1224　Dimitrijević, Kosta *and* Miloš Teodorović. Uput za crkveno i manastirsko knjigovodstvo i računovodstvo (Instruction for

Bookkeeping of Churches and Monasteries). Beograd, 1927. 420 p. (DLC)

1225 Djordjević, Jovan. Radnja Blagoveštenskog sabora naroda srpskog u Sremskim Karlovcima (Council of the Serbian People at Sremski Karlovci). Novi Sad, 1861. (DLC)

1226 Dučić, Nicifor. (a) Književni radovi. Knjiga V: 1. Hrišćanski brak. 2. Primjedbe na projekat: zakona o uredjenju niže i više bogoslovije. 3. Zakona o crkvenijem vlastima. 4. Improvizacija pri pretresu Zakona o crkvenijem vlastima u Narodnoj Skupštini. 5. Uporedjenje novoga zakona o crkvenijem vlastima sa zakonom od 1862 (Literary Works. Book 5: 1. Christian Marriage. 2. Comments on the Draft of the Law on the Organization of the Lower and Higher Theological schools; 3. on the Law on Church Authorities in the Kingdom of Serbia. 4. Deliberation of this law in the National Assembly; 5. Comparison of this Law with the Law of 1862). Beograd, 1898. 370 p.; (b) Primjetbe na projekat zakona o crkvenim vlastima Istočne pravoslavne crkve u Kraljevini Srbiji (Comments on the Draft of the Law on Church Authorities of the Serbian Orthodox Church in the Kingdom of Serbia). Beograd, 1889.

1227 Durković, Jakšić, Lj. Razvitak osnovnog crkvenog zakona u Šumadiji u prvoj polovini 19. veka, 1804–1847 (Development of the Basic Church Law in Šumadija in the First Half of the Nineteenth Century, 1804–1847). Beograd, 1948. 28 p.

1228 Grujić, Radoslav. (a) Srednjevekovno srpsko parohisko sveštenstvo (Medieval Serbian Parish Clergy). Skoplje, 1923; (b) Gde je osnov našim narodno-crkvenim saborima? (Where is the Foundation of our National Church Councils?). n.p., 1908; (c) Prvi privilegijalni narodno-crkveni sabor 1708 (First National Church Council of 1708). n.p., 1908.

1229 Janić, Vojislav and Milenko M. Janošević, editors. Zakon o Srpskoj pravoslavnoj crkvi; Ustav Srpske pravoslane crkve (Law on the Serbian Orthodox Church; Constitution of the Serbian Orthodox Church). Beograd, 1932. 295 p. (DLC)

1230 Jeremić, Jovan. (a) Priložak rešavanju našeg crkvenog pitanja (Contribution to the Solution of our Church Problem). Sr. Karlovci, 1914. 103 p. (DLC); (b) Predlog zakona o Srpskoj pravoslavnoj crkvi i njegova vrednost (Draft of the Law on the

Serbian Orthodox Church and its Value). Sremski Karlovci, 1925. 28 p.; (c) Gde je Karlovačka Mitropolija? (Where is the Metropolitan Diocese of Karlovci?). Sr. Karlovci, 1923; (d) Još nešto o Saborskom izbornom redu od 1870 (Additional Comments on the Rules of Electoral Procedure of 1870 for the Church Council). Srem. Karlovci, 1901.

1231 Joannovič, Eftimij. Načatki cerkovnoga prava drevnija pravoslavnija vostočnija cerkve (Beginning of the Ancient Church Law of the Eastern Orthodox Church). Novi Sad, 1844. 2 v.

1232 Jovanović, Evgenije. (a) Crkovno pravo istočne crkve u Austrijskoj državi (Church Law of the Eastern Orthodox Church in Austria). Karlstat, 1842. 189 p.; (b) O sudjeh cerkovnih (Ecclesiastical Courts). V Karlštadtskago, 1844. 95 p. (DLC)

1233 Jokanović, Jovan. Dokazi o antikanoničnosti jedne osude prvostepenog crkvenog suda Srpske pravoslavne zvorničko-Tuzlanske eparhije (Uncanonical Nature of a Judgment Rendered by the Ecclesiastical Court of Zvornik-Tuzla). Sarajevo, 1925. 70 p. (DLC)

1234 Kazimirović, Radovan. Crkveno-pravne rasprave (Ecclesiastical and Legal Essays). Beograd, 1922.

1235 Klicin, Mita. Uredba o uredjenju crkvenih, školskih i fundacionih dela grčko-istočne srpske mitropolije od 10 avgusta 1868 (Decree on the Organization of the Ecclesiastical, Educational and Charitable Affairs of the Eastern Orthodox Metropolis of August 10, 1868 as Amended). Sremski Karlovci, 1909. 222 p.

1236 Lanović, Mihailo. Crkvena uprava u Srbiji (Church Administration in Serbia). *Mjesečnik*, 1917: 245–251, 300–309, 380–384, 449–453, 553–569, 625–639. (DLC)

1237 Ljubibratić, Savo. Nacrt ustava i samo-upravno uredjenje Srpske pravoslavne crkve (Draft of the Constitution and Self-Government of the Serbian Orthodox Church). Sarajevo, 1925. 102 p.

1238 Marković, Čed. Političko-pravno pitanje religije (Political and Legal Problem of Religion). Beograd, 1924. 16 p.

1239 Miladinović, Žarko. (a) Tumač povlastica, zakona, uredaba i drugih naredjenja srpske narodne crkvene avtonomije u Ugarskoj, Hrvatskoj i Slavoniji (Commentary on Privileges, Laws, Decrees, etc., of the Serbian Orthodox Church Autonomy in Hun-

gary, Croatia and Slavonia). Novi Sad, 1897. 486 p. (DLC); (b)
Jus inspectionis . . . Vrhovni državni nadzor ili Država i samouprava (The State and the Self-Government of the Archbishopric
at Sremski Karlovci). Sremski Karlovci, 1909. 98 p. (DLC)
1240 Milaš, Nikodim. (a) Zbornik pravila koja su primljena pravoslavnom crkvom (Collection of Canons Accepted by the Eastern Orthodox Church). Zadar, 1884. 380 p.; 2d rev. ed. Novi
Sad, 1886. 381 p. (DLC) Covers the material traditionally included in Nomokanon or Krmčija (*Kormchaia*); (b) Pravila
(Kanones) Pravoslavne Crkve, s tumačenjima (Canons of the
Eastern Orthodox Church and Commentary). Novi Sad, 1875–
1896. 2 v. (DLC); Russian translation: St. Petersburg 1911–1912;
(c) Pravila pravoslavne crkve (Canons of the Eastern Orthodox
Church), 1st ed. Zadar, 1873: I, 44 p., II, 88 p., III, 168 p; 2d.
ed. Panchevo, 1878; 3d ed. 1880; (d) Pravoslavno crkveno pravo
(Eastern Orthodox Ecclesiastical Law). Zadar, 1890. 655 p. (DLC).
Russian translation, St. Petersburg, 1897. German translation
under the title Das Kirchenrecht der Morgenländischen Kirche.
Übersetzt von A. R. von Pessić. Zara, 1897. 621 p. (DLC); 2d ed.
Mostar, 1905. 742 p. (DLC); 2nd ed. in Serbian, Mostar, 1902.
784 p.; 3d ed. in Serbian, Beograd, 1926. 904 p. (DLC); Bulgarian
translation, Sofia, 1904.; (e) Crkeno Kazneno Pravo (Church
Criminal Law). Mostar, 1911. 636 p. (DLC); (f) Slavenski apos-
toli Kiril i Metodije i istina pravoslavlja (Cyril and Methodius
and the Truth about the Eastern Orthodox Church). Zadar, 1881.
387 p.; (g) Dostojanstva u pravoslavnoj crkvi (Authorities in
the Serbian Orthodox Church). Zadar, 1879. 167 p.; (h) Ustav
Pravoslavne Konzistorije u Knjaževini Crnoj Gori (Constitution
of the Serbian Orthodox Consistory in the Principality of Montenegro). Cetinje, 1904; (i) Istorijsko-kanonički pogled na Ustanovljenje Srpsko-Rumunske Mitropolije (Historical and Canonical Study on the Creation of the Serbo-Romanian Metropolis).
Zadar, 1873.

All works of Nikodim Milaš (58 items) published up to 1926 are
listed in No. 1240d (1926, pp. 903–904).

1241 Mitrović, Čedomilj. (a) O zakonodavnim granicama izmedju
Crkve i Države (Legislative Boundary between Church and State).
Beograd, 1900. 34 p. (DLC); 2d ed. Beograd, 1928. 32 p. (DLC);

(b) Crkveno pravo (Ecclesiastical Law). Beograd, 1918? 220 p.
Mimeographed. (DLC); 1929, 243 p.; (c) Bračno pravo (Marriage Law). Beograd, n.d. 102 p. Mimeographed. (DLC); 2d
ed. 1921, 228 p.; (d) Iz crkvenog i bračnog prava (Ecclesiastical
and Marriage Law). Beograd, 1909. 228 p. (DLC); (e) Vladičanstvo i monaški čin (Bishopric and Monastic Orders). Sarajevo,
1908. 19 p.; (f) Kaludjerstvo i njegovo socijalno značenje (Monasticism and its Social Meaning). Beograd, 1901. 16 p. (DLC);
(g) O pravu proglašavanja svetaca u staro doba (Right to Proclaim Saints in Ancient Times). Sarajevo, 1908. 28 p.

1242 Niketić, Gojko, editor. Crkveno zakonodavstvo Srpske pravoslavne crkve (Legislation Concerning the Serbian Orthodox
Church). Beograd, v. 1, 1926. 171 p. (Zbirka zakona, sv. 77)
(DLC); Beograd, 1931. 162 p. (Zbirka zakona, sv. 115) (DLC);
Beograd, 1933. 278 p. (Zbirka zakona, sv. 218). (DLC)

1243 Nikolajević, Djordje. Protoprezviter i njegovo dostojanstvo
po kanonima svetim i po istoriji crkvenoj (Archpriest and His
Authority under the Canons of the Church and According to
Church History). n.p., n.d.

1244 Pahorukov, Nikolaj, editor. Zakon o Srpskoj Pravoslavnoj
Crkvi. Ustav Srpske Pravoslavne Crkve (Law of the Serbian
Orthodox Church and Constitution of the Serbian Orthodox
Church). Beograd, 1932. 120 p.

1245 Palmov, I. S. Noveishee ustroistvo pravoslavnoi Chernogorskoi Tserkvi po Ustavu Sv. Sinoda ot 30 dekabria 1903 goda
i Ustavu pravoslavnykh konsistorii ot 1 ianvaria 1904 goda (The
Organization of the Montenegrin Orthodox Church under the
Constitution of the Holy Synod of December 30, 1903 and the
Constitution of the Consistories of January 1, 1904). Reprint
from Khristianskoe Chtenie (St. Petersburg), 1905: 679–698, 811–
832, 3–19.

1246 Pavlović, St. Srpski Narodni Sabor u Sremskim Karlovcima
godine 1869 (Serbian National Council at Sremski Karlovci in
1869). Novi Sad, 1870.

1247 Petković, Tod. and Čedomilj Mitrović. Zbornik pravila, uredaba, i naredaba Arhijerejskog Sabora pravoslavne Srpske crkve
u Kraljevini Srbiji (Collection of Rules, Decrees, and Ordinances

of the Episcopal Council of the Serbian Orthodox Church in the Kingdom of Serbia). Beograd, 1900. 410 p.

1248 Petranović, Gerasim. Pravoslavni crkveno-narodni Sinod, držan u Zadru 1808 (National Synod of the Serbian Orthodox Church Held at Zadar 1808). Reprint from *Magazin,* 1870. Zadar, 1871. 95 p.

1249 Popović, Atanasije. Crkva u oblasti prava (Church and Law). Sremski Karlovci, 1920. 40 p.

1250 Popović, Mihailo I. Istorijska uloga Srpske Crkve u čuvanju narodnosti i stvaranju države (Historical Role of the Serbian Church in Preserving Nationality and the Creation of the State). Beograd, 1933. 329 p. (DLC)

1251 Pržić, Ilija, *editor.* Zakonodavstvo Srpske pravoslavne crkve (Legislation of the Serbian Orthodox Church). Beograd, 1939. 440 p. (DLC)

1252 Radojčić, Nikola. Sveti Sava i avtokefalnost srpske i bugarske crkve (St. Sava and Autocephaly of the Serbian Orthodox and Bulgarian Churches). *Glas Srpske Kraljevske Akademije,* Book 91. Beograd, 1939.

1253 Rajković, Dj. Srpski Narodno-Crkveni Sabor 1769 (Council of the Serbian Orthodox Church of 1769). n.p., 1872.

1254 Ruvarac, Dimitrije. (a) Postanak i razvitak crkveno-narodne avtonimije (Origin and Development of Selfgovernment of the Serbian Orthodox Church). U Karlovcima, 1899. 286 p. (DLC); (b) O srpskoj narodno-crkvenoj autonomiji, 1690–1903 (Autonomy of the Serbian Orthodox Church, 1690–1903). Sremski Karlovci, 1926. 28 p.; (c) Jesmo li imali narodno-crkvenu autonomiju (Did We Have National Church Autonomy?). Sr. Karlovci, 1926; (d) Srpski narodni sabor održan 1774 u Karlovcima (Council of the Serbian Orthodox Church Held in 1774 at Karlovci). Reprint from *Spomenik Srpske kraljevske akademije,* 1929.

1255 Ružičić, Nikanor. (a) Nomokanon Srpske crkve (Collection of Church Canons of the Serbian Orthodox Church). Beograd, 1882. 2 v.; (b) Kratki istorijski pregled uzajamnih odnosa izmedju srpske i grčko-carigradske crkve (Historical Survey of Mutual Relations between the Serbian Orthodox and the Greek Orthodox Church of Constantinople). Beograd, 1875. 158 p.

1256 Sava, episkop Žički. Važi li za crkvu raščinjenje svcštenih lica kad je ono posledica presuda gradjanskih sudova (Whether the Church is Bound by a Judgment of a Civil Court Unfrocking Priests). Beograd, 1908. 56 p.

1257 Solovjev, Aleksandar. Srpska crkvena pravila iz XIV veka (Serbian Church Canons of the Fourteenth Century). Reprint from *Glasnik Skopskog Naučnog Društva,* 1935.

1258 Stojadinović, Milan M. Srpsko zakonodavstvo o izdržavanju sveštenstva (Serbian Legislation on Support of the Clergy). Beograd, 1909. 103 p.

1259 Stojanović, Stevan. Pomoćna knjiga za praktičnu upotrebu postupka za sudove u Srpskoj pravoslavnoj crkvi u sporovima o razvodu braka (Manual for Practical Use of Procedure in Courts of the Serbian Orthodox Church Adopted in Divorce Cases). Tuzla, 1935. 200 p.

1260 Troicki, Sergije. (a) Problem crkvenog zakonadavstva (Problem of Church Legislation). Niš, 1925; (b) Predosnova gradjanskog zakonika i naše versko zakonodavstvo (Draft of the Civil Code and our Religious Legislation). Reprint from *Spomenica Dolencu, Kreku, Kušeju, i Skerlju,* Ljubljana, 1937. 74 p.; (c) Novo zakonodavstvo o Srpskoj crkvi i njegovi komentatori (New Legislation on the Serbian Orthodox Church and its Commentators). Beograd, 1932; (d) Crkvena jurisdikcija nad pravoslavnom diasporom (Church Jurisdiction over Eastern Orthodox Churches which are under no Particular Geographical Jurisdiction). Sremski Karlovci, 1932. 127 p. (DLC)

1261 Vlačić, Ljubomir. Zbirka zakona, naredaba, i riješenja crkvene, gradjanske, i školske vlasti koja se tiče crkve, crkvene administracije, i škole u dalmatinsko-istrijskoj eparhiji (Collection of Laws, Ordinances, and Decisions of the Church, Civil, and Educational Authorities Pertaining to the Diocese of Dalmatia and Istria). Zadar, 1906. 543 p.

1262 Vučetić, Ilija. Zbrika uredaba u stvarima Srpske pravoslavne narodno-crkvene autonomije (Collection of Decrees on National Self-Government of the Serbian Orthodox Church). Novi Sad, 1897. 199 p.

1263 Vučković, Jovan. Nepravoslavnost srodnika kao smetnja rukopoloženju (Not Belonging to the Serbian Orthodox Church of Relatives as an Impediment to Ordination). Sremski Karlovci, 1912.

1264 Živković, Teofan. Srbska narodna crkva na kanonično-istoričnom temelju svom (Serbian National Church and its Canonical and Historical Foundation). Temišvar, 1868.

c Roman Catholic Church

See also Nos.: 220; 449a; 1413; 1428; 1438; 1444; 2319c; 2396.

1265 Belaj, F. Katoličko Crkveno Pravo (Catholic Ecclesiastical Law). Zagreb, 1901. 633 p.

1266 Crnica, Ante. (a) Kanonsko Pravo Katoličke Crkve (Canon Law of the Catholic Church). Split, 1937., 797 p.; (b) Priručnik kanonskog prava katoličke crkve (Manual on Canon Law of the Catholic Church). Zagreb, 1945. 441 p.

1267 Dalla Costa, Angelo. Zakon Czarkovni (Code of the Church for Croatian Priests). U Mneczi, 1778. 2 v. (DLC)

1268 Gross, K. Udžbenik Crkvenog Prava Katoličke crkve (Textbook on Canon Law of the Catholic Church). Zagreb, 1930. 456 p.

1269 Konkordat pred Narodnom skupštinom (Concordat before the National Assembly). Beograd, 1937. 145 p. (DLC)

1270 Kušej, Rado. (a) Konkordat, ustava in verska ravnopravnost (Concordat, Constitutional and Religious Equality). Ljubljana, 1937. 73 p.; (b) Cerkveno pravo Katoliške Cerkve (Ecclesiastical Law of the Catholic Church). 1st ed. Ljubljana, 1923. 488 p.; 2d ed. 1927. 695 p. (DLC); (c) Katoliška cerkev in njeno pravo v povojni dobi (Catholic Church and its Rights after the War). Reprint from *Zbornik znanstvenih razprav*, 1930. 28 p.; (d) Posledice državnega preobrata na polju patronatnega prava (Consequences of the Changed Government Position in Patronage Rights). Ljubljana, 1923.

1271 Lanović, Mihajlo. Konkordat Jugoslavije s Vatikanom (Concordat between Yugoslavia and the Vatican). Beograd, 1925. 107 p. (DLC)

1272 Matina, Mato. Obranbeni zakon za svećenike (Conscription of the Clergy). Zagreb, 1892. 65 p. (Hrvatski zakoni, XVII).

1273 Nestorović, Dj. B. Konkordat izmedju Srbije i Vatikana (Concordat between Serbia and the Vatican). Beograd, 1902.

1274 Odar, Alojzij, *editor*. Zakonik Crkenoga prava (Codex Juris Canonici). Ljubljana, 1944. 1054 p. (DLC)

1275 Ritig, Svetozar. Povijest i pravo slovenštine u crkvenom bogoslužjenju, sa osobitim obzirom na Hrvasku (History and the Right to Use Old Slavonic in Religious Services, Especially with Regard to Croatia). Zagreb, 1910. 224 p. (DLC)

1276 Šarić, Ivan. Spomen knjiga iz Bosne (Commemorative Book of Bosnia in Honor of Bishop Josip Strossmayer. Bishopric of Bosnia. Catholic Church in Bosnia. Cathedral of Djakovo). Zagreb, 1901. 227 p. (DLC)

1277 Turk, Josip. Prvotna Charta Caritatis (Original *Charta Caritatis*). Ljubljana, 1942. 56 p. (DLC)

1278 Vatikan i Jugoslavija, 1 deo (Vatican and Yugoslavia, Part I). Beograd, 1953. 180 p. (DLC)

1279 Vojnović, Lujo. Konkordat sa sv. Stolicom i naše nacijonalno pitanje (Concordat with the Holy See and our National Problem). Zagreb, 1923. 60 p. (DLC).

1280 Zakon o konkordatu izmedju Srbije i Svete Stolice u Rimu. (Law on the Concordat between Serbia and the Holy See). Beograd, 1921. 15 p. (DLC)

7 Civil Service

1281 Zakon o državnim službenicima (Law on Government Employees). 2d ed. Beograd, 1948. 96 p. (DLC); 3d ed. 1949. 106 p. (Zbirka zakona FNRJ, Nos. 57, 47). (DLC); 1958, 200 p. (Zbirka saveznih propisa, Br. 152). (DLC)

1282 Zakon o javnih uslužbencih z navodilom za izvajanje določb IV. dela zakona (Law on Public Servants and Instructions for Putting into Force the Provisions of the Fourth Part of the Same Law). Ljubljana, 1958. 198 p. (DLC)

1283 Baltić, Aleksandar, *editor*. (a) Komentar zakona o državnim službenicima (Commentary on the Law on Government Employees). Beograd, 1949. 325 p. (DLC); 1950. 309 p. (DLC); (b) Opšta teorija o pojmu javnog službenika (Concept of the Public Servant). Beograd, 1939. 266 p. (DLC)

1284 Baltić, A. *and* J. Jovanović. Zakon o državnim službenicima (Law on Government Employees, Annotated). Beograd, 1955. 68 p. (DLC)

1285 Baltić, Aleksandar, Jovan Jovanović *and* Vlada Nikolić, *comp.* Zbirka propisa o platama službenika (Collection of Provisions on Salaries of Clerical Employees). Beograd, 1952. 353 p. (DLC)

1286 Zakon o ustanovljenju prava na penziju i o penzionisanju državnih službenika (Law Establishing the Right of Retirement of Government Employees). Beograd, 1947. 91 p. (Zbirka zakona FNRJ, br. 13). (DLC)

1287 Propisi o dodacima na decu (Provisions on Children's Allowances). Beograd, 1952. 75 p. (DLC)

1288 Zakon o činovnicima i ostalim državnim službenicima gradjanskoga reda (Law on Government Civil Employees). 5th ed. Beograd, 1928. 280 p. (DLC); 1931. 332 p. (DLC); 285 p. (DLC) (Zbirka zakona, sv. 51, 11, 179), 1931. 191 p. (DLC); 1938. 248 p. (DLC); 1940. 350 p. (DLC) (Zbirka zakona, sv. 53). (DLC)

1289 Zakon o činovnocima gradjanskog reda (Law on Government Civil Employees). Beograd, 1861. 26 p. (DLC)

1290 Pevačević, Živko, *comp.* Zbirka propisa o putnim i selidbenim troškovima državnih službenika i radnika i službenika privrednih organizacija (Collection of Provisions on Travel and Transfer Expenses of Government Employees and Employees of Economic Enterprises). Beograd, 1955. 117 p. (DLC)

1291 Uredba o putnim i selidbenim troškovima (Decree on Travel and Transfer Expenses). Beograd, 1953. 39 p. (DLC); 1954. 21 p. (DLC)

1292 Zbirka propisa o putnim i selidbenim troškovima (Collection of Provisions on Travel and Transfer Expenses of Government Employees, Annotated). Beograd, 1949. 104 p. (DLC). Dodatak zbirci propisa (Appendix to the Collection of Provisions). 1951. 26 p. (DLC)

1293 Predpisi o nazivih in plačah uslužbencev državnih organov (Provisions on Classification and Salaries of Government Employees). Ljubljana, 1952. 430 p. (DLC)

1294 Zbirka propisa o platama službenika državnih organa i ustanova (Collection of Provisions on Salaries of Employees of Government Agencies and Institutions). Beograd, 1954. 112 p. (DLC); 1955. 153 p. (DLC)

1295   Zbirka propisa o strukama i platama državnih službenika (Collection of Provisions on the Classification and Salaries of Government Employees). Beograd, 1947. 511 p. (Zbirka zakona FNRJ, br. 64).

1296   Jovanović, Jovan, *comp.* (a) Zbirka propisa o platama službenika državnih organa i ustanova (Collection of Provisions on Salaries and Wages of Government Employees). Beograd. 1957. 247 p. (DLC); (b) Zbirka propisa o službenicima. Plate i zvanja, stručni ispiti, rang škola i tećajeva, putni i selidbeni troškovi (Collection of Provisions on Employees). Beograd, 1954. 447 p. (DLC); (c) Zbirka propisa o javnim službenicima. Drugi deo (A Collection of Provisions on Public Servants. Second Part). Beograd, 1959. 294 p.; (d) Zbirka propisa o javnim službenicima (A Collection of Provisions on Public Servants). Beograd, 1960. 870 p. (DLC)

1297   Arandjelović, Drag. O odgovornosti države i činovnika prema trećim licima (Liability of the State and Employees for Damage to Third Persons). Beograd, 1906.

1298   Bogosavljević, Adam M. Prestanak službe državnih službenika (Termination of Government Service). Beograd, 1937. 218 p. (DLC)

1299   Cavalieri, Vinko Celso. Disciplinski propisi po Zakonu od 31 jula 1923 o činovnicima (Disciplinary Provisions According to the Law on Government Civil Employees of July 31, 1923). Zagreb, 1924. 272 p. (DLC)

1300   Državna služba i državne sluge (Civil Service and Government Employees). U Beču, Pečatnia Srmenskoga Manastira, 1859. 89 p. (DLC)

1301   Esih, Vinko, *editor.* Zakon o pensionom osiguranju službenika (Law on Pensions for Employees). Zagreb, 1938. 85 p. (DLC)

1302   Ilić, Mihailo, *editor.* Uredba o razvrstavanju i rasporedjivanju činovnika i ostalih državnih službenika gradjanskoga reda (Decree Concerning Classification of Government Civil Employees). Beograd, 1927. 494 p. (Zbirka zakona, sv. 6). (DLC)

1303   Kostić, Laza M. Iz činovičkog prava (Civil Service Law). Beograd, 1928. 142 p. (DLC)

1304 Krbek, Ivo. Lica u državnoj službi (Individuals in Government Service). Zagreb, 1948. 178 p. (DLC)

1305 Lazić, Bogosav. Činovnički pensioni fond i porodično penziono pravo državnih službenika (Government Employees Pension Fund). Beograd, 1938. 752 p. (DLC)

1306 Niketić, Gojko, editor. (a) Zakon o činovnicima (Law on Government Employees). Beograd, 1935. 750 p. (DLC); (b) Zakonodavstvo o činovnicima (Legislation on Employees, Second Book). Beograd, 1932. 312 p. (DLC); (c) Zakoni, uredbe i pravilnici o izmenama i dopunama u zakonu o činovnicima (Amendments and Supplements to Laws, Decrees and Regulations on Government Employees). Beograd, 1930. 169 p. (Zbirka zakona, sv. 164). (DLC); (d) Pravilnici o polaganju državnih stručnih ispita (Regulations Concerning Civil Service Professional Examinations). Beograd, 1926. 2 v. (Zbirka zakona, sv. 74). (DLC)

1307 Paunović, Živojin M. Zakon o činovnicima od 31 jula 1923 (Law on Government Civil Employees of July 31, 1923). Beograd, 1924.

1308 Pravilnici o polaganju državnih stručnih ispita (Regulations on Civil Service Examinations). Beograd, 1926. 2 v. (Zbirka zakona, sv. 72. 74). (DLC)

1309 Protić, St. M., editor. Uredba o naknadi troškova državnim službenicima učinjenih prilikom službenog putovanja i seobe (Decree on Travel and Transfer Expenses of Government Employees). Beograd, 1928. 157 p. (DLC)

1310 Dilber, Nikola, editor. Zakon o penzijskom osiguranju (Law on Pensions). 3rd ed. Beograd, 1961. 334 p.

1311 Vizjak, Albert. Penziono osiguranje službenika (Employee Pensions). 2d ed., Beograd, 1938. 349 p. (DLC)

1312 Vragović, Aleksandar, editor. Zakon o činovnicima od 31. Marta 1931 god. (Law on Government Employees of March 31, 1931). Zagreb, 1931. 152 p. (DLC)

1313 Zakon o suzbijanju zloupotreba u službenoj dužnosti od 30 marta 1929 (Law Suppressing Abuse in the Performance of Official Duties of March 30, 1929). Beograd, 1929. 16 p. (Zbirka zakona, sv. 134). (DLC)

8   Contracts and Torts

See also Nos.: 434s; 771; 778; 1124; 2309.

1314   Arandjelović, D. (a) O pravu opcije u privatnom pravu (The Right of Option in Private Law). *Branič*, 1927: 1–3; (b) O odgovornosti za naknadu štete (Liability for Damages). Beograd, 1st ed?; 2d ed. 1923. 71 p. (DLC); (c) Odgovornost gostioničara prema putnicima zbog pretrpljene štete u gostionici na unesenim stvarima (Responsibility of Innkeepers for Property Damage Incurred by their Customers on the Inn's Premises). Beograd, 1906. 30 p.; (d) Oštećenje preko polovine kod teretnih ugovora (Damages for Disproportionate Consideration in Non-gratuitous Contracts). *Branič*, 1905: 401–420; (e) Osnovi obligacionog prava sa naročitim obzirom na Gradjanski Zakonik Kr. Srbije. Opšti deo (Principles of Contracts and Torts with Special Reference to the Serbian Civil Code. General Part). Beograd, 1st ed. 1929. 199 p.; 2d ed. 1936. 205 p. (DLC)

1315   Avakumović, G. Promena valute i pravatno-pravni poslovi. (Currency Reform and Private Transactions). Beograd, 1923. 44 p.

1316   Bajič, S. Navezna pogodba (Standard Contracts). *Zbornik znanstvenih razprav*, 1942: 43–73. (DLC)

1317   Bajalović, Ljubomir. Kupoprodajni ugovor (Purchase and Sale Contract). Beograd, 1956. 54 p. (DLC)

1318   Blagojević, B. T. (a) Gradjanska odgovornost liječnika (Civil Responsibility of Physicians). *Mjesečnik*, 1940: 35–51; (b) Gradjanskopravni obligacioni ugovori (Civil Law Contracts). 1st ed. Beograd, 1947. 216 p. (DLC); 2d ed. 1952. 187 p. (DLC); (c) Ugovori po pristanku; formularni ugovori (Standard Contracts). Beograd, 1934. 172 p. (DLC)

1319   Blagojević, V. O naknadi štete pričinjene motornim vozilima (Compensation for Damage Caused by Motor Vehicles). Beograd, 1932. 41 p.

1320   Cigoj, Stojan. Odškodninsko pravo (Right to Indemnification). Ljubljana, 1960. 310 p. (DLC)

1321   Djordjević, Živomir S. Problem ekvivalentnosti u obligacionom pravu (Adequacy of Performance and Counterperformance). Beograd, 1958. 112 p. (DLC)

1322   Eisner, B. Pad valute kao problem privatnog prava (Currency Depreciation as a Problem of Private Law). Sarajevo, 1923. 42 p.

1323   Finžgar, A. Darila med zakonci (Donations between Spouses). *Zbornik znanstvenih razprav*, 1956: 5–22.

1324   Gams, A. Odgovornost za radnje trećih lica u privatnom pravu (Civil Responsibility for Acts of Third Parties). Beograd, 1940. 186 p.

1325   Jakšić, S. Obligaciono pravo. Opšti deo (Contracts and Torts. General Part), 1st ed.?; 2nd rev. ed. Sarajevo, 1957. 482 p. (DLC); 3rd ed. 1960. 2 v. (General and Special Parts).

1326   Kalodjera, M. Naknada neimovinske štete (Compensation for Mental Suffering). Zagreb, 1941. 399 p.

1327   Kapor, Vladimir. (a) Ugovor o kupovini i prodaji robe. (Purchase and Sale of Goods). Beograd, 1956. 158 p. (DLC); 2nd rev ed. 1957. 170 p. (DLC); (b) Uticaj promenjenih okolnosti na ispunjenje privrednog ugovora (Economic Contracts under Changed Conditions). *Arhiv*, 1952: 401–419. (DLC)

1328   Konstantinović, M. (a) Obligaciono pravo. Opšti deo (Contracts and Torts. General Part). Beograd, 1952. 215 p. (DLC); (b) Osnov odgovornosti za prouzrokovanu štetu (Legal Foundation of the Concept of Damages). *Arhiv*, 1952: 296–305. (DLC)

1329   Krbek, I. Odgovornost države za štetu (Civil Liability of the State). Zagreb, 1954. 155 p.

1330   Lapajne, S. (a) Obrestovano posojilo in denarno posojilo de lege lata et ferenda (Lending of Money at Interest under the Law in Force and in Theory). Ljubljana, *Zbornik znanstvenih razprav* 1940: 30–47 (DLC); (b) Pogodbena nezvestoba (Violation of Contractual Obligations). *Slovenski pravnik* 1931: 164–184, 237–256; (c) Regresni zahtevi našega državljanskega prava (Recourse Action of the Payer under Yugoslav Law). *Zbornik znanstvenih razprav*, 1934: 98–129. (DLC); (d) Reparacije civilnega prava (Compensation for Damages in Civil Law). Ljubljana, 1927. 85 p.; (e) Spori v pogledu vzročne zveze (Question of Causation). *Zbornik znanstvenih razprav*, 1934: 133–166.

1331   Lazarević, A. Osnovi obligacionog prava Opšti deo (Elements of Contracts and Torts). Skopje, 1956–1960. 2 v.

1332 Loza, B. Pitanje oblika i visine naknade štete prouzrokovane deliktom (Torts). *Godišnjak Pravnog Fakulteta u Sarajevu,* 1956: 185–199. (DLC)

1333 Lukić, Ž. O konvencionalnoj kazni (Contractual Penalty). *Arhiv,* 1922: 21–30, 100–106, 183–202. (DLC)

1334 Marković, Č. Reparacija moralne štete (Compensation for Mental Suffering). *Arhiv,* 1922: 81–92, 198–205, 257–279. (DLC)

1335 Matijević, I. O zakonskom založnom pravu porabodavca (The Tenant's Property as Security for Landlord's Lien). Beograd, 1938. 80 p.

1336 Maurović, Ivan. (a) Nacrt Predavanja o Općem privatnom pravu. Pravo Obligacija. Opći dio obligacija (Outline for a Lecture on Civil Law. Contracts and Torts. General Part). Zagreb, 1938. 96 p. (DLC); (b) Posebni dio obligacija (Special Part of Contracts and Torts). Zagreb, 1937. 65 p. (DLC); (c) O principu culpae i causae u odštetnom pravu općega gradj. zakona (Negligence and Causation in Actions for Damages under the General Civil Code). *Mjesečnik,* 1902, Nos. 9–12; 1903, Nos. 1–3. (DLC)

1337 Rucner, Josip. Naknada štete prouzročene pogonom motornih vozila. Kauzalna odgovornost za štetu. Pozitivni propisi cestovnog saobraćajnog prava (Liability for Damage Caused by Operating Motor Vehicles. Causation. Substantive Traffic Provisions). Zagreb, 1959. 235 p. (DLC)

1338 Mudrovčić, J. Rastu li novčane tražbine, kad valuta pada? (Revaluation of Claims in Connection with Currency Depreciation). Zagreb, 1925. 88 p. (DLC)

1339 Nedeljković, B. (a) Prodajni nalog po srpskom gradjanskom zakoniku (Order to Sell under the Serbian Civil Code). *Arhiv,* 1931: 214–225.; (b) Ugovor u korist trećeg (Contract for the Benefit of a Third Party). *Arhiv,* 1937: 233–246. (DLC)

1340 Nikolajević, Borko. Uvodni pojmovi obligacionog prava (Basic Introduction to Contracts and Torts). Beograd, 1956.

1341 Novaković, Radivoje K. Šteta i njena naknada (Damages). Beograd, 1940. 651 p. (DLC)

1342 Obšte uzanse za promet robom (Usages Governing Trade in Commodities). Beograd, 1954. 55 p. (DLC)

1343 Pantelić, D. Sef-obveze i odgovornost banke (Responsibility of Banks for Safe Deposits). *Arhiv,* 1938: 69–89, 216–225. (DLC)

1344 Pavlović, Djordje. (a) O obveznostima i ugovorima uopšte §§ 531–560 Gradjanskog zakonika (Obligations and Contracts under Sections 531–560 of the Serbian Civil Code). Beograd, 1869. 431 p. (DLC); ed. 1892, under slightly varied title, 487 p.; (b) Objašnjenje gradjanskog zakonika. O jemstvu §§ 827–846 (Commentary on Sureties. Sections 827–846 of the Serbian Civil Code). 1st ed. Beograd, 1871. 160 p. (DLC); 2nd ed. 1879. 176 p. (DLC)

1345 Perić, Boško. O odnosu izmedju kontraktualne i deliktne odgovornosti (Contractual and Tort Liabilities). *Arhiv*, 1953: 108–119. (DLC); (b) O pravnom Značaju označenih prelaza na ulicama (Legal Significance of Marked Cross-Walks). *Godišnjak Društva za Uporedno Pravo*, 1938: 129–150.

1346 Perić, Živojin M. (a) Gradjansko pravo. Predavanja . . . O posebnim ugovorima (Civil Law. Lectures. Individual Contracts). Beograd, 1927, 366 p. (DLC); (b) Karakterne osobine ugovora o poklonu (Donation: Main Features). *Arhiv*, 1924: 161–175, 252–271, 336–361. (DLC); (c) O poništaju ugovora zbog ncizvršenja (Rescission for Failure to Perform the Contract). Beograd, 1903. 49 p.; (d) O ugovoru o prodaji i kupovini (Sale and Purchase Contracts). Beograd, 1920–21. 3 v. (DLC); (e) O ugovoru o poklonu (Donation). *Arhiv*, 1926; 241–258, 359–396. (DLC)

1347 Pliverić, M. (a) O naknadi štete učinjene motornim vozilima (Liability for Damage Caused by Motor Vehicles). *In* Spomenica kongresa pravnika, 1931: 137–177; (b) Odgovornost za pomoćnika ispunjavanja obveze (Liability for Damage Caused by Agents in the Performance of Contractual Duties). *In* Spomenica Dolencu, Kreku, Kušeju in Škerlju, 1937: 161–201. (DLC)

1348 Poličević, M. O ugovorima koji se zaključuju korespondencijom (Contracts by Correspondence). Beograd, 1897. 89 p.

1349 Poznić, B. O nepravičnom obogaćenju (Unjust Enrichment). *Pravna misao*, 1939: 107–122. (DLC)

1350 Bartoš, M. Državni intervencionizam u tražbenim odnosima (Government Intervention in Damage Controversies). *Arhiv*, 1936: 104–108. (DLC)

1351 Puhan, I. Dogovorito za Podarot vo Semejnoto i Naslednoto Pravo (Donations among Relatives and Inheritance Law). *Pregled*, 1956: 29–43.

1352 Radičević, Rikard. Prikaz propisa o valorizaciji (Rules and Regulations on Valorization). Zagreb, 1946. 36 p. (DLC)

1353 Ristić, R. (a) O deliktnim obligacijama (Torts). Novi Sad, 1934, 174 p. (DLC); (b) Teorija objektivne odgovornosti (Theory of Strict Civil Responsibility). Novi Sad, 1934. 141 p. (DLC)

1354 Rižnar, V. *and* J. Štempihar. Zakonita ureditev obročnih poslov (Regulations Concerning Sales on the Installment Payment Plan). *In* Spomenica kongresa pravnika, 1939: 167–207.

1355 Salihagić, B. Ugovor o doživotnom izdržavanju u korist trećeg u svijetlu odredaba Zakona u nasledjivanju (Contract of Support for Life for the Benefit of Third Persons under the Inheritance Law). *Anali,* 1956: 285–399. (DLC)

1356 Spaić, V. Pitanje naknade neimovinske štete u našem pravu (The Problem of Compensation for Mental Suffering under Yugoslav Law). *Arhiv,* 1953: 120–129. (DLC)

1357 Smole, A. Problem odškodnine za idealno škodo in problem civilno—pravnega varstva osebnosti v kapitalizmu, v družbi s socialistično orijentacijo in v socijalizmu (Compensation for Mental Suffering and Protection of the Individual in Capitalist, Socialist—Oriented and Socialist Societies). *Pravnik,* 1956: 270–289. (DLC)

1358 Štempihar, Jurij. (a) Civilno pravo; osnutek posebnega dela obveznosti (Civil Law; An Outline of the Special Part on Contracts and Torts). Beograd, 1952. 121 p. (DLC); (b) Spolnitvene in jamčevalne napake pri kupni pogodbi (Vendor's Warranties). *Pravnik,* 1956: 199–208. (DLC); (c) Vrednota, valorizacija in zasebno pravo (Currency, Valorization and Private Law). *Slovenski pravnik,* 1939: 101–119, 157–177. (DLC)

1359 Goldštajn, Aleksandar. Posebne uzance i poslovni običaji (Special Usages and Customes of the Trade). *Zbornik pravnog fakulteta* (Zagreb), 1961: 32–41. (DLC)

1360 Urošević, L. Klauzula *rebus sic stantibus* (The Clause *Rebus sic stantibus). Pravosudje,* 1937: 10–17, 85–93. (DLC)

1361 Vuković, M. (a) Medjuugovorni odnosi (Contractual Relationship). *Zbornik Pravnog fakulteta u Zagrebu,* 1955: 163–181. (DLC); (b) Obavezno pravo I (Contracts and Torts I). Zagreb, 1956. 350 p.; (c) Odgovornost za štetu u gradjanskom pravu (Damages in Civil Law). Zagreb, 1951. 120 p.

1362 Zebić, Milorad. Valorizacija (Valorization). Beograd, 1927. 73 p. (DLC)

1363 Georgijević, Radovan. Problematika posebnih uslova materijalne odgovornosti vojnih lica i gradjanskih lica na službi u Jugoslavenskoj narodnoj armiji (Civil Liability of Military Personnel and Civilian Employees of the Yugoslav Army). *Naša Zakonitost* (Zagreb), 1962: 236–252. (DLC)

1364 Zuglia, Srećko. Prirodne obaveze u teoriji i u srpskom privatnom pravu (Natural Obligations in Theory and in the Serbian Civil Law). Subotica, 1924. 40 p.

1365 Uredba o likvidaciji zemljoradničkih dugova od 25 septembra 1936 sa pravilnicima i ostalim odredbama za njeno izvršenje (Decree on the Liquidation of Peasant Debts). Beograd, 1st ed.?; 2d ed. 1938. 310 p. (DLC)

1366 Zakon o zastarelosti potraživanja (Law on the Statute of Limitations of Contractual and Tort Liabilities). Beograd, 1954. 14 p.; 3rd ed. 1956. 15 p.; 4th ed. 1959. 19 p. (DLC)

9 Cooperatives

See also Nos.: 2260b; 2290; 2292; 2312; 2331; 2413; 2415; 2423; 2425a; 2425g; 2444.

1367 Bilimović, Aleksandar. Načrt zadružnega zakona (Draft Law on Co-operatives). Reprint from *Zbornik znanstvenih razprav (Ljubljana)*. 1936. 25 p. (DLC)

1368 Češljarević, Josif K. Zakon o privrednim zadrugama (Law on Economic Co-operatives). Beograd, 1937. 128 p. (DLC)

1369 Esih, Vinko, *editor*. Zakon o privrednim zadrugama (Law on Economic Co-operatives). Zagreb, 1937. 86 p. (DLC)

1370 Gajić, Vaso. Zadrugarstvo i njegovi zadaci u izgradnji socijalisma (The Co-operatives and their Role in the Building of Socialism). Sarajevo, 1951. 219 p. (DLC)

1371 Jelašić, Josip *and* Bogumil Korlević, *editors*. Zakon o privrednim zadrugama od 24 rujna 1937 (Law on Economic Co-operatives). Zagreb, 1942. 230 p. (DLC)

1372 Krbek, Ivo. Pravna konstrukcija hrvatske kućne zadruge (Legal Structure of Croatian Family Cooperatives). *Arhiv*, 1938: 47–52. (DLC)

1373 Jovanović, Bogoljub. Zadrugarstvo i zadružna izgradnja sta-
nova (The Co-operative Movement and Co-operative Housing).
Beograd, 1936. 190 p. (DLC)

1374 Kapor, V. Imovinsko—pravni odnosi članova seljačkih radnih zadruga u našoj sudskoj praksi (Property Relationships of
the Members of the Peasant Working Co-operatives in the Yugoslav Court Practice). *Arhiv,* 1952: 71–76.

1375 Lazarov, Stojan. Organizacija na rabotata i stopanskata smet-
ka bo selanskite rabotni zadrugi (Organization and Management of Farmers' Cooperatives). Skopje, 1951. 78 p.

1376 Marković, Bogdan St. (a) Ekonomski i pravni odnosi kod
zemljoradničkih zadruga u Srbiji (Economic and Legal Relationships in the Serbian Farmers' Cooperatives). Beograd, 1909.
190 p.; (b) Komentar Zakona o zemljoradničkim i zanatskim
zadrugama (Commentary on the Law on Farmers' and Artisans'
Co-operatives). Beograd, 1921. 85 p.

1377 Marković, Golub. (a) Komentar zakona o privrednim za-
drugama (Commentary on the Law on Economic Co-operatives).
Beograd, 1938. 320 p. (DLC); (b) Zadruge i njihov razvoj u
Velikoj Britaniji, Nemačkoj, Švajcarskoj, Danskoj, i Jugoslaviji
(The Co-operative Movement in Great Britain, Germany, Nether-
lands, Denmark and Yugoslavia). Beograd, 1937. 224 p.

1378 Osnovni Zakon o Zemljoradničkim Zadrugama (Basic Law
on Peasant Co-operatives). Beograd, 1949. 61 p. (DLC)

1379 Petrović, Mladen. Zemljoradničke zadruge (Farmers' Co-
operatives). Beograd, 1954. 99 p. (DLC)

1380 Popović, Vojin, *joint editor.* Priručnik o organizaciji rada
u seljačkoj radnoj zadruzi (Handbook on the Organization of
Work in the Peasant Working Co-operatives). Beograd, 1950.
158 p. (DLC)

1381 Propisi o štedno-kreditnom poslovanju zemljoradničkih zadruga (Rules and Regulations on the Operation of the Savings
and Credit Operations of Farmers' Co-operatives). Beograd, 1949.
54 p. (DLC)

1382 Rastovčan, P. (a) Pravo zemljoradnićkih zadruga (Law on
Farmers' Co-operatives). Zagreb, 1950. 99 p. (DLC); (b) Zadružno pravo (Co-operative Law). Zagreb, 1948. 120 p. (DLC)

1383 Regan, Djuro. Radne norme i obračun zarade u seljačkim

radnim zadrugama (Working Standards and Computation of Members, Earnings in the Peasant Working Co-operatives). Zagreb, 1950, 165 p. (DLC)

1384 Škerlj, M. (a) Nadzor v gospodarskih zadrugah (Control over the Economic Co-operatives). *Slovenski Pravnik,* 1940: 231–244; (b) Poništavanje odluka skupštine po Zakonu o privrednim zadrugama (Invalidation of Decisions Passed by the Assemblies of Co-operatives). *Arhiv,* 1939: 8–25.

1385 Stjepanović, Branko, *editor.* Propisi o Zadrugama (Regulations on Co-operatives). Beograd, 1952. 91 p. (DLC)

1386 Todorović, M. (a) O prelaznim oblicima zemljoradničkih zadruga (Transitional Forms of Farmers' Co-operatives). *Komunist,* 1949: 129–141; (b) O radnoj zadruzi (Peasant Working Co-operatives). *Komunist,* 1952: 70–97.

1387 Ugledna pravila proizvodjačko-uslužnih zanatskih zadruga (Bylaws of Co-operatives of Producers and Artisans). Cetinje, 1950. 29 p.

1388 Ugledna pravila za seljačke radne zadruge (Bylaws of Peasant Working Co-operatives). Zagreb, 1949. 110 p. (DLC)

1389 Uredba o zemljoradničkim zadragama (Decree on Farmers' Co-operatives). Beograd, 1954. 31 p. (DLC)

1390 Urbanić, F. Udrugarstvo (Laws and Regulations on Co-operatives). Zagreb, 1877. 256 p.

1391 Vučković, M. (a) Neutralno zadrugarstvo, kapitalizam i socijalizam (Neutral Co-operatives, Capitalism and Socialism). Beograd, 1936. 160 p.; (b) Zadrugarstvo (The Co-operative Movement). Beograd, 1947, 160 p. (DLC)

10 Corporations and Partnership

See also Nos.: 2332; 2337; 2412; 2443b.

1392 Bajkić, Velimir. (a) Akcionarska društva i pravo nadzora Ministarstva trgovine i industrije (Corporations and their Supervision by the Ministry of Finance). Beograd, 1926. 81 p. (DLC); (b) Akcionarsko društvo i politička vlast (Corporations and Government Authority). *Arhiv,* 1926: 385–398. (DLC); (c) Osnivanje akcionarskih društva u Srbiji (Organization of Corporations in Serbia). *Arhiv,* 1913: 263–273; 1914: 48–51. (DLC)

1393 Marković, Lazar. O pravnoj prirodi javnog trgovačkog društva (Legal Nature of Full Partnerships). *Arhiv*, 1907:390–399. (DLC)

1394 Mirković, Dj. (a) Dve teorije o pravnoj prirodi trgovačkih društava (Two Theories on the Legal Nature of Partnership). Beograd, 1934. 31 p.; (b) Javno trgovačko društvo kao pravno lice, s naročitim osvrtom na srpsko zakonodavstvo (Full Partnership as a Corporate Body, with Special Reference to Serbian Law). Beograd, 1934. 84 p.; (c) Pravna priroda pravila trgovačkih društava, s naročitim osvrtom na akcionarska i društva s. o.j. (Legal Nature of Corporate Bylaws, with Special Reference to Joint Stock Companies and Companies with Limited Liability). Beograd, 1940. 126 p.; (d) Pravna priroda trgovačkih društava (Legal Nature of Commercial Companies). *Arhiv*, 1945: 415–430.

1395 Pliverić, M. O jamstvu članova javnog i komanditnog trg. društva za društvene obaveze (Liabilities of Partners for Obligations of a Full or Limited Partnership). *Mjesečnik*, 1909: 761–774, 999–1014, 1130–1144.

1396 Rastovčan, Pravo. (a) Trgovačka društva (Commercial Companies). Zagreb, 1951. 120 p. (DLC); (b) Trgovačka društva, glavni nosioci privrede u kapitalizmu (Commercial Companies as Principal Agents of Capitalist Economy). Zagreb, 1951. 120 p.; 1958. 255 p. (DLC)

1397 Storoženko, Jakov A. Trgovačko preduzeće i privatno pravo (Commercial Enterprises and Private Law). Beograd, 1941. 202 p. (DLC)

1398 Stražnicki, M. O reformi prava dioničkih društava (Reform of Yugoslav Corporation Law). Zagreb, 1922.

1399 Škerlj, M. (a) Osebne trgovinske družbe po novejših zakonih (Commercial Partnership in Modern Legislation). *Razprave Akademije znanosti in umetnosti. Pravni razred*, 1943: 219–290; 1945: 1–132; (b) Pravila naših delniških družb (Status of our Commercial Companies). Ljubljana, 1926. 215 p.

1400 Zebić, Milorad. (a) Akcijsko pravo Kraljevine S.H.S. (Yugoslav Corporation Law). Beograd, 1928. 354 p. (DLC); (b) Prestanak i likvidacija akcijskih društava (Liquidation of Corporations). Beograd, 1935. 303 p. (DLC); (c) Uporedna razmatranja iz akcijskog prava (Reflections on Comparative Corporation

Law). Beograd, 1930. 60 p. (DLC); (d) Zakoni i raspisi o akcionarskim društvima (Corporation Laws and Regulations). Beograd, 1925. 205 p. (DLC)

11 Domestic Relations, Civil Status, *prodična zadruga*

See also Nos.: 339b; 345b; 744; 771; 1112e; 1118; 1655; 2022; 2247; 2319h; 2319k; 2319o; 2345a; 2373b; 2396; 2417; 2425e; 2425d.

a   Domestic Relations and Civil Status

1401   Osnovni zakon o braku. Zakon o državnim matičnim knjigama (Basic Law on Marriage. Law on Civil Status Registry). Beograd, 1st ed. ?; 2d ed., 1948. 77 p. (DLC)

1402   Žepić, Zvonimir, *editor*. Zakoni i propisi o ženidbi (Provisions Governing Marriage). Zagreb, 1937. 233 p. (DLC)

1403   Zakoni o državnim matičnim knjigama, o ličnim imenima i o overavanju potpisa, rukopisa i prepisa (Laws on Civil Status Registry, Names, and Certification of Manuscripts and Copies). Beograd, 1948. 93 p. (DLC)

1404   Zakon o vršenju starateljstva [od 6 februara 1950] (Guardianship Law). Beograd, 1950. 23 p. (DLC)

1405   Zakoni o starateljstvu i usvojenju (Laws on Guardianship and Adoption). Beograd, 1947. 35 p. (DLC)

1406   Zakon o starateljstvu od 25 okt. 1872, i Zakon o postavljanju sudija za vanparnična dela (Law on Guardianship of October 25, 1872 and on the Appointment of Judges in Non-adversary Proceedings). Beograd, 1872. 45 p. (DLC)

1407   Zakon o ličnim imenima (Law on Personal Names). Beograd, 1929. 24 p.; 2nd ed., 1930. 57 p. (DLC)

1408   Alagić, T. O razlozima koji raskidaju bračnu vezu, i o sudskom postupku u parnicama za raskid braka (Grounds for Divorce and Procedure in Divorce Cases). Sombor, 1892. 104 p.

1409   Andrijević, A. Naš brak i reforma njegova (Our Marriage and its Reform). Veliki Bečkerek, 1919. 73 p.

1410   Arandjelović, D. Nekoliko reči o mirazu, spremi i udomljenju (Dowry and Paraphernalia). Beograd, 1905. 35 p.

1411 Bakić, Vojislav. (a) Priručnik za Porodično pravo (Handbook on Domestic Relations). Beograd, 1951. 286 p.; (b) Položaj vanbračne dece u FNRJ (Status of Illegitimate Children in FPRY). Beograd, 1957. 138 p. (DLC); (c) Porodica i porodično pravni odnosi u Jugoslaviji (The Family and Family Relations in Yugoslavia). Beograd, 1960. 215 p. (DLC)

1412 Begović, Mehmed Dž. Porodično pravo (Domestic Relations). 1st ed. Beograd. 1946–1947. 3 v.; 2d ed. 1952, 1 v. 210 p.; 3d ed. 1957, 1 v., 219 p. 4th ed. 1959. 228 p. (DLC); 5th ed. 1961. 230 p.

1413 Belić, Matija, editor. Zbirka kanonskih propisa o braku (Canon Law Provisions on Marriage). Zagreb, 1937. 468 p. (DLC)

1414 Bogišić, V. (a) O obliku nazvanom inokoština u seoskoj porodici Srba i Hrvata (Inokoština in Serbian and Croatian Peasant Families). Beograd, 1884. 60 p.; (b) O položaju porodice u pravnoj sistemi (Status of the Family Under the Law). Beograd, 1893. 52 p. (DLC)

1415 Božić, A. Položaj žene u privatnom pravu kroz istoriju do danas (Legal Status of the Wife in Private Law Throughout History up to Date). Beograd, 1939. 223 p.

1416 Curinaldi, A. Priručnik parbenog postupka kod crkvenih ženidbenih sudova (Procedure in Marriage Cases Before Ecclesiastical Courts). Split, 1930. 224 p.

1417 Eisner, Bertold. (a) Porodično pravo (Domestic Relations). Zagreb, 1950. 260 p.; (b) Privatno-pravni položaj žene po današnjem pravu Jugoslavije (Women Under Present Yugoslav Law). In Spomenica Mauroviću, 1934: 325–419. (DLC)

1418 Finžgar, A. Rodbinsko pravo (Domestic Relations). Ljubljana, 1957. 178 p.

1419 Graber, Vilim. Prava djece, s osobitim obsirom na brak, obitelj i nasljedstvo (Status of Children, Marriage, Family, and Inheritance). Zagreb, 1893. 2 v. (DLC)

1420 Hiršl, Jakov. O sudskom postupku u bračnim sporovima (Court Procedure in Marriage Suits). Zagreb, n. d., 45 p. (DLC)

1421 Janković, Dimitrije. Mešoviti brak u pravoslavnoj crkvi (Mixed Marriages in the Orthodox Church). Sarajevo, 1906.

1422 Jelisavčić, J. Udata žena u Gradjankom pravu (Married Woman and Civil Law). Beograd, 1897. 51 p.

1423 Jovanović, Petar. Srodstvo kao bračna smetnja prema bračnim pravilima Srpske pravoslavne crkve (Kinship as a Marriage Impediment under the Rules of the Serbian Orthodox Church). Tuzla, 1936. 96 p.

1424 Jovičić, Miloš M. (a) Kako da se u novom Gradjanskom zakoniku uredi pravni položaj vanbračne dece (Status of Children Born out of Wedlock in the New Civil Code). Reprint from Spomenica Kongresa Pravnika, Beograd, 1937. 27 p.; (b) Pravni odnosi u porodici (Domestic Relations). Beograd, 1935. 38 p.

1425 Kastl, Dragan. Priručnik dječje zaštite i starateljstva (Handbook on the Protection of Children and on Guardianship). Zagreb, 1951. 130 p. (DLC)

1426 Lanović, Mihailo. Zbirka matičnih propisa, valjanih u Kraljevini Hrvatskoj i Slavoniji (Collection of Provisions on Civil Status Registry in Force in the Territory of the Kingdom of Croatia and Slavonia). Zagreb, 1908. 408 p. (DLC)

1427 Lazarević, Adam. O državnoj intervenciji u porodičnim odnosima (Government Interference in Domestic Relations). Beograd, 1927. 112 p. (DLC)

1428 Liebald-Ljubojević, Julij. Katoličko ženitbeno pravo obzirom na gradjanske zakone (Roman Catholic Marriage Law with Reference to Civil Law). Osijek, 1878. 221 p. (DLC)

1429 Lovrić, E. Ženidba i njezini bitni momenti (Marriage and its Essential Elements). Zagreb, 1900. 41 p.

1430 Marinković, K., A. Božić, M. Prodanović, D. Golović and R. Lukić, editors. Priručnik saveznih propisa o pravima žena i dece (Handbook of the Federal Provisions Governing the Rights of Married Women and Children). Beograd, 1950. 172 p. (DLC)

1431 Marković, Lazar. Porodično pravo (Domestic Relations). Beograd, 1920. 274 p. (DLC)

1432 Mitrović, Čedomilj. (a) O bračnim parnicama (Marriage Suits). Beograd, 1906. 106 p.; (b) Sud za bračne sporove u Srbiji od oslobodjenja do izdanja Gradjanskog zakonika (Courts for Marital Litigations in Serbia from the Liberation to the Promulgation of the Civil Code). Beograd, 1924; 2d ed. 1929. 32 p.

1433 Milaš, Nikodim. (a) Reforma bračnog prava u Austriji (Reform of the Marriage Law in Austria). Reprint from *Arhiv*, 1908.

36 p.; (b) Rukopoloženje kao smetnja braku (Ordination as a Marriage Impediment). 1st ed. .; 2nd ed. 1907. 16 p. (DLC)

1434 Perić, Živojin M. Lično bračno pravo, o srpskom gradjanskom zakoniku (Marriage Law under the Serbian Civil Code). Beograd, 1934. 90 p.

1435 Porodično pravo; savezni zakoni (Domestic Relations; Federal Provisions). 1st ed., Beograd. 1949. 69 p.; 2d ed. 1954. 68 p.; 4th ed. 1959. 94 p. (DLC); 5th ed. 1960. 94 p.

1436 Priručnik za porodično pravo (Handbook on Domestic Relations). Zagreb, 1954. 185 p. (DLC)

1437 Prokop, Ana. (a) Komentar Osnovog zakona o braku (Commentary on the Basic Law on Marriage). Zagreb, 1953. 246 p.; (b) Odnosi roditelja i djece po zakonodavstvu FNRJ (Parent and Child under the Law of the FPRY). Zagreb, 1954. 108 p.; (c) Prava žene nove Jugoslavije u braku i porodici (Rights of a Married Woman in the Family in Present-Day Yugoslavia). Beograd, 1950. 112 p. (DLC); (d) Pravna zaštita maloljetnika u našem porodičnom zakonodavstvu (Protection of Minors in Our Domestic Relations). *In* Zbornik Pravnog fakulteta u Zagrebu, 1951: 181–204; (e) Ravnopravnost žene, brak i porodica, po ustavu FNRJ (Equal Status of Women under the Federal Yugoslav Constitution). Zagreb, 1946. 56 p. (DLC); (f) Starateljstvo po zakonodavstvu FNRJ (Guardianship under the Law of the FPRY). Zagreb, 1956. 103 p.; (g) Usvojenje po zakonodavstvu, FNRJ (Adoption under the Law of the FPRY). Zagreb, 1948. 123 p. (DLC); (h) Utvrdjivanje i osporavanje bračnog očinstva (Proof and Denial of Paternity). *In* Zbornik Pravnog fakulteta u Zagrebu, 1954: 59–70. (DLC); (i) *editor.* Komentar o osnovnom zakonu o braku (A Commentary on the Basic Law on Marriage). *In* Školska knjiga. Štamparija Vjesnik (Zagreb), 1960: 205–480.

1438 Ruvarac, Dimitrije. O razvodu mešovitih brakova u Hrvatskoj i Slavoniji (Divorce of Mixed Marriages in Croatia). Sr. Karlovci, 1907. 24 p.

1439 Ružičić, Nikanor. Tablice raznovrsnih primera srodstva (Chart of the Various Kinds of Kinship). Beograd, 1886. 175 p. (DLC)

1440 Tomac, Dragutin. Ustav i bračno pravo (Constitution and Domestic Relations). Zagreb, 1925. 187 p. (DLC)

1441 Troicki, Sergije. Hrišćanska filozofija braka (Christian Concept of Marriage). Beograd, 1934. 254 p.

1442 Veselinović, Stevan. O braku sveštenoslužilaca (Marriage of Priests). Beograd, 1907.

1443 Vlačić, Ljubomir. Austrijsko bračko pravo (Austrian Marriage Law). Spljet, 1909. 208 p.

1444 Zuglia, Srećko. Nepostojeći brak i njegove pravne posljedice (Null and Void Marriage and its Effects). *Zbornik Pravnog fakulteta u Zagrebu,* 1955.

b Family Community Property (*Kućna i porodična zadruga*)

See also Nos.: 1815; 2247; 2259b, c; 2290; 2292; 2331; 2413; 2417; 2423; 2425a and g; 2444; 2451.

1445 Ilić, Ananije V. Sistem prava o Kućnoj zajednici u Crnoj Gori (System of Law on Family Community Property in Montenegro). Beograd, 1936. 203 p. (DLC)

1446 Spaić, Vojislav. Pitanje okućnice u našem pravu (Homesteads under Our Law). *Arhiv,* 1949: 638–650. (DLC)

1447 Krišković, V. Hrvatsko pravo kućnih zadruga (Croatian Law on Family Community Property). Zagreb, 1925. 124 p. (DLC)

1448 Perić, Živojin M. (a) Zadružno pravo po Gradjanskom zakoniku Kraljevine Srbije (Family Community Property under the Serbian Civil Code). Beograd, v. 1, 1924; v. 4, 1920. 2 v. (v. 2 and 3 never published?) (DLC); (b) Porodično zadružno pravo u Hrvatskoj i Slavoniji (Family Community Property in Croatia and Slavonia). Beograd, 1926. 38 p. (DLC)

1449 Vežić, Milivoj, *editor.* Zakoni i naredbe o zadrugah u Hrvatskoj i Slavoniji (Laws and Decrees on Family Community Property in Croatia and Slavonia). Zagreb, 1880. 242 p. (DLC)

1450 Zakon od 3. ožujka 1874 o zadrugah (Law of March 3, 1874 on Family Community Property). Zagreb, 1875. 90 p. (DLC)

12 Economic Law

See also: Ch. 11, A, 2f.; Nos.: 868; 992; 1043; 1748.

1451 Antonijević, Zoran. Privredno pravo. Bankarski poslovi i hartije od vrednosti (Economic Law. Banking Transactions and Negotiable Instruments). Beograd, 1960. 170 p. (DLC)

1452 Arandjelović, Dragoljub *and* Dušan Subotić. Komentar zakona o likvidaciji moratornog stanja (Commentary on the Law Providing for the Liquidation of the War-Moratorium). Beograd, 1920. 240 p. (DLC)

1453 Bačić, Z. Privredni sporovi u FNRJ (Economic Disputes in the FPRY). Beograd, 1957. 146 p.

1454 Balog, Nikola. Poslovi privrednog prava (Economic Transactions). Beograd, 1952. 355 p.

1455 Bartoš, Milan. Zastupanje stranih privrednih preduzeća u Jugoslaviji (Representation of Foreign Economic Enterprises in Yugoslavia). *Yugoslovenska revija*, 1956: 237–245.

1456 Blagojević, B. T. Pravni položaj i pravni poslovi državnih privrednih poduzeća (Status of Government-Economic Enterprises and their Legal Transactions). Beograd, 1948. 264 p.

1457 Čobeljić, Djordje. (a) Privredno pravo. Uvodni deo i privredne organizacije (Economic Law. Introductory Part. Economic Organizations). Beograd, 1959. 140 p.; (b) Privredno pravo sa osnovima gradjanskog prava i radnim odnosima u privredi (Economic Law along with Civil Law Principles and Labor Relations in the Economy). Beograd, 1960. 336 p. (DLC)

1458 Društveni plan N.R. Crne Gore (Social Plan of the P.R. of Montenegro). Titograd, 1954– (DLC v. 1)

1459 Geršković, L. Osnovni principi novih privrednih propisa (Basic Principles of the New Economic Regulations). *Arhiv*, 1952: 267–295. (DLC)

1460 Goldštajn, A. (a) Pravni odnosi preduzeća (Legal Relations of Government Enterprises). Beograd, 1957. 116 p.; (b) Konvencionalna kazna u privrednim ugoovrima (Contractual Penalty in Economic Contracts). *Arhiv*, 1949: 650–668. (DLC); (c) Zaključenje privrednog ugovora (The Making of Economic Contracts). *Narodni pravnik*, 1950: 25–37.

1461 Hristov, A. Nekoliko pitanja o uticaju plana na privredne ugovore (Planning and Economic Contracts). *Arhiv*, 1950: 254–275. (DLC)

1462 Ilić, Ananije V. (a) O upravljanju državnim privrednim preduzečima (Management in Government-Economic Enterprises)

Sarajevo, 1951. 59 p.; (b) Mesto privrednog prava u sistemu socijalističkog prava FNRJ (The Place of the Economic Law in the Yugoslav Socialist Legal System). *Godišnjak Pravnog fakulteta u Sarajevu*, 1953: 83–101; (c) Poslovanje privrednih organizacija (Transactions of Economic Organizations). *Ibid.*, 1956: 85–115; (d) Privredno pravo FNRJ (Yugoslav Economic Law). Sarajevo, 1949–51. 2 v. (DLC); 1957. 576 p.; 2nd ed. 1959. 668 p. (DLC)

1463 Jović, Milan V. Ingerencija policije u obrtne delatnosti gradjana (Interference of the Police in the Business Activities ot Citizens). Niš, 1939, 170 p.

1464 Kidrić, B. (a) O državnim privrednim preduzećima (Government Economic Enterprises). Zagreb, 1946. 45 p.; (b) Privredni problemi FNRJ (Economic Problems of the FPRY). Zagreb, 1950. 298 p. (DLC)

1465 Kongres radničkih saveta Jugoslavije, 25–27 juni 1957 (Congress of the Workers' Councils of Yugoslavia of June 25–27, 1957). Beograd, 1957. 788 p.

1466 Kovač, P. *and* Dj. Miljević. Samoupravljanje proizvodjača u privredi (Self-Government of the Producers in Economy). Beograd, 1958. 184 p. (DLC)

1467 Lazarević, A. (a) O pojmu i pravnoj prirodi upravljanja (Concept of Management and its Legal Nature). *Godišnik na Pravno-ekonomskiot fakultet vo Skopje,* 1955, 1956: 301–346; (b) Pitanje pravne ličnosti radnih kolektiva (Workers' Collectives as Legal Entities). *Anali,* 1954: 185–193; (c) Problem gradjansko-pravne odgovornosti radnih kolektiva prema društvenoj Zajednici i zaštita opšte narodne imovine (Civil Responsibility of Workers' Collectives and Protection of Social Property). *Godišnik na Pravno-ekonomskiot fakultet vo Skopje,* 1954, 1955: 11–85.

1468 Ljubibratić, Drago. O pitanju prava upravljanja (The Problem of Law of Management). *Arhiv,* Beograd, 1953: 155–162.

1469 Jovanović, Vladimir. Privredno pravo. Privredne organizacije (Economic Law. Economic Organizations). Beograd, 1961. 326 p.

1470 Miljević, Djordje, Stevan Blagojević *and* Miloje Nikolić. Razvoj privrednog sistema FNRJ (Development of the Economic System of the FPRY). Beograd, 1st ed. ?; 2nd ed. 1955: 191 p.

1471 Mikić, Vladimir V. (a) Osnovi državnog i društvenog uredjenja i radnog prava FNRJ (Principles of the Governmental and
Social Setup and the Labor Law of the FPRY). Beograd, 1959.
108 p.; 2nd ed. 1960. 172 p.; (b) —— *and* Miodrag Pavlović.
Osnovi državnog i društvenog uredjenja FNRJ. Udžbenik za
stručne škole (Principles of the Governmental and Social Setup
of the FPRY. Textbook for Professional Schools). 2nd ed. Beograd, 1960. 84 p.

1472 Mirković, Jovan, Branko Medješki *and* Miodrag Šaponjić.
Zbirka propisa o zanatstvu (Laws Governing the Handicraft
Trade). Beograd, 1954. 113 p. (DLC)

1473 Vučkovački, Dušan. (a) Udžbenik prava za srednje ekonomske i ostale srednje škole. Državno i društveno uredjenje FNRJ
(Textbook on Law for Schools on Economics. Government and
Social Setup of the FPRY). 4th ed., Zagreb, 1958. 194 p. (DLC);
5th ed. 1960. 192 p.; 6th ed. 1961. 192 p.; (b) *coauthor*. Udžbenik prava za ekonomske i druge stručne škole. Privredno i radno
pravo (Textbook on Law for Economic and Other Professional
Schools. Economic and Labor Law). 2nd ed. Zagreb, 1961. 186 p.

1474 Niketić, Gojko. Zakon o radnjama (Trade Law). Beograd,
1936. 2 v.

1475 Pavičević, M. Sindikati i trudbeničko upravljanje privredom
(Trade Unions and Labor Management). *Komunist* (Beograd),
1951: 131–158.

1476 Petrović, Vojislav J. (a) Razvitak privrednog sistema FNRJ
posmatran kroz pravne propise (Evolution of the Economic System of the FPRY Viewed from a Legal Point). Beograd, 1954–
58. 5 v. (DLC); (b) Pravo za studente Ekonomskog fakulteta
(Law for Students of the Faculty of Economics). Beograd, 1960.
328 p. (DLC); (c) Radni odnosi u javnoj službi i privrednim
organizacijama (Labor Relations in Public Service and Economic Organizations). 2nd ed. Beograd, 1960. 210 p.; (d) Državno
uredjenje i privredni sistem FNRJ (Government Setup and
Economic System of the FPRY). Beograd, 1960. 184 p.

1477 Pretnar, S. Pravna struktura podjetja (Legal Structure of
Economic Enterprises). *Ljudski pravnik,* 1952: 187–194.

1478 Rastovčan, P. (a) Deset godina našeg privrednog zakonodavstva (Ten Years of Our Economic Legislation). *Nova Jugo-*

slavija, 1954: 213–241; (b) Državna privredna poduzeća (Government Economic Enterprises). Zagreb, 1949. 228 p.; (c) Naša socijalistička izgradnja u svitlu privrednog zakonodavstva (Building-Up of Our Socialism in the Light of the Economic Legislation). *Zbornik Pravnog fakulteta,* 1951: 205–254; (d) Pravni položaj privrednih produzeća u FNRJ (Legal Status of the Economic Enterprises in Yugoslavia). Beograd, 1957. 110 p. (DLC)

1478[1] Savezni društveni plan za 1962 godinu sa ekspozeom Avda Huma (Federal Social Plan for 1962 with the Exposé by Avdo Humo). Beograd, 1962. 85 p.

1479 Simić, Nikola Dj. Industrijska, zanatska, i radnička politika, i zakonodavstvo (Industrial, Crafts and Labor Policy and Legislation). Beograd, 1926. 208 p.

1480 Sirotković, Jakov. (a) Novi privredni sistem FNRJ; osnove, organizacioni oblici, i metode upravljanja (The New Yugoslav Economic System; its Foundations, Organizational Forms and Methods of Management). Zagreb, 1954. 187 p. (DLC); (b) Planiranje narodne privrede FNRJ. Opći dio (Planning of the National Economy of the FPRY. General Part). Zagreb, 1951. 162 p. (DLC); (c) Društveno planiranje u Jugoslaviji (Social Planning in Yugoslavia). Beograd, 1958. 130 p. (DLC); (d) *co-author.* Privredno planiranje u Jugoslaviji (Economic Planning in Yugoslavia). Zagreb, 1959. 90 p. (DLC)

1481 Sladović, E. Zanatsko pravo (Handicraft Law). Beograd, 1926. 270 p.

1482 Subotić, Dušan M. Zakonodavstvo o moratoriumu za Kraljevinu Srbiju 1912–1919 (Serbian Moratorium Laws, 1912–1919). Beograd, 1919. 187 p.

1483 Kapor, Vladimir *and* Zoran Antonijević. Privredno pravo (Economic Law). Beograd, 1961. 227 p.

1484 Vajner, Zdenko. (a) Financijsko poslovanje (Financial Management). Zagreb, 1959. 272 p.; (b) Organizacija poslovanja privrednih poduzeća. Opći dio (Organization of the Economic Enterprises' Management. General Part). Zagreb, 1950. 2 v.; (c) Principi organizacije i poslovanja poduzeća (Principles of Organization and Management of Economic Enterprises). Zagreb, 1955. 416 p.

1485 Žigrović- Pretočki, Ivan. Obrtni Zakon (Trade Law). Zagreb, 1886. 116 p.

1486 Vuković, Mihailo. (a) Privredni sistem FNRJ (Economic System of the FPRY). Sarajevo, 1955. 95 p.; 2nd ed. 1956. 123 p. (DLC); (b) Gradjansko pravo s naročitim osvrtom na privredne odnose (Civil Law with Reference to Economic Conditions). Zagreb, 1952. 148 p. (DLC)

1487 Zakonodavstvo o radnjama (Trade Legislation). Beograd, 1932. 2 v. (DLC)

' 13 Education

See also: Ch. 11, A, 2g; No. 2432.

1488 Uvodni zakon za Splošni zakon o šolstvu (Introductory Law to the General Law on Education). Ljubljana, 1958. 96 p. (DLC)

1489 Opšti zakon o upravljanju školama (General Law on School Management). Beograd, 1955. 47 p. (DLC)

1490 Opći zakon o univerzitetima (General Law on Universities). Beograd, 1954. 78 p. (Zbirka saveznih zakona, br. 119) (DLC); 2d ed. 1958. 73 p. (Zbirka saveznih zakona, br. 163). (DLC)

1491 Kovačević, Milivoje, *editor*. Zakon o univerzitetima (Law on Universities). Beograd, 1956. 52 p. (Zbirka propisa N.R. Srbije, br. 2). (DLC)

1492 Sveučilištni zakoni i provedbena naredba o državnim ispitima (Law on Universities and Decree Enacting it). Zagreb, 1895. 67 p. (DLC)

1493 Prednacrt Statuta pravnog fakulteta u Beogradu (Draft of the Statute for the Law School of Belgrade). Beograd, 1956. 16 p. (DLC)

1494 Uputstvo o polaganju doktorskih ispita na teološkim fakultetima . . . na RKT. Bogoslovskom Fakultetu Sveučilišta u Zagrebu (Directions for Passing the Examination for a Doctor's Degrec in the Theological School of the University of Zagreb). Zagreb, 1951. 16 p. (DLC)

1495 Zakon u muzejima. Uredba o organizaciji i radu zemaljskog muzeja u Sarajevu (Law on Museums. Decree on the Organization of the Activities of the Museum of Sarajevo). Sarajevo, 1958. 33 p. (DLC)

1496 Teodorović, Dragoslav, *joint editor.* Zbirka saveznih i republičkih zakona i propisa za Bosnu i Hercegovinu iz oblasti školstva, 1945–1956 (Collection of Federal and Republican Laws and Provisions for Bosnia and Herzegovina Relating to Education, 1945–1956). Sarajevo, 1957. 430 p. (DLC)

1497 Nastavni plan i program za osnovne škole N.R. Crne Gore (Educational Plan and Program for the Schools of the P.R. of Montenegro). Cetinje, 1953. 51 p. (DLC)

1498 Prijedlog zakona o narodnim školama (Draft of the Law on Elementary Schools). Zagreb, 1951. 18 p. (DLC)

1499 Predlog na zakonot za narodnite osnovni učilišta (Draft of the Law on People's Elementary Schools). Skopje, 1952. 24 p. (DLC)

1500 Uredba o Višoj islamskoj šerijatsko-teološkoj školi u Sarajevu (Decree on the Higher Islamic Sheriat-Theological School). Beograd, 1937. 21 p. (DLC)

1501 Zakon o obaveznom telesnom vaspitanju (Law on Compulsory Physical Education). Beograd, 1937. 56 p. (DLC)

1502 Prosvetni šematizam (Educational Handbook). Zagreb, 1932. 1586 p. (DLC)

1503 Zakon o narodnijem školama u knj. Crnoj Gori (Law on Elementary Schools of the Principality of Montenegro). Cetinje, 1907. 43 p. (DLC)

1504 Zakon, naredbe . . . za osnovne škole u knjaževini Crnoj Gori, 1884–1902 (Law, Ordinances . . . for Elementary Schools in the Principality of Montenegro, 1884–1902). Cetinje, 1902. 319 p. (DLC)

1505 Baralić, D. Student prava (The Law School Student). Beograd, 1940–1941. 92 p.

1506 Ilić, Mihailo, *editor.* Zakon o srednjim školama i zakon o učiteljskim školama (Law on Secondary Schools and Law on Teachers' Colleges). Beograd, 1930. 113 p. (Zbirka zakona, sv. 26). (DLC)

1507 Marčić, Stjepan A. Gradjanska nauka i socijalno zakonodavstvo (Civics and Social Legislation). Split, 1932. 168 p. (DLC)

1508 Marković, Mil. *and* Zar. R. Popović. Prosvetni zbornik zakona i naredaba po kojima . . . se upravljaju škole i druge prosvetne ustanove u Kraljevini Srbiji (Educational Manual for Schools and Other Educational Institutions in Serbia). Beograd, 1895. 1306 p. (DLC)

1509 Niketić, Gojko, editor. (a) Zakon o narodnim školama od 5 decembra 1929 (Law on Elementary Schools of December 5, 1929). Beograd, 1930. 87 p. (DLC); 4th ed. 1935. 75 p. (Zbirka zakona, sv. 158) (DLC); (b) Zakon o srednjim školama od 31. augusta 1929 (Law on Secondary Schools). Beograd, 1932. 83 p. (Zbirka zakona, sv. 181) (DLC); (c) Uredba o učiteljskim disciplinskim sudovima (Decree on Disciplinary Boards for Teachers). Beograd, 1927. 31 p. (Zbirka zakona, 81). (DLC)

1510 Petković, Vujica. Nastavni plan i program za osnovnu i višu narodnu školu (Educational Plan and Program for Elementary and Secondary Schools). Beograd, 1937. 290 p. (DLC)

1511 Radovanović, Ljubomir V., editor. Uredba o izdržavanju narodnih škola od 9 septembra 1936 (Decree on Support of Elementary Schools of September 9, 1936). Beograd, 1937. 176 p. (Zbirka zakona, sv. 2). (DLC)

1512 Stanišić, Staniša S., editor. Najnoviji učiteljski zbornik. Zakoni, raspisi . . . (Teachers' Manual of Laws, Regulations, etc.). 4th ed. Beograd, 1928. 261 p. (DLC)

1513 Stojanović, Dušan. Uredba o podizanju školskih zgrada (Decree Concerning the Erection of School Buildings). Beograd, 1931. 106 p. Mimeographed. (DLC)

14 Elections

See also: Ch. 11, A, 2h; and Nos. 416; 531; 541; 2264; 2297.

1514 Zakon o pravima i dužnostima, izboru i opozivu saveznih narodnih poslanika (Law on the Election and Recall of Federal People's Representatives). Preface by Jovan Djordjević. Beograd, 1957. 91 p. (DLC)

1515 Zakon o volitvah ljudskih poslancev za Ljudsko Skupščino FLRJ (Law on the Election of People's Representatives to the Federal National Assembly). Beograd, 1950. 147 p. (DLC)

1516 Zakon za izbiranje narodni pratenici na narodnata skupština na FNRJ (Law on the Election of People's Representatives to the National Assembly of the FPRY). Beograd, 1950. 137 p. (DLC)

1517 Legge sulle elezioni dei deputati all 'Assemblea Popolare della Repubblica Federativa Popolare di Jugoslavia. Zagreb, 1950. 48 p. (DLC)

1518 Zakon o izboru i opozivu odbornika narodnih odbora (Law on the Election and Recall of Members of People's Committees). Beograd, 1953 (?). 79 p. (DLC)

1519 Zakon o biračkim spiskovima sa objašnjenjima (Law on Voters' Lists Annotated). 2nd ed. Beograd, 1947. 72 p. (Zbirka zakona FNRJ, br. 8). (DLC)

1520 Predlog Zakonu o izboru narodnih poslanika Narodne Skupštine NR Srbije (Draft of the Law on the Election of Representaives to the Assembly of the People's Republic of Serbia). Beograd, n.d. 15 p. (DLC)

1521 Prijedlog zakona o izboru narodnih zastupnika za sabor Narodne Republike Hrvatske. Prijedlog zakona o izmjenama i dopunama zakona o administrativno-teritorijalnoj podjeli NR Hrvatske od 17 svibnja 1950 (Draft of the Law on the Election of Representatives to the National Assembly of the PR of Croatia, Draft of the Law on the Amendment of the Territorial Division). Zagreb, 1950. 19 p. (DLC)

1522 Zakon o pravicah in dolžnostih ter o volitvah in odpoklicu republiških ljudskih poslancev v LR Sloveniji (Law on the Election and Recall of Representatives of the PR of Slovenia). Ljubljana, 1957. 150 p. (DLC)

1523 Obrazci k zakonu o volitvah in odpoklicu odbornikov ljudskih odborov (Forms for the Law on the Election and Recall of Members of People's Committees). Ljubljana, 1952. 86 p. (DLC)

1524 Zakon o izboru narodnih poslanika za narodnu Skupštinu NR Bosne i Hercegovine od 5 Oktobra 1950 i zakon o opozivu narodnih pretstavnika sa objašnjenjima (Laws on the Election and Recall of People's Representatives to the National Assembly of the PR of Bosnia and Herzegovina of October 5, 1950 Annotated). Sarajevo, 1950. 152 p. (DLC)

1525 Zakon za pravata i dolžnostite, izborot i otpovikuvanjeto na narodnite pratenici na narodno sobranie (Law on the Election and Recall of Representatives to the Assembly of the PR of Macedonia). Skopje, 1958. 137 p. (DLC)

1526 Izbornite zakoni za izbor pratenici na Narodnoto sabranie na NRM i za izbor odbornici na narodnite odbori (Laws on the Election of Representatives to the National Assembly of the PR of Macedonia and of Members of People's Committees). Skopje, 1953. 211 p. (DLC)

1527 Zakon za izbor na odbornici na narodnite odbori (Law on the Election of Members of the People's Committees). Skopje, 1948. 34 p. (DLC)

1528 Odluka o pravima i dužnostima, izboru i opozivu narodnih poslanika Narodne Skupštine Autonomne Pokrajine Vojvodine (Decree on the Election and Recall of Representatives to the National Assembly of the Autonomous Region of Voyvodina). Novi Sad, 1953. 77 p. (DLC)

1529 Zakon o izboru narodnih poslanika za Narodnu skupštinu i Zakon o biračkim spiskovima sa autentičnim tumačenjima (Law on the Election of Representatives to the National Assembly and Law on Voters' Lists, Annotated). Beograd, 1938. 110 p. (DLC)

1530 Zakon o izboru narodnih poslanika za Narodnu skupštinu Kraljevine Srba Hrvata i Slovenaca (Law on the Election of Representatives to the National Assembly of the Kingdom of the Serbs, Croats and Slovenes). Beograd, 1922. 32 p. (DLC)

1531 Zakon o volilnih imenikih. Zakon o volitvah narodnih poslancev za narodno skupščino (Law on Voters' List. Law on the Election of Representatives to the National Assembly). Ljubljana, 1931. 47 p. (DLC)

1532 Zakon o biračkim spiskovima i zakon o izboru narodnih poslanika za narodnu skupštinu, sa tumačenjima ministarstva i obrascima izdatim od strane Ministarstva unutrašnjih Poslova (Law on Voters' Lists and Law on the Election of People's Representatives to the National Assembly). Beograd, G. Kon, 1931. 90 p. (DLC)

1533 Zakon o izboru narodnih poslanika za narodnu skupštinu sa zakonom o biračkim spiskovima i uputstvima (Law on the Election of People's Representatives to the National Assembly). 3d ed. Beograd, 1927. 113 p. (DLC)

1534 Zakon o izboru narodnih poslanika za ustavotvornu skupštinu Kraljevine Srba, Hrvata i Slovenaca (Law on the Election of People's Representatives to the Constitutional Assembly of the Kingdom of Serbs, Croats and Slovenes). Beograd, 1920. 134 p. (DLC)

1535 Privremeni zakon o izborima članova narodnoga predstavništva (Temporary Law on the Election of Members of the National Assembly). Beograd, 1901. 105 p. (DLC)

1536 Saborski izbori. Zakoni o zaštiti sloboda izbora, o izbornome redu i o uredjenju Sabora (Elections of Croatian National Assembly). Zagreb, 1908. 64 p. (DLC)

1537 Zakoni ob izbornom redu i ob uredjenju sabora kraljevinah Dalmacije, Hrvatske i Slavonije (Law on the Election and Organization of the National Assembly of the Kingdoms of Dalmatia, Croatia and Slavonia). Zagreb, 1892. 52 p. (DLC)

1538 Zakon o izborima narodnijeh poslanika Crne Gore (Law on the Election of Members of the National Assembly of Montenegro). Cetinje, 1907. 30 p. (DLC)

1539 Zakon za izbor zemaljskog poslanika u Ugarskoj osim Erdelja (Law on the Election of the Representative of Voyvodina in Hungary). Novi Sad, 1875. 36 p. (DLC)

1540 Derenčin, Marijan. Izborna reforma (Election Reform). Zagreb, 1899. 140 p.

1541 Djordjević, Jovan. Komentar zakona o pravima i dužnostima, izboru i opozivu saveznih narodnih poslanika (Commentary on the Law on the Election and Recall of People's Representatives to the National Assembly). Beograd, 1953. 307 p. (DLC)

1542 Kostić, Laza M. (a) Zakon o izboru senatora od 30 septembra 1931 sa komentarom (Law on the Election of Senators of September 30, 1931 Annotated). Beograd, 1938. 278 p.; (b) Statistika izbora narodnih poslanika Kraljevine SHS, održanih 18 marta 1923 (Statistics Concerning the Election of Representatives of the Kingdom of the S.C.S. of March 18, 1923). Beograd, 1923.

1543 Kangrga, Milenko. Gradjanin u izborima (The Role of Citizens in the Elections). Beograd, 1953. 22 p. (DLC)

1544 Perić, Živojin. Političko izborno pravo u Bosni i Herzegovini

(Election Law in Bosnia and Herzegovina). Reprint from *Narod*. Mostar, 1908. 28 p.

1545 Polić, Ladislav. Izborni zakon za Narodnu skupštinu (Election Law for the National Assembly). Zagreb, 1927. 105 p.

1546 Protić, Božidar. Zakon o biračkim spiskovima i zakon o izboru narodnih poslanika za narodnu skupštinu, sa uputstvima (Law on Voters' Lists. Law on the Election of Representatives to the National Assembly Annotated). 2nd ed. Beograd, 1927. 136 p.

1547 Rašić, Voj. Biračko pravo (Voters' Rights). Beograd, 1905.

1548 Ristić, Živojin. Izborni zakoni Srbije. Doktorska teza (Election Laws in Serbia. Doctoral Thesis). Beograd, 1935. 183 p.

1549 Soški, Luka. Zakon za zaštitu slobode izbora od 1 ožujka 1907 (Law of March 1, 1907 Protecting Free Elections). Zagreb, 1907. 56 p. (DLC)

1550 Tasić, Djordje. Žensko pravo glasa i demokratija (Women's Right to Vote and Democracy). Beograd, 1921. 51 p.

1551 Veljović, Radul. Statistički pregled izbora narodnih poslanika za 1903, 1905, 1906, i 1908 godinu (Statistical Review of the Election of Representatives in 1903, 1905, 1906, and 1908). Beograd, Izdanje Narodne Skupštine, 1910.

15 Finance and Taxation

See also Nos.: 2274; 2306; 2357; 2358; 2390; 2402.

a Budget

1552 Dakić, Strahinja. Budžetski sistem FNRJ (Budgetary System of the FPRY). Beograd, 1951. 166 p. (DLC)

1553 Dakić, Strahinja, *editor*. Osnovni zakon o budžetima sa komentarom (Basic Law on Budgets, annotated). Beograd, 1956. 168 p.

1554 Dakić, Strahinja *and* Slobodan Turčinović, *editors*. Zakon o budžetima sa ostalim propisima o finansiranju državnih organa (Law on Budgets with Regulations on Financing of Government Agencies). Beograd, 1953. 195 p. (DLC)

1555 Guć, Nedeljko, *editor*. Zbirka propisa o budžetima i ustanovama sa samostalnim financiranjem (Collection of Provisions on Budgets and Institutions with Independent Financing). Zagreb, 1956. 198 p. (DLC)

1556 Uputstva za izvršenje budžeta (Directions for the Execution of the Budget by the National Bank of the FPRY). Beograd, 1954. 188 p. (DLC)

1557 Budžet Federativne Narodne Republike Jugoslavije, 1951, 1955, 1956, 1957 i 1958 (Budget of the FPRY, 1951, 1955, 1956, 1957 and 1958). (DLC)

1558 Predlog budžeta FNRJ (Draft of the Budget of the FPRY). Beograd, 1951–53, 1957. (DLC)

1559 Ekspozei o budžetu FNRJ za 1951 godinu (Presentation of the Budget for 1951 by Josip Broz-Tito, Edvard Kardelj, Boris Kidrič, D. Radosavljević). Beograd, 1951. 76 p. (DLC)

1560 Zakon o opštedržavnom završnom računu za godinu (Law on the Final General Audit of the Government). Beograd. (DLC: 1948, 1949, 1950)

1561 Predlog zakona o završnom računu o izvršenju budžeta FNRJ za godinu . . . (Draft of the Law on the Final Audit Concerning the Execution of the Budget for the Year). Beograd. (DLC: 1957)

1562 Budžet. Finansijski zakon za . . . Državnih rashoda i prihoda kraljevine SHS. Vrhovna državna uprava . . . ministarstva . . . za . . . (Budget. Financial Law for . . . Budget of Appropriations and Expenditures of the Kingdom SCS. Supreme Government Administration . . . Ministries in [varying numbers for each year] . . . for . . .). Beograd, 17 v. (DLC: 1920/21, 1922/23, 1924/25, 1926/27, 1929/30, 1932/33,—1934/35, 1936/37—1939/40)

1563 Predlog Finansijskog zakona za . . . godinu. Predlog budžeta državnih prihoda kraljevine SHS . . . Predlog budžeta rashoda . . . Vrhovna državna uprava ministarstva . . . (Draft of the Financial Law for . . . Draft of the Budget on the Government Appropriations of the Kingdom of the SCS . . . Draft of the Budget for Expenditures . . . Supreme Government Administration. Ministries . . .). Sarajevo and Beograd. (DLC: 1922, 1926/27)

1564 Budžetska debata. Ekspozeji i govori (Budget Debate. Exposés and Speeches). Beograd, 1949. 238 p. (DLC)

1565 Kostić, Laza and Adam Maksimović, editors. Zbornik finansijskih zakona od 1919 do 1939/40 godnu (Collection of Financial Laws, 1919–1940). Novi Sad, 1940. 990 p. (DLC)

1566 Uredba o prenosu kredita predvidjenih u državnom budzetu za . . . godinu na Banovinu Hrvatsku . . . (Decree Transferring Credits Appropriated in the Budget for . . . to the *Banovina* of Croatia). Sarajevo, 1939. 147 p. (DLC)

1567 Uputstva za izvršenje budžeta državnih rashoda i prihoda za . . . godinu (Directions for the Execution of the Budget on Government Appropriations and Expenditures for . . .). Beograd. (DLC: 1937/38)

1568 Todorović, Randjel V. Budžet, sastav i izvršenje prava, dužnosti i odgovornosti naredbodavaca . . . (Budget Draft, Rights and Duties Delegated to Agencies). Beograd, 1930. 605 p. (DLC)

1569 Završni račun državnih prihoda i rashoda Kraljevine Srbije za . . . godinu (Final Audit of Government Appropriations and Expenditures for the Kingdom of Serbia for . . .). Beograd. (DLC: 1905, 1912)

1570 Zakon o državnom budžetu (Law on the Budget for Montenegro). Cetinje, 1906. 26 p. (DLC)

1571 Propisi i tehnička uputstva za II narodni zajam . . . (Provisions and Directions for the Second People's Loan). Beograd, 1950. 32 p. (DLC)

1572 Djinić, Božidar, *editor*. Zbirka propisa o doprinosu za stambenu izgradnju (Collection of Provisions on Building Construction). Beograd, 1956. 103 p. (Nova Administracija, sv. 60). (DLC)

b Budget Office

1573 Zakon o državnom računovodstvu (Law on the Governmental Budget Office). 5th ed. Beograd, 1932. 294 p. (Zbirka zakona, sv. 25). (DLC)

1574 Uredba o državnom računovodstvu (Decree on the Governmental Budget Office). Beograd, 1941. 114 p. (DLC)

1575 Pravilnik o izvršenju uredbe o državnom računovodstvu od 10. marta 1941 (Regulation on the Enforcement of the Decree on the Governmental Budget Office). Beograd, 1941. 160 p. (DLC)

1576 Sagadin, Stevan. Ugovori i nabavke prema Zakonu o državnom računovodstvu (Contracts and Acquisitions According to the Law on the Government Budget Office). Reprint from Spomenica Mauroviću. Beograd, 1934. 24 p.

1577 Todorović, Ran. V. Objašnjenje i izvršenje zakona o državnom računovodstvu (Enforcement of the Law on the Government Budget Office, Annotated). Beograd, 1926. 507 p. (DLC)

1578 Zakon o državnoj kontroli od 5. januara 1949 (Law on the Comptroller General's Office of January 5, 1949). 3rd ed. Beograd, 1950. 70 p. (DLC)

1579 Ilić, Mihailo, editor. Zakon o Glavnoj kontroli (Law on the Comptroller General's Office). Beograd, 1926. 169 p. (DLC); 1929. 170 p. (Zbirka zakona, sv. 19) (DLC); 1931. 75 p. (Zbirka zakona, sv. 112). (DLC)

1580 Popović, Alek., editor. Odluke Glavne Kontrole Kraljevine SHS, i zakonodavstvo o Glavnoj Kontroli (Decisions of the Comptroller General of the Kingdom SCS and Legislation on the Comptroller General's Office). Beograd, 1926. 328 p.

1581 Stjepanović, Nikola. Opšta teorija o Glavnoj Kontroli Kraljevine Jugoslavije (General Principles of the Comptroller General's Office). Beograd, 1938. 153 p.; 2nd ed. 1938. 180 p. (DLC)

1582 Zakon o organizaciji finansijske kontrole (Law on Governmental Accounting). 2nd ed. Beograd, 1926. 255 p. (Zbirka zakona, sv 15). (DLC)

1583 Radovanović, Ljub., editor. Zakon o organizaciji Finansijske Kontrole od 28. februara 1922 (Law on the Organization of Governmental Accounting). Beograd, 1937. 530 p. (DLC)

1584 Zakon o organizaciji finansijske uprave (Law to Organize the Office of Financial Policy Management). Beograd, 1930. 94 p. (Zbirka zakona, sv. 32). (DLC); 1937. 175 p. (Zbirka zakona, sv. 7). (DLC)

1585 Finansijska služba za 1924–1928 godinu (Employment in Fiscal Offices for 1924–1928). Beograd, 1924–1928. 5 v. (DLC)

1586 Petrović, Mita. Finansije i ustanove obnovljene Srbije do 1842 s jednim pogledom na raniji istorijski razvoj finansiskog uredjenja u Srbiji (Finances and Reorganization of Serbian Agencies up to 1842). Beograd, 1897–1899. 3 v.

c Taxation

1587 Zakon o porezima sa ostalim poreskim propisima (Law on Taxation and Regulations). Beograd, 1947. 110 p. (DLC); 4th ed. Beograd, 1948. 167 p. (DLC); 5th ed. Beograd, 1949. 326 p. (DLC)

1588　Šćekić, Mihailo, *editor.* (a) Zbirka propisa o porezima (Collection of Provisions on Taxation). Beograd, 1956. 488 p. (DLC); (b) Zakon o porezu na nasledja i porezu na poklone (Law on Inheritance and Gift Taxes). Beograd, 1955. 52 p. (DLC)

1589　Uredba o prinudnoj naplati poreza (Decree on the Compulsory Collection of Taxes). Beograd, 1953. 88 p. (DLC)

1590　Milatović, Sava, *editor.* Uredba o porezu na dohodak (Decree on Income Tax). Beograd, 1954. 175 p. (DLC)

1591　Tonić, Bogoljub, *editor.* (a) Zbirka propisa o porezu na promet (Collection of Sales Tax Provisions). 3d ed. Beograd, 1955. 159 p. (DLC); 4th ed. 1956. 183 p. (DLC); (b) Uredba o porezu na promet (Decree on the Sales Tax). Beograd, 1954. 55 p. (DLC); 2nd ed. 1954. 80 p. (DLC)

1592　Zakon sa pravilnikom o neposrednim porezima (Law on Direct Taxation and Regulation). Beograd, 1928. 336 p. (DLC)

1593　Zakon o neposrednom porezu (Law on Direct Taxation). 2nd ed. Beograd, 1927. 105 p. (Zbirka zakona, sv. 3) (DLC); 1928. 114 p. (Zbirka zakona, sv. 91). (DLC)

1594　Privremeni zakon o državnoj trošarini od 27 juna 1921. (Temporary Law on Excise Tax). Zagreb, 1921? 238 p. (DLC)

1595　Biljegovni i pristojbeni zakon za Bosnu i Hercegovinu. Objavljen 31 jula 1886 (Law on Stamp Fees for Bosnia and Herzegovina of July 31, 1886). Sarajevo, 1886. 139 p. (DLC)

1596　Dukanac, Ljubomir S. Osnovni problemi porezivanja (Basic Problems of Taxation). Beograd, 1938. 339 p. (DLC)

1597　Jocković, Aleksandar. Uput za naplatu službeničkog poreza i prireza (Instruction for the Collection of Payroll Taxes). 2nd ed. Beograd, 1941. 130 p. (DLC)

1598　Kocian, Samuel. (a) Biljegovina i pristojbe (Stamp Fees). Zagreb, 1889. 460 p. (Hrvatski zakoni, XIII); (b) Zakoni i propisi o izravnih porezih, priručnik (Laws and Provisions on Direct Taxation. Manual). Zagreb, 1888. 863 p. (DLC)

1599　Lunaček, Valdemar *and* Mate Škarić, *editors.* Zbornik zakona o neposrednim porezima (Collection of Laws on Direct Taxation). Zagreb, 1931. 973 p. (Zakoni Kraljevine Jugoslavije, knj. X). (DLC)

1600　Nikolić, Djuradj. Društveni porez u Kraljevini Jugoslaviji (Corporate Tax). Beograd, 1934. 115 p. (DLC)

1601 Spasojević, Voj. St. *and* Voj. J. Božanović, *editors*. Poreski zbornik; zakon sa pravilnikom o neposrednim porezim (Handbook on Taxation; Law on Direct Taxation and its Regulation). Beograd, 1931. 589 p. (DLC)

1602 Sušec, Štefan, *editor*. (a) Zakon o neposrednih davkih z dne 8. februarja 1928 (Law on Direct Taxation of February 8, 1928). Ljubljana, 1935. 552 p. (DLC); (b) Zakon o državni trošarini s trošarinskim pravilnikom in komentarjem (Excise Tax Law and its Regulation, annotated). Ljubljana, 1939. 372 p. (DLC); (c) Takse (Taxes). Ljubljana, 1937–1940. 3 v. (DLC)

1603 Šćekić, Mihailo V. *and* Mile Mikić, *editors*. (a) Poreski zakoni sa komentarom (Laws on Taxation, annotated). Beograd, 1933. 704 p. (DLC); 2nd ed. 1940. 975 p. (DLC); (b) Poreski zbornik sa komentarom (Tax Law Collection, annotated). Beograd, 1938. 756 p. (DLC)

1604 Šijan, Dušan *and* Dušan Letica, *editors*. Izravni porezi i nameti, biljezi i pristojbe u Bosni i Hercegovini (Direct Taxation and Stamp Fees in Bosnia and Herzegovina). Mitrovica, 1910. 162 p. (DLC)

1605 Trivanović, Gaja *and* Marin Puharić. Zbornik propisa o porezu na poslovni promet sa komentarom (Collection of Provisions on the Sales Tax, annotated). Beograd, 1940. 800 p. (DLC)

1606 Žilić, Franjo *and* Miroslav Šantek, *editors*. Propisi o nasljednoj i darovnoj taksi (Provisions on Inheritance and Gift Taxes). Zagreb, 1938. 91 p. (DLC)

1607 Radulović, Jovan M., *editor*. (a) Zbirka svih propisa o taksama sa objašnjenjima (Collection of All Provisions on Taxes, annotated). Beograd, 1956. (DLC); 3d ed. Beograd, 1958. 471 p.; (b) Zakon o taksama i propisi o opštinskim taksama (Law on Fees and Provisions Concerning Local Taxation). Beograd, 1955. 182 p. (Biblioteka Novo Zakonodavstvo II, knj. 2). (DLC)

1608 Djinić, Božidar, *editor*. (a) Zbirka propisa o taksama (Collection of Provisions on Taxes). Beograd, 1955. 214 p.; (b) Nove tarife o taksama: tarifa zakona o taksama i tarifa o sudskim taksama (New Tariffs on Taxes and Court Fees). Beograd, 1952. 112 p. (DLC); 2nd ed. 1952. 120 p. (DLC); (c) Takse (Taxes). Zagreb, 1960. 268 p.

1609   Priručnik o sudskim taksama (Manual on Court Fees). Zagreb, 1950. 59 p. (DLC)

1610   Zakon o taksama sa komentarom (Law on Taxation, annotated). 5th ed. Beograd, 1949. 113 p. (Zbirka propisa iz oblasti finansija, br. 2). (DLC)

1611   Zakon o taksama (Law on Taxation). Beograd, 1932. 249 p. (DLC)

1612   Pravilnik za izvršenje zakona o taksama (Regulation for the Enforcement of Taxes). Beograd, 1924. 349 p. (DLC); 2nd ed. 1933. 326 p. (DLC)

1613   Kocijan, Samuel, editor. Tumač i riječnik uredovnoj zbirci zakona i propisa o biljegovini i pravnoj pristojbi (Commentary of and Dictionary for the Official Collection of Laws and Provisions on Stamp Fees). Zagreb, 1908. 756 p. (DLC)

1614   Mihalinović, Franjo and Josif Trtanj, editors. Zakon o sudskim taksama (Law on Court Fees). Sarajevo, 1930. 75 p.

1615   Oglar. Davčno-sodni trgovsko-pisarniški praktični priročnik za vsakogar (Practical Handbook on Taxation). Ljubljana, 1935. 430 p. (DLC)

1616   Pavlič, Bogumil and Frank Mahkovec, editors. Zakon o taksah (Law on Taxation). Ljubljana, 1932. 199 p. (DLC)

1617   Petrović, Petar I., Rad. Marinković and Drag. Pavlović, editors. Zakon o taksama (Law on Taxation). Beograd, 1932. 727 p. (DLC)

1618   Lovčević, Jov. Porezi. Posebni deo. Poreski sistem FNRJ (Taxation. Special Part. Tax System of the FPRY). Beograd, 1950. 242 p. (DLC)

1619   Radovanović, Radomir. Poreski sistem (Tax System). Beograd, 1953. 123 p. (DLC)

d   Customs

1620   Živković, Sreten and Milutin Popović, Carinski priručnik (Handbook on Customs Duties). Beograd, 1957. 169 p. (DLC)

1621   Carinski Zakon od 23 januara 1899 godine (Law on Customs Duties of January 23, 1899). Beograd, 1920. 55 p. (DLC)

1622   Komentar carinske tarife (Commentary on Customs Tariffs). Beograd, 1920. 1048 p. (DLC)

1623   Borisavljević, Petar, *editor*. Predlog zakona o opštoj carinskoj tarifi (Draft of the Law on the General Customs Tariff). Beograd-Zemun, 1927. 810 p. (DLC)

1624   Gospodnetić, Franjo *and* Konrad Šmid, *editors*. Opšta carinska tarifa (General Customs Tariff). Zagreb, 1923. 540 p. (DLC); 1925. 298 p. (DLC).

1625   Ivanović, Milan K. Studije za carinsko pravo (Study on Customs Duty Laws). Zagreb, 1938. 183 p. (DLC)

1626   Prpić, Dragutin, Slobodan Sterdjević *and* Dragomir Stojković, *editors*. Predlog zakona o opštoj carinskoj tarifi, sa uvoznim i izvoznim carinama (Draft of the Law on the General Customs Tariff and Import and Export Duties). Beograd, 1940. 573 p. (DLC)

1627   Radovanović, Ljub., *editor*. Carinski zbornik Kraljevine Jugoslavije (Manual on Customs Duty of the Kingdom of Yugoslavia). Beograd, 1934. 1364 p. (DLC)

1628   Radulović, Jovan S. *and* Vladimir L. Ristić, *editors*. Carinski godišnjak Kraljevine Jugoslavije (Yearbook on Customs Duties of the Kingdom of Yugoslavia). Beograd, 1936. 1000 p. (DLC)

1629   Carinski zakon sa ekspozeom Nikole Minčeva i registrom (Law on Customs Duties. Exposé by Nikola Minčev. Registry). Beograd, 1959. 82 p. (DLC)

1630   Stojanović, Josif K., Vlada Dr. Stojanović *and* Milorad D. Sokolović, *editors*. Carinski zakon (Law on Customs Duties). Beograd, 1920. 411 p. (DLC)

1630[1]   Uredba o privremenoj općoj carinskoj tarifi . . . za robu koji gradjani uvoze odnose unose iz inozenostva (A Decree Concerning the Temporary General Customs Tariff . . . on Goods Imported by Citizens from Abroad). Beograd, 1961. 214 p. (DLC)

e   Monopolies

1631   Zakon o državnim monopolima (Law on Government Monopolies). Beograd, 1932. 61 p. (Zbirka finansijskih zakona, sv. 38) (DLC); 70 p. (Zbirka zakona, sv. 52). (DLC)

1632   Monopolski zakoni (Monopoly Laws). Beograd, 1923. 2 v. (Zbirka zakona, sv. 26–27). (DLC)

1633 Zakoni o konversiji državnih dugova, Uredba o samostalnoj monopolskoj upravi, o monopolu duvana; o monopolu soli, o ustanovljenju novih državnih monopola (Laws on Conversion of Public Debts; Decree on Independent Monopoly Administration; Salt Monopoly; Creation of New Government Monopolies). Beograd, 1926. 151 p. (DLC)

1634 Devečerski, Živ. St., *editor.* Uredba o samostalnoj upravi državnih monopola Kraljevine Jugoslavije (Decree on the Independent Administration of Government Monopolies). Beograd, 1933. 160 p. (DLC)

16 Forensic Medicine

See also No. 984.

1635 Čoporda, Milivoj. Sudska veterinarska medicina (Forensic Veterinary Medicine). Beograd, 1950. 404 p. (DLC)

1636 Gerasimović, D. Sudska Medicina. Knjiga prva (Forensic Medicine. Book I). Beograd, 1888–1890. 3 v.

1637 Jevtić, Dušan M. (a) Sudska psihijatrija (Forensic Psychiatry). Beograd, 1951. 348 p. (DLC); (b) Sudska psihopatologija (Forensic Psychopathology). 2nd ed. Beograd, 1960. 552 p.

1638 Jovanović, Milan. Manual Sudskog lekarstva za pravnike (Handbook on Forensic Medicine for Lawyers). Beograd, 1868. 224 p.

1639 Medović, Aćim. Državno lekarstvo za pravnike i lekare. Deo prvi (Legal Medicine for Lawyers and Physicians. Part 1). Beograd, 1866. 443 p.

1640 Milovanović, Milovan. Sudska medicina (Forensic Medicine). Beograd, 1926. 302 p. (DLC); 1960. 408 p.

1641 Pešić, Svetozar. Sudska medicina (Forensic Medicine). Zagreb, 1919; 2d ed. Beograd, 1921. 378 p. (DLC)

1642 Vasić, Milan V. Iz Sudske Medicine i javne higijene (Forensic Medicine and Public Health). Beograd, 1893. 165 p.

1642[1] Winterhalter, Mato. Sudsko veterinarstvo. Pravni i opći dio (Forensic Veterinary Medicine. Legal and General Part). Zagreb, Slavonski Brod, 1961. 85 p. Mimeographed.

17 Government Arbitration and Economic Courts

See also Nos.: 201; 202; 2280.

1643 Zakon o privrednim sudovima (Law on Economic Courts). Beograd, 1954. 43 p. (DLC)

1644 Srzentić, Nikola, *editor.* Zakon o privrednim sudovima sa objašnjenjima (Law on Economic Courts and Commentary). Beograd, 1956. 74 p. (DLC)

1645 Zakon o državnoj arbitraži (Law on Government Arbitration). 1st ed.?; 2d ed. 1949. 68 p. (DLC); 3d ed. 1950. 92 p. (DLC)

1646 Zakon o rešavanju imovinskih sporova putem državne arbitraže, od 12 decembra 1946 (Law Settling Property Controversies by Government Arbitration, Dec. 12, 1946). Beograd, 1947. 100 p. (Zbirka zakona FNRJ, br. 62)

1647 Propisi o radu arbitražnih vještaka i popis vještaka za NRH za 1952 godinu (Provisions Concerning the Work of Experts in Arbitration Cases and List of Experts of the PRC for 1952). Zagreb, 1952. 120 p. (DLC)

1648 Goldštajn A. Neki problem pravosudja—privredno sudstvo (A Problem in the Administration of Justice—Economic Courts). *Arhiv,* 1954: 382–398. (DLC)

1649 Šmit, Vladimir. Zadružne organizacije pred privrednim sudovima. Priručnik (Cooperative Organizations before Economic Courts. Manual). Zagreb, 1957. 168 p. (DLC)

1650 Zuglia, S. Rješavanje imovinskih sporova putem državne arbitraže (Settlement of Property Disputes by Government Arbitration). *In* Zbornik Pravnog Fakulteta u Zagrebu, 1948: 299–331.

18 Inheritance

See also Nos.: 771; 1351; 2260b; 2292; 2319f; 2319i; 2319r; 2425e; 2435.

1651 Zakon o nasledjivanju, sa objašnjenjima i napomenama (Inheritance Law, annotated). Beograd, 1955. 206 p. (DLC)

1652 Zakon o zadužbinama (Law on Trust Estates). Beograd, 1927. 31 p. (DLC)

1653 Arandjelović, Dragoljug. (a) Nasledno pravo s naročitim obzirom na gradjanski zakonik Kraljevine Srbije (Inheritance Law with Special Reference to the Serbian Civil Code). Beograd, 1925. 176 p.; (b) O izjednačenju muških i ženskih srodnika u zakonskom nasledjivanju (Equal Status for Male and Female Relatives as Intestate Heirs). Beograd, 1925. 13 p.

1654   Arandjelović, D. and M. Begović. Nasledno pravo (Inheritance Law). Beograd, 1940. 207 p.

1655   Bakić, V. Nasledno-pravni položaj vanbračnog deteta (Inheritance of Illegitimate Children). Anali, 1954: 266–280.

1656   Blagojević, B.T. (a) Nasledno pravo FNRJ (Inheritance Law of the FPRY). Beograd, 1955. 436 p. (DLC); 2d ed. 1958. 399 p. 3rd ed. 1960. 399 p. (DLC); (b) Osnov prava nasledja (Foundation of the Right of Inheritance). Branič, 1935: 173–183, 238–244; (c) Zakonsko nasledjivanje u svojini izmedju bračnih drugova (Intestate Inheritance of Property among Spouses). Arhiv, 1939: 222–237; (d) Nasledno-pravni položaj usvojenih lica (Inheritance Status of Adopted Persons). Pravosudje, 1940: 262–273; (e) Nasledjivanje kod zadužbina (Inheritance of Trust Estates). Pravosudje, 1940: 297–305.

1657   Bušatlić, Hafiz Abdulah. Porodično i nasljedno pravo Muslimana (Domestic Relations and Inheritance Law of Moslems). Sarajevo, 1926. 189 p. (DLC)

1658   Cemović, M. Krvna srpska zajednica i neravnopravnost odiva po srpskom naslednom pravu (Blood Relationship and Discrimination against Female Relatives in the Serbian Inheritance Law). Arhiv, 1907: 7–20.

1659   Danić, D. Intestatsko nasledno pravo (Intestate Inheritance Law). Beograd, 1933. 81 p.

1660   Djordjević, A. (a) Nasledno pravo (Inheritance Law). Beograd, 1904. 156 p.; (b) Nasledno pravo Kraljevine Srbije (Serbian Inheritance Law). Beograd, 1910. 136 p.

1661   Djurković, Evg. Pravo nasledija za obšću slaveno-serbskago u madjarskoj naroda polzu sočineno i izdano (Inheritance Law of the Serbs of Hungary). Budim, 1823. 221 p.

1662   Farkas, Lj. Materijalno i formalno pravo u ostavinskim stvarima u Bosni i Hercegovini (Substantive and Procedural Inheritance Law in Bosnia and Herzegovina). Mjesečnik, 1910: 22–32, 121–137, 205–216, 325–342, 400–416, 515–527, 592–604.

1663 Finžgar, A. (a) Dedno pravo (Inheritance Law). Ljubljana, 1953. 114 p.; (b) Pridobitev dediščine (Acceptance of Inheritance). *Pravnik,* 1956: 145–157.; (c) Zbirka razprav iz dednega prava (A Collection of Writings on Inheritance Law). Ljubljana, 1960. 153 p.

1664 Jovanović, M. Pravo reprezentacije u nasledju (Representation in Inheritance Law). Beograd, 1924. 74 p.

1665 Krstić, Dj. Nasledje na seoskim dobrima (Inheritance of Peasant Property). *Arhiv,* 1929: 178–188, 265–282, 346–358. (DLC)

1666 Marković, L. Nasledno pravo (Inheritance Law). Beograd, 1930. 392 p. (DLC)

1667 Matanović, A. Nasledno običajno pravo u Crnoj Gori (Customary Inheritance Law of Montenegro). *Arhiv,* 1928: 349–358, 461–468. (DLC)

1668 Miljković, Dušan Lj. Ugovori o nasledjivanju (Inheritance Contracts). Beograd, 1913. 30 p.

1669 Milovanović, M. Intestatsko nasledno pravo (Law on intestate Succession). Beograd, 1884. 54 p. (DLC)

1670 Nedeljković, B. (a) Porodica i nasledstvo (Family and Inheritance). *Arhiv,* 1940: 8–26. (DLC); (b) Prvenstvo muških srodnika nad ženskim u srpskom nasljednom pravu (Precedence of Male over Female Relatives in Serbian Inheritance Law). *Pravna misao,* 1940: 430–451.

1671 Nestorović, Dj. B. Kako se piše testament po našem Gradjanskom Zakoniku (How to Draw a Will under the Serbian Civil Code). Beograd, 1898. 44 p.

1672 Perić, Živojin M. Zadružno nasledno pravo po Gradjanskom zakoniku Kr. Srbije (Inheritance Law of Family Communities under the Serbian Civil Code). Beograd, 1913. 174 p. (DLC)

1673 Ćosić, Filip. Braća i sestre kao nužni naslednici (Brothers and Sisters as Forced Heirs). *Pravni Život* (Beograd) No. 2, 1962: 48–55. (DLC)

1674 Silajdžić, Alija O. (a) Testamenat u šeriatskom pravu (Wills in Sheriat Law). Sarajevo, 1941. 136 p. (DLC); (b) Nasljedno pravo (Inheritance Law). Sarajevo, 1959. 112 p.

1675 Škuljić, Abdulah. Šeriatsko nasljedno pravo (Sheriat Inheritance Law). Sarajevo, 1941. 115 p. (DLC)

1676   Stojanović, Marko. (a) Može li pisac testamenta biti svedok testamenta? (Can a Person Employed as Scribe of a Will be a Testamentary Witness?). Beograd, 1880. 66 p.; (b) Zakoni red nasledja po Gradjanskom Zakoniku za Kraljevinu Srbiju (Intestate Succession under the Serbian Civil Code). Beograd, 1870; 2d ed. 1897. 49 p.

1677   Leskovic, Stanislav. Stvarno dedno in zemljiško knjižno pravo (Inheritance of Realty and Land Registry Law). 2nd ed. Ljubljana, 1959. 108 p.

1678   Tomović, B. Nasledno običajno pravo u Crnoj Gori (Montenegrin Customary Inheritance Law). Beograd, 1926. 118 p. (DLC)

1679   Bogišić V. Nasledno i porodično pravo u Crnoj Gori (Inheritance Law and Domestic Relations in Montenegro). *Pravni Zbornik,* 1936: 36–45.

19   Judicial System

See also: Ch. 11, A, 2i.

a   The Bar

See also No. 2360.

1680   Zakon o advokaturi od 10 aprila 1957 godine (Law on Attorneys of April 10, 1957). Beograd, 1957. 72 p. (DLC)

1681   Program za polaganje stručnog ispita u pravnoj struci sa objašnjenjima i literaturom (Program for Taking Professional Examinations in the Legal Branch with Annotations and Literature). Beograd, 1951. 46 p. (DLC)

1682   Ilić, Mihailo, *editor.* Zakon o advokatima za kraljevinu SHS (Law on Attorneys of the Kingdom of Yugoslovia). Beograd, 1929. 80 p. (DLC); 1929. 60 p. (DLC) ; 2d ed. 1929. 77 p. (DLC)

1683   Niketić, Gojko, *editor.* Zakon o advokatima od 17 marta 1929 (Law on Attorneys of March 17, 1929). 2d ed. Beograd, 1929. 77 p. (DLC)

1684   Živadinović, Milan Ž., *editor.* Zakon o advokatima (Law on Attorneys). Beograd, 1941. 752 p.

1685   Prvi Kongres Pravnika Jugoslavije (First Convention of

Yugoslav Lawyers Held from October 3 to 6, 1954 in Belgrade). Beograd, 1954. 35 p. (DLC)

1686   Jovanović, Stojan. Spomenica sedme glavne skupštine kongresa pravnika Kraljevine Jugoslavije u Beogradu dana 22–24 septembra 1935 (Commemorative Volume of the Seventh Convention of Yugoslav Lawyers Held from September 22 to 24, 1935). Beograd, 1935.

1687   Ugovor o socijalnom osiguranju advokata od 28. dec. 1959 godine. Pravilnik o vodjenju poslovnih knjiga advokata (Lawyers' Social Security Contracts of December 28, 1959. Regulation Concerning Lawyers' Business Books). Novi Sad, 1960. 12 p.

1688   Šilović, Josip, editor. Spomen-knjiga na proslavu dvadetpetgodišnjice obstanka Pravničkog društva u Zagrebu, dana 3. ožujka 1900 (Commemorative Volume on the 25th Anniversary of the Lawyers' Association at Zagreb on March 3, 1900). Zagreb, 1900. 178 p. (DLC)

1689   Cenić, Dj. D. Mogu li pensionari biti pravozastupnici? (May Retired Persons Practice Law?). Beograd, 1881. 29 p. (DLC)

1690   Jovanović, Vasa I. O advokaturi (The Legal Profession). Beograd, 1921. 16 p.

1691   Jurašić, Ivan. Narodni hrvatski odvjetnik (The Croatian Attorney). Rijeka, 1878. 645 p. (DLC)

1692   Hinković, Dr. Odvjetnički red od 24 srpnja 1852 (Decree on Attorneys of July 24, 1852). Zagreb, 1883. 66 p. (DLC)

1693   Nešić, Milutin. O srpskom pravništvu (The Serbian Lawyer). Beograd, 1905. 32 p. (DLC)

b   Courts and Public Prosecutors

See also: Special Topics: Government Arbitration and Economic Courts; Nos.: 2319w; 2339a; 2368; 2372; 2411; 2429; 2439; 2441a.

1694   Sodstvo. Organizacijski zakoni in drugi predpisi (Judiciary. Laws on Organization and other Provisions). Ljubljana, 1957. 268 p. (DLC)

1695   Zakon o sudovima sa objašnjenjima (Law on Courts with Notes). Beograd, 1954. 70 p. (DLC)

1696   Srzentić, Nikola. Zakon o sudovima (Law on Courts). 2d ed. Beograd, 1956. 66, 73 p. (DLC)

1697 Srzentić, Nikola, Vladimir Kalember *and* Ranko Radaković. Zakon o uredjenju narodnih sudova, sa komentarom (Law on the Organization of People's Courts, annotated). Beograd, 1949. 158 p. (Zbirka zakona FNRJ, br. 12). (DLC)

1698 Uloga sudija-porotnika u našem pravosudju (Role of Judge-Assessors in our Administration of Justice). Beograd, 1948. 47 p. (DLC)

1699 Zbirka zakonitih predpisov za uporabo v kazenskem sodstvu (Collection of Laws for Use in Criminal Courts). Ljubljana, 1947. 152 p. (DLC)

1700 Zakon o sudijama redovnih sudova (Law on Judges of Regular Courts). Beograd, 1929. 40 p. (Zbirka zakona, sv. 9). (DLC)

1701 Zakon o uredjenju redovnih sudova za kraljevinu SHS od 18. januara 1929 (Law on the Organization of Regular Courts in the Kingdom of Yugoslavia of January 18, 1929). Beograd, 1929. 59 p. (Zbirka zakona sv. 1) (DLC); 1929. 48 p. (Zbirka zakona, 119). (DLC)

1702 Zakon o ureditvi rednih sodišč za kraljevino SHS (Law on the Organization of Regular Courts). Ljubljana, 1929. 96 p. (DLC)

1703 Sudsko organizaciono zakonodavstvo (Legislation on the Organization of the Judiciary). Zagreb, Themis, 1929. 328 p. (DLC)

1704 Zakon o ustanovljenju sreskih i okružnih sudova na području apelacionog suda u Beogradu (Law Establishing County and District Courts within the Jurisdiction of the Court of Appeals in Belgrade and the Court of Appeals in Skoplje). Beograd, 1931. 41 p. (DLC)

1705 Zakon o uredjenju šerijatskih sudova i o šerijatskim sudijama od 21 marta 1929 (Law on the Organization of Sheriat Courts and Sheriat Judges of March 21, 1929). Beograd, 1929. 25 p. (DLC)

1706 Jovanović, Milenko. Porota u pravosudju Jugoslavije (Jury in the Administration of Justice of Yugoslavia). Beograd, 1958. 125 p. (DLC)

1707 Jovanović, Stojan, Matijević Ivo *and* Čulinović Fedro, *editors.* Spomenica skupštine udruženja sudija (Volume Commemorating the First Convention of Yugoslav Judges Held on the 5th and 6th of June 1933). Beograd, 1933. 108 p. (DLC)

1708 Zakoni Kraljevine Srbije o ustrojstvu prvostepenih i viših sudova (Laws of the Kingdom of Serbia On the Organization of Courts of Original Jurisdiction and Higher Courts). Beograd, 1891. 146 p. (DLC)

1709 Ustrojstvo sudova za Knjažestvo Srbiju (Organization of Courts; Code of Civil Procedure and Bankruptcy Proceedings for the Principality of Serbia). Beograd, 1879. 31, 186, 67 p. (DLC)

1710 Zakon o istražnim sudijama (Law on Investigating Judges). Beograd, 1890. 11 p. (DLC)

1711 Zakon od 3 listopada 1876 o mjestnim sudovima i o postupku pred njimi (Local Courts for Small Claims and Procedure). Zagreb, 1876. 29 p. (DLC)

1712 Kranjčić, Stjepan. Zakoni o umirovljenju, o vlasti sudačkoj... (Law on Retirement, Judicial Power, Organization of Courts, and District Attorneys). Zagreb, 1892. 137 p.

1713 Osnova zakona o ustavu za sudove (Draft of Constitutional Provisions for the Judiciary in Bosnia and Herzegovina). Sarajevo, 1911. 105 p.

1714 Sudski poslovnik za sudove I i II stepena (Rules for Courts of First and Second Resort). Zagreb, 1933. 176 p. (DLC)

1715 Uredba o sodnem poslovniku za sodišča prve in druge stopnje (Rules for Courts of First and Second Resort). Ljubljana, 1933. 341 p. (DLC)

1716 Agatonović, Agoston Franjo. Uredbe o poslovnom redu za redovne krivične sudove i državna tužioštva (Decrees on Rules for Criminal Courts and District Attorneys). Zagreb, 1930. 301 p. (DLC)

1717 Niketić, Gojko, editor. Uredba o sudskom poslovniku (Decree on Rules for Courts of First and Second Resort). Beograd, 1933. 570 p. (DLC)

1718 Matijević, Ivo, editor. Sudski poslovnik (Rules for the Courts). Beograd, 1933. 892 p. (DLC)

1719 Meichsner, Eugen. Sudski poslovnik za sudove prvog i drugog stepena (Rules for Courts of First and Second Resort). Beograd, 1933. 392, 150 p. (DLC)

1720 Rušnov, Adolf, *editor.* Gradjanski sudovnik od 16 veljače 1853 i zakon o poslovnom redu sudbenih vlasti od 3 svibnja 1853 (Rules in Civil Matters). Zagreb, 1885. 125 p. (DLC)

1721 Zakon o nutrnjoj uredbi i o poslovnom redu sudbenih vlasti (Law on the Internal Organization and Rules for Courts). Zagreb, 1873. 162 p. (DLC)

1722 Brkić, Milan, *editor.* Zakon o javnom tužioštvu sa komentarom (Law on the Office of the Public Prosecutor). Beograd, 1956. 64 p. (DLC)

1723 Zakon o javnom tužioštvu sa objašnjenjima (Law on the Office of the Public Prosecutor, Annotated). Beograd, 1946. 27 p. (DLC)

1724 Sajovic, Rudolf. Javni tožilec v civilni pravdi (The Public Prosecutor in Civil Cases). Ljubljana, 1948. 33 p. (DLC)

1725 Ilić, Mihailo, *editor.* (a) Zakon o državnom tužioštvu (Law of the Public Prosecutors). Beograd, 1929. 24 p. (DLC); 1929, 30 p. (Zbirka zakona, sv. 129). (DLC); (b) Uredba o poslovnom redu za državna tužioštva (Decree on Rules for the Public Prosecutors). Beograd, 1930. 53 p. (DLC)

1726 Bayer, V. Problem sudjelovanja nepravnika u savremenom kaznenom sudovanju (Problem of Laymen Participation in the Present Administration of Justice in Criminal Cases). Zagreb, 1940.

1727 Hočevar, M. Splošni nadzor javnega tožilstva (General Supervision by the Public Prosecutor). Ljubljana, 1949. 41 p.

1728 Čubinski, Mihail Pavlović. Nove sudske reforme (New Judicial Reforms). Beograd, 1925. 109 p. (DLC)

1729 Čulinović, Ferdo. Pravosudje u Jugoslaviji (Administration of Justice in Yugoslavia). Zagreb, 1946. 285 p. (DLC)

1730 Danić, D. O sudskoj vlasti (Judicial Power). Beograd, 1932. 31 p. (DLC)

1731 Devečerski, Živan St., *editor.* Zakon o sudskim taksama (Law on Court Fees). Beograd, 1930. 182 p. (DLC)

1732 Grabnar, Drago. Priročnik za ekonomsko-finančno poslovanje pri sodiščih LRS (Manual for the Economic and Financial Operation of Courts of the PRS). Ljubljana, 1953. 452 p. (DLC)

1733 Legradić, R. *and* M. Besarović. Narodni sudovi i javno tužioštvo u novoj Jugoslaviji (People's Court and Office of the Public Prosecutor). Beograd, 1948. 80 p.

1734 Matijević, I. *and* J. Vesel. O odgovornosti države i sudija za štetu (Liability of Government and Judges for Damages). Zagreb, 1930. 156 p. (DLC)

1735 Perić, Živojin. (a) Granice sudske vlasti (Limit of Judicial Powers). Beograd, 1899. 143 p. (DLC); (b) O ulozi sudske vlasti po srpskom zakonodavstvu (Role of Judicial Power under Serbian Legislation). Beograd, 1909. 37 p.; (c) O sudskoj nezavisnosti (Judge's Independence). Beograd, 1899. 23 p. (DLC)

1736 Tasić, Dj. O jemstvima sudske nezavisnosti (Guarantee of Judge's Independence). Beograd, 1935. 16 p.

1737 Ugrić, Jevrem. Sudijska vlast i odgovornost sudija (Judicial Power and Liability of Judges). Beograd, 1930. 91 p.

1738 Vragović, Aleksa, *editor.* Zakoni i drugi propisi o sudovima (Laws and Other Provisions on Courts, Judges, District Attorneys and Lawyers). Zagreb, 1929. 232 p. (DLC)

1739 Zuglia, Srećko. Sudovi i ostali organi koji učestvuju u vrešenju gradjanskog pravosudja (Courts and other Agencies which Participate in the Administration of Justice in Civil Cases). Zagreb, 1956. 240 p. (DLC)

c Notaries Public

1740 Zakon o javnim beležnicima (Law on Notaries Public). Beograd, 1930. 134 p. (DLC)

1741 Agatonović, Agoston Franjo, *editor.* Zakon o javnim beležnicima (Law on Notaries Public). Zagreb, 1931. 296 p. (DLC)

1742 Ili, Mihailo, *editor.* Zakon o javnim beležnicima (Law on Notaries Public). Beograd, 1931. 156 p. (DLC)

1743 Stanoš, Ivo. Da li je potrebno javno bilježništvo?. (Are Notaries Public Necessary?). *Mjesečnik,* 1925: 298–301. (DLC)

1744 Žilić, Franjo *and* Miroslav Šantek. Zakon o javnim bilježnicima (Law on Notaries Public, Annotated). Zagreb, 1934. 316 p. (DLC)

1745 Niketić, Gojko, *editor.* Uredba kojom se odredjuje tarifa o nagradama javnih beležnika (Notaries Public's Fees). Beograd, 1931. 85 p. (DLC)

1746   Pappafava, Vladimir. Bilježnički obraznik (Forms for Notaries Public). 1st ed. Zadar, 1895. 505 p.; 2d ed. 1896. 505 p. (DLC)

20   Labor Law

See also: Ch. 11, A, 2j; Nos.: 132; 508; 521; 1059; 1061; 1064; 1089; 1457b; 1465; 1473b; 1475; 2347; 2383; 2362a; 2389a.

1747   Bajič, Stojan. (a) Delovno pravo (Labor Law). Ljubljana, 1936. 220 p.; (b) Delavsko in nameščensko pravo (Labor and Employment Law). Ljubljana, 1933. 360 p. (DLC); (c) Delovnopravni zbornik (Collection of Labor Laws and Regulations). Ljubljana, 1940; (d) Kolektivni spor (Labor Disputes). *Slovenski Pravnik,* 1940: 57–72; (e) O prekočasnem delu (Compensation for Overtime Work). *Ibid.,* 1934: 172–273; (f) Osnovi radnog prava (Elements of Labor Law). Beograd, 1937. 208 p.; (g) O strajku sa zauzimanjem fabrika (Seizing of Factories by Strikers). *Arhiv* 1939: 616–619. (DLC)

1748   Baltić, Aleksandar. (a) Radno pravo FNRJ (Labor Law of the FPRY). Beograd, 1951. 156 p. (DLC); (b) Osnovi radnog prava FNRJ (Principles of Labor Law of the FPRY). Beograd, 1955. 271 p.; 1958. 387 p. (DLC); (c) Ustavno uredjenje, privredno i radno zakonodavstvo (Constitutional Setup, Economic and Labor Legislation). 2nd ed. Beograd, 1955. 319 p.; 3rd ed. 1958. 539 p.; 4th ed. 1958. 675 p. (DLC); (d) Pregled pozitivnih propisa radnog prava FNRJ (Review of Current Labor Laws and Regulations). Beograd, 1949. 131 p. (DLC); (e) Sistem plata radnika i službenika (System of Wages and Salaries). Beograd, 1952. 98 p. (DLC); (f) Radni odnos i pravo upravljanja (Employee Relationship and Labor Management). *Arhiv,* 1957: 265–275. (DLC); (g) *editor.* Zbirka propisa o radnim odnosima (Collection of Rules and Regulations on Labor Relations). 2nd ed. Beograd, 1955. 214 p. (DLC); 3rd ed. 1956. 279 p. (DLC)

1749   Cota, Zlatko *and* Zdravko Popović. Radni staž. Utvrdjivanje radnog i posebnog staža i radna knjižica (Period of Employment. Establishment of Regular and Special Periods of Employment. Employment Identity Card). Beograd, 1960. 479 p.

1750   Blagoev, B. I. Trudot kako predmet na pravoto (Labor

as a Legal Subject). *Godišnik na pravno-ekonomskiot fakultet vo Skopje*, 1956: 25–70.

1751 Blagojević, B. T. Radnički štrajkovi u svetlosti prava (Labor Strikes Seen from a Legal Angle). *Socijalni arhiv*, Beograd, 1940: 89–102.

1752 Buzuk, Radomir. Radni odnosi radnika i službenika u privredi (Employer-Employee Relations in Economy). Zagreb, 1st ed.?; 2d rev. ed. 1956, 254 p. (DLC)

1753 Despotović, M. Pravo na rad i radničko samoupravljanje (The Right to Work and Labor Self-Government). *Ahriv*, 1957: 284–292.

1754 Dilber, N. Samoupravljanje službom i sredstvima socijalnog osiguranja (Self-Government in the Field of Social Security). *Narodna država* (Beograd), 1952: 260–271. (DLC)

1755 Dimitrijević, P. *and* V. Petrović. Radno privredno zakonodavstvo (Labor Legislation). Zagreb, 1949. 312 p.

1756 Gojković, Emilo R., *editor.* Uredba o utvrdjivanju minimalnih nadnica, zaključivanju kolektivnih ugovora, pomirenju i arbitraži (Decree Fixing Minimum Wages, Collective Bargaining, Conciliation, and Arbitration). Beograd, 1937. 85 p. (DLC)

1757 Ivčić, Milivoj, *editor.* Zbirka propisa o higijenskim i tehničkim zaštitnim mjerama pri radu (Collection of Technical and Health Protection Labor Regulations). Zagreb, 1957. 684 p. (DLC)

1758 Josipović, Djordje. Registar propisa o radnim odnosima, zaštiti rada i socijalnom osiguranju (Register of Labor and Social Welfare Rules). Sarajevo, n.d. 44 p. (DLC)

1759 Kaclerović, Triša. Radničko zakonodavstvo u Srbiji pre Prvog Svetskog Rata (Pre-World War I Serbian Labor Legislation). Beograd, 1952. 66 p. (DLC)

1760 Laković, Milan, *editor.* Zbirka propisa o stručnom osposobljenju i zvanjima radnika (Collection of Regulations on the Professional Training and Qualification of Workers). Beograd, 1950. 79 p.

1761 Lapčević, Dragiša. Položaj radničke klase i sindikalni pokret u Srbiji (Labor and Trade Unions in Serbia). Beograd, 1928. 411 p. (DLC)

1762 Bašić, Hrvoje. Neposredno učešće radnog kolektiva u upravljanju preduzečima (Direct Participation of Workers and Employees in the Management of Enterprises). *Pravni zbornik* (Titograd), 1961: 69–78. (DLC)

1763 Djuranović-Janda, Saša. Žena u radnom odnosu (Women in Labor Relations). Zagreb, 1960. 329 p. (DLC)

1764 Perić, Boško K. Radno pravo (Labor Law). Sarajevo, 1949. 289 p.; 1950. 634 p. (DLC)

1765 Perić, I. P. Jugoslavensko socijalno zakonodavstvo (Yugoslav Social Welfare Legislation). Beograd, 1931. 472 p. (DLC)

1766 Pešić, Ratko *and* Ratko Maričić. Propisi o otkazivanju radnog odnosa, o materijalnom obezbedjenju radnika i službenika, i o organizaciji posredovanja rada (Rules and Regulations on the Termination of Labor Contracts, Unemployment Benefits, and Labor Exchange, Annotated). Beograd, 1952. 178 p.

1767 Politeo, Ivo. (a) Radno pravo (Labor Law). Zagreb, 1934. 276 p. (DLC); (b) Trgovački i ostali privatni nameštenici, prema službodavcima i zakonu na temelju zakona o radnjama od 5. XI. 1931 (Employer-Employee Relations under the Trade Law of September 5, 1931). Zagreb, 1932. 279 p. (DLC)

1768 Popović, S. Radni odnosi u FNRJ (Labor Relations in the FPRY). Beograd, 1950. 194 p. (DLC); 1950. 212 p. (DLC)

1769 Popović, Teofilo. Pravni položaj inspekcije rada u FNRJ (Legal Status of Labor Inspection). Beograd, 1958. 100 p. (DLC)

1770 Popović, Teofilo, *joint editor*. Zbirka propisa o materjalnom obezbedjenju i drugim pravima lica van radnog odnosa (Collection of Regulations Concerning the Social Benefits of non-Employed Persons). Beograd, 1956. 207 p. (DLC)

1771 Radnička komora za Vojvodinu. Položaj radničke klase. Privredne i socijalne prilike radnika u Vojvodini (Conditions of Labor in the Voyvodina). Novisad, 1927. 176 p. (DLC)

1772 Reisman, Avguštin. Delovno pravo (Labor Law). Maribor, 1933. 190 p.

1773 Savez sindikata Jugoslavije. (a) Finansisko poslovanje sindikalnih organizacija (Financial Operation of the Trade Unions). Beograd, 1955. 60 p. (DLC); (b) Pravilnik o godišnjim skupštinama sindikalnih organizacija (Rules on the Annual Meetings of the Trade Unions). Beograd, 1951. 20 p. (DLC)

1774 J. Dj. Radničko samoupravljanje i društvene nauke (Workers' Self-Management and Social Science). *Arhiv,* 1960: 4–10. (DLC)

1775 Simonovski, Živko, *editor.* O zaštiti rada. Zbornik materijala za sindikalne aktiviste o zaštiti rada (Collected Material on Labor Protection for Trade-Union Officials). Beograd, 1950. 167 p. (DLC)

1776 Svetek, L. Delovna pogodba in Delovnopravno razmerje po našem pravu (Labor Contract and Employer-Employee Relations in Yugoslav Law). *Ljudski pravnik,* 1950: 140 152, 191–204.

1777 Šarić, Veljko. Primjena propisa o radnim odnosima (Regulation of Employer-Employee Relations). 1st ed. Zagreb, n.d. 68 p.; 2nd ed. 1951. 67 p. (DLC)

1778 Tintić, Nikola. (a) Osnovi Radnog Prava (Elements of Labor Law). Zagreb, 1955. 256 p.; (b) Radnički odbori u kapitalističkim zemljama i organi radničkog samoupravljanja u FNRJ (Workers' Committees in Capitalistic Countries and Labor Self-Government in the FPRY). *Pregled,* 1954: 209–217, 293–303.

1779 Tomić, Todor *and* Branko Medješki, *editors.* Zbirka propisa o platama u privredi (Wages and Salaries in Economy). Beograd, 1952. 208 p. (DLC)

1780 Živković, Radomir Lj. (a) Savremeno pravno uredjenje radnih odnosa (Contemporary Regulation of Labor Relations). Beograd, 1957. 73 p.; (b) Problem pravne prirode ugovora o radu (Legal Aspect of Labor Relations). Beograd, 1940. 311 p.

1781 Materijal za proučvanje radnog prava (Material for Study of Labor Law). Beograd, 1946. 2 v. (DLC)

1782 O delovnih razmerjih v gospodarstvu (Labor Problems). Ljubljana, 1958. 327 p. (DLC)

1783 Kyovsky, R. Pravica do dela (Labor Law). *Zbornik znanstvenih razprav,* 1955: 91–124. (DLC)

1784 Pravila o polaganju majstorskih ispita od 17 januara 1929 (Rules and Regulations Governing Skilled Workmen's Examinations). Beograd, 1929. 155 p. (DLC)

1785 Magerl, Milivoj. Ostvarivanje prava iz radnog odnosa (Realization of Rights Deriving from Labor Relations). Zagreb, 1959. 103 p. (DLC)

1786 Mirjanić, Blagoje *and* Milenko Grujić. Radno zakonodavstvo (Labor Legislation). Beograd, 1960. 77 p.

1787 Uredba o izbranim odborima (Decree on the Organization of Arbitration Boards). Beograd, 1937. 123 p. (DLC)

1788 Zakon o inspekciji rada (Labor Inspection Law). 1st ed. Beograd, n.d.; 2d ed. 1948. 86 p. (DLC)

1789 Zakon o radnim odnosima, sa izmenama i dopunama od 28 juna 1958 (Law on Employer-Employee Relations, amended). Beograd, 1958. 163 p. 2nd ed. 1959. 126 p. (DLC)

1790 Zakon o zaštiti radnika (Labor Protection Law). Beograd, 1922. 57. p.

1791 Zbirka propisa o radnim odnosima (Collection of Labor Rules and Regulations). Beograd, 1948. 352 p.; 2nd ed. 1955. 240 p.; 3rd ed. 1956. 277 p. (DLC)

1792 Priručnik za primenu Zakona o radnim odnosima (Manual on the Application of the Law on Labor Relations). Milan Laković, Slavko Bujdić and Teofilo Popović, editors. 3rd ed. Beograd, 1960. 330 p. (DLC)

1793 Tomić, Teodor, editor. Zbirka propisa o radnim odnosima (Collection of Provisions on Labor Relations). Beograd, 1960. 300 p. (DLC); 2nd ed. 1961. 275 p. (DLC)

21 Land Reform

See also Nos.: 2275; 2289; 2307; 2338.

1794 Agrarna reforma; uredbe, naredbe i raspisi (Land Reform; Decrees, Regulations and Circulars). Beograd, 1920–1925. 2 v. (DLC)

1795 Agrarni propisi u Bosni i Hercegovini (Rules and Regulations on Land Tenure in Bosnia and Herzegovina). Sarajevo, 1946. 189 p. (DLC)

1796 Agrarni zbornik (Collection of Land Laws and Regulations on Land Tenure). Beograd, 1924. 303 p. (DLC)

1797 Zakon o beglučkim zemljama u Bosni i Hercegovini (Law Concerning the Estates of the Former Ottoman Feudal Landowners in Bosnia and Herzegovina). Beograd, 1929. 24 p. (DLC)

1798 Zakon o dobrovoljcima (Law on War Volunteers). Beograd, 1928. 29 p. (DLC)

1799 Zakon o poljoprivrednom zemljišnom fondu opštenarodne

imovine i dodeljivanju zemlje poljoprivrednim organizacijama (Law on the Land Reserve Fund and Allocation of Land to Farming Organizations). Beograd, 1953. 36 p.

1800 \Zakon za selsko-stopanskiot zemjišen fond na opštonarodniot imot i za dodeluvanje zemja na selsko-stopanskite organizacii (Law on the Land Reserve Fund and Allocation of Land to Farming Organizations). Beograd, 1953. 39 p. (DLC); Skopje, 1956. 77 p. (DLC)

1801 Zakonodavstvo o likvidaciji agrarne reforme (Legislation on the Liquidation of the Land Reform). Beograd, 1932. 291 p. (DLC)

1802 Bjelovučić, N. Z. Rješenje Dubrovačkog kmetstva i polovništva (Solution of the Problem of Tenancy in the Region of Dubrovnik). Dubrovnik, 1927.

1803 Bösendorfer, Josip. Agrarni odnosi u Slavoniji (Land Tenure in Slavonia). Zagreb, 1950. 264 p. (DLC)

1804 Čaldarević, Vladimir, Fadil Imamović and Mustafa Kamarić, editors. Agrarni propisi u Bosni i Hercegovini (Rules and Regulations Governing Land Tenure in Bosnia and Herzegovina). Sarajevo, 1946. 189 p.

1805 Ćerimović, Mehmed Ali. O vakufu (Trust Estates under Sheriat Law). Sarajevo, 1935. 62 p. (DLC)

1806 Erić, Milivoje. Agrarna reforma u Jugoslaviji, 1918–1941 god. (Land Reform in Yugoslavia, 1918–1941). Sarajevo, 1958. 547 p. (DLC)

1807 Krbek, Ivo. Nacionalizacija zemljišnih zajednica i krajiških imovnih općina (Nationalization of Land Communities in the Krajina). Zagreb, 1948. 30 p.

1808 Lalošević, Joca. Nacrt zakona o ekspropriaciji velikih poseda i o novom uredjenju agrarnih odnosa, i njegove obrazloženje (Draft Law Providing for the Nationalization of Large Estates, and the Reorganization of Land Tenure). Sombov, 1923.

1809 Majstorović, Bogdan, editor. (a) Zibrka propisa o agrarnoj reformi i poljoprivrednom zemljišnom fondu (Collection of Regulations on Land Reform and the Land Reserve Fund). Beograd, 1st ed.?; 2d end.? 3d rev. ed. 1956. 49 p. (DLC); (b) Zbirka propisa NR Srbije o agrarnoj reformi i o upravljanju sa opštenarodnom imovinom (Collection of Rules and Regulations of the

PR of Serbia Governing the Land Reform and Administration of People's Property). Beograd, 1956. 176 p. (DLC)

1810   Medini, Milorad. O postanku i razvitku kmetskih i težačkih odnošaja u Dalmaciji (Origin and Development of Land Tenancy in Dalmatia). Zadar, 1920. 123 p.

1811   Milosavljević, Brana. Zemljišni maksimum (Limitation of the Amount of Land Admitted to Private Ownership). Beograd, 1st ed.?; 2d ed.?; 3d ed. 1954. 57 p. (DLC)

1812   Nešović, Slobodan M., editor. Zakon o agrarnoj reformi i kolonizaciji (Law on Land Reform and Colonization). Beograd, 1st ed?; 2d ed. 1948. 273 p. (DLC)

1813   Mihletić, S. Agrarna reforma i kolonizacija u Hrvatskoj (Land Reform and Colonization in Croatia). Zagreb, 1952.

1814   Ristić, Teofan Dj. Borba za zemlju i naša agrarna reforma (Struggle for the Possession of Land and the Yugoslav Land Reform). Beograd, 1938. 96 p.

1815   Stipetić, V. Agrarna reforma i kolonizacija u FNRJ godine 1945–1948 (Land Reform and Colonization Policy of the FPRY in 1945–1948). Zagreb, 1954. 431 p.

1816   Tašner, Joža and Albin Radikon, editors. Zakon o likvidaciji agrarne reforme na velikim posedima (Law on the Liquidation of the Land Reform on Large Estates, annotated). Beograd, 1931. 165 p. (DLC)

1817   Truhelka, Čiro. Historička podloga agrarnog pitanja u Bosni (Historical Background of the Land Tenure Problem in Bosnia). Sarajevo, 1915. 110 p. (DLC)

22   Maritime Law

See also Nos.: 221; 378f; 1081; 2260a; 2300; 2319a, h; 2340; 2422.

1818   Bačić, V. A. Uvod u medjunarodno pomorsko javno i ratno pravo (Introduction to International Public Maritime and War Law). Beograd, 1933. 208 p.

1819   Brajković, V. (a) Pomorsko pravo (Maritime Law). Zagreb, 1949 [in Coauthorship with G. Badovinac]; 2nd ed. 1949; 304 p. (DLC); (b) Uvod u medjunarodno pomorsko javno i ratno pravo (Introduction to International Public- and War- Maritime Law). Beograd, 1922. 208 p.

1820 Cigoj, S. Havarije pomorskog prava (Average in Maritime Law). *Pravnik,* 1956: 365–400.

1821 Domazetović, F. Pribrežno more (Coastal Waters). *Mjesečnik,* 1922: 161–174.

1822 Jakaša, B. Zapljena tereta u ratu (Seizure of Cargoes in Wartime). *Mornarički glasnik,* 1956: 697–714.

1823 Katičić, N. Teritorijalno more (Territorial Waters). *Jugoslovenska revija,* 1955: 231–251.

1824 Maksimović, M. Ugovor o pomorskom osiguranju (Contract of Maritime Insurance). Beograd, 1957. 201 p. (DLC)

1825 Mirković, Djordje Ž. (a) O prirodi pravnih odnosa koji vezuju kapetana broda za vlasnika ili opremitelja (Legal Nature of the Shipowner-Shipmaster Relationship). *Arhiv,* 1933: 110–125; (b) Pravni pojam broda (The Legal Concept of a Vessel). *Arhiv,* 1933: 33–53. (DLC)

1826 Mogan, Julije. (a) O brodovlasniku i njegovoj odgovornosti (Responsibility of the Shipowner). *Arhiv,* 1921: 114–126. (DLC); 188–197. (DLC); (b) O srazu brodova (Collision of Vessels). *Mjesečnik,* 1918: 227–234, 274–283. (DLC); (c) Pomorski vozarski ugovor (Freightage). Rijeka, 1915. 136 p.

1827 Osnova trgovačkog pomorskog zakona za Jugoslavensku državu (Draft of the Yugoslav Code on the Merchant Marine). Split, 1919. 108 p. (DLC)

1828 Pilić, V. Pomorsko osiguranje u spoljnoj trgovini (Maritime Insurance in Foreign Trade). Beograd, 1955. 101 p. (DLC)

1829 Primožić, A. Prava i dužnosti brodskog osoblja u trgovačkoj mornarici (Rights and Duties of the Crew of a Merchant Ship). Zagreb, 1932. 86 p. (DLC)

1830 Sambrailo, B. Kodifikacija medjunarodnog prava otvorenog mora i UN (Codification of the International Law Governing the High Seas, and the United Nations). *Anali Jadranskog Instituta,* 1956: 157–204.

1831 Savin, Špiro. Pomorski prijevozi, havarije i osiguranja (Maritime Shipping, Average and Insurance). Zagreb, 1950. 206 p. 2nd ed. 1958. 196 p. (DLC)

1832 Subotić, Ivan V. *and* Slavko Stojković. Hipoteka na rečnim brodovima u slovenskim državama (Lien on Internal Navigation Vessels in the Slavic Countries). *Pravosudje,* 1933: 604–615.

1833   Škarica, V. Hipoteka na morske brodove (Lien on Seagoing Vessels). *In* Spomenica Kongresa Pravnika, 1932: 132–152.

1834   Špehar, Milan. (a) Odgovornost brodara osvrtom i na Haška pravila (Responsibility of Shipowners with Reference to the Hague Rules). Zagreb, 1939. 208 p.; (b) Savremeni smjerovi Pomorskog prava, s obzirom na našu kodifikaciju (Contemporary Trends in Maritime Law with Reference to Codification). Zagreb, 1937. 48 p.

1835   Šuc, A. Regime of Merchant Vessels in the Yugoslav Coastal Sea. *Jugoslovenska revija*, 1956: 65–71.

1836   Tomašić, Lj. Pomorsko pravo (Maritime Law). Zagreb, 1924. 111 p. (DLC)

1837   Verona, Ante. Pomorsko pravo (Maritime Law). Zagreb, 1927. 183 p. (DLC)

1838   Zbornik za pomorsko pravo (Manual on Maritime Law). Zagreb, 1951– (DLC: v. 1, 3, 4)

1839   Uredba o nadležnosti za vodjenje postupka u pomorskim prekršajima (Decree on the Jurisdiction of the trials of Maritime Petty Offenses). Split, 1950. 74 p. (DLC)

1839[1]   Zbirka pomorskih propisa (Collection of Maritime Provisions). Vlado Medanić, Ilija Čolović *and* Dušan Mijatović, *comp.* Beograd, 1958– (DLC: v. 1, 3)

23   Military Penal Law

See also No. 2409c.

1840   Dabić, Ljub. A. (a) Vojni Kazneni Zakonik sa Objašnjenjem (Military Criminal Code, Annotated). Beograd, 1922. 116 p. (DLC); (b) Komentar Vojnog Krivinog Zakonika (Commentary on the Military Criminal Code). Beograd, 1930. 178 p. (DLC)

1841   Marinković, Dragutin. Vojni kazneni zakonik sa Zakonom o vojnom disciplinskom sudu i Zakonom o postupku vojnih sudova u krivičnim delima (Military Criminal Code, with the Law on the Military Disciplinary Court and the Law on Military Criminal Procedure). Beograd, 1928. 304 p. (DLC)

1842   Mićović, Milutin B. Članci i rasprave iz oblasti vojnog krivičnog zakonodavstva (Articles and Studies on Military Criminal Legislation). Beograd, 1938. 147 p.

1843   Nikitović, Časlav M. *and* Miloš B. Carević. Osnovi vojnog krivičnog prava; posebni deo (Elements of the Yugoslav Military Criminal Code, Special Part). Beograd, 1928. 189 p. (DLC)

1844   Pavlović, Gojko. Nekoliko reči o izveštaju Skupštinskog Anketnog Odbora o vojnom sudstvu (A Few Words on the Report of the Parliamentary Committee Charged with the Investigation of Military Justice). Beograd, 1937.

1845   Urošević, Spasoje. Uput za vodjenje informativnog izvidjaja i prethodne krivične istrage u mornarici (Instruction Concerning Preliminary Inquiry and Investigation in the Navy). Zemun, 1939. 226 p. (DLC)

1846   Vojni Krivični Zakonik Kr. Jugoslavije od 11 februara 1930 (Yugoslav Military Criminal Code of February 11, 1930). Beograd, 1930. 56 p. (Zbirka zakona, sv. 152). (DLC); *idem,* 78 p. (Zbirka zakona, sv. 34). (DLC)

1847   Vojni krivični zbornik Kraljevine Jugoslavije (Collection of Military Penal Laws). Beograd, 1st and 2d ed.? 3d ed. 1925. 167 p. (DLC); 1930. 56 p. (DLC)

1848   Zakon o ustrojstvu vojnih sudova. Zakonik o postupku vojnih sudova u krivičnim delima i vojni kazneni zakon (Laws on the Organization of Military Courts, Military Criminal Procedure, and Military Criminal Law). Beograd, 1901. 12, 92, 36, 7 p. (DLC)

1849   Zakon o vojnim krivičnim delima od Septembra 1948 (Military Criminal Law of September 1948). Beograd, 1949. 34 p. (DLC)

1850   Zakon o vojnom disciplinskom sudu od 12 Januara 1899 (Law on Military Disciplinary Courts of January 12, 1899). Solun, 1918. 14 p. (DLC)

1851   Živanović, Toma. Osnovi vojnog krivičnog prava. Opšti deo (Principles of Military Criminal Law. General Part). Beograd, 1924. 194 p. (DLC)

24 Nationality Law (Citizenship)

See also: Ch. 11, A, 2k; Nos.: 2278c; 2319n; 2319af; 2343a; 2397; 2433a.

1852 Zakon o državljanstvu sa Pravilnikom za izvršenje zakona (Law on Citizenship and Regulation for Putting it into Force). 3d ed. Beograd, 1958. 47 p. (Zbirka saveznih propisa, br. 160). (DLC)

1853 Krbek, Ivo. *and* Negoslav Ocokoljić. Zakon o državljanstvu, sa komentarom (Law on Citizenship, Annotated). Beograd, 1948. 170 p. (Zbirka zakona FNRJ, br. 18). (DLC)

1854 Pirkmajer, Otomar. (a) Zakon o državljanstvu sa tumačenjem (Law on Citizenship, Annotated). Beograd, 1929. 438 p. (DLC); (b) Zakon o državljanstvu z razlago (Law on Citizenship, Annotated). Maribor, 1929. 297 p. (DLC)

1855 Zakon o državljanstvu Kraljevine SHS (Law on Citizenship of the Kingdom of Yugoslavia). Beograd, 1929. 39 p. (Zbirka zakona, sv. 2) (DLC); 2nd ed. 1929. 97 p. (Zbirka zakona, sv. 109). (DLC)

1856 Blagojević, Borislav T. (a) Državljanstvo, s naročitim obzirom na pravo FNRJ (Citizenship with Regard to the Laws of the FPRY). 2nd ed. Beograd, 1947. 210 p.; (b) Osnovi nauke o državljanstvu (Basic Principles on Nationality Laws). Beograd, 1938. 148 p. (DLC); (c) Višestruko državljanstvo (Plural Nationality). *Mjesečnik,* 63. 1937: 411–437.

1857 Cvjetković, Branko. Državljanstvo i zavičajnost (Citizenship and Home and Support Right). Beograd, 1940. 95 p. (DLC)

1858 Lapajne, Stanko. Razvoj in sedanje stanje našega državljanskega prava (Development in the Present Status of Our Nationality Law). Ljubljana, 1934. 48 p. (DLC)

1859 Mnenja k predhodnemu načrtu državljanskega zakonika za Kraljevino Jugoslavijo (Opinions on the Draft of the Law on Citizenship for the Kingdom of Yugoslavia). Ljubljana, 1938. 464 p. (DLC)

1860 Perić, Živojin M. (a) Državljanstvo i brak (Citizenship and Marriage). *Slovenski pravnik,* 1927: 70–80; (b) O Narodnosti u Srpskom Zakonodavstvu (Nationality in Serbian Legislation). Reprint from *Barnič.* Beograd, 1905. 39 p.

1861 Practicus, *editor.* Zavičajno pravo. Zakon od 30. travnja 1880 ob uredjenju zavičajnih odnošaja u Kraljevinah Hrvatskoj i Slavoniji (Law of April 30, 1880 on Home and Support Right Valid in Croatia and Slavonia). Zagreb, 1894. 318 p. (DLC)

1862 Vesel, Josip. Zakon o državljanstvu Kraljevine SHS od 21 septembra 1928, sa tumačenjima (Yugoslav Law on Citizenship of Sept. 21, 1928, Annotated). Sarajevo, 1928.

25 Negotiable Instruments

See also Nos.: 769; 1425; 1451; 2319s; 2401a; 2403; 2442.

1863 Bajalović, Ljubomir. Menično i čekovno pravo FNRJ (Lectures on Negotiable Instruments of the FPRY). Beograd, 1947. 87 p.; 2nd ed. 1958. 109 p. (DLC)

1864 Bartoš, Milan. Menični zakon i čekovni zakon (Law on Negotiable Instruments). Beograd, 1929. 248 p. (DLC)

1865 Bartoš, Milan, Zoran Antonijević *and* Vlada Jovanović. Menično i čekovno pravo (Negotiable Instruments). Beograd, 1953. 307 p. (DLC)

1866 Čimić, Ernest. (a) Mjenični i čekovni zakon od 29 novembra 1928, sa tumačenjima (Law on Bills and Notes of November 29, 1928, Annotated). 1st ed.?; 2d ed. Zagreb, 1930. 314 p. (DLC); (b) Mjenično pravo u Kraljevini SHS (Yugoslav Law on Bills and Notes). Zagreb, 1925. 238 p.

1867 Deželić, Branko *and* Stanko Deželić. Mjenično pravo za školsku i svakidašnju potrebu (Handbook on Bills and Notes Law). Zagreb, 1923.

1868 Djordjević, Andra. (a) Menično pravo Kraljevine Srbije (Law on Bills and Notes of Serbia). Beograd, 1904. 400 p.; 1905. 375 p.; (b) Nauka o Meničnom pravu (Teaching on Bills and Notes). Beograd, 1881. 149 p.

1869 Eisner, Bertold. Ženevske konvencije o čeku (Geneva Convention on Checks). Zagreb, 1932. 60 p.

1870 Gospavić, Obrad. (a) Čekovno pravo Kraljevine Jugoslavije (Law on Checks of Yugoslavia). Beograd, 1931. 134 p.; 1933. 189 p.; (b) Osnovi meničnog prava (Principles of Bills and Notes Law). Beograd, 1933. 189 p. (DLC)

1871 Janković, Dragutin. Komentar meničnog zakona i zakona o čeku (A Commentary on the Law on Bills and Notes and on the Check Law). Beograd, 1930. 233 p. (DLC)

1872 Jovanović, Radivoje. Hartije na donosioca (Instruments Payable to the Bearer). Beograd, 1933. 100 p.

1873 Karajovanović, Dj. Menično pravo (Law on Bills and Notes). Beograd, 1901; 1920.

1874 Konjar, Anton. Zakon o menici in Zakon o čeku (Law on Bills and Notes and Check Law). Ljubljana, 1949. 38 p. (DLC)

1875 Kramer, Rudolf. Menice, menični protesti, in drugo, po novom meničnom zakonu (Bills and Notes, their Protest and other Questions under the New Law). Ljubljana, 1930. 178 p.

1876 Marković, Lazar. Menično jemstvo (Endorsement of Bills and Notes). Beograd, 1906.

1877 Menični Zakon i čekovni Zakon (Law on Bills and Notes, and Check Law). Beograd, 1929. 77 p. (DLC)

1878 Menični Zakon Kraljevine Jugoslavije (Law on Bills and Notes of the Kingdom of Yugoslavia). Beograd, 1929. 108 p. (DLC)

1879 Mišić, Dušan. Čekovno pravo. Zakon o čeku od 29 novembra 1928 (Law on Checks of November 29, 1928). Beograd, 1931. 192 p.

1880 Nestorović, Djordje B. (a) Menično pravo (Law on Bills and Notes). Beograd, 1909. 246 p. (b) Menično pravo u teoriji i sudskoj praksi (Bills and Notes Law in Theory and Practice). Beograd, 1912. 319 p. (DLC)

1881 Nestorović, Dj. B. and S. Pešić. Vučena menica, s naročitim pogledom na odredbe našeg trgovačkog zakonika (The Bill of Exchange in Serbian Law). Beograd, 1887. 78 p.

1882 Pavlović, Toma. Osnovi meničnog prava i komentar novog meničnog zakona (Elements of the Bills and Notes Law, and a Commentary on the New Yugoslav Law). Novi Sad, 1934. 429 p. (DLC)

1883 Poličević, Mihailo S. Teorija meničnog pokrića (Theory of the Bills and Notes Coverage). Arhiv, 1909.

1884 Premužić-Tomašićki, Konstantin. Mjenbeno pravo i mjenbeni zakon, sa potrebitim uzorcima (The Law on Bills and Notes, with the Pertinent Forms). Sarajevo, 1913. 119 p. (DLC)

1885 Protić, Kosta J. Blanko menica (Blank Bills and Notes). Beograd, 1938. 104 p.

1886 Radojičić, Spasoje. (a) Haška konferencija za izjednačenje Meničnog prava (The Hague Conference for the Unification of the Law on Bills and Notes). Beograd, 1911; (b) Izjednačeno menično pravo (The Law on Bills and Notes Unified). Beograd, 1914. 34 p.

1887 Rastovčan, Pavao. Vrijednosni papiri, menica, ček (Securities and Negotiable Instruments). Zagreb, 1950. 73 p. (DLC); 1955. 112 p.

1888 Salavari, Franjo. Repetitorij trgovačkoga i mjeničnoga prava (Digest of Commercial Law and of the Law on Bills and Notes). Zagreb, 1st ed.?; 2nd ed. 1925. 195 p.

1889 Stražnicky, M. (a) Tumač zakona o čeku od 19 Novembra 1929 (Commentary on the Check Law of November 19, 1929). Zagreb, 1931. 211 p.; (b) Tumač zakona o mjenici (Commentary on the Law on Bills and Notes). Zagreb, 1929. 491 p.; (c) Udžbenik mjeničnoga prava (Textbook on Bills and Notes). Zagreb, 1932. 207 p. (DLC)

1890 Subotić, D. Seljak i njegova pasivna menična sposobnost (Peasants and Their Capacity to Issue Bills and Notes). Beograd, 1927. 47 p.

1891 Škerlj, M. (a) Menično pravo (Law on Bills and Notes). Ljubljana, 1922. 287 p. (DLC); (b) Naša nova zakona o menici in o čeku in njiju slovensko besedilo v Uradnem listu FNRJ (The New Yugoslav Laws on Negotiable Instruments and their Translation into Slovenian in the Official Gazette). *Zbornik znanstvenih razprav,* 1948: 197–242.

1892 Tucaković, Miloš T. (a) Menično pravo (Law on Bills and Notes). Beograd, 1896. 306 p. (DLC); (b) Domicilirana menica (Bills and Notes Limited as to the Place of Payment). Beograd, 1895. 179 p.

1893 Vinter, Vilim. Tumač mjenbenom zakonu (Commentary on the Law on Bills and Notes). Zagreb, 1882.

1894 Vrbanić, Fr. Mjenbeni zakon. Tumač z. čl. xxvii: 1876 (Bills and Notes Law. Commentary on the Law No. xxvii of 1876 for Croatia-Slavonia). Zagreb, 1886. 704 p. (DLC)

1895 Vrbanić, Juraj. (a) Čekovno pravo /Z. čl. 58, 1908/ (Check

Law No. 58 of /1908/ for Croatia-Slavonia). Zagreb, 1909. 120 p. (DLC); (b) Mjenično pravo Kraljevine SHS (Law on Bills and Notes of Yugoslavia). Zagreb, 1929. 228 p. (DLC)

1896 Zakon mieničnii Kralievstva Ungarie s magjarskog na serbskii dialekt preven' Eugeniem' ot' Gjurkovič (Law on Bills and Notes of the Hungarian Kingdom. Translated from Hungarian into Serbian by Eugene Gjurkovich). U Pešti, 1840. 236 p., [20] p. (DLC)

1897 Zakon o čeku za Kraljevinu S.H.S. (Law on Checks of Yugoslavia). Beograd, 1929. 51 p. (DLC)

1898 Zakoni o menici i čeku (Laws on Negotiable Instruments). Beograd, 1st and 2nd ed.?; 3rd ed. 1953. 67 p. (DLC); 4th ed.?; 5th ed. 1958. 60 p. (DLC)

26 Patents, Trade-Marks, Copyright

See also: Ch. 11, A, 2m; Nos.: 773; 1112c; 2319ac; 2325; 2386; 2407; 2443a; 2445.

1899 Iznajditeljska delavnost in njena ureditev v naši državi (Invention Activities and our Legislation). Ljubljana, 1951. 140 p. (DLC)

1900 Radojković, Živan. Svjetska konferencija o autorskom pravu (World Conference on Copyright). Arhiv, 1960: 162–167. (DLC)

1901 Šuman, Janko. (a) Zakonski propisi iz oblasti industrijske svojine (Provisions of Law on Patents and Trade-Marks). Beograd, 1925. 426 p. (DLC); 1929. 285 p. (DLC); Zagreb, 1930. 199 p.; 1931. 695 p. (DLC); (b) Komentar zakona o zaštiti autorskog prava i medjunarodnih propisa (Commentary on the Law on Copyright and International Provisions). Beograd, 1935. 579 p. (DLC); 1936. 579 p.; (c) Zakonski propisi iz autorskog prava, sa motivima (Provisions of Law on Copyright, annotated). Zagreb, 1930. 199 p. (DLC).

1902 Bogdanović, Andrija. Zaštita prava industrijske svojine (Protection of Patents and Trade-Marks). Beograd, 1956. 51 p. (DLC)

1903 Niketić, Gojko, editor. (a) Zakon o zaštiti industrijske svojine (Law on Protection of Patents and Trade-Marks). Beograd, 1928. 168 p. (Zbirka zakona, sv. 94) (DLC); (b) Zakon o zaštiti autorskog prava sa . . . zakonom o Bernskoj konvenciji (Law on Copyright and Law on the Bern Convention). Beograd, 1933. 121 p. (Zbirka zakona, sv. 213). (DLC)

1904 Perić, Živojin M. Naučna svojina (Literary Property). Reprint from *Glasnik Uprave za zaštitu industrijske svojine*. Beograd, 1925. 24 p.

1905 Pretnar, Stojan. (a) Vloga in pomen patenta v družbeno-ekonomski ureditvi naše države (Role and Meaning of Patents in our Social and Economic Setup). Ljubljana, 1951. 23 p. (Knjižnica pravne fakultete v Ljubljani, 9). (DLC); (b) *editor*. Zakon o patentih in tehničnih izboljšavah (Law on Patents and Trade-Marks and Technical Improvements). Ljubljana, 1961. 130 p.

1906 Spaić, Vojislav. (a) Autorsko pravo (Copyright). Sarajevo, 1957. 377 p. (DLC); (b) *editor*. Zakon o autorskom pravu (Law on Copyright). Beograd, 1958. 96 p. (DLC)

1907 Štempihar, Jurij. Avtorsko pravo (Copyright). Ljubljana, 1960. 217 p. (DLC)

27 The Press

See also: Ch. 11, A, 21; Nos.: 774; 2314c; 2315.

1908 Zakon o Udruženjima, zborovima i drugim javnim skupovima, zakon o štampi i zakon o izdavanju i raspačavanju omladinske i dečje književnosti i štampe (Law on Associations, Meetings, and other Public Gatherings, Law on the Press, and Law on the Issuance and Distribution of Literature and Printings for Youth and Children). Beograd, 1947. 41 p. (Zbirka zakona FNRJ, br. 14). (DLC)

1909 Zakon o štampi . . . (Law on the Press and Decree Concerning the Settlement of Relations between Newspapermen and Newspaper Owners). Beograd, 1929. 63 p. (Zbirka zakona, sv. 10) (DLC); 2–4 eds.?; 5th ed. 1930. 53 p. (Zbirka zakona, 68) [DLC); 1938. 82 p. (Zbirka zakona, sv. 30). (DLC)

1910 Zakon o tisku (Law on the Press). Ljubljana, 1925. 43 p. (Zbirka zakonov, sv. 18). (DLC)

1911 Agatonović, Agoston Franjo, *editor*. Zakon o štampi (Law on the Press). Zagreb, 1930. 450 p. (Kazneno zakonodavstvo, knj. 2). (DLC)

1912 Zakon o štampi i drugim vidovima informacija (Law on the Press and Other Kinds of Information). Preface by Bogdan Osolnik. Beograd, 1960. 53 p. (DLC)

1913 Henigsberg, Lavoslav. Komentar štamparskog prava (Commentary on the Law of the Press). Beograd, 1932. 184 p. (DLC)

1914 Muha, M. Zakon o štampi od 6 augusta 1925 (Law on the Press of August 6, 1925). Zagreb, 1926. 92 p.

1915 Pejanović, Djordje. Štamparije u Bosni i Hercegovini, 1529–1951 (Publishing Houses in Bosnia and Herzegovina, 1529–1951). Sarajevo, 1952. 76 p. (DLC)

1916 Zakon o štampi (Law on the Press, as Amended). Beograd, 1904. 25 p. (DLC)

1917 Zakoni o štampi (Laws on the Pres). Beograd, 1884. 332 p. (DLC)

1918 Zakon o štampi od 12 marta 1881, sa izmenama i dopunama od 12 juna 1882 (Law on the Press of March 12, 1881, as Amended). Beograd? 1882? 15 p. (DLC)

1919 Zakon o pečatnji (štampi) Kneževine Srbije (Law on the Press in the Principality of Serbia). Kragujevac, 1870. 23 p.

1920 Zakon o štampi u Knjaževini Crnoj Gori (Press Law of the Principality of Montenegro). Cetinje, 1905. 26 p. (DLC)

1921 Uredba o vojnoj cenzuri za vreme rata (Decree on Military Censorship During the War). Sarajevo, 1919. 22 p. (DLC)

1922 Kruszelnicki, Franjo. Zakon o štampi za Bosnu i Hercegovinu (Law on the Press for Bosnia and Herzegovina). 191?. 136 p. (DLC)

1923 Zakon o štampi za Bosnu i Hercegovinu (Law on the Press for Bosnia and Herzegovina). Sarajevo, 1906. 39 p. (DLC)

1924 Dolenc, Metod. Pravica na popravek po zakonu o tisku (Right to Have Newspaper Statements Corrected). Reprint from Spomenice VI glavne skupštine Kongresa Pravnika u Zagrebu. Zagreb, 1934. 13 p.

1925 Frank, Stanko. Osnovi prava o štampi (Principles of the Law on the Press). Zagreb, 1927. 173 p. (DLC)

1926 Ilić, Mihailo. Šta treba izmeniti u zakonu o štampi (What

Should be Changed in the Law on the Press). Beograd, 1937. 35 p.

1927 Jakšić, Vl. Postanak i razviće štampe u Srbiji (Creation and Development of the Press in Serbia). *Pravda,* Nos. 13 and 14, 1872.

1928 Knaflič, Vladimir. Traktat o tisku (Treatise on the Press). Ljubljana, 1930. 198 p.

1929 Milovanović, G. O slobodnoj štampi uopšte (On the Free Press in General). Beograd, 1901. 254 p. (DLC)

1930 Podbrežnik, Fran, *editor.* Godišnjak štampe Kraljevine Jugoslavije (Yearbook of the Press of the Kingdom of Yugoslavia). Beograd, 1937–? (DLC v. 1, 1937)

1931 Predlog uredbe o Državnoj štampariji Kraljevine Jugoslavije (Draft of the Decree on the Government Printing Office of the Kingdom of Yugoslavia). Beograd, n.d. 16 p. (DLC)

1931[1] Skerlić, Jovan. Istorijski pregled srpski štampe, 1791–1911 (Historical Survey of the Serbian Press, 1791–1911). Beograd, 1911. 81 p. (DLC)

1932 Vesel, Josip. (a) Pravo na ispravku po Zakonu o štampi (Right to Have Newspaper Statements Corrected). Beograd, 1934. 18 p.; (b) Paušalne klevete po zakonu o štampi (Libels under the Law of the Press). Beograd, 1932. 41 p. (DLC)

28 Property Law

See also: Ch. 11, A, 2n; Nos.: 435d; 744; 754b; 778; 1446; 2250; 2293b; 2430; 2436; 2457; 2467b.

1933 Agić, Oskar. Pravoužitničko pravo krajišnika (Rights of the Members of the Peasant Communities of the Krayna). Vinkovci, 1925. 63 p. (DLC)

1934 Cavalieri, Celso. Tumač zakonu od 6 travnja 1906 o nužnim prolazima (Commentary on the Law on the Right of Way of April 6, 1906). Zagreb, 1917. 470 p. (DLC); 2nd ed. 1928. 386 p. (DLC)

1935 Komentar opšteg zakona o stambenim zajednicama. Božidar Popović; Zakona o poslovnim zgradama i prostorijama. Vojislav Popović; Zakona o svojini na delovima zgrada. Alojzij Finžgar (Commentary on the General Law Concerning Dwelling Communities by Božidar Popović; the Law on Business Buildings and Premises by Vojislav Popović; the Law on Ownership of Individual Portions of Buildings by Alojzij Finžgar). Beograd, 1960. 368 p.

1936 Čimić, Ernest. Zakon o smetanju posjeda od 8 maja 1890, sa tumačem (Law on Trespass of May 8, 1890, with a Commentary). Zagreb, 1929. 96 p. (DLC)

1937 Čulinović, F. (a) Komentar zakona o izdavanju tapija (Commentary on the Law on Land Title Certificates). Požarevac, 1932. 238 p. (DLC); (b) Komentar zemljišno-knjižnih zakona (Commentary on the Laws on Land Title Registers). Beograd, 1931. 728 p. (DLC); (c) O zemljišno-knjižnim upisima (Recording in Land Title Registers). Zagreb, 1930. 93 p.; (d) Zemljišno-knjižno pravo (Land Register Law). Beograd, 1933. 207 p. (DLC)

1938 Djordjević, Andra. O pravu svojine i pravnim odnošajima na vodama u Srbiji (Property and Water Rights in Serbia). Reprint from *Policijski glasnik*, 1905. 42 p.

1939 Farkaš, Lj. Zemljišno zakonodavstvo u Bosni i Hercegovini (Land Property Legislation in Bosnia and Herzegovina). *Arhiv*, 1925: 169–182, 266–283, 388–399. (DLC)

1940 Finžgar, A. (a) Posebni primeri upotrebe splošnega ljudskega premoženja (Individual Examples of the Use of Public Domain). Ljubljana, 1951. 30 p.; (b) Stvarno pravo (Property Law). Ljubljana, 1952. 143 p.

1941 Gams, A. (a) O diskusiji o socijalističkoj svojini (Controversy over Socialist Ownership). *Anali*, 1955: 414–426; (b) Stvarno Pravo (Property Law). 1st ed. Beograd, 1949. 197 p.; 2d ed. 1955. 267 p.; 3rd ed. 1961. 350 p. (DLC); (c) Dopunski materijal iz stvarnog prava. Društvena svojina nad stambenim zgradama (Additional Material on Property Law. Social Ownership of Dwelling Houses). Beograd, 1960. 30 p.

1942 Geršković, Leon, *editor*. Zakon o prometu zemljišta i zgrada sa komentarom (Law Providing for the Sale and Purchase of Real Property, annotated). Beograd, 1955. 78 p. (DLC)

1943 Geršić, Gliša. Priroda državine i osnova njene pravne zaštite; sa kritičnim pogledom na naš gradjanski zakonik (Legal Nature of Possession and its Legal Protection with Reference to the Serbian Civil Code). Beograd, 1885. 93 p. (DLC)

1944 Gojković, Gavra, *editor*. Komasacija zemljišta (Land Surveying and Boundary Settlement). Zagreb, 1926. 65 p. (DLC)

1945 Haladi, Franjo, *editor*. (a) Zakon od 22 lipnja 1902, o komasaciji zemljita (Land Surveying and Boundary Settlement Act of June 22, 1902). Zagreb, 1922. 524 p. (DLC); (b) Tumač zakona o nuždnim prolazim (Commentary on the Law on the Right of Way). Zagreb, 1906. 788 p. (DLC); (c) Zakon od 25 travnja 1894 o uredjenju zemljišnih zajednica i zakon od 1. svibnja 1895 o uredjenju plemenite obćine turopoljske (Law on the Organization of Agricultural Communities of April 25, 1894, with the Law on the Organization of the Noble Commune of Turopolje of May 1, 1895). Zagreb, 1898. 249 p. (DLC)

1946 Ivšić, M. Problem seljačke svojine (Problem of Peasant Property). *Mjesečnik*, 1933: 59–72, 155–169.

1947 Jokanović V. Socijalistička svojina u FNRJ (Socialist Ownership in the FPRY). *Arhiv*, 1952: 315–345

1948 Rajić, Rajko. Šta je stambena zajednica (What is a Community of Dwellings). Beograd, 1960. 80 p. (DLC)

1949 Jovanović, Mih. P. (a) Državina, njena zaštita i održaj (Possession, Legal Protection and Custody). Beograd, 1925. 196 p.; (b) Svojina, njen pravni i socijalnopolitički značaj (Ownership and its Social-Political Implications). Reprint from *Arhiv*, 1921. 45 p. (DLC)

1950 Kadlec, Karel. Agrární právo v Bosně a Herzegovině (Land Tenure Law in Bosnia and Herzegovina). Prague. 1903. 140 p. (DLC)

1951 Komadinić, Milan. Agrarno-pravni odnosi nove Srbije (Land Tenure in New Serbia). Beograd, 1914. 115 p.

1952 Kosorić, Veselin, *joint editor*. Priručnik pravnih pravila o nepokretnoj opštenarodnoj imovini (Manual of Rules and Regulations Governing Real Property of the People). Sarajevo, 1956. 2 v. (DLC)

1953 Košutić, M. (a) Tumač k Zakonu o zemljišnim knjigama (Commentary on the Law on Land Title Registers). Zagreb, 1930. 743 p. (DLC); (b) Gruntovno pravo (Land Title Law). Zagreb, 1910. 463 p.; (c) Tumač Zakonu o zemljišnoknjižnim diobama (Commentary on the Law on the Partitioning of Land in Land Title Registers). Zagreb, 1931. 424 p. (DLC)

1954 Vedriš, Martin. Vlasništvo stana (Ownership of One's Own Apartment). *Zbornik pravnog fakulteta* (Zagreb), 1955: 194–205. (DLC)

1955 Krstić, Djordje. (a) Individualna i kolektivna svojina na zemljištu i individualizam težaka (Individual and Collective Property of Land and the Individualistic Orientation of Peasants). *Arhiv*, 1929:428–442; (b) Zakon o seoskom posjedu u Bosni i Hercegovini (Law on Peasant Tenures in Bosnia and Herzegovina). Sarajevo, 1928. 64 p.

1956 Kukoljac, Milorad V. Zemljišno-knjižno pravo; osnovni pojmovi (Elements of the Land Title Register Law). Beograd, 1937. 114 p. (DLC)

1957 Kojić, Živojin. Zbirka obrazaca po intabulacionim, zemljišnoknjižnim i vanparničnim stvarima (Collection of Forms for Mortgage, Land Title Register, and Non-Contentious Procedure). Beograd, 1st ed. (?); 2d ed. 1939. 484 p. (DLC)

1958 Lapajne, St. Pripombe k naši in moderni posestni zaščiti (Protection of Possession in Modern and Yugoslav Law). Ljubljana, 1936. 28 p.

1959 Legradić, R. Teorija stvarnog prava i stvarno pravo FNRJ (Theory of the Property Law and Property Law of the FPRY). Skopje, 1957. 258 p.

1960 Mallin, I. (a) Zaštita posjeda (Protection of Possession). Zagreb, 1891. 199 p.; (b) Zakon od 22 prosinca 1890, kojim se preinačuju odn. nadopunjuju njeke ustanove postupka u poslovih urbarskih (Law Amending Certain Provisions of the Procedure for the Liquidation of Feudal Tenancy of December 22, 1890). Zagreb, 19–?. 324 p. (DLC)

1961 Marković, Č. Ukoliko je preporučljivo ograničenje prava svojine (How Far Should the Right of Private Property be Limited). *Pravosudje*, 1933: 596–604.

1962 Marković, L. Hipotekarno pravo (Mortgage Law). Beograd, 1911. 197 p.

1963 Matić, Dragoslav D. Zemljišno-knjižni postupak (Rules of Procedure in Land Title Register Matters, with Forms). Beograd, 1936. 192 p. (DLC)

1964 Zbirka zakona iz stambene oblasti sa ekspozejom Lidije Šejtunc (Collection of Laws on Housing. Preface by Lidija Šejtunc). Beograd, 1959. 213 p.; 2nd ed. 1960. 322 p.

1965 Pašić, N. Šta je svojina? (What is Ownership?). Beograd, 1942. 81 p. (DLC)

1966 Pavlović, Dj. Hipotekarno pravo u Kneževini Srbiji (Mortgage Law in Serbia). Beograd, 1868. 262 p. (DLC)

1967 Perović, M. O socijalističkoj svojini i njenom pravnom izražavanju (Socialist Ownership as Expressed in Law). *Naša stvarnost*, 1955: 407–427.

1968 Petrović, Jelenko S. Okuće ili zaštita zemljoradničkog minimuma (Protection of Homesteads). Beograd, 1930. 448 p. (DLC)

1969 Radanović, Božidar *and* Miodrag Matejić, *editors*. (a) Osnovni zakon o eksproprijaciji (Law on the Right of Eminent Domain). Beograd, 1st, 2d and 3d ed. (?); 4th ed. 1953. 126 p.; 5th ed. 1954. 122 p. (DLC); (b) Komentar zakona o eksproprijaciji (Commentary on the Law on Eminent Domain). Beograd, 1957. 155 p. (DLC)

1970 Rušnov, Adolfo, *editor*. Komentar k Gruntovnom pravu (Commentary on the Land Title Register Law). Zagreb, 1881. 260 p.

1971 Rušnov, Adolfo *and* Antun Goglia. Gruntovni zakoni (Laws on the Land Title Register). Zagreb, 1886. 326 p.

1972 Spaić, V. (a) Stvarno pravo (Property Law). Sarajevo, 1949. 252 p.; (b) Priroda Naše državne svojine (Nature of State Property in Yugoslavia). *Pregled* (Sarajevo), 1949: 28–39; (c) Priroda prava upravljanja opštenarodnom imovinom (Concept of Law of Management of the People's Property). *Narodna uprava* (Sarajevo), 1952: 29–37.

1973 Spevec, Franjo Josip. Posjed stvari i posjed prava prema svome najnovijem razvoju (Possession of Tangible Property and Choses in Action). Zagreb, 1907. 44 p. (DLC)

1974 Spendé, Anton. Zemljišna knjiga (Land Title Register). Ljubljana, 1937. 164 p. (DLC)

1975 Već, Hinko *and* Antun Goglia, *editors*. Zakoni i naredbe tičući se gruntovnice i izvlastbe (Laws and Regulations Governing Land Title Registers and the Right of Eminent Domain). Zagreb, 190– (?) 551 p. (DLC)

1976 Vežić, Milivoj, *editor*. Urbar Hrvatsko-Slavonski (Code of Feudal Tenancy for Croatia-Slavonia). Zagreb, 1882. 610 p. (DLC)

1977 Vuković, Mihailo. Osnovi Stvarnog prava (Elements of Property Law). Zagreb, 1950. 211 p.

1978 Živadinović, Stevan. Pravo raspolaganja i svojina (Property and Disposal of Property). Beograd, 1938. 145 p. (DLC)

1979 Zakon o bivšim kmetskim selištima i stečenim beglucima (Law on Resettlement of Bosnian Peasants). Beograd, 1928. 51 p. (DLC)

1980 Urbarski sustav kraljevinah Hrvatske i Slavonije (Code of Feudal Tenancy for the Kingdoms of Croatia and Slavonia). Translated from Latin by Franjo Žigrović Pretočki. Zagreb, 1880. 64 p. (DLC)

1981 Zakonodavstvo o eksproprijaciji (Legislation on Eminent Domain). Beograd, 1929. 88 p. (DLC)

1982 Zakon o izdavanju tapija na području kasacionog sudu u Beogradu i velikog suda u Podgorici od 30 maja 1931 (Law on the Issuing of Ownership Certificates in the Territories under the Jurisdiction of the Supreme Courts of Belgrade and Podgorica of May 30, 1931). Beograd, 1938. 95 p. (DLC)

1983 Zakon o prometu zemljišta i zgrada (Law on the Sale and Purchase of Real Property). Zagreb, 1954. 14 p. (DLC)

1984 Zakon o zemljišnim knjigama i zakon o unutrašnjem uredjenju, osnivanju i ispravljanju zemljišnih knjiga (Law on Land Title Registers with the Law on their Organization, Setting-Up and Rectifications). Beograd, 1930. 164 p. (DLC)

1985 Osnovni zakon o ekspropriaciji (Basic Law on Eminent Domain). Beograd, 1949. 48 p. (DLC)

1986 Gruntovni red i naknadne mu naredbe (Law on Land Title Registers with Pertinent Rules and Regulations). Zagreb, 1876. 160 p. (DLC)

29 Public Health

See also Nos.: 2111; 2248.

1987 Dilber, Nikola *and* Miroslav Nikitović, *editors*. Osnovni zakon o zdravstvenom nadzoru nad životnim namirnicama (Basic

Law on Sanitary Control of Foodstuffs). Beograd, 1956. 91 p.; 1957. 124 p. (DLC)

1988 Hudjber, Nikola, Krunoslav Filipčić *and* Josip Kucel, *editors.* Zbirka veterinarskih i stočarskih propisa (Collection of Provisions on Veterinary Medicine and Cattle). Zagreb, 1957. 659 p. (DLC)

1989 Zbirka predpisov o higijeni živil (Collection of Provisions on Meat and Dairy Control). Ljubljana, 1954. 160 p. (DLC)

1990 Zbirka zdravstvenih predpisov (Collection of Provisions on Public Health). Lljubljana, 1947. 396 p. (DLC)

1991 Zakon o lekarima od 14 januara 1931 (Law on Physicians of January 14, 1931). Beograd, 1938. 233 p. (Zbirka zakona, sv. 37). (DLC)

1992 Dolžan, Janko, *editor.* Nova zdravstvena zakonodaja (New Legislation on Public Health). Ljubljaa, 1931. 406 p. (DLC)

1993 Konstantinovich, Bogoljub, *editor.* Zbornik sanitetskog zakonodavstva (Collections of Public Health Legislation). Beograd, 1934. 1072. (DLC)

1994 Zakon o zdravstvenih domovih in zdravstvenih postajah. Zakon o bolnicah (Public Health Laws, Slovenia. Hospitals). Ljubljana, 1956. 190 p. (DLC)

1995 Zakon o suzbijanju polnih bolesti sa Pravilnikom (Law on Venereal Diseases and Regulations). Beograd, 1935. 48 p. (Zbirka zakona, sv. 231). (DLC)

1996 Zbirka zakona, uredbi, pravilnika i propisa o apotekama (Collection of Laws, Decrees, Regulations and Provisions on Pharmacies). Beograd, 1932. 441 p. (DLC)

1997 Zakon od 24. siječnja 1894 o uredjenju zdravstvene službe u Kraljevinah Hrvatskoj i Slavoniji i zakon od 11. Travnja 1894 o ljekarničtvu (Law of January 24, 1894 on Public Health Service in the Kingdom of Croatia and Slavonia and Law on Pharmacies of April 11, 1894). Zagreb, 1894. 27 p. (DLC)

30 Roman Law

See also Nos.: 2467c; 2467d.

1998 Andrassy, Ljudevit. Rimska pravna povijest (History of Roman Law). Zagreb, 1913. 160, 158 p. Mimeographed. (DLC)

1999 Arandjelović, Dragoljub. Predavanja iz Rimskog Prava (Lectures on Roman Law). Beograd, 1938. 428 p.

2000 Bakotić, Lujo. Justinianove Institucije (Justinian's Institutes). Beograd, 1912.

2001 Blagojević, Borislav. (a) Gradjanski postupak u Rimskom Pravu (Civil Procedure in Roman Law). Beograd, 1955. 89 p. (DLC); 1957. 89 p. (DLC); (b) Rimsko pravo (Roman Law Lectures). Beograd, 1946–1951. 2 v. (DLC)

2002 Brozović, A. Rimsko nasljedno pravo (Roman Inheritance Law). Bakar, 1879. 195 p.

2003 Egersdorfer, Aleksandar. (a) Predavanja o rimskom pravu (Lectures on Roman Law). Zagreb, 1919. 117 p.; 350 p.; 163 p.; (b) Predavanja o pandektama (Lectures on Pandects). Zagreb, 1915–1917. 2 v.; (c) Rimski civilni parbeni postupnik (Roman Civil Procedure). Zagreb, 1913. 88 p. Mimeographed. (DLC)

2004 Eisner, Bertold and Marijan Horvat. Rimsko pravo (Roman Law). Zagreb, 1948. 646 p.

2005 Geršić, Gl. (a) Sistem Rimskoga privatnoga prava (System of Private Roman Law). Beograd, 1882. 283 p.; (b) Nešto o pravništvu uopšte i o potrebi Rimskog prava po svesno pravništvo (About Law in General and the Need for Roman Law). Vila, 1866. 695 p.

2006 Graber, Vilim. Prinos k razvoju pojma obveze u Rimskom pravu (Contribution to the Development of the Principle of Obligation in Roman Law). Zagreb, 1898. 69 p. (DLC)

2007 Horvat, Marijan. (a) Rimsko pravo (Roman Law). Zagreb, 1952. 212 p. (DLC); 1954. 215 p.; 3rd ed. 1958. 432 p. (DLC); (b) Rimska pravna povijest (History of Roman Law). Zagreb, 1943; (c) Bona fides u razvoju Rimskog obveznoga prava (Good Faith in the Development of Roman Contract and Tort Law). Zagreb, 1939. 160 p.

2008 Korošec, Viktor. Očrt Rimskega prava (Outline of Roman Law). Ljubljana, 1948. 191 p.; 1953. 160 p.; 1955. 130 p. (DLC); 1960. 98 p.

2009 Korošec, Viktor and Gregor Krek. Zgodovina in sistem Rimskega zasebnega prava (History and System of Private Roman Law). Celje, 1937.

2010 Lešjanin, Rajko. Institucije Justinijanovog Rimskog Prava (Justinian Institutes). Beograd, 1857. 553 p. (DLC)

2011 Milosavljević, Ž. Rimsko privatno pravo i njegov uticaj na Europska zakonodavstva i pravničko obrazovanje (Roman Private Law and its Influence on European Legislation). Beograd, 1889. 87 p.

2012 Puhan, Ivo. Rimsko pravo (Roman Law). Skopje, 1956. 3 v. Mimeographed. (DLC)

2013 Radovanović, Mihailo M. Justinianove Institucije (Justinian's Institutes). Beograd, 1864. 293 p. (DLC)

2014 Stojčević, Dragomir. (a) Rimsko Pravo (Roman Law). 2d ed. Beograd, 1947– (DLC); 1951– (DLC); 3rd ed. 1960– (DLC v. 2, pt. 2); 6th ed. 1957–; 7th ed. 1960– (DLC); (b) Rimsko pravo. Obligaciono pravo (Roman Law. Contracts and Torts). Beograd, 1957. 158 p. (DLC)

2015 Strohal, I. Miraz za vrijeme braka po rimskom pravu (Dowry During Marriage under Roman Law). Zagreb, 1898. 110 p.

31 Sheriat Law

See also Nos.: 1657; 1674; 1675; 1705; 1805; 2254

2016 Zakonodavstvo o Islamskoj verskoj zajednici Kraljevine Jugoslavije (Legislation on the Mohammedan Religion in Yugoslavia). Beograd, 1932. 124 p. (DLC)

2017 Farkaš, Lj. Nasljedno pravo muslimana u Bosni i Hercegovini po hanifetskom redu (Mohammedan Inheritance Law in Bosnia and Herzegovina under the Hanifé School). *Mjesečnik,* 1929: 330–365. (DLC)

2018 Kruszelnicki, Franjo. Postupak pred šerijatskim sudovima u Bosni i Hercegovini (Procedure before Sheriat Courts in Bosnia and Herzegovina). Zagreb, 1917. 79 p. (DLC)

2019 Bušatlić, Abdulah. Šerijasko-sudski postupnik (Procedure in Sheriat Courts). Sarajevo, 1927. 239 p. (DLC)

2020 Uredba o vodjenju matica rodjenih i umrlih muslimana u Kraljevini SHS i Pravilnik (Decree on Vital Statistics of Moslems and Regulation for its Enforcement in the Yugoslav Kingdom). Beograd, 1928.

2021 Medžele i ahkjami šerije (Ottoman Civil Code). Reprint from *Bosansko-hercegovački zakoni, sv.* 4. Sarajevo, 1906.

2022 Begović, Mehmed. (a) Šerijatsko bračno pravo (Sheriat Marriage Law). Beograd, 1936. 148 p.; (b) O izvorima šerijatskog prava (Sources of Sheriat Law). Reprint from *Arhiv,* 1933. 24 p.

2023 Sladović, Eugen. Islamsko pravo u Bosni i Hercegovini (Mohammedan Law in Bosnia and Herzegovina). Beograd, 1926. 151 p. (DLC)

32 Social Security (Including War Veterans) and Insurance Law

See also: Ch. 11, A, 2, o; Nos. 1185; 1754; 1798; 2350.

2024 Arsov, Lj. Socijalno osiguranje u FNRJ (Social Security in the FPRY). *Komunist,* 1950: 181–212. (DLC)

2025 Blagojević, B. T. Pravni problemi osiguranja kod nas (Problems of Insurance in Yugoslavia). *Anali,* 1953: 278–310.

2026 Bole, Josip. Praktična objašnjenja zakonskih propisa o socijalnom osiguranju (Comments on Social Security Laws and Regulations). Beograd, 1951. 342 p.

2027 Boncelj, J. Preosnova individualnega zavarovalstva (Reform of the System Governing the Insurance of Persons). Ljubljana, 1953. 40 p.

2028 Brejc, T. Novi zakon o socijalnem zavarovanju (New Law on Social Security). *Delo,* 1950: 1–15.

2029 Dilber, N. (a) Naše novo socijalno osiguranje (New Yugoslav Social Security System). Beograd, 1947. 190 p.; (b) Novi sistem invalidskog osiguranja u Jugoslaviji (New Disability Insurance System). Beograd, 1959. 166 p.

2030 Gavrilović, M. Nauka o osiguranju (Theory on Insurance). Beograd, 1930. 141 p.

2031 Gojković, Emilo R. (a) Zakon o osiguranju radnika od 14 maja 1922, objašnjen sporednim zakonodavstvom i praksom (Commentary on the Social Security Law of May 14, 1922). Beograd, 1936. 695 p.; (b) Zakon o pensionom osiguranju službenika (Law on Civil Servants' Retirement Pension Insurance). Beograd, 1938. 264. (DLC)

2032 Jovanović, Vladimir. Prava osigurača prema trećem odgovornom licu (Rights of Insurers against Third Persons). Beograd, 1957. 178 p. (DLC)

2033 Kapor, V. Obavezno osiguranje robe u našem železničkom transportu (Compulsory Insurance of Goods Transported by Rail). *Anali*, 1953: 317–332. (DLC)

2034 Krajčević, Franjo. Radnička zaštita i radničko osiguranje (Protection of Labor and Social Security). Zagreb, 1927. 30 p.

2035 Lukić, Živan. Ugovor o osiguranju života (Contract of Life Insurance). Beograd, 1929. 142 p. (DLC)

2036 Macan, Josip. Invalidsko pitanje (The Question of Disabled War Veterans). Beograd, 1921.

2037 Milovanović, Milorad. Izjednačenje prava ugovornog osiguranja (On the Unification of the Rules and Regulations Governing Insurance). *In* Spomenica Kongresa Pravnika (Beograd), 1935: 114–132. (DLC)

2038 Nedić, Božidar. Problem obezbedjenja invalida i savremeno invalidsko zakonodavstvo (The Problem of Disabled War Veterans and the Present Legislation). Beograd, 1936. 134 p.

2039 Nikolić, N. Ugovor o osiguranju (Insurance Contracts). Beograd, 1957. 282 p. (DLC)

2040 Novaković, Drag. O. Invalidski Zakon s komentarom (Law on Disabled War Veterans, Annotated). Beograd, 1926. 510 p.

2041 Novaković, Radivoje. (a) Invalidsko pitanje i nepovratnost sile zakona (The Problem of Disabled War Veterans and the Principle of Non-Retroactivity of the Law). Beograd, 1936. 74 p.; (b) Invalidsko pitanje i stečena prava invalida (The Problem of Disabled War Veterans and the Principle of Vested Rights). Beograd, 1913. 41 p.; (c) Ko nije ratni invalid? Ko ima pravo po invalidskoj uredbi od 1 aprila 1936 (Persons Enjoying the Status of Disabled War Veterans under the Law of April 1, 1936). Beograd, 1936. 31 p.

2042 Perić, B. Socijalno osiguranje umetnika u FNRJ (Social Insurance of Artists in the FPR of Yugoslavia). Beograd, 1957. 191 p.

2043 Perić, Živojin. O stečenim pravima invalida (Vested Rights of Disabled War Veterans). Reprint from *Arhiv*, 1932. 16 p. (DLC)

2044 Perić, Živojin *and* Milan Bartoš. Izjednačenje prava o osiguranju (Unification of the Insurance Law). *In* Spomenica Kongresa pravnika, 1935: 71–85. (DLC)

2045 Pešić, R. Nastanak i razvitak socijalnog osiguranja u Jugoslaviji (Origin and Development of Social Security in Yugoslavia). Beograd, 1957. 210 p.

2046 Poličević, Mihailo S. O ugovorima o osiguranju života (Life Insurance Contracts). *Arhiv,* 1907: 58–65, 192–201. (DLC)

2047 Urbanc, A. Zavarovalno pravo (Insurance Law). Ljubljana, 1939. 256 p.

2048 Vesić, Budimir, *editor.* (a) Novi propisi o ratnim vojnim invalidima (New Rules and Regulations on Disabled War Veterans). Beograd, 1957. 98 p. (DLC); (b) Zbirka propisa o ratnim i mirnodobskim vojnim invalidima, sa objašnjenjima (Collection of Rules and Regulations Governing the Status of War- and Peacetime Disabled Armed Forces Personnel, Annotated). Beograd, 1st ed.?; 2nd ed. 1953. 180 p. (DLC); (c) Zbirka propisa o ratnim i mirnodobskim vojnim invalidima (Collection of Rules and Regulations Governing the Status of War and Peacetime Disabled Armed Forces Personnel). Beograd, 1959. 153 p.; 2nd ed. 1961. 176 p.

2049 Vujnović, Gojko. Naše socijalno osiguranje (Our Social Security). Beograd, 1950. 101 p.

2050 Invalidski zakon 4 jula 1929 (Law on Disabled War Veterans). Beograd, 1929. 80 p. (DLC)

2051 Invalidski zakon od 17 novembra 1925 sa pravilnikom (Law on Disabled War Veterans of November 17, 1925 with Regulation). Beograd, 1926. 95 p. (DLC)

2052 Novi propisi o ratnim vojnim invalidima, sa uputstvima i objašnjenjima (New Rules and Regulations on Disabled War Veterans, Annotated). Beograd, 1952. 47 p. (DLC)

2053 Pravila za: (a) Dobrovoljno osiguranje (Voluntary Insurance). Beograd, 1951. 15 p. (DLC); (b) Osiguravanje na dobitok (Cattle Insurance). Skopje, 1954. 34 p. (DLC); (c) Osiguranje od posledica nesrećnog slučaja (Accident Insurance). Beograd, 1952. 36 p. (DLC); (d) Osiguranje od šteta uslijed požara i drugih prirodnih dogadjaja (Insurance Against Fire and Other Acts of God). Beograd, 1952. 14 p. (DLC); (e) Osiguranje od šteta uslijed provalne kradje (Insurance against Burglary). Beograd, 1949. 16 p. (DLC), 18 p. (DLC); (f) Osiguranje od šteta uslijed zakonske odgovornosti (Insurance against Liability for Damages). Beograd, 1951. 13 p. (DLC); (g) Osiguranje stakla od šteta uslijed loma (Insurance of Glasswork against Breakage). Beograd, 1949. 13 p. (DLC); (h) Osiguranje stoke (Cattle Insurance). Beograd, 1952. 31 p. (DLC); (i) Osiguranje strojeva, strojnih naprava, instalacija i aparata (Insurance of Machines, Machinery, Installations, Apparatus). Beograd, 1949. 14 p. (DLC); (j) O osnivanju, sastavu i radu komisija za pregled osiguranika i uputstvo (Regulation on the Organization and Tasks of Commissions Charged with the Examination of Policy Holders). Beograd, 1952. 27 p. (DLC); (k) Za nezgodno zavarovanje (Accident Insurance). Murska Sobota, 1956. 20 p. (DLC); (l) Za zavarovanje posenkov in plodov proti škodam po toči (Crop Insurance). Ljubljana, 1953. 12 p. (DLC); (m) Za zavarovanje proti škodi zaradi zakonitega jamstva (Insurance against Liability for Damages). Beograd, 1951. 13 p. (DLC)

2054 Pravilnik o organizaciji i poslovanju Narodnog Invalidskog Fonda od 21 Septembra 1939 (Regulation Providing for the Setting Up and Working of the Disabled War Veterans' Fund). Beograd, 1939. 23 p. (DLC)

2055 Pravilnik za izvršenje uredbe o ratnim invalidima i ostalim žrtvama rata (Regulation on the Implementation of the Decree on Disabled War Veterans and Other War Casualties). Zagreb, 1939. 133 p. (DLC)

2056 Zakon o invalidskom osiguranju, sa ekspozeom Mome Markovića (Law on Disability Insurance. Preface by Moma Marković). Beograd, 1958. 237 p. (DLC); 1959. 191 p. (DLC)

2057 Ugovor o socijalnom osiguranju katoličkih svećenika-članova udruženja katoličkih svećenika "Dobri Pastir" za N R Bosnu i Hercegovinu (Social Insurance Contract of Roman-Catholic Priests, Members of the "Good Shepherd Society" in the P.R. of Bosnia and Herzegovina). Sarajevo, 1958. 17 p. (DLC)

2058 Uredba o socijalnom osiguranju sveštenika. Ugovor o socijalnom osiguranju sveštenika Islamske vjerske zajednice u FNRJ (Decree on the Social Insurance of Priests. Contract Providing for the Social Insurance of Moslem Priests). Sarajevo, 1952. 21 p. (DLC)

2059 Uredba o zbrinjavanju nezaposlenih radnika (Decree on Unemployment Benefits). Beograd, 1938. 93 p.

2060 Zakon o invalidskem zavarovanju (Law on Disability Insurance). Ljubljana, 1958. 261 p. (DLC); 1959. 201 p. (DLC)

2061 Zakon o mirovinskom osiguranju sa tablicama za preračunavanje mirovine (Law on Retirement Pension Insurance). Beograd, 1958. 150 p. (DLC)

2062 Zakon o osiguranju radnika od 14 maja 1922 (Social Security Law of May 1, 1922). Zagreb, 1922. 124 p. (DLC)

2063 Zakon o pensionom osiguranju službenika (Law on the Retirement Pension Insurance of Clerical Workers). Zagreb, 1938. 85 p. (DLC)

2064 Zakon o ratnim vojnim invalidima. Zakon o mirnodopskim vojnim invalidima (Law on War- and Peace-Time Disabled Armed Forces Personnel). Beograd, 1951. 26 p. (DLC)

2065 Zbirka predpisov o varstvu mater in otrok (Collection of Provisions on Mother and Child Welfare). Ljubljana, 1948. 105 p. (DLC)

2066 Zbirka propisa o ratnim vojnim invalidima, sa objašnjenjima (Collection of Rules and Regulations on Disabled War Veterans, Annotated). Beograd, 1951. 152 p. (DLC)

33 Transportation

2067 Uredba o organizaciji, poslovanju i upravljanju Jugoslovenskim željeznicama (Decree on the Organization, Operation and Management of Yugoslav Railways). Subotica, 1954. 52 p. (DLC)

2068 Uredba o platama radnika i službenika železničkih transportnih preduzeća (Decree on Wages and Salaries of Railway Employees). Beograd, 1954. 104 p. (DLC)

2069 Tarifa za prevoz putnika, prtljaga i ekspresne robe na prugama Jugoslovenskih željeznica (Tariff on the Transportation of Passengers and Goods by Yugoslav Railways). Subotica, 1952. 2 v.

2069[1] Brajković, Vladimir. Medjunarodno transportno pravo (International Transportation Law). Zagreb, 1957. 92 p. (DLC)

2070 Nedeljković, Jovan, *editor.* Zakonske osnove prevoženja robe željeznicom (Provisions of Law Concerning Transportation of Goods by Railways). Beograd, 1950. 454 p. (Zbirka zakonskih propisa, knj. 5). (DLC)

2071 Zakon o željeznicama javnog saobraćaja (Law on Public Railways). Beograd, 1932. 157 p. (Zbirka zakona, sv. 200). (DLC)

2072 Vuković, Ivo, *editor.* Željezničko-saobraćajna uredba Kraljevine Jugoslavije (Decree on Railroad Transportation of the Kingdom of Yugoslavia). Zagreb, 1931. 291 p. (DLC)

2073 Niketić, Gojko, *editor.* Željczničko policijski zakon (Law on the Policing of Railways). Beograd, 1927. 51 p. (Zbirka zakona, sv. 13). (DLC)

2074 Zbirka propisa iz oblasti auto-saobraćaja. Plate i radni odnosi radnika (Collection of Provisions on Motor Transportation. Wages and Labor Relations of Employees). Beograd. 1949–50. 5 v. (DLC: 2–5)

2075 Tošić, Branislav L. Zbirka propisa NR Srbije iz oblasti saobraćaja (Collection of Provisions on Transportation of the People's Republic of Serbia). Beograd, 1950. 304 p. (DLC)

2076 Uredba o saobraćaju na javnim putevima (Decree on Public Road Transportation). Zagreb, 1951. 58 p. (DLC)

2077 Zakon o državnim putovima (Law on State Highways). Beograd, 1929. 133 p. (Zbirak zakona, sv. 135). (DLC)

2078 Deronja, Mehmen H. *and* Stjepan I. Forgić, *editors.* Saobraćajna i komercijalna služba (Transportation and Commercial Service). Beograd, 1936. 1024 p. (DLC)

2079 Cigoj, Stojan. (a) Transportno pravo (Transportation Law). Ljubljana, 1959. 105 p.; (b) Prevoz blaga po železnici (Railway Transportation of Goods). Ljubljana, 1960. 200 p.

2080 Tihomirov, Konstantin *and* Jovan M. Jovanović, *editors.* Zakon o državnom saobraćajnom osoblju (Law on Government Transportation Personnel). Beograd, 1936. 666 p. (Željezničko zakonodavstvo, sv. 1); 2nd ed. 1940. 981 p. (DLC)

2081 Zakon o državnom saobraćajnom osoblju od 22 juna 1931 (Law on Government Personnel Employed in Transportation of June 22, 1931). Beograd, 1931. 134 p. (Zbirka zakona, sv. 187) (DLC); 1931. 170 p. (Zbirka zakona, sv. 42). (DLC)

34   Trials

See also: Ch. 11, A, 2, p.; Nos. 2239; 2241; 2241[1]; 2242; 2258; 2273; 2326; 2354; 2416; 2450.

2082   Mihailović, Draža, *codefendant*. Sudjenje članovima . . . organizacije (Trial of Members of the Political and Military Organization of . . . Stenographic Records). Beograd, 1945. 576 p. (DLC)

2083   ———. Izdajnik i ratni zločinac (Records of the Trial). Beograd, 1946. 540 p. (DLC)

2084   Stepinac, Alois, *codefendant*. Sudjenje Lisaku, Stepincu i dr. (Trial of Lisak, Stepinac et al.). Zagreb, 1946. 494 p. (DLC)

2085   ———. 1000 Lojzekovih Grijeha (One Thousand Sins of Stepinac). n.p., 1946. 60 p. (DLC)

2086   Pribičević, Adam, *codefendant*. Obtužnica od 12 sijećnja 1908 (Bill of Charges). Zagreb, 1909. 107 p. (DLC)

2087   ———. Stenografski zapisnik (Stenographic Record of the Trial). Zagreb, 1909. 2 v. (DLC)

2088   ———. Govori branitelja (Pleadings of Counsels for Defense). Zagreb, 1909. 471 p. (DLC)

2089   Branilački govor dra. Nikole Tolnauera, branioca Aleksandra Sohra u krivičnoj parnici protiv dra. Svetozara Grgina i drugova (Arguments of the Defense Counsel Dr. Nicolas Tolnauer in the Criminal Case against Dr. Svetozar Grgin and others. From the Stenographic Records). Zagreb, 1935. 293 p. (DLC)

2090   Hinković, Hinko. Veleizdajnička parnica (Trial for Treason. Appeal from the Judgment of the District Court of Zagreb). Zagreb, 1911. 32 p. (DLC)

2091   Bayer, Vladimir. Ugovor s djavlom; procesi protiv čarobnjaka u Europi a napose u Hrvatskoj (Contract with the Devil. Trials of Magicians in Europe, particularly in Croatia). Zagreb, 1953. 798 p. (DLC)

2092   Bogičević, Vojislav. Sarajevski atentat (Assassination in Sarajevo). Sarajevo, 1954. 455 p. (DLC)

2093   Djukanović, Ilija. Ubistvo kneza Mihaila i dogadjaji o kojima se nije smelo govoriti (Murder of Prince Mihailo and the Events which could not be Discussed). Beograd, 1935. 352 p. (DLC)

2094 Grujić, Radoslav M. Apologija Srpskog naroda u Hrvatskoj i Slavoniji. Povodom Optužnice kr. drž. odvjetnika u Zagrebu od 12. Januara 1909 (Defense of the Serbian People in Croatia and Slavonia in Connection with the Information of the District Attorney in Zagreb, January 12, 1909). Novi Sad, 1909. 293 p. (DLC)

2095 Levi, Jakov. Zločin protiv pravosudja. O antijugoslovenskom i antidemokratskom Budipeštanskom procesu Rajku i ostalima (Crime against the Administration of Justice. The Budapest Trial of Rajk and others). Beograd, 1950. 132 p. (DLC)

2096 Maksimović, St. Sudjenja u kneževini Srbiji pre pisanih zakona iz arhive Požarevačkog magistrata (Trials in the Principality of Serbia under Customary Law). Požarevac, 1898. 179 p. (DLC)

2097 Novak, Lujo. Iza kulisa jedne presude (Behind the Scenes of a Judgment). Zagreb, 1933. 124 p. (DLC)

2098 O Sofiskom Procesu (Trial of Sofia). Beograd, 1950. 79 p. (DLC)

2099 Tajne Emigrantskih zločinaca. Ispovijest Jelke Pogorelec o Gustavu Perčecu i Drugovima (Secrets of Emigrant Criminals. Jelka Pogorelec's Confession Concerning Perčec and Others). Zagreb, 1933. 38 p. (DLC)

2100 Živanović, Milan Ž. Solunski proces hiljadu devetsto sedamnaeste (Saloniki Trial in 1917). Beograd, 1955. 755 p. (DLC)

35 Unfair Competition

See also No.: 2362b.

2101 Darvaš, E. Nelojalna konkurencija (Unfair Competition). Beograd, 1933. 126 p.

2102 Eisner, B. Zaštita od nelojalne konkurencije (Protection from Unfair Competition). Mjesečnik, 1924: 362–385. (DLC)

2103 Politeo, Ivo. Zakon o suzbijanju nelojalne utakmice od 4 aprila 1930 (Law on Unfair Competition of April 4, 1930). Zagreb, 1930. 55 p. (DLC)

2104 Pretnar, S. (a) Nedopustna konkurencija (Unfair Competition). Ljubljana, 1957. 122 p.; (b) Pravna problematika kon-

kurence v naši državi (Legal Problems of Competition in Yugoslavia). *Zbornik znanstvenih razprav,* 1956: 143–182. (DLC)
2105 Šuman, J. Nelojalna utaknica (Unfair Competition). Beograd, 1939. 311 p. (DLC)
2106 Zakon o suzbijanju nelojalne konkurencije (Law on Unfair Competition). Beograd, 1930. 26 p. (DLC)

11

BIBLIOGRAPHY OF BOOKS AND ARTICLES IN FOREIGN LANGUAGES

A   In English

See also Nos.: 20; 21; 75; 210; 211; 212; 213; 214; 258; 321; 327; 329; 535; 975; 1117; 1835.

Mention is first made of publications which are comprehensive in scope, covering translations of laws and decrees of Yugoslavia. These are followed by publications arranged according to topic. Under each topic the translations of laws and decrees are entered first and these are followed by jurisprudential writings.

1   Comprehensive Collections of Translations of Yugoslav Laws and Decrees and General Works

2107   Collected Yugoslav Laws. Beograd, Association of Jurists of the F.P.R.Y., 1950– (DLC: 2–3, 1952)

> So far three numbers, called series, containing translations of various Yugoslav laws have been published. The first series covers constitutional laws and government organization; the second, nationality laws, elections, and laws on associations, meetings and assemblies; the third, laws concerning business enterprises and domestic relations.

2108   Zalar, Charles. Yugoslav Communism. A Critical Study. Prepared for the Subcommittee to Investigate the Administration of the Internal Security Act and Other Internal Security Laws of the Committee on the Judiciary, United States Senate,

87th Congress, 1st session. Washington, Government Printing Office, 1961. 387 p. (DLC)

2109   International Labour Office. Legislative Series. Geneva, 1919– (DLC)

> Contains translations of practically all labor laws and occasionally some other laws of general importance. Early volumes in this series contain legislation issued by the Serb-Croat-Slovene Kingdom. Such entries are identified by the letters S.C.S. Later legislation issued by the Kingdom of Yugoslavia and by the F.P.R.Y. is identified by the abbreviation Yug. Translation of each law is printed as a separate pamphlet.

2110   Food and Agricultural Legislation in Yugoslavia. Published by the Food and Agriculture Organization of the United Nations. Rome, 1, 1952– (DLC)

> Contains translations of a selection of laws and regulations of various countries. Issued in three editions, English, French and Spanish. Appears quarterly in folders, each containing separate leaflets covering the country and particular laws in full, excerpts, or summaries.

2111   International Digest of Health Legislation. Yugoslavia. World Health Organization, Geneva. Quarterly, 1, 1948– (DLC)

> Appears quarterly in two separate editions, English and French, and contains translations of selected health laws and regulations of various countries giving the text in full, excerpts or summaries.

2112   Gsovski, V. New Codes in the New Slavic Countries (Czechoslovakia, Poland, Yugoslavia). Washington, D.C., 1934: 159–198. Reprint from *Comparative Law Bulletin of the American Bar Association,* 1933.

2113   Gsovski, V. *and* K. Grzybowski, *editors.* Government, Law and Courts in the Soviet Union and Eastern Europe. London, Stevens & Son, N.Y., F. Praeger, 1959. 2 v. (DLC)

> Covers Yugoslavia in Chapters: 12: 316–460; 26: 803–838; 28: 853–855; 40: 1101–1124; 48: 1362–1391; 57: 1571–1604; 68: 1878–1902.

2114   Jaszenko, Kiril. (a) Civil Law. Yugoslavia. *In* No. 2113: 1362–1391. (DLC); (b) The [Yugoslav] Code of Civil Procedure.

Highlights, 1958: 225–228. (DLC); (c) Milovan Djilas. The New Class. Book review. *Ibid.,* 1957: 431–434. (DLC); (d) Statute of Limitation. *Ibid.,* 1954: 80–82. (DLC)

2115 Maksimovich, B., F. Gjupanovich *and* K. Jaszenko. Survey of Legislation. *Highlights,* 1953–1: 19–20; 1953–2: 18–21; 1953–3: 16–19; 1953–6: 17–24. (DLC)

2116 Maksimovich, B. *and* K. Jaszenko. Survey of Laws and Treatises for 1955–1956. *Highlights,* 1957: 27–46. (DLC)

2117 Plamenatz, Ilija P. Yugoslav Abbreviations. A Selective List. Washington, 1959. 185 p.; 2nd ed. 1962. 198 p. (DLC)

2 By Subject Matter

a Banking and Foreign Exchange

2118 Currency Law of the Kingdom of Yugoslavia. May 11, 1931. *In* No. 20, pp. 229–230; Law Concerning the National Bank of the Kingdom of Yugoslavia, June 17, 1931, *id.,* pp. 205–227; Regulation Concerning Foreign Exchange, October 7, 1931, *id.,* pp. 455–560.

b Church and State

2119 Churches and Religion. Washington, 1950. 15 p. (National Committee for a Free Europe. Mimeographed) (DLC)

2120 Ivičević, Petar. About the Law on the Legal Status of Religious Communities. *In* Nos. 258, 1954.

c Constitutional Law

2121 Act Respecting Associations, Assemblies and Private Meetings, dated 18th September 1931. *In* No. 2109, 1931 (Yug. 3).

2122 Constitution [of Serbia] of 5 (18) June 1903. *In* Herbert F. Wright, *editor.* The Constitutions of the States at War 1914–1918. Washington, Government Printing Office, 1919: 554–586. (DLC)

2123 Constitution [of Montenegro] of 6 (19) December 1905. *Ibid.:* 407–429. (DLC)

2124 Constitution of the Kingdom of the Serbs, Croats, and Slovenes of June 28, 1921. *In* Howard Lee McBain *and* Lindsay Rogers, *editors.* The New Constitutions of Europe. New York, Doubleday-Page, 1923: 348–378 (DLC); B. Shiva Rao, *editor.* Select Constitutions of the World. Madras, 1934: 45–77. (DLC)

2125 Constitution of the Federal People's Republic of Yugoslavia of January 31, 1946. Washington, Embassy of the F.P.R.Y., 1946. 48 p. (DLC); Beograd, Office of Information, 1947. 86 p. (DLC); Beograd, 1951. 87 p. (DLC). *Also in* No. 2107, No. 5, first series. 2nd ed.

2126 Constitution of the P.R. of Serbia [of January 17, 1947]. *In* No. 2107, first series.

2127 General Law on People's Committees [of April 1, 1952]. *In* No. 258, 1952: I-XVII. *Also in* No. 2107, first series.

2128 General Law on the Organization of Communes and Districts [of June 17, 1955]. Excerpts. *In* No. 258, No. 3, July-September 1955: 28–31. (DLC)

2129 Minić, Miloš. The Constitutional Law of the People's Republic of Serbia. *In* No. 258, Nos. 1–2, 1953: 4–17. (DLC)

2130 Law of State Administration. *In* No. 258, 1956: 37–55.

2131 Law on Associations, Meetings and other Assemblies [of June 21, 1945]. *In* No. 2107, second series.

2132 Vučković, M. Basic Principles of the Organization and Functioning of the Federal Executive Council. *In* No. 258, Nos. 1–2, 1959: 15–23. (DLC)

2133 Law Concerning the Constituent Assembly [of August 21, 1945]. *In* Five Laws Bearing on the Forthcoming Elections. London, Yugoslav Information Office, 1945: 31–34. (DLC)

2134 Law Prohibiting Incitement to National, Racial and Religious Hatred and Discord [of July 11, 1946]. Beograd, Office of Information attached to the Government of the F.P.R.Y., 1947. 13 p. (DLC)

2135 New Fundamental Law of Yugoslavia; Fundamental Law Pertaining to the Bases of the Social and Political Organization of the Federal People's Republic of Yugoslavia and of the Federal Organs of State Authority [of January 13, 1953]. Beograd, Union of Jurists' Associations of Yugoslavia, 1953. 99 p. (DLC)

2136 Manifest[o] from the King to the Serb-Croat-Slovene Nation of January 6, 1929. *In* Milton H. Andrew, *editor.* Twelve Leading Constitutions. Compton, Calif., 1931: 379–381 (Amer. Univ. Series). (DLC)

2137 Statute of the Autonomous Province of Voyvodina in the People's Republic of Serbia [of May 24, 1948]. *In* No. 258, No. 4, 1950: 50–58. *Also in* No. 2107, first series.

2138 Statute of Kosovo and Metohija. *In* No. 2107, first series.

2139 Adamovitch, A. Judicial Control of Administrative Acts [in Yugoslavia]. *Highlights,* 1958: 289–298. (DLC)

2140 Baerlein, Henry P. B. The Birth of Yugoslavia. London, 1922.

2141 Beard, Charles A. *and* George Radin. The Balkan Pivot: Yugoslavia. New York, 1929. 325 p.

2142 Bishop, William W., Jr. Judicial Decisions: Alien's Right to Estate, Consular Functions. In re Arbulich's Estate. *The American Journal of International Law,* January 1953. (DLC)

2143 Byrnes, Robert F., *editor.* East-Central Europe under the Communists. Yugoslavia. New York, 1957. 488 p.

2144 Djordjević, Jovan. (a) Local Self-Government in Yugoslavia. *American Slavic and East European Review* (New York), 1953: 188 200. (DLC); (b) Yugoslavia's New System of Government. *The Fortnightly* (London), April, 1953. (DLC)

2145 Gershković, Leon. The System of Producers' Councils in Yugoslavia. *International Labor Review* (Geneva,), 1955: 34–59. (DLC)

2146 Jaszenko, Kiril *and* B. Maksimović. Yugoslavia; The Regime and the Origin. *In* No. 2113, pp. 396–460.

2147 Kardelj, Edvard. (a) On the Law on People's Committees. *In* No. 258, Nos. 1–2, 1952: 6–29; (b) The New Organization of Municipalities and Districts. *Ibid.,* No. 3, 1955: 3–27; (c) Our State Administration under the New Conditions. *Ibid.,* No. 2, 1956: 3–20; (d) On the Further Development of the Social and Legal System. *Ibid.,* No. 1, 1957: 3–11. (DLC); (e) Four Factors in the Development of Socialist Social Relations. Beograd, 1960. 34 p.

2147[1] Landy, Paul. Reforms in Yugoslavia. *Problems of Communism* (Washington, D. C.), v. 10, No. 6, 1961: 24–33.

2148 Lukić, Radomir. The State Organization of Yugoslavia. Beograd, 1955. 59 p.

2149   Maksimović, B. (a) Constitutional Amendments. *Highlights,* 1954: 200–202. (DLC); (b) Experiment in Legislative Technique. *Ibid.,* 1954: 385–386. (DLC)

2150   The Organization of the State Administration, *In* No. 258, 1956–2: 21–25. (DLC)

2150[1]   Peaslee, Amos J. Constitution of Nations. Concord, 1950. 3 v. Yugoslavia, v. 3, 1950: 518–541. (DLC); 2nd ed. 1956. 3 v. Yugoslavia, v. 3, 1956: 753–791. (DLC)

2151   Pejović, Andrija. On the Law of the Organs of Internal Affairs. *In* No. 258, 1956–3: 57–64. (DLC)

2152   Peselj, B. M. (a) Legal Trends in People's Democracies: the Satellite States. *George Washington Law Review,* 1954: 513–53; (b) Contemporary Croatia in the Yugoslavia Federation; Its Constitutional Status and Socio-Economic Position. *Journal of Croatian Studies,* New York, v. 2, 1961; (c) The Socialist Character of Yugoslav Law. *Review,* London. 1961: 75–112. (DLC)

2153   The State Administration of the People's Republics, Autonomous Units, Districts and Communes. *In* No. 258, 1956–2: 26–36. (DLC)

2154   Survey of the Reorganization in the State Administration of the Federative People's Republic of Yugoslavia. *In* No. 258, 1950–2/3: 33–45. (DLC)

d   Criminal Law and Procedure

2155   Code of Criminal Procedure [of September 10, 1953]. Beograd, Union of Jurists' Associations of Yugoslavia, 1954. 79 p. (DLC) *Also in* No. 258, 1953: 25–76. (DLC)

2156   Criminal Code [of March 2, 1951]. Beograd, Federation of Jurists' Associations of Yugoslavia, 1951. 79 p.; 1960. 124 p. (DLC)

2157   Criminal Code (Unified Text). *In* No. 258, Nos. 3–4, 1959: 1–156. (DLC)

2158   New [Yugoslav] Code of Criminal Procedure. *Highlights,* 1954: 47–48; 259–264. (DLC)

2159   Kukavica, Radmila. The Substance of the Amendments and Supplements to the Code of Criminal Procedure. *In* No. 258, Nos. 1–2, 1960: 8–12. (DLC)

2160   Donnelly, R. C. The New Yugoslav Criminal Code. *Yale Law Journal,* 1952: 510–39. (DLC)

2161 Givanovitch, Thomas. The Tripartite System of Criminal
Law. *Revue internationale de droit pénal*, 1926: 87–98.
2162 Gjupanovich, Fran. Criminal Law. Yugoslavia, Ch. 40. *In*
No. 2113: 1101–1122. (DLC)

e Domestic Relations

2163 Basic Law on Marriage of April 3, 1946; Law on Guardianship of April 1, 1947; Law on Adoption of April 1, 1947; Law
on the Relationship between Parents and Children of December
1, 1947. *In* No. 2107, third series.
2164 American Jewish Joint Distribution Committee. European
Legislation on Declarations of Death. Survey concluded on January 1, 1949. Paris, 1949. 199 p.
2165 Yugoslav Family Legislation. *In* No. 258, 1951: 1–45.
2166 Cohn, Herman. The Foreign Laws of Marriage and Divorce.
v. 1: The Countries of the European Continent. Tel Aviv, 1937.

> A concise and precise presentation of the rules of marriage and
> divorce from Albania to Yugoslavia (all Europe) with references
> to the code provisions. Still useful in spite of the changes in some
> countries.

2167 Federation of Women's Societies of Yugoslavia. Woman's
Equality under the Yugoslav Legislation. Beograd, 1956. 29 p.
2168 Vreeland, Hamilton. Validity of Foreign Divorces. A Study
Concerning the Extraterritorial Recognition of Divorce Decrees.
Chicago, 1938. 355 p. (DLC) Yugoslavia: p. 309.

f Economic Law

2169 Basic Law Concerning the Management of State Economic
Enterprises and Higher Economic Associations by the Workers'
Collectives [of July 2, 1950]. *In* No. 258, No. 2–3, 1950: 75–82.
Also in No. 2109, 1950 (Yug. 2) *and* No. 2107, third series.
2169[1] Bogosavljević, M. *and* M. Pešaković. Workers' Management
of a Factory in Yugoslavia. Beograd, 1959. 107 p. (DLC)
2170 Decree Concerning Handicraft Establishments and Handicraft Undertakings, dated 26 January 1954. *In* No. 2109, 1954
(Yug. 1). (DLC)

2171 Fundamental Law Concerning Cooperative Societies, dated 18 July 1946. *In* No. 2109, 1946 (Yug. 7). (DLC)

2172 Law against Illicit Speculation and Economic Sabotage, April 23, 1945. Law No. 241, *Sl. L.*, No. 26, 1945. Amended by Law No. 382, *ibid.*, No. 56, 1956. (DLC: MELP)

2173 Law Concerning Management of Governmental Enterprises [of June 21, 1946]. Law No. 391, *Sl. L.*, No. 43, 1950. (DLC: MELP)

2174 Law on the Five Year Plan [of April 28, 1947]. Beograd, Office of Information Attached to the Government of the F.P. R.Y., 1947. 166 p. (DLC)

2175 The Law on Planned Management of National Economy [of December 29, 1951]. *In* No. 2107, third series.

2176 Law on Nationalization of Tenements and Building Lots. *In* No. 258, Nos. 1–2, 1959: 38–46. (DLC)

2177 Summary Review of Federal Laws Characteristic of Recent Changes in the Structure and Organization of the Socialist Economy in the F.P.R.Y. (1944–1949). *In* No. 258, 1950–2/3: 46–74. (DLC)

2178 Adamovitch, A. Industrial Management [in Yugoslavia]. *Highlights,* 1957: 165–178. (DLC)

2179 Gjupanovich, F. Arbitration and Economic Courts. Yugoslavia. *Highlights,* 1957: 347–350. (DLC)

2180 Jaszenko, Kiril. (a) Economic Planning in Yugoslavia. *Highlights,* 1956: 291–294; (b) Foreign Trade. [Yugoslavia]. *Ibid.,* 1954: 177–180. (DLC)

2181 Management of Housing [in Yugoslavia]. *Highlights,* 1954: 117–119. (DLC)

2182 Rastovčan, P. On the Interrelationship of Economic Enterprises and their Relationship toward Third Persons. *In* No. 258, 1957: 102–111. (DLC)

2183 Valko, Laszlo. International Handbook of Cooperative Legislation. State College of Washington. 1954. 273 p. (DLC)

g Education

2184 General Law on Education in Yugoslavia. Beograd, 1959. 111 p. (DLC)

2185 General Law on Universities [of June 15, 1954]. *In* No. 258,

July-December 1954: 47–55. General Law on Faculties and Universities (Revised Text). *Ibid.* Nos. 3–4, 1960: 62–87. (DLC)

2185[1] Crvenkovski, Krste. Higher Educational and Vocational Training in Yugoslavia. *Ibid.,* Nos. 3–4, 1960: 7–25. (DLC)

2185[2] Lukić, Radomir. Teaching Reform at the Faculty of Law in Beograd. *Ibid.,* Nos. 1–2, 1959: 34–37. (DLC)

2186 Maksimovich, B. New Law on Universities. Yugoslavia. *Highlights,* 1954: 342–346. (DLC)

2187 Turosienski, Severin K. Education in Yugoslavia. Washington, D.C., 1939. 146 p. (DLC)

h Elections

2188 Five Laws Bearing on the Forthcoming Elections . . . together with a Commentary on these by Milan Bartoš and a Diagrammatic Representation of the Constituent Assembly. London, 1945. 51 p. (DLC)

> This work contains the translation of the Laws on: the Election of the Members of the Constituent Assembly [of August 22, 1945]; the Electoral Lists [of August 10, 1945]; the Election of the Members of the National Assembly [no date]; the Recall of Members of the National Assembly; and the Registers of Electors.

2189 Basic Provisions of the Law on the Recall of the People's Deputies of the National Assembly of the F.P.R. of Yugoslavia. *In* No. 258, 1950: 29–33. (DLC)

2190 Djordjević, Jovan. (a) The Electoral System and the Results of the Elections for the Federal People's Assembly. *In* No. 258, 1954; (b) The New Electoral System for the National Assembly. *In* No. 258, 1950–1: 9–12. (DLC); (c) Some Basic Principles and Institutions of the New Yugoslav Electoral Law. *Review of International Affairs,* 1953–18: 13–15. (DLC); (d) The Yugoslav Election System. *Ibid.* No. 1, 1958: 15–24.

i Judicial System

2191 Law on Courts of Justice [of July 1, 1954]. *In* No. 258, July-December, 1954: 38–46.

2192 Law on Economic Courts [of July 1, 1954]. *Ibid.* July-December, 1954: 55–60.

2193 Law on the Organization of People's Courts [of May 17, 1946]. Beograd, Jugoslovenska Knjiga, 1948. 51 p. (DLC)

2194 Gjupanovich, F. (a) Administration of Justice by Administrative Authorities. Yugoslavia. *In* No. 2113. (DLC); and also *in Highlights,* 1957: 219–222; (b) Arbitration and Economic Courts /in Yugoslavia/. *Ibid.,* 1957: 347–350; (c) Attorneys in Yugoslavia. *Ibid.,* 1958: 410–419; (d) The Judicial System of Yugoslavia. *Ibid.,* 1954: 47–48; 259–264; (e) The New Judiciary Act of Yugoslavia. *Ibid.,* 1955: 35–38; (f) Organization of the Bar. *Ibid.,* 1955: 165–166; (g) The Status of the Legal Profession in Yugoslavia. Reprint from *The American University Law Review,* v. 8, No. 2, 1959: 117–122. (DLC)

2195 Goldstajn, Aleksander. (a) The Practice of Economic Courts. *In* No. 258. 1956–3: 33–57; (b) Yugoslavia: Reform of Economic Courts. *American Journal of Comparative Law,* 1955: 600–603. (DLC)

2196 Jovanović, Milenko. From the Practice of the Regular Courts. *In* No. 258, 1956–3: 12–32. (DLC)

2197 Srzentić, Nikola. The Organization of Law Courts in Yugoslavia. Beograd, 1955. 32 p.

j Labor Law

2198 Adamovitch, Alexander. (a) Contemporary Yugoslav Trade Unions. *Highlights,* 1956: 319–332; (b) Industrial Management in Yugoslavia. *Ibid.,* 1957: 165–178; (c) Worker and Factory. Yugoslavia. *In* No. 2113. (DLC)

2199 Djordjević, Jovan. Essential Characteristics of the New System of Managing State Economic Enterprises and Higher Economic Associations. *In* No. 258, 1950: 13–28.

2200 Finžgar, A. The Rights of the Organs of Workers' Self-Government toward General People's Property. *In* No. 258, 1957: 78–85.

2201 Marshal Tito on Management of State Economic Enterprises and Higher Economic Associations by Workers' Collectives. *In* No. 258, 1950: 3–7.

2202 Uvalić, Radivoj. The Management of Economic Undertakings by the Workers in Yugoslavia. *International Labor Review,* 1954: 235–254. **(DLC)**

2203   Yerémitch, Douchan M. Problems of Agricultural Labor in Yugoslavia. *International Labor Review,* August 1938. (DLC)

k   Nationality Law

2204   Act of August 23, 1945, to Deprive of Yugoslav Nationality Officers and Non-Commissioned officers of the Former Yugoslav Armed Forces. *In* Laws Concerning Nationality. New York, United Nations, 1954: 553–563 (United Nations Legislative Series). (DLC)

2205   Nationality Law of July 1, 1946 of the F.P.R.Y. *Ibid.,* pp. 554–652. *Also* in No. 2107, second series. Amendments of December 2, 1947. *Ibid.,* pp. 562–653 (DLC); of December 1, 1948. *Ibid.,* p. 563.

2206   Law of Nationality of September 21, 1928. *In* Flournoy, Richard *and* Manley Hudson. Nationality Laws. New York, Oxford Univ. Press, 1929: 389–402. (DLC)

2207   A New Law of Nationality for the Kingdom of the Serbs, Croats and Slovenes [of September 1, 1928]. Typed report. U. S. Consulate in Beograd, 1929 44 p. (DLC)

2208   McMillin, Stewart E. A New Law of Nationality for the Kingdom of the Serbs, Croats and Slovenes. Beograd, 1929. 44 p. Mimeographed. (DLC)

2209   Peritch, J. Basic rules of the Yugoslav Law Concerning Nationality. *American Journal of International Law,* 1930: 728–37.

2210   United Nations, Commission on the Status of Women, Nationality of Married Women. New York, 1950. 74 p. (DLC)

l   The Press

2211   Law Concerning the Press [of August 24, 1945]. *In* Five Laws Bearing on the Forthcoming Elections. London, Yugoslav Information Office, 1945: 38–42. (DLC)

2212   Law on the Press [of April 1, 1947]. Beograd, Office of Information Attached to the Government of the F.P.R.Y., 1948. 25 p. (DLC) *Also in* No. 2107, second series.

2212[1]   Law on the Press and Other Forms of Information [of November 9, 1960]. *In* No. 258, Nos. 3–4, 1960: 26–59. (DLC)

2213   Shearman, M. and O. T. Rayner, *editors.* The Press Laws of Foreign Countries. London, Foreign Office of Great Britain, 1926. 328 p. (DLC)

>   A compilation of the laws or provisions on the press of 51 countries. Most of these are in English translations except those which are issued originally in French.

m   Patents, Trade Marks, Copyright

2214   Bureau Voor Technische Adviezen, Amsterdam. Manual for the Handling of Applications for Patents, Designs and Trade Marks throughout the World. 1st ed. Amsterdam, 1927; 2d ed. 1936, loose-leaf. (1936–50)

2215   Yugoslavia. Copyright Statute. *In* UNESCO, Copyright Laws and Treaties of the World. Paris, 1961. Item 1, p. 1–11. (DLC)

2216   Popović, Delija. Trademark Provisions in Yugoslavia. *Trade Mark Reporter* (New York), 1954: 1376–77. (DLC)

2217   Radojković, Živan. Copyright in Yugoslavia. *Revue internationale du droit d'auteur* (Paris), 1956: 58–93. (DLC)

n   Property Law

2218   Agricultural Laws and Regulations in Yugoslavia 1945–1953. Vladimir Gsovski, *editor.* New York, 1954. 57 p. Mimeographed. (DLC)

2219   Decree No. 25 of November 21, 1944, Concerning the Transfer into Government Ownership of Enemy Property, Government Administration of Property Belonging to Absent Persons, and Sequestration of Property Alienated by Force by the Occupying Forces, with the Amendment of July 31, 1946. *In* Translation of Yugoslav Laws on Agrarian Reform and Colonization. New York, Mid-European Studies Center, 1952. (DLC)

2220   Basic Law on Expropriation, April 1, 1947. Law No. 209. *Ibid.*

2221   Executive Order on the Procedure for the Appraisal and the Determination of Compensation for Nationalized Property, November 17, 1947. Law No. 716, 1947. *Ibid.*

2222   Law Concerning the Treatment of Property which the Owners were Forced to Abandon during the Occupation and Property

Taken from them by the Occupying Forces and their Collaborators, May 24, 1945. No. 36, 1945. Amended by Law No. 54, 1946 and Law No. 740, 1946. *Ibid.*

2223 Law No. 605 of August 23, 1945, on Land Reform and Colonization, with the Amendment of March 18, 1946. *Ibid.*

2224 Law on Confiscation and Execution of Confiscation, June 9, 1945. Law No. 359, Amended by Law No. 432 and Law No. 747, 1946. *Ibid.*

2225 Law on Nationalization of Private Economic Enterprises, December 6, 1946. Law No. 677, amended by Law No. 269, 1948. (DLC)

2226 Law on Seizure of War Profits Acquired during the Period of Enemy Occupation, May 24, 1945. Law No. 320, amended by Law No. 355, 1946. (DLC)

2227 Adamovitch, Alexander. (a) Land and Peasant. Yugoslavia. *In* No. 2113; (b) Postwar Farming [in Yugoslavia]. *Highlights,* 1957: 519–526. (DLC)

2228 Brašić, R. M. Land Reform and Ownership in Yugoslavia, 1919–1953. New York, 1954. 109 p.

2229 Doman, N. R. Compensation for Nationalized Property in Post-War Europe. *International Law Quarterly,* 1950: 323–42. (DLC)

2230 Dowson, *Sir* Ernest *and* V. L. O. Sheppard. Land Registration. London, 1952. 211 p.

2231 Postwar Nationalization of Foreign Property in Europe. *Columbia Law Review,* 1948: 1125–61. (DLC)

2232 Peselj, Branko M. International Aspect of the Recent Yugoslav Nationalization Law. *American Journal of International Law,* v. 53, no. 2, April 1959: 428–432.

o Social Security and War Veterans

2233 Decree on the Organization of Social Insurance Institutes. Beograd, 1956. 18 p. (DLC)

2234 Law on Pension Insurance. Beograd, 1958. 87 p. (DLC)

2235 Dilber, Nikola. Principles of the New Law on Social Insurance. *In* No. 258, 1950–1: 13–18.

2236 Vesić, Budimir. Protection of Disabled War Veterans in Yugoslavia. Beograd, 1955. 39 p.

p   Trials

See also Nos.: 2258; 2326; 2355; 2416; 2450.

2237   Adamovitch, A. Notes on a Belgrade Trial. *Highlights,* 1959: 175–182. (DLC)
2238   Austro-Magyar Judicial Crimes. Prosecutions of the Yugoslavs. Political Trials, 1908–1916. Chicago. The Yugoslav Committee in North America, 1916 (?). 96 p. (DLC)
2239   The Case of Archbishop Stepinac. Washington, Embassy of the F.P.R.Y., 1947. 96 p. (DLC)
2240   Gjupanovich, Fran. The Djilas Case. *Highlights,* 1957: 411–415. (DLC)
2241   O'Brien, Anthony Henry. Archbishop Stepinac. The Man and his Case. 1st ed. Lublin, n.d.; 2d ed. [1947]. 83 p. (DLC)
2241[1]   Pattee, Richard. The Case of Cardinal Stepinac. Milwaukee, 1953. 499 p. (DLC)
2242   The Trial of Dragoljub-Draža Mihailović. Beograd, 1946. 552 p. (DLC)

B   In French

See also Nos.: 54; 209; 222; 223; 228; 259; 306b; 316; 321; 326; 965e.

2243   Adamovitch, Alexandre. La responsabilité ministerielle d'après la Constitution du Royaume des Serbes, Croates, et Slovènes. Paris, 1926. 184 p. (DLC)
2244   Andrassy, Georges. (a) Règlement des questions de frontières entre la Yougoslavie d'une part, et l'Italie, l'Autriche, et la Hongrie d'autre part. *Annuaire,* 1934: 115–136. (DLC); (b) Les traités d'arbitrage et de conciliation conclus par la Yougoslavie. *Annuaire,* 1931: 75–95. (DLC)
2245   Andrassy, Georges *and* Milan Bartoš. Jurisprudence des tribunaux et des autorités Yougoslaves en matière de droit international. *Annuaire,* 1937: 237–257. (DLC)

2246   Arandjelović, Drag. *and* Georges Popovitch Les Conférences Balkaniques et l'unification du droit des pays balkaniques. *Annuaire,* 1934: 27–35. (DLC)

2427   Ardant, Gabriel. (a) La famille yougoslave au Monténégro, d'après la nouvelle codification. *Réforme sociale* (Paris), v. 6, No. 68, 1888: 408–413; (b) Une nouvelle méthode de codification du droit civil. *Ibid.,* 1888: 614–618; (c) La zadrouga, la famille patriarcale et le régime de communauté dans les Balkans depuis l'indépendance. *Ibid.,* 1886: 141–162 p.

2248   Arrêté de S. E. Le Gouverneur Général des Provinces Illyriennes sur l'organisation du service de santé. Trieste, 1812.

2249   Atanatskovitch, Milena. La protection de la femme en Yougoslavie. *Les Balkans,* 1934.

2250   Aucoc, Léon. Code général des biens pour la principauté de Monténégro. *Séances et travaux de l'Académie des sciences morales et politiques* (Paris), v. 139, 1893: 310–312.

2251   Babinet, Louis. Communication de deux études de M. Jovanović sur le Monténégro. *Bulletin de la Société de Législation Comparée* (Paris), 1885/1886: 248–257.

2252   Bartoš, Milan. (a) Le droit international sur la faillite en Yougoslavie. *Annuaire,* 1934: 241–258. (DLC); (b) Exposé de droit international privé, notamment de droit international commercial selon la législation et la jurisprudence yougoslave en Serbie. Paris, 1927, 308 p.

2253   Bartoš, Milan *and* Ilija Pržić. Premier Congrès des juristes des états slaves. *Annuaire,* 1934: 36–58. (DLC)

2254   Begovitch, Mehmed. (a) De l'évolution du droit musulman en Yougoslavie. Alger, 1930. 182 p.; (b) Législation relative aux affaires musulmanes en Yougoslavie. *Annuaire,* 1934; 265–289. (DLC)

2255   Biderman, H. J. Législation autonome de la Croatie et aperçu de l'histoire du droit croate. *Revue de droit international,* (Gand), 1876: 215–292. (DLC)

2256   Blagoyevitch, Borislav. (a) Exéquatur des jugements étrangers selon la loi yougoslave sur les exécutions et saisies-exécutions. *Annuaire,* 1934: 275–289. (DLC); (b) De l'influence du civil au criminel et du criminel au civil dans la législation yougoslave. Paris, 1936. 15 p.; (c) Les preuves et l'assistance judiciare devant les tribunaux yougoslaves. *Annuaire,* 1937: 177–210. (DLC)

2257 Bochkovitch, Miloutin. La banque nationale de Serbie. Paris, 1919. 179 p.

2258 Bogičević, Miloš. Le procès de Salonique, juin 1917. Paris, 1927. 183 p. (DLC)

2259 Bogišić, Valtazar. (a) À propos du Code Civil du Monténégro. Paris, 1886. 23 p.; 2d ed., 1888. 19 p.; (b) D'une forme particulière de la famille rurale chez les Serbes et les Croates. *Revue du droit international et de législation comparée* (Paris), 1884; (c) De la forme dite *inokosna* de la famille rurale chez les Serbes et les Croates. *Ibid.,* 1884; (d) Droit civil au Monténégro. Paris, 1888; (e) Modifications introduites dans la nouvelle édition du Code civil du Monténégro. Paris, 1900. 14 p.

2260 Brajković, V. (a) Étude historique sur le droit maritime privé du littoral yougoslave. Marseille, 1933. 348 p.; (b) La notion et le fondement de l'héritage dans le zadrouga yougoslave. *Annales de la Faculté de droit d'Aix* (Aix-en-Provence), 1931; 3–19.

2261 Brunswik, Benoît. Recueil de documents diplomatiques relatifs au Montenegro (1699–1876). Constantinople, Weiss, 1876. 152 p.

2262 Cigoj, S. Les règles de conflits de lois du droit yougoslave en matière de succession. *Yugoslovenska revija,* 1956: 138–152.

2263 Code général des biens pour la Principauté du Monténégro de 1888. Paris, 1892. (DLC)

2264 Čemerlić, Hamdija. Les systèmes électoraux en Yougoslavie. Paris, 1937. 175 p. (DLC)

2265 Chotch, Pierre. Le Monténégro, pages d'histoire diplomatique. Paris, Figuière, 1920. 89 p.

2266 Dareste, R. Les Slavs du Sud. *In* Études d'histoire du droit. 2d ed. Paris, 1908. (DLC)

2267 Dareste, R. *and* A. Rivière. Code général des biens pour la Principauté du Monténégro de 1888. Paris, 1892. 285 p.

2268 Décret sur l'organisation de l'Illyrie. Paris, 1811.

2269 Delarue, Henri. Le Monténégro. Histoire, description, moeurs, usages, législation, constitution politique, documents, et pièces officielles. Paris, 1862. 183 p.

2270   Dickel, Karl. (a) Étude sur le nouveau Code Civil du Monténégro. Reprint from *Revue générale du droit* (Paris), 1891. 76 p.; (b) Monténégro. *La législation pénale comparée* (Paris), 1894: 241–244.

2271   Dietz, J. Loi du 22 février 1880 concernant l'administration de la Bosnie et de l'Herzégovine, confiée à l'Autriche-Hongrie par le traité de Berlin du 13 juillet 1878. *Annuaire de législation étrangère* (Paris), 1880: 270–273.

2272   Djordjević, Vladan. La Serbie au Congrès de Berlin. Paris, 1891.

2273   Dragoun, Theodore. Le dossier du Cardinal Stepinac. Paris, 1958. 286 p. (DLC)

2274   Dzoulizibaritch, Dragolioub. Le Dinar serbe et l'évolution financière de la Serbie depuis 1914. Nancy, 1925. 192 p.

2275   Frangeš, Otto. La réforme agraire en Yougoslavie. *International Review of Agriculture* (Rome), mars-août 1934. (DLC)

2276   Gachitch, Y. De l'émission des billets de banque en Yougoslavie. Bordeaux, 1923. 106 p.

2277   Givotitch, V. (a) La participation de la Yougoslavie à la vie internationale. *Annuaire*, 1934: 13–21. (DLC); (b) Situation actuelle des minorités nationales en Yougoslavie. *Annuaire*, 1937: 113–123. (DLC)

2278   Godyévatz, Anna. (a) Compétence de la Cour Permanente de Justice Internationale ratione personae et ratione materiae par rapport au différend concernant les emprunts serbes. *Annuaire*, 1934: 208–217. (DLC); (b) Liste des traités et des engagements internationaux de la Serbie de 1870 à 1914. *Annuaire*, 1934: 305–343. (DLC); (c) Nationalité de la femme dans la nouvelle loi yougoslave. *In* Documents de la III-ème Conférence Balkanique. Bucarest, 1932.; (d) La situation de la femme en Yougoslavie suivant le droit civil et suivant les lois spéciales. *Ibid.*

2279   Glouchtchévitch, M. Le Self-government local en Serbie. Paris, 1911. 244 p.

2280   Goldstajn, A. La jurisprudence des tribunaux économiques. *Le nouveau droit yougoslave*, 1956: 35–59.

2280[1]   Guillite, Paulette. L'organisation de l'information en Yougoslavie: Un exemple d'autogestion sociale. *Annales de la Faculté de Droit* (Liège), 1961: 453–461. (DLC)

2281 Haumant, Emile. La formation de la Yougoslavie. Paris, 1930. 752 p.

2282 Horvatski, Milan. La Constitution de Vidovdan. Grenoble, 1923.

2283 Janković, D. La convention collective de travail et les lois du 25 mars 1919 et du 12 mars 1920. Lyon, 1920. 136 p.

2284 Jaquin, Pierre. La question des minorités entre l'Italie et la Yougoslavie. Paris, 1929. 221 p.

2285 Karitch, Slobodan Mil. De l'organisation du Parlement yougoslave d'après la Constitution de 1931. Lyon, 1932. 130 p.

2286 Koyitch, D. S. L'annexion de la Bosnie et de l'Herzégovine et le droit international public. Paris, 1910. 152 p.

2287 Krunsky, B. L'annexion de la Bosnie et de l'Herzégovine en 1908. Paris, 1912. 185 p. (DLC)

2288 Lapajne, S. Le Droit international privé en matière d'adoption. *Annuaire,* 1934: 230–240. (DLC)

2289 Lapradelle, Albert Geouffre de. Causes célèbres du droit des gens. La réforme agraire yougoslave devant la justice internationale. Paris, 1930. 434 p. (DLC)

2290 Laveleye, Emile de. Les communautés de famille et de village. *Revue d'économie politique* (Paris), 1888.

2291 Lazarevitch, Adam. De l'exécution des jugements autrichiens en Yougoslavie. *Annuaire,* 1934: 271–274. (DLC)

2291[1] Loi sur la presse et autres formules d'information. Beograd, Union des Associations de Juristes de Yougoslavie, 1960. 58 p. (DLC)

2292 Markovitch, Givan T. La transmission du patrimoine d'une personne décédée dans la zadrouga serbe. Paris, 1929. 166 p.

2293 Marcovitch, Lazare. (a) Le problème constitutionnel Serbo-Croate-Slovène. Genève, 1924. 31 p.; (b) Le régime immobilier en Serbie et la nécessité urgente de sa réforme. *Revue de l'Institut de droit comparé* (Bruxelles), 1912.

2294 Miletitch, Strachimir. Les droits sociaux et individuels dans la société anonyme en droit serbe. Fribourg (Suisse), 1921. 185 p. (DLC)

2295 Miletitch, Voukadine. Le mouvement des idées constitutionnelles en Yougoslavie depuis la fin de la Grande Guerre. Paris, 1934. 143 p. (DLC)

2296 Miliouche, B. L'organisation municipale en Yougoslavie. Paris, 1934. 220. p.

2297 Milochevitch, M. Le suffrage politique dans les constitutions de Serbie jusqu'à la Constitution de Vidovdan. Paris, 1929.

2298 Milochevitch, Voislav. Les monopoles en Yougoslavie. Paris, 1923. 170 p. (DLC)

2299 Mirkine Guetzévitch, B. Yougoslavie. *Annuaire de l'Institut international de droit public* (Paris), 1932: 726–828.

2300 Mirković, Dj. Navire et patrimoine de mer. Bordeaux, 1932. 311 p.

2301 Mitrović, Pero. Convention sur la pêche dans la Mer Adriatique. *Annuaire,* 1937: 98–104. (DLC)

2302 Mitrovitch, A. de. L'aviation au point de vue économique et juridique. Beograd, 1929. 124 p. (DLC)

2303 Montbel, G. La condition politique de la Croatie-Slavonie dans la Monarchie Austro-Hongroise. Paris. 1st ed.?; 2d ed. 1910. 314 p. (DLC)

2304 Mousset, Albert. Le Royaume des Serbes, Croates, et Slovènes. Paris, 1926. 316 p.

2305 Moyltch, Sava. Le parlement économique. Paris, 1927. 146 p.

2306 Murko, Vladimir. L'évolution de la dette publique yougoslave. *Revue de science et de législation financière,* 1954.

2307 Myovitch, Dobrivoye. La réforme agraire en Voïvodine. Nancy, 1938. 166 p.

2308 Namysłowski, Władysław. Situation juridique de l'église orthodoxe dans le Royaume des S.H.S. *Revue diplomatique, mensuelle consacrée aux questions de politique étrangère,* 1919.

2309 Našić, S. L'action en résolution dans les contrats. Paris, 1909. 192 p.

2310 Nikitovitch, Tchaslav M. L'affaire du Monastère de Saint Naoum. Paris, 1927. 144 p.

2311 Nikolayévitch, Rad. L'extradition en Yougoslavie. *Annuaire,* 1937: 225–234. (DLC)

2312 Novakovitch, Dragolioub. La zadrouga. Paris, 1905. 188 p.

2313 Novakovitch, Mileta. La commission riveraine du Danube, et la Serbie, 1856–1858. *Annuaire,* 1934: 64–73. (DLC)

2314 Pavlovitch, G. (a) De la condition juridique des étrangèrs en Serbie. Paris, 1884; (b) Loi du 3/15 février 1880, sur le règlement des questions agraires dans les nouveaux territoires de la Principauté de Serbie. *Annuaire de législation étrangère* (Paris), 1881: 716–724; (c) Loi du 12/12 mars 1881, sur la presse en Serbie, et Loi du 1/13 avril 1881 sur les associations et les réunions en Serbie. *Annuaire de législation étrangère* (Paris), 1881: 732–741, 741–747.

2315 Pavlovitch, Voja. La législation sur la liberté de la presse en Yougoslavie. Paris, 1928. 258 p. (DLC)

2316 Pavkovitch, Dragolioub. De l'intervention de l'état dans le gestion des forêts particulières en Yougoslavie. Nancy, 1935. 119 p.

2317 Pechitch, Paul. La participation de la Yougoslavie à la solution pacifique des conflits internationaux. Paris, 1939. 293 p.

2318 Perić, Boshko K. Contribution juridique en vue de l'élaboration d'un code civil yougoslave. Paris, 1936. 377 p. (DLC)

2319 Péritch, J. M. (a) Appendice à l'étude sur la constitution du Royaume de Serbie du 6 avril 1901. Reprint from *Bulletin de la Société de législation comparée*. Paris, 1903. 15 p.; (b) Application du principe de territorialité des lois aux différents instituts du droit privé suivant le droit international privé en Yougoslavie. *Journal du droit international*, 1930: 332–351; (c) Compétence des tribunaux civils serbes en matière de procés matrimoniaux des ressortissants serbes de religion catholique. Concordat entre le Vatican et la Serbie. Divorce ou question d'état civile. Bruxelles, 1932; (d) De la compétence judiciaire en matière matrimoniale dans le Royaume de Yougoslavie. Reprint from *Annuaire* (Beograd-Paris), 1934. 15 p. (DLC); (e) Conception du droit international privé d'après la doctrine et la pratique en Yougoslavie. Paris, 1929. 154 p. (DLC); (f) Les conceptions sociales dans le droit de succession ab intestat. Paris, 1935. 22 p.; (g) De l'amnistie en droit pénal serbe par rapport à la question des régicides. Reprint from *Revue générale du droit, de la législation et de la jurisprudence* (Paris), 1907. 56 p.; (h) De l'unification du droit de mariage dans les pays slaves. Beograd, 1933. 16 p.; (i) De la capacité de succéder des sujets roumains en Serbie. Reprint from *Le mouvement économique* (Bucarest), 1905. 23; (j) De la cession de créances dans le droit civil serbe. Padova, 1935. 45 p.; (k) De la compétence judiciaire en matière matrimoniale dans le Royaume de Yougoslavie. *An-*

nuaire, 1934: 217–229; (DLC) (1) De la condition juridique des bosniaques et des herzegoviniens en pays étrangers. Bruxelles, 1902. 60 p.; (m) De la forme du mariage dans le droit international privé d'après la législation serbe. Bruxelles, 1912. 19 p.; (n) De la nationalité suivant la législation serbe. Paris, 1900. 37 p.; (o) De la nullité et de la dissolution du mariage dans la législation serbe. London, 1913. 57 p.; (p) Le délit de rébellion en droit pénal serbe et français. Paris, 1921. 19 p.; (q) Des communautés de famille en droit serbe. Paris, 1911. 24 p.; (r) Le droit de succession en droit international privé yougoslave. Bruxelles, 1930; (s) Le droit international et interprovincial dans les nouvelles lois yougoslaves sur la lettre de change et sur le chèque du 29 novembre 1928. *Annuaire*, 1931: 177–213. (DLC); (t) Le droit international privé et la guerre, par rapport à la Serbie. Bayonne, 1920. 7 p.; (u) Droit international privé yougoslave. Livres parus au cours des années 1929–1930. *Revue de droit international privé*, 1933; (v) Influence de la codification civile nationale sur le progrès de l'unification juridique internationale. Bruxelles, 1910. 32 p.; (w) La loi serbe sur l'inamovibilité des juges. Paris, 1901. 1 p.; (x) Le mariage en droit international privé suivant la législation yougoslave. I. La législation serbe. Leyde, 1939. 50 p.; (y) Le monarque constitutionnel. Reprint from *Revue générale du droit* (Paris), 1904. 16 p.; (z) Le mysticisme dans le droit de succession. *Archiv für Rechts- und Wirtschaftsphilosophie*, 1922/23: 457–468; (aa) Les principaux traits caractéristiques de la constitution du Royaume des Serbes, Croates, et Slovènes de 28 juin 1921. *Revue internationale de sociologie* (Paris), 1928; (ab) Principes fondamentaux de la législation yougoslave sur le régime foncier. Paris, 1939. 30 p.; (ac) La propriété scientifique. Beograd, 1924. 37 p.; (ad) Quelques particularités du droit civil yougoslave. Paris, 1928. 27 p.; (ae) Le réorganisation politique de l'Etat Yougoslave. Genève, 1937. 8 p.; (af) Le traité de Berlin et la question de la nationalité par rapport à la Principauté de Serbie. Paris, 1900. 36 p.; (ag) Les travaux d'unification du droit civil en Yougoslavie, spécialement l'unification du droit des communautés de famille ou "zadrougas." Bruxelles, 1926; (ah) L'unification du droit privé maritime en Yougoslavie. *Revue de la marine marchande* (Paris), 1924.

2320   Perić, Ž. *and* M. Bartoš. La condition de la femme en Yougoslavie. Paris, 1938. 28 p.

2321   Picot, E. Les Serbes de Hongrie, leur histoire, leur privilèges, leur Église, leur état politique et social. Prague, 1873. 474 p. (DLC)

2322   Pop-Kocitch, Jivoine. Étude juridique sur l'incorporation de territoires macédoniens à la Serbie. Paris, 1935. 127 p.

2323   Popovitch, Georges. La Yougoslavie et la Société des Nations. *Annuaire,* 1937: 11–30. (DLC).

2324   Popovitch, Georges *and* Drag. Arandjelović. Les Conférences Balkaniques et l'unification de droit des pays balkaniques. *Annuaire,* 1934: 27–35. (DLC)

2325   Popovitch, Radomir. La législation yougoslave sur la propriété industrielle. Lyon, 1924. 44 p.

2326   Le Procès d'Agram et l'union européenne. Paris, 1909. 30, 4 p. (DLC)

2327   Protitch, Milan. Banque nationale du royaume des Serbes, Croates, et Slovènes. Paris, 1922. 256 p.

2328   Pržić, Ilija. Le problème des rapports entre le droit interne et le droit international et ses discussions dans la science juridique yougoslave. *Annuaire,* 1937: 129–151. (DLC)

2329   Radovanovitch, Voyslav M. (a) Le Danube et l'application du principe de la liberté de la navigation fluviale. Genève, 1925. 336 p.; (b) L'Entente Balkanique devant le Droit International. *Revue de droit international et de législation comparée,* 1935: 688–735. (DLC)

2330   Radović, Andrija. La question du Monténégro présentée par A. Radovitch, R. Bochkovitch et I. Voukotitch. Paris, 1919. 51 p. (DLC)

2331   Rivière, Albert. Note sur la zadrouga en Croatie. *Bulletin de la Société de législation comparée,* 1888.

2332   Rosendorf, Richard. La réforme du droit des Sociétés par Action en Yougoslavie. *Annales de droit commercial et industriel* (Paris), 1936.

2333   Rosendorf, Richard *and* Joseph Henggeler. Droit fiscal international du globe. Zurich, 1937. 3 v.

2334 Salaville, S. Le Concordat de la Serbie avec le Saint-Siège. *Echos d'Orient,* 1915: 459–68.

2335 Smirnoff, M. L'aviation civile en Yougoslavie. Beograd, 1959. 51 p.

2336 Smodlaka, S. J. La justice administrative en Yougoslavie. Paris, 1931. 183 p.

2337 Soubotine, Stevan. Du régime des sociétés par actions en Serbie. Caen, 1921. 142 p.

2338 Srebreno-Dolinski, Tschédomir. La réforme agraire en Yougoslavie. Paris, 1921.

2339 Srzentić, Nikola. (a) L'organisation des tribunaux en Yougoslavie. Beograd, 1955. 44 p. (DLC); (b) Les problèmes posés sur les délits économiques. *Le nouveau droit yougoslave,* 1955: 49–66.

2340 Stražnicky, M. Les sources du droit maritime privé yougoslave. *Annuaire,* 1937: 155–176. (DLC)

2341 Styepanovitch, Nikola. Les réformes constitutionelles et administratives en Yougoslavie. *Revue internationale des sciences administratives,* 1954.

2342 Subotić D. Aperçu du système pénitentiare de la Yougoslavie. Paris, 1935. 30 p.

2343 Subotić, I. (a) Effets de la dissolution de l'Autriche-Hongrie sur la nationalité de ses ressortissants. Paris, 1926. 315 p.; (b) Le nouveau régime juridique du secteur de Danube dit des Cataractes et des Portes-de-Fer. *Annuaire,* 1934: 77–111. (DLC)

2344 Tchiritch, Slavko M. La question de Fiume. Paris, 1924. 200 p.

2345 Tchirkovitch, Stévan. (a) La code de la famille en Yougoslavie. *Revue internationale de droit comparé,* 1951; (b) Liste des traités, accords et engagements internationaux du Royaume de Yougoslavie y compris les lois et les décisions d'ordre international de 1919 à 1935. *Annuaire,* 1934: 345–349. (DLC); (c) Règlement des questions de frontière entre le Royaume de Yougoslavie et ses voisins balkaniques: Albanie, Grèce, Bulgarie, et Roumanie. *Annuaire,* 1934: 136–155. (DLC)

2346 Thalac. Le droit public de la Principauté de Serbie. *Le Nord* (Paris), 1859.

2347 Todorovitch, Dragoslav B. Le droit syndical et les doctrines syndicalistes. Paris, 1934. 400 p.

2348   Tomitch, Zoran S. La formation de l'Etat Yougoslave. Paris, 1927. 244 p.

2349   Ubicini, Jean Henry Abdolonyme. (a) Constitution de la Principauté de Serbie. Paris, 1871. 168 p. (DLC); (b) Les Serbes de Turquie. Études historiques, statistiques, et politiques sur la Principauté de Serbie, le Monténégro, et les pays serbes adjacents. Paris, 1865. 336 p.

2350   Vesić, Budimir. La protection des invalides de guerre en Yougoslavie. Beograd, 1955. 37 p. (DLC)

2351   Vesnitch, Milenko. (a) L'annexion de la Bosnie-Herzégovine et le droit international. Paris, 1909; (b) Le système pénitentiaire en Serbie et les projets de sa réorganisation. Saint-Petersbourgh, 1893.

2352   Vilimanovitch, Miloïko. Zone libre serbe à Salonique. Paris, 1926. 130 p.

2353   Vošnjak, Begumil. (a) L'administration française dans les pays yougoslaves, 1809–1813. *Revue des sciences politiques* (Paris), 1917; (b) Les origines du Royaume des Serbes, Croates, et Slovènes. *La revue des sciences politiques* (Paris), 1920; (c) Le Pacte Balkanique. *Annuaire,* 1937: 31–43. (DLC)

2354   Yourichitch, Evgeniye. Le procès Tito-Mihailovitch. Paris, 1950. 190 p.

2355   Yovanovitch, Miloutine. (a) Le régime absolu yougoslave institué le 6 janvier 1929. Paris, 1930. 197 p.; (b) La réforme administrative en Yougoslavie. Paris, 1932. 104 p.

2356   Yovanovitch, Nikodié. Étude sur la Constitution du Royaume des Serbes, Croates, et Slovènes du 28 juin 1921. Paris, 1924. 420 p.

2357   Yovanovitch, Slobodan. Le contrôle budgétaire en Yougoslavie. Paris, 1938. 127 p. (DLC)

2358   Živković, Jovan. La garantie des emprunts publics du Royaume de Yougoslavie. Paris, 1931. 114 p.

2359   Žujović, Mladen J. Le pouvoir constituant dans les constitutions serbes. Paris, 1928. 330 p. (DLC)

C   In German

See also Nos.: 10; 16; 30; 36; 37; 38; 43; 49; 50; 53; 70; 311a-b; 321; 401b; 407.

2360   Advocaten—Ordnung vom 24. Juli 1852. Agram, 1873. 167 p. (DLC)

2361   Barlovac, C. R. Das serbische Parlament. Heidelberg, 1895. 63 p.

2362   Bilimović, Aleksander. (a) Arbeitsrecht des Koenigreiches der Serben, Kroaten und Slovenen. *Zeitschrift für Ostrecht, 3*/1929: 369–388. (DLC); (b) Das Kartellrecht Jugoslawiens. *Zeitschrift für Osteuropäisches Recht, 1936–1937:* 67–80. (DLC)

2363   Civil—Process—Ordnung für Bosnien und Hercegowina. Wien, 1906. 188 p. (DLC)

2364   Costa, Heinrich. Zur Geschichte der Handels- und Gewerbsgesetzgebung in Illyrien. *Triester Zeitung,* issues 178 and 179, 1856.

2365   Demmelhuber, Peter. Das Kmetenwesen in Bosnien und der Herzegowina. Erlangen, 1934. 73 p.

2366   Dennewitz, Bodo (unter Mitarbeit von Boris Meissner). Die Verfassungen der modernen Staaten. Eine Dokumentensammlung. Jugoslawien: Erster Band. Hamburg, 1947: 22–24.

2367   Dickel, Karl. Über das neue bürgerliche Gesetzbuch für Montenegro . . . Marburg, Hessen, 1889. 112 p. (DLC)

2368   Djermekov, D. Richter und Gerichte in Jugoslawien. *Zeitschrift der Akademie für deutsches Recht, 3/1936.*

2369   Djurić, Dimitrije Dj. Das öffentliche Recht im mittelalterlichen Serbien. Freiburg (Schweiz), 1926. 79 p. (DLC)

2370   Dolenc, Method. (a) Der allgemeine Teil des jugoslavischen Strafgesetzentwurfes in seinen Grundzügen. *Zeitschrift für Ostrecht, 1927:* 502–514. (DLC); (b) Die neuesten Aenderungen in den strafrechtliche Gesetzen Jugoslawiens. *Zeitschrift für Ostrecht, 1932:* 427–432; (c); Strafrechtliche Sanktionen der Freiheitsentziehung in Jugoslawiens. *Zeitschrift für osteuropäisches Recht, N. F. 2, 1935–36:* 248–261; (d) Die strafrechtliche Bekämpfung des Kommunismus im Königreiche Jugoslawien. *Zeitschrift der Akademie für deutsches Recht, Juni* 1936; (e) Strafrechtliches aus Jugoslawien. *Zeitschrift für osteuropäisches Recht,* 2/1926: 462–486. (DLC)

2371 Egloff, Willy. Die bosnisch-herzegowinische Annexionskrise 1908–1909 in der schweizerischen Presse. Würzburg, 1935. 81 p.

2372 Eichler, Eduard. Das Justizwesen Bosniens und der Herzegovina. Wien, 1889. 395 p. (DLC)

2373 Eisner, Bertold. (a) Die Rechtsstellung der ausländischen Handelsgesellschaften in Jugoslawien nach dem neuen jugoslawischen Handelsgesetz. Reprint from Mèlanges Streit (Athens), 1939; (b) Das Eherecht im jugoslawischen Vorentwurf. *In* Spomenica Dolencu, Kreku, Kušeju in Škerlju, 1937: 567–643 (DLC); (c) Das neue Zivilprozessrecht in Jugoslawien. Berlin, 1933. 18 p. (d) Die Schuldverhältnisse, das Erbrecht, die Ersitzung, und die Verjährung im Vorentwurf zu einem jugoslawischen Zivilgesetzbuch. *Annuario di Diritto Comparato e di Studi Legislativi* (Roma), v. 14, 2/1938; (e) Der Vorentwurf eines Zivilgesetzbuches für das Königreich Jugoslawien. Roma, 1938. 200 p.; (f) Die Zivilrechtsprechung der ordentlichen Gerichte Jugoslawiens 1945–1953. *Zeitschrift für ausländisches und internationales Privatrecht* (Berlin-Tübingen), 1954: 296–321. (DLC)

2374 Frank, Stanko. Die theoretischen Grundlagen des jugoslawischen Strafrechtes. *Revue internationale de la théorie de droit,* 1932–33.

2375 Friedrichs, K. Serbische Kulturautonomie im Habsburgstaate. *Nation und Staat* (Wien), 1930.

2376 Geller, Leo. Bosnisch-hercegovinische Verfassungs- und politische Grundgesetze. Wien, 1910. 136 p. (DLC)

2377 Gesetzbuch Daniel's I, Fürsten und Gebieters von Montenegro und der Berda. Wien, 1859. 38 p.

2378 Das Gesetzbuch Petars I, Bishofs von Montenegro. *Slavische Rundschau,* Juli 1929.

2379 Giegl, Julius. Verfassungsgesetze der Länder Bosnien und Hercegovina. Wien, 1910. v. 110 p. (DLC)

2380 Gjordjević, N. Die Selbständigkeit der serbischen Kirche. Sr. Karlovci, 1922.

2381 Goršić, Franz. (a) Die Rechtsstellung der Ausländer in Yugoslawien. *Zeitschrift für osteuropäisches Recht,* N. F. 3, 1936–37:

353–370; (b) Zum neuen jugoslawischen Zivilprocessgesetz. *Zeitschrift für Ostrecht,* June 1933. (DLC)

2382 Grünberg, Karl. Die Agrarverfassung und das Grundentlastungsproblem in Bosnien und der Herzegowina. Leipzig, 1911. 120 p. (DLC)

2383 Hallstein, Walter (Rostock). Das Aktienrecht des jugoslawischen Handelsgesetzentwurfes 1932. *Zeitschrift für ausländisches und internationales Privatrecht,* 1934. (DLC)

2384 Handausgabe der Gesetze für das Herzogtum Krain. Laibach, 1910. 2 v.

2385 Hassenstein, Karl. Das Königreich Südslawien. Entstehung, Rechtsnatur, und Stellung zur deutschen Minderheit. Erlangen, 1934. 44 p .

2386 Hoffman, Willy. Das jugoslawische Urheberrechtsgesetz. *Börsenblatt für den deutschen Buchhandel* (Leipzig), 131/1930.

2387 Hollman, A. H. Agrarverfassung und Landwirtschaft Jugoslawiens. Berlin, 1931. 136 p.

2388 Holzer, Erwin. Die Entstehung des jugoslawischen Staates. Berlin, 1929. 107 p.

2389 Holzman, Hugo. (a) Fremde als Arbeiter und Angestellte in Jugoslawien. Zagreb, 1935. 318 p.; (b) Unifiziertes Handelsgesetz für das Königreich Jugoslawien. Zagreb, 1938. 251 p.

2390 Janković, V. S. System der direkten Steuern in Serbien. Berlin, 1904. 76 p. (DLC)

2391 Jiriček, Jos. Die Serbischen Privilegien. Verhandlungs-Congresse und Synoden. *Österreichische Revue,* 7, 8/1864.

2392 Jovanović, Dragoslav. Das Verhältnis zwischen der Staatsverfassung und dem normalen Gesetze in Jugoslawien. *Zeitschrift für Ostrecht,* 1929: 47–55. (DLC)

2393 Jovanović, Milan P. Montenegrinische Rechtsgeschichte. *Zeitschrift für vergleichende Rechtswissenschaft* (Stuttgart), v. 15, 1885.

2394 Jugoslawien. *In* A. Bergman. Internationales Ehe- und Kindschaftsrecht. 1st ed. Berlin, 1925–1926. 3 v.; 2d ed. Berlin, 1938–1940. 2 v.; 3d ed. Frankfurt a/Main, 1952, loose leaf. (DLC)

2395 Kauschansky, D. M. (a) Das Eherecht Jugoslawiens. Tübingen, 1929. 32 p.; (b) Das Ehescheidungsrecht Jugoslawiens. München, 1929. 15 p.; (c) Hauptzüge des altserbischen Eherechts.

Zeitschrift für vergleichende Rechtswissenschaft (Stuttgart), v. 4, 1927; (d) Das internationale Eherecht Jugoslawiens in seinen Beziehungen zu anderen europäischen und aussereuropäischen Rechten. *Revue de droit international, de sciences diplomatiques et politiques,* janvier-mars, avril-juin 1933.

2396 Kazimirovitsch, Radovan. Das serbische Ehescheidungsrecht im Vergleich mit dem russischen und deutschen. Bonn, 1911.

2397 Konstantinovic, Michael. Die Staatsangehörigkeit in Jugoslawien unter besonderer Berücksichtung der Friedensverträge. *Zeitschrift für Ostrecht,* 7, 8, und 12, 1926. (DLC)

2398 Krek, Gregor. (a) Grundzuege des Verfassungsrechtes des Königreichs der Serben, Kroaten und Slovenen. *Zeitschrift für osteuropäisches Recht,* 1 and 2/1925–1926; (b) Zum jugoslawischen Zivilprozessgesetz. *Zeitschrift für osteuropäisches Recht,* 1934. (DLC)

2399 Krek, Gregor *and* Milan Škerlj. Die österreichischen Zivilprozessgesetze im Königreiche der Serben, Kroaten, und Slowenen. Reprint from Nachtrag III aus Neumanns Kommentar zu den Zivilprocessgesetzen. 4. Aufl. Vienna, 1928. 224 p. (DLC)

2400 Kršnjavi, Izidor. Das staatsrechtliche Verhältnis Kroatiens zu Ungarn. Wien, 1907.

2401 Lachner, Hugo. (a) Das neue jugoslavische Wechselgesetz im Vergleich mit dem deutschen. *Zeitschrift für Ostrecht* (Berlin), 1930: 17–22; (b) Das neue Zivilprozessrecht Jugoslawiens. Wien, 1933–1934. 2 v. (DLC)

2402 Laufer, Otto. Die Steuergesetznovelle vom 18. v. 1930 sammt Durchführungsverordnung. Novi Sad, 1930. 16 p.

2403 Laufke, Franz. Das Wechselrecht der Tschechoslowakei, Polens, und Südslawiens. *Zeitschrift für ausländisches und internationales Privatrecht,* 1930: 268–349.

2404 Lehman, Heinrich (Koeln). Kritische Bemerkungen zum Entwurf eines Handelsgesetzbuches für das Königsreich Jugoslawien. Reprint from Festschrift für Dolenz, Krek, Kušelj und Škerlj. Ljubljana, 1936. 47 p.

2405 Leitmaier, Victor. (a) Der Serbische Civilprocess nebst Concoursordnung und einem Anhange über den Rechtshilfvertrag zwischen Österreich-Ungarn und dem Königreiche Serbien vom 6 Mai 1881. Wien, 1885. 292 p. (DLC); (b) Der Serbische Strafprozess, in Vergleichung mit der Österreichischen Strafprozessordnung des Deutschen Reiches. Wien, 1884. 172 p.

2406 Lovrić, E. Das Eherecht im Rechtsgebiete Kroatien-Slavonien. Berlin, 1937. 52 p.

2407 Löwenbuch, Ivan. Das jugoslavische Gesetz über den Schutz des Urheberrechtes. *Schaffen und Wettbewerb* (Prag), No. 7, 8/1930.

2408 Lubenoff, Georg. (a) Die jugoslawische Freizone in Saloniki. *Zeitschrift für ausländisches öffentliches Recht und Völkerrecht,* 2/1931: 166–230; (b) Die Verfassung Jugoslawiens vom 3. September 1931. *Ibid.,* 1933: 402–444.

2409 Maklecow, Alexander. (a) Jugoslawien: I Gesetzgebung, II Gesetzentwürfe, III Grundsätzliche Gerichtsentscheidungen, IV Literarische Neuerscheinungen. *Zeitschrift für die gesamte Strafrechtswissenschaft,* 4, 5/1935; (b) Das neue jugoslavische Strafgesetz und die Kommentare dazu. *Zeitschrift für Ostrecht,* 1930: 749–752; (c) Das neue Militärstrafgesetzbuch Jugoslawiens. *Zeitschrift für Strafrechtswissenschaft,* 1931; (d) Das neue jugoslawische Jugendstrafrecht. *Zeitschrift für die gesamte Strafrechtswissenschaft,* 1931: 346–359; (e) Die Rechtsprechung zum jugosl. Strafgesetzbuch v. 27. Januar 1929. *Zeitschrift für osteuropäisches Recht,* N. F. 1 Jg. H. 5, 1935; (f) Der strafrechtliche Schutz des Staates in Jugoslawien. *Zeitschrift für osteuropäisches Recht,* 1936: 149–164.

2410 Marcuse, Hugo. Die Verfassung des Königreichs Serbien von 6. April 1901. Berlin, 1902. 42 p.

2411 Markovitsch, B. Über das serbische Schwurgericht im Vergleiche mit dem deutschen, französischen und englischen Schwurgericht. Freiburg, 1899. 95 p. (DLC)

2412 Markowitsch, Lazar. Das Problem der Sonderrechte der Körperschaftsmitglieder. Berlin, 1910. 177 p. (DLC)

2413 Mayer, A. Die bäuerliche Hauskommunion in den Königreichen Kroatien und Slavonien. Heidelberg, 1910. 174 p.

2414 Merk, Walther. Das Handelsregister nach dem Entwurf des südslawischen Handelsgesetzbuches. *In* Festschrift für Dolenz, Krek, Kušelj und Škerlj. Ljubljana, 1936. 36 p.

2415 Miler, Ernest. Die Hauskommunion der Südslaven. *In* Jahrbuch der internationalen Vereinigung für vergleichende Rechtswissenschaft und Volkswirtschaftslehre. Berlin, 1898. 24 p.

2416 Miletić, Svetozar, *defendant*. Das Urtheil der Budapester K. Gerichtstafel und die Berufung in Hochverrathsprocesse Miletics. Neusatz, 1878. 87 p. (DLC)

2417 Milowanowitsch, Georg. Das altserbische Familienrecht. Breslau, 1910. 95 p. (DLC)

2418 Munda, August. Das jugoslawische Strafgesetzbuch vom 2. März 1951. Berlin, 1952. 110 p. (DLC)

2419 Neubecker, Friedrich Karl. Der Entwurf eines Strafgesetzbuches für das Königreich Serbien. *In* Festschrift der Berliner Juristischen Fakultät für Professor v. Martitz. Berlin, 1911. (DLC)

2420 Neugebauer, J. L. Die Süd-Slawen und deren Länder, in Beziehung auf Geschichte, Kultur, und Verfassung. Leipzig, 1851.

2421 Nikosavić, Blagoje. Die Agrarverfassung und der landwirtschaftliche Kredit Jugoslawiens. Berlin, 1935. 85 p.

2422 Ostojitsch, Relja. Das verkehrswirtschaftliche Problem der Donauschiffahrt insbesondere der Jugoslawischen Donauschiffahrt. Berlin, 1933. 160 p.

2423 Pantschewitsch, B. Das landwirtschaftliche Genossenschaftswesen in Südslawien. Leipzig, 1930. 92 p.

2424 Pappafava, Vladimir. Rechts- und Justizverhältnisse und das Urkund- und Beurkund-ungswesen in Montenegro. Wien, 1910. 20 p. (DLC)

2425 Péritch, J. (a) Ein Beispiel bürgerlichen Agrarkommunismus. Die serbische Familiengenossenschaft oder Zadruga. Glarus (Schweiz), 1919, p. 10; (b) Das Civilprozessrecht in Serbien. Berlin, 1931. 28 p.; (c) Das Eherecht im Rechtsgebiet Serbien. Reprint from *Rechtsverfolgung im internationalen Verkehr* (Berlin), IV/1935; (d) Die Ehescheidung nach serbischem Recht. *Ostrecht,* 1927: 1–33; (e) Die Frau im serbischen Erbrecht. *Zeitschrift für osteuropäisches Recht,* 1926: 486–508; (f) Die politische Fortentwicklung des jugoslawischen Staates. Reprint from *Neue Züricher Zeitung,* Zürich, 1928. 16 p.; (g) Die serbische Familiengenossenschaft. Berlin, 1911. 36 p.; (h) Serbische Verfassung. *Mitteilungen der internationalen Vereinigung für vergleichende Rechtswissenschaft und Volkswirtschaftslehre* (Berlin),

März 1905; (i) Unifizierung der Strafgesetzgebung im Königreiche der Serben, Kroaten, und Slovenen. Reprint from *Monatsschrift für Kriminalpsychologie und Strafrechtsreform*. Heidelberg, 1926; (j) Die Wiederaufnahme des Strafverfahrens nach der neuen Jugoslavischen STPO vom 16. Februar 1929. *Ibid.*, 1930.

2426 Pitamic, Leonida. Die Verfassung des Königreiches der Serben, Kroaten, and Slovenen. Reprint from *Zeitschrift für öffentliches Recht* (Wien-Leipzig), 1927. 31 p.

2427 Pliverić, Josip. (a) Beiträge zum ungarisch-kroatischen Bundesrechte. Agram, 1886. 540 p.; (b) Der kroatische Staat. Agram, 1887. 136 p. (DLC)

2428 Pliverić, M. Das in Kroatien geltende allgemeine Privatrecht. Berlin, 1942. 42 p.

2429 Popović, Georg. Recht und Gericht in Montenegro. Agram, 1877. 90 p. (DLC)

2430 Posilović, Stjepan. Das Immobilar-Recht in Bosnien und Herzegowina. Agram, 1894. 241 p. (DLC)

2431 Reutz, Alexander von. Verfassung und Rechts-Zustand der Dalmatinischen Küsten-Städte und Inseln im Mittel-Alter. Dorpat, 1841. 415 p. (DLC)

2432 Rühlmann, Paul. Das Schulrecht der Deutschen Minderheit in Jugoslawien im Rahmen der Minderheitenrechtlichen Gesamtproblematik. Berlin, 1932. 126 p. (DLC)

2433 Sagadin, Stefan. (a) Das Staatsangehörigheitsrecht des Königreiches Jugoslawien. *In* Das Recht der Staatsangehörigkeit der europäischen und der aussereuropäischen Staaten (Berlin), VII/1934; (b) Die verfassungsrechtliche Entwicklung Jugoslawiens seit 1926. *Zeitschrift für osteuropäisches Recht*, N. F. 2, 1935–36: 1–23.

2434 Schoen, Josef. Das bosnische-herzegowinische, österreichische, ungarische und kroatische Handelsrecht in ihren Verschiedenheiten. Wien, 1913. 386 p. (DLC)

2435 Schweissguth, Edmund. (a) Entwicklung und Grundbegriffe des Erbrechtes der Föderativen Volksrepublik Jugoslawien. München, 1955. 194 p. (DLC); (b) Die Entwicklung des Bundesverfassungsrechts der Föderativen Volksrepublik Jugoslawien. Frankfurt, Verlag für Internationalen Kulturaustausch 1960. 307 p. (DLC)

2436   Shek, Adalbert. Allgemeines Gesetzbuch über Vermögen für das Fürstenthum Montenegro. Berlin, 1893. 191 p. (DLC)

2437   Sladović, Eugen. Der Unabhängige Staat Kroatien. *Zeitschrift für osteuropäisches Recht,* N. F. 9, 1942: 1–41.

2438   Sperl, Hans. Das jugoslavische Zivilprozess- und Exekutionsrecht. Ein Beitrag zur Beurteilung der neuesten Gesetzgebung in Jugoslawien. Ljubljana, 1936. 121 p. (DLC)

2439   Srzentić, N. Der Aufbau des Gerichtswesens in Jugoslawien. *Rechtswissenschaftlicher Informationsdienst* (Berlin), 20. Mai 1956.

2440   Strafprocessordnung für Bosnien und die Hercegovina. Wien, 1906. 391 p. (DLC)

2441   Subotitsch, Dušan M. (a) Kassationshof in Jugoslawien. *In* J. Magnus. Die Höchsten Gerichte der Welt. Berlin, 1929. (DLC); (b) Der Vorentwurf zu einem neuen serbischen Strafgesetzbuch. *Deutsche Juristen-Zeitung* (Berlin), 1912.

2442   Šapčanin, Sava. Die passive Wechselfähigkeit des Bauern nach dem Geltenden Recht des Königreichs der Serben, Kroaten und Slovenen insbesondere nach den in Serbien Geltenden Vorschriften, und de lege ferenda. *Zeitschrift für Ostrecht,* 1928: 572–589. (DLC)

2443   Škerlj, Milan. (a) Das jugoslavische Gesetz zum Schutze des gewerblichen Eigentums. *Zeitschrift für Ostrecht,* 5–6/1927; (b) Das Gesetz über Gesellschaften mit beschränkter Haftung. Wien, 1906. 189, 16 p.

2444   Šribar, Cvetko. Die rechtliche Entwicklung und die social-politische Bedeutung der Südslawischen Hausgenossenschaft Zadruga. Köln, 1934. 75 p.

2445   Šuman, Janko. (a) Der Schutz des industriellen Eigentums in Jugoslawien. Berlin, 1929. 207 p. (DLC); (b) Das gewerbliche Eigentumsrecht in Jugoslawien. Wien, 1921. 167 p. (DLC)

2446   Spiller, K. Die neue jugoslawische Zivilprozessordnung vom 13. VII. 1929. *In* Gesetzgebung und Rechtspraxis des Auslandes, v. 6, 1930.

2447   Tassitsch, G. Ein jugoslawisches Werk über den Staat. Zugleich Gedanken zu einigen grundsätzlichen Problemen der modernen Rechtstheorie. *Zeitschrift für öffentliches Recht*, 1928.

2448   Tauber, Leonid. (a) Das ständige Schiedsgericht der Handelskammer in Belgrad. *Zeitschrift für osteuropäisches Recht*, N. F., 1937–38: 543–552; (b) Das neue Handelsgesetzbuch des Königreichs Jugoslawien. *Ibid.*, N. F., 1938–39: 69–83.

2449   Tkalac, E. I. Das Staatsrecht des Fürstenthums Serbien. Leipzig, 1858. 286 p.

2450   Übersberger, Hans. Der Saloniki-Process . . . Berlin, 1933. 746 p. (DLC)

2451   Utiešenović, Ognieslav M. Die Hauskommunionen der Südslaven. Wien, 1859. 277 p. (DLC)

2452   Zivilprozessordnung der Föderativen Volksrepublik Yugoslawien. (Berichte des Osteuropa-Instituts an der Freien Universität Berlin, Heft 33; Rechtwirtschaftliche Folge, No. 12). Berlin, 1957. 129 p .(DLC)

D   In Italian

See also Nos.: 13; 14; 15; 19; 42; 46; 54; 71; 317; 321; 410c; 1517.

2453   Alimena, Bernardino. La legislazione penale del Montenegro. Reprint from *Giustizia Penale*. Roma, 1896. 20 p. (DLC)

2454   Carena, Annibale. Dalla costituzione del Vidov-Dan alla costituzione jugoslava del 3 settembre 1931. Reprint from *Annali di scienze politiche* (Pavia), 1931. (Milano), 1931. (DLC)

2455   Codice civile generale del Principato del Montenegro. Traduzione italiana . . . di Antonio Martecchini. Spalato, 1900. 318 p. (DLC)

2456   Codice penale. Beograd, 1951. 77 p. (DLC)

2457   Della Golia, Todaro A. La seconda edizione del Codice generale dei beni del Montenegro. Palermo, 1901. 53 p.

2458   Fabri, A. Effetti giuridici delle annessioni territoriali, con speciale riguardo alle annessioni di Fiume e della Dalmazia nei rapporti italo-jugoslavi. Padova, 1931.

2459   Fra Michel da Spalato. Statuti di Spalato [Edizione permessa dal Comune di Spalato, proprietario del Codice Membranaceo portante la data del 17 febbraio 1395]. Spalato, n.d. 435 p. (DLC)

2460   Fumagalli, Primo. La Costituzione di Vidovdan. Reprint from *Europa Orientale* (Roma), 1928 and 1929.

2461   Gatta, Enrico. La Costituzione jugoslava del 1931. Firenze, 1947. 177 p. (DLC)

2462   Giannini, Amadeo. La Costituzione jugoslava del 1931. Roma, 1935. 44 p. (DLC)

2462^1 Jurić, Dušan. L'ordinamento statale e sociale della Jugoslavia. Beograd, 1961. 94 p.

2463   Madirazza, Franz. Storia e costituzione dei comuni Dalmati. Spalato, 1911. 583 p. (DLC)

2464   Pagliano, Emilio. La Costituzione del Montenegro. Roma, 1906.

2465   Peritch, J. M. (a) Gli elementi non giuridici nel diritto. Reprint from *Rivista internazionale di filosofia del diritto* (Roma), 1934. (DLC); (b) Istituti del diritto civile jugoslavo relativi alla materia agraria. Reprint from *Rivista di diritto agrario* (Firenze), 1932. 31 p. (DLC)

2466   Tasić, Djordje. (a) Il diritto positivo come valore e il diritto naturale. Roma, 1930. 35 p.; (b) Sul concetto di diritto soggetivo. Reprint from *Rivista internazionale di filosofia del diritto* (Roma), marzo-aprile, 1928. (DLC)

2466^1 Tito, Josip Broz. Costruzione del socialismo e ruolo e compiti dell' Unione socialista del popolo lavoratore della Jugoslavia. Rijeka, 1960. 84 p.

2467   Zocco-Rosa, Antonio. (a) La nuova edizione del Codice Civile montenegrino ed il diritto romano; la gestione di affari (Art. 587–594). Catania, 1899; (b) La nuova edizione del codice generale dei beni del Montenegro. Roma, 1898; (c) Il Codice del Montenegro ed il diritto romano. Reprint from *Rivista scientifica del diritto* (Roma), v. 1, 1897. 83 p.; (d) Il codice civile dei beni del Montenegro ed il diritto romano, con speciale riguardo al titolo de digesti de diversis regulis juris. Catania, 1897. 16 p.

12

INDIVIDUAL LAWS OF PRIMARY IMPORTANCE

The list of the most important laws of Yugoslavia is broken down according to the main stages in the development of the Yugoslav laws and government. A more detailed picture is given in Chapter I. What follows is merely a brief list presenting characteristic legislation in each period.

Part I covers the opening stage in the formation of one state Yugoslavia—from hitherto independent Serbia, Montenegro and separate parts of Austria-Hungary. In this part, only the laws enacting provisions uniformly applicable throughout all of Yugoslavia are listed. They are identified by date.

Part II covers the next stage in the achivement of the legal and political unity of Yugoslavia—from 1929 to 1941.

The period of occupation from 1941 to 1943 is not covered, since its legal continuity was interrupted when Yugoslavia was resurrected.

Part III covers Yugoslav laws from the beginning of the activities of the Anti-Fascist Council of National Liberation of Yugoslavia in 1943, to the present.

Each law is cited by the date and the number under which it appears in the particular part of *Službene Novine* or *Službeni List*.

A   1918-1929

During the first years of Yugoslavia's existence some Serbian laws were extended to the whole of the Kingdom. This was true of military law and also of the following laws:

Law of 1862 Establishing an Executive Branch of the Government, extended by the Edict of December 7, 1918; Law of 1886 on the Stock Exchange, extended by the Law of May 15, 1922; Law of 1904 on Public Schools, amended and put into effect by the Law of April 4, 1919; Law of April 21, 1922 Extending the Provisions of Chapters IX and X of the Criminal Code of the Kingdom of Serbia.

Uniform laws were enacted during this period covering the following subjects: Age of Majority, July 31, 1919; Free Medical Care, October 25, 1921; Labor Inspection, December 31, 1921; Protection of Industrial Property, February 17, 1922, superseded, April 27, 1928; Police Forces, February 18, 1922; Protection of Labor, February 28, 1922; Social Security, May 14, 1922; State Council and Administrative Courts, May 22, 1922; Voters' Lists, May 30, 1922; Responsibilities of Ministers, July 20, 1922; Protection of Children and Youth, July 24, 1922; Election of People's Representatives, July 27, 1922; Organization of the Army and Navy, June 9, 1923; Press, August 25, 1925, amended, January 8, 1929 and October 3, 1931; Financial Adjustments of Corporation Assets, August 7, 1926; Nationality, September 21, 1928; Attorneys at Law, November 12, 1928; Checks and Promissory Notes, November 29, 1928.

B   1929-1941

As stated in the introduction, this period is marked by an increased number of uniform nationwide laws enacted by the Yugoslav legislature.

1 Armed Forces

Organization of the Army, Navy [and Air Force], September 6, 1929, No. 463; National Defense, July 14, 1930, No. 357.

2 Church and State

Old Catholic Church, December 18, 1923, No. 204; Serbian-Orthodox Church, November 16, 1929, No. 543; Religious Communities of Jews, December 24, 1929, No. 624; German Evangelic-Christian Church of the Augsburg Confession, December 22, 1930, No. 625; Evangelic-Christian Churches and the Reformed Christian Church, April 28, 1930, No. 204; Slovak Evangelic-Christian Church of the Augsburg Confession, July 16, 1932, No. 477.

3 Civil Law and Commercial Law

Personal Names, February 19, 1929, No. 104; Rent Control, April 27, 1929, No. 222; Bankruptcy, November 22, 1929, No. 567; Compulsory Composition Outside of Bankruptcy, November 22, 1929, No. 568; Copyright, December 29, 1929, No. 629; Land Records, May 18, 1930, No. 307; Unfair Competition, April 4, 1930, No. 185; Commercial and Industrial Enterprises, November 5, 1931, No. 558; Cooperatives of Producers, September 11, 1937, No. 463; Commercial Code for the Kingdom of Yugoslavia, October 2, 1937, No. 572 [This law never went into effect].

4 Civil Procedure

Code of Civil Procedure, July 13, 1929, No. 396; effective, July 9, 1930, No. 384; Attachment and Execution, July 9, 1930, No. 364.

5 Criminal Law and Procedure

Protection of Public Safety and Order in the State, January 6, 1929, No. 9; Criminal Code, January 27, 1929, No. 73; Military Criminal Code, February 11, 1930, No. 77; Code of Criminal Procedure, February 16, 1929, No. 97; Execution of Punishments, February 16, 1929, No. 102; Putting into Effect the Criminal Code, the Code on Criminal Procedure, and the Law on Execution of Punishments, February 16, 1929, No. 103.

6   Education

Elementary Schools, December 5, 1929, No. 591; Secondary Schools, August 31, 1929, No. 454; Universities, June 28, 1930, No. 315; Supreme Council of Education, July 2, 1931, No. 329.

7   Elections

Voters' Lists, September 6, 1931, No. 428; Election of Representatives to the National Assembly, September 10, 1931, No. 448; Election of Senators, September 30, 1931, No. 473.

8   Government, Central and Local

Power of the King and Organization of the Executive Branch of the Government, January 6, 1929, No. 8; The Supreme Legislative Council and Boards of Experts Attached to the Ministry of Justice, January 31, 1929, No. 55; Organization of the Executive Branch of the Government, March 31, 1929, No. 166; Creation of the Executive Branch of the Government, June 8, 1929, No. 301; Organization of the Government Administration, June 19, 1929, No. 143; Name of the Kingdom and its Division into Administrative Provinces, October 3, 1929, No. 489; Provincial Administration, November 7, 1929, No. 529; Police Forces, September 27, 1930, No. 497; General Administrative Procedure, November 9, 1930, No. 571; Civil Service, March 31, 1931, No. 150.

9   Judicial System

Organization of the Courts, January 18, 1929, No. 40; Judges of Regular Courts, January 8, 1929, No. 14; Court for the Protection of the State, January 8, 1929, No. 15 and December 31, 1929, No. 648; Organization of Sheriat Courts and Sheriat Judges, March 21, 1929, No. 149; Public Prosecutors, March 21, 1929, No. 148; Attorneys at Law, March 17, 1929, No. 145; Notaries Public, September 1, 1930, No. 472.

10   Land Reform

Land Reform for Large Estates, June 19, 1931, No. 312.

11   War Veterans

Disabled Veterans, July 4, 1929, No. 350.

C   Since 1943

The foundations for postwar legislation in Yugoslavia were laid down during the war, in November 1943, when the Anti-Fascist Council of National Liberation of Yugoslavia declared itself the supreme legislative body. Hence, the list below begins with enactments dating from that time.

1   Administrative Law and Procedure

Abolition of the State Council and Administrative Courts, April 23, 1945, No. 244; amended, March 18, 1946, No. 154; Administrative Disputes, April 10, 1952, No. 249; amended, March 28, 1953, No. 88; Administrative Procedure Act, December 19, 1956, No. 658.

2   Air Law

Aerial Navigation, June 1, 1949, No. 392 amended, December 12, 1951, No. 534; Use of Parachutes by Civilians, September 3, 1955, No. 461; Non-Military Gliders, September 10, 1955, No. 559.

3   Aliens

Employment of Experts, Foreign Citizens, July 22, 1955, No. 438; amended, February 20, 1956, No. 63; superseded, Use and Exchange of Foreign Experts, February 2, 1957, No. 68; Sojourn and Movement of Foreigners, January 15, 1959, No. 149.

4   Armed Forces

The Yugoslav Army, March 2, 1945; Yugoslav National Army, July 5, 1955, No. 302; Military Service of Citizens of Yugoslavia,

April 1, 1946, No. 179; amended, December 12, 1946, No. 712; December 2, 1947, No. 772; April 28, 1948, No. 271; January 5, 1949, No. 21; February 28, 1951, No. 120; February 3, 1953, No. 29; superseded, National Defense, June 20, 1955, No. 315; amended, March 29, 1957, No. 153; November 4, 1961, No. 649; Fulfilment of Military Duties, May 28, 1957, No. 289; Military Academy of Medicine, April 13, 1960, No. 194.

5 Banking, Foreign Exchange, Currency

Credit System, October 26, 1945, No. 831; amended, August 21, 1946, No. 484; October 8, 1951, No. 429; repealed, November 16, 1954, No. 615; Credits for Trade Transactions and other Short Term Credits, January 26, 1954, No. 31; affirmed, January 29, 1954, No. 96; Short Term Credits, July 17, 1956, No. 415; Loans for Investments in the Economy, January 26, 1954, No. 30; affirmed, January 29, 1954, No. 96; Banks and Savings-Banks, January 26, 1954, No. 34; affirmed, January 29, 1954, No. 96; amended, March 15, 1954, No. 152; affirmed, December 30, 1954, No. 676; Amounts Which May Be Withdrawn from Savings Accounts Established with the National Bank of the F.P.R.Y., July 29, 1948, No. 576; Transactions with Savings Accounts Established with Government Banks, Local Savings Banks, and Cooperatives, February 16, 1949, No. 141; Savings Accounts, February 17, 1949, No. 136; Union of Government Investment Bank of the F.P.R.Y. and Government Farm Cooperative Credit Banks with the National Bank of the F.P.R.Y., and Abolition of Municipal Banks, March 20, 1952, No. 147; Yugoslav Investment Bank, July 12, 1956, No. 397; Banks, March 15, 1961, No. 118; Foreign Exchange Transactions, September 2, 1945, No. 630; amended, October 23, 1946, No. 604; January 5, 1949, No. 9; October 8, 1951, No. 429; January 26, 1954, No. 60; Elaboration of the Plan for Import and Plan for Distribution of Imported Goods, May 23, 1947, No. 360; superseded, Supervision of Imports and Exports, January 22, 1948, No. 53; amended, October 14, 1948, No. 776; superseded, Export and Import of Goods and Foreign Exchange Transactions, June 25, 1952, No. 413; superseded, Foreign Exchange Transactions, December 28, 1954, No. 641 and December 6, 1955, No. 574; amended, May 21, 1956, No. 281; July 11, 1956, No. 377; May 16, 1957, No. 254; February 12, 1958, No. 69;

Foreign Exchange Transactions, January 18, 1961, No. 6; Withdrawal and Exchange of Occupation Currency, April 5, 1945, No. 198; Legal Rates for the Withdrawal of Occupation Currency and Settlement of Claims, April 5, 1945, No. 223; affirmed, November 9, 1946, No. 647; Payment on Receipts Issued on the Exchange of Occupation Currency and Disposition of Frozen Assets, June 7, 1945, No. 346; amended, October 26, 1946, No. 616; Coinage of Small Denominations of the DFY, July 23, 1945, No. 478; amended, October 4, 1946, No. 575; Fixing of the Official Rate of the Dinar, December 27, 1951, No. 571.

6 Church and State

Creation of the Government Commission for Religious Affairs, August 21, 1945, No. 584; February 26, 1959, No. 164; Legal Status of Religious Denominations, May 27, 1953, No. 151.

7 Civil Procedure

Procedure to Expedite Court Proceedings, May 4, 1955, No. 190; Code of Civil Procedure, January 23, 1957, No. 25, and No. 26; amended, December 31, 1961, No. 760.

8 Civil Service

Civil Service Employees, July 23, 1946, No. 436; amended, December 11, 1946, No. 713; April 28, 1948, No. 333; May 7, 1948, No. 334; January 5, 1949, No. 19; January 23, 1950, No. 96; February 28, 1951, No. 120; superseded, Public Servants, December 25, 1957, No. 664; amended, November 5, 1958, No. 748; January 7, 1959, No. 5; December 30, 1959, No. 849; July 6, 1960, No. 379; December 31, 1960, No. 689.

9 Constitutional Law

Declaration of November 29, 1943, of the Second Session of the Anti-Fascist Council of National Liberation of Yugoslavia, February 1, 1945, No. 1; affirmed, November 9, 1946, No. 647; Decree of December 30, 1943, on the Supreme Legislative and Executive Body of Yugoslavia, and the National Committee for

Liberation of Yugoslavia as Temporary Organs of the Supreme People's Powers during the Liberation War, February 1, 1945, No. 2; amended, March 7, 1945, No. 140; affirmed, November 9, 1946, No. 647; Decree of November 29, 1943, Depriving the Yugoslav Cabinet Abroad of Its Status as a Legitimate Government and Prohibiting King Peter II Karadjordević from Returning to the Country, February 1, 1945, No. 3; affirmed, November 9, 1946, No. 647; Agreements between the Committee for National Liberation of Yugoslavia and the Royal Yugoslav Government, June 16, 1944, and November 1, 1944, March 9, 1945, No. 133, 134; Delegation of the King's Powers to the Royal Regency, January 29, 1945, No. 135; Repeal and Invalidation of All Laws Enacted Before April 6, 1941, as well as Those Issued During Enemy Occupation, February 3, 1945, No. 51; amended, October 23, 1946, No. 605; December 23, 1946, No. 744; Proclamation of the Federal People's Republic of Yugoslavia, November 30, 1945, No. 881; Proclamation of the Anti-Fascist Council of National Liberation of Yugoslavia as the Temporary National Assembly of the DFY, August 11, 1945, No. 557; affirmed, November 9, 1946, No. 647; Constituent Assembly, August 21, 1945, No. 594; amended, June 17, 1946, No. 351; Presidency of the Constituent Assembly, December 7, 1945, No. 888; Presidium of the National Assembly of the F.P.R.Y., July 23, 1946, No. 413; amended, March 2, 1951, No. 138; January 1, 1952, No. 7; Constitution of the Federal People's Republic of Yugoslavia, January 31, 1946, No. 54; Extension of the Constitution, Laws, and Other Provisions of Yugoslavia to the Territory Incorporated by the Peace Treaty with Italy, September 15, 1947, No. 549; Constitutional Law, January 13, 1953, No. 19, and No. 20; amended, September 8, 1953; No. 292; January 30, 1954, No. 87; March 11, 1954, No. 145; Application of the Constitution, Laws and Other Federal Provisions [of Yugoslavia] in Territory Over Which the Civil Administration of Yugoslavia Was Extended by International Treaties, October 26, 1954, No. 551; Repeal of Chapter XIV of the Constitution of 1946, December 8, 1954, No. 609; Delegation of Powers to the Cabinet of the F.P.R.Y. to Legislate on Economic Matters, February 4, 1946, No. 72 (superseded, Planning Management of National Economy, Decmber 29, 1951, No. 569); to Introduce the New Financial

System and Other Economic Measures, October 2, 1951, No. 408; to Create Social Funds, April 1, 1952, No. 171; to Issue Decrees Bringing the Activities of the National Economy into Conformity with the New Economic System, April 8, 1952, No. 200. Affirmation of Decrees Issued by the Federal Executive Council and Delegation of Legislative Powers in the Economic Field, January 29, 1954, No. 96; Assemblies, Conventions and other Public Meetings, August 25, 1945, No. 612; amended, June 21, 1946, No. 350; April 1, 1947, No. 217; January 17, 1951, No. 429; Delegation of Powers to Federal and Republic Agencies, April 16, 1958, No. 346; amended, May 6, 1959, No. 321; March 8, 1961, No. 98; Organization and Functioning of the Federal Executive Council, May 16, 1958, No. 371; amended, May 27, 1959, No. 380; Organization and Functioning of the Federal Secretariat for Internal Affairs and on the General Principles for the Organization of Agencies for Internal Affairs in the Republics, July 12, 1958, No. 574; amended, March 15, 1961, No. 135; Organization of the Secretariat for National Defense, July 12, 1958, No. 602; amended, May 24, 1961, No. 337.

10   Contracts and Torts

Regulation of Prewar Obligations, October 27, 1945, No. 841; amended, August 14, 1946, No. 474; Final Liquidation of Farmers' Debts, October 27, 1945, No. 851; amended, October 4, 1946, No. 573; Contracts Relating to the Economy, December 9, 1946, No. 722; repealed, December 28, 1954, No. 642; Transactions Involving Land and Buildings, June 23, 1954, No. 290; amended, May 4, 1955, No. 193; December 3, 1958, No. 812; superseded, December 31, 1958, No. 890.

11   Cooperatives

On Cooperatives, July 18, 1946, No. 412; amended, December 11, 1946, No. 713; January 17, 1951; No. 53; February 28, 1951, No. 120; repealed in part, November 16, 1954, No. 615; Farmers' Cooperatives, June 6, 1949, No. 411; amended, January 17, 1951, No. 53; February 28, 1951, No. 120; September 29, 1951, No. 419; superseded, January 26, 1954, No. 46; amended, August 8, 1956, No. 466; October 3, 1956, No. 515; April 28, 1958, No. 348;

Unified Text, May 10, 1961, No. 310; Property Relations and Reorganization of Farmers' Labor Cooperatives, March 30, 1953, No. 83.

12   Criminal Law and Procedure

Types of Punishment, July 5, 1945, No. 436; amended, October 22, 1945, No. 781; August 14, 1946, No. 473; Petty Offenses, December 4, 1947, No. 789; amended, October 11, 1948, No. 754; January 21, 1950, No. 98; October 8, 1951, No. 428; December 31, 1955, No. 633; January 14, 1959, No. 22; Approval of Provisions Issued by Federal Government Agencies Concerning Petty Offenses, June 25, 1956, No. 344; Criminal Code, General Part, December 4, 1947, No. 776; Criminal Code, March 2, 1951, No. 134; February 28, 1951, No. 120; amended, July 2, 1959, No. 559, and 560; Code of Criminal Procedure, October 12, 1948; No. 818; Code of Criminal Procedure, Semptember 30, 1953, No. 321, and 322; amended, December 28, 1959, No. 848; February 3, 1960, No. 49; Execution of Punishments, October 12, 1948, No. 788; amended, December 14, 1949, No. 802; superseded, Execution of Punishment, Safety Measures and Educational and Corrective Measures, October 8, 1951, No. 436; superseded, June 21, 1961, No. 405; Economic Offenses, April 20, 1960, No. 218.

13   Domestic Relations, Civil Status

Marriage, April 3, 1946, No. 182; amended, April 28, 1948, No. 270; February 28, 1951, No. 120; April 25, 1955, No. 184; Parent-Child Relations, December 1, 1947, No. 761; amended, December 8, 1956, No. 665; Adoption, April 1, 1947, No. 235; amended, April 10, 1952, No. 262; Guardianship, April 1, 1947, No. 234; amended, February 28, 1951, No. 120; Personal Names, December 1, 1947, No. 767; amended, December 14, 1949, No. 802; January 17, 1951, No. 53; October 8, 1951, No. 429; Declaration of Death of a Person Unaccounted for Pursuant to Evidence of Death, April 26, 1952, No. 259; Civil Status Registry, April 1, 1946, No. 183; amended, January 5, 1949, No. 20; January 17, 1951, No. 53; February 28, 1951, No. 120; October 8, 1951, No. 429.

14 Economic Law

General Economic Plan and Government Planning Agencies, May 25, 1946, No. 302; superseded, Planned Management of the National Economy, December 29, 1951, No. 569; The Five-Year Plan for the Development of the Yugoslav National Economy, 1947-1951, April 28, 1947, No. 280; amended, December 30, 1950, No. 657; Social Plan of the F.P.R.Y. for 1952, April 1, 1952, No. 169; for 1953, December 27, 1952, No. 727; for 1954, March 24, 1954, No. 146; (amended, June 15, 1954, No. 288; July 5, 1954, No. 375; October 25, 1954, No. 561; November 25, 1954, No. 611; December 30, 1954, No. 674); for 1955, December 30, 1954, No. 666; (amended, April 25, 1955, No. 185; November 10, 1955, No. 530); for 1956, March 30, 1956, No. 135; (amended, December 6, 1956, No. 51); for 1957, December 31, 1956, No. 693; (amended, February 28, 1957, No. 119; March 29, 1957, No. 155; October 18, 1957, No. 558; December 6, 1957, No. 630); for 1958, December 28, 1957, No. 665; for 1959, November 28, 1958, No. 846; for 1960, December 30, 1959, No. 845; for 1961, December 31, 1960, No. 685; for 1962, December 31, 1961, No. 752; Social Plan for the Economic Development of Yugoslavia, 1957–1961, December 25, 1957, No. 662; 1961–1965, December 31, 1960, No. 684; Government Economic Enterprises, July 24, 1946, No. 437; repealed, November 16, 1954, No. 615; Management of Government Economic Enterprises and Economic Associations by Workers' Collectives, July 2, 1950, No. 391; amended, February 28, 1951, No. 120; Organization of Economic Enterprises and [Retail] Stores, December 18, 1953, No. 424; affirmed, January 29, 1954, No. 8; amended, July 10, 1954, No. 379; affirmed, March 19, 1955, No. 110; amended, November 10, 1954, No. 571; affirmed, December 30, 1954, No. 676; amended, April 27, 1956, No. 187; Liquidation of Economic Enterprises and [Retail] Stores, December 18, 1953, No. 425; affirmed, January 29, 1954, No. 96; amended, November 21, 1956, No. 615; Management of Basic Means of Economic Organizations, December 23, 1953, No. 433; amended, June 10, 1954, No. 267; July 19, 1954, No. 393; February 9, 1955, No. 44; March 9, 1956, No. 95; January 3, 1957, No. 1; June 8, 1957, No. 297; July 19, 1957, No. 401; December 9, 1957, No. 637; Means of Economic Enterprises, December 28, 1957, No. 667; Handicraft [Retail] Stores and Handicraft Enterprises, January 26, 1954, No. 48; affirmed, January 29, 1954, No. 96; Hotels and Restaurants, January 26, 1954, No. 63; affirmed, January 29, 1954, No. 8; amended, November 10, 1954, No. 571; affirmed, December 30, 1954, No. 676; Mining Law, July 2, 1959, No. 512; Association and Business Cooperation in the Economy, July 13, 1960, No. 404.

15   Education

Seven Year Elementary Education, October 26, 1945, No. 801; amended, July 9, 1946, No. 385; Creation of the Council of Academies of the F.P.R.Y., May 29, 1948, No. 365; amended, May 23, 1949, No. 380; Degree of Doctor of Science, October 12, 1948, No. 765; superseded, July 5, 1955, No. 303; Ranks of Schools, April 1, 1952, No. 195; amended, July 26, 1952, No. 520; June 4, 1953, No. 171; December 15, 1953, No. 479; July 26, 1955, No. 451; July 15, 1956, No. 412; July 31, 1957, No. 526; August 9, 1957, Nos. 547, 548, 549; Universities, June 30, 1954, No. 304; amended, December 29, 1955, No. 634; Faculties and Universities, Unified Text, July 20, 1960, No. 433. Management of Schools, March 16, 1955, No. 84; Scholarships, July 13, 1955, No. 349; amended, December 8, 1956, No. 666; Schools of Administration, July 11, 1956, No. 374; Scholarship for Foreign Study, July 17, 1956, No. 428; Organization of Schools of Administration, October 22, 1956, No. 546; Organization of Scientific Work, August 14, 1957, No. 462; Education, June 28, 1958, No. 535; Organization and Functioning of the Council of Education of Yugoslavia, March 11, 1959, No. 181; Protection of Monuments, April 16, 1959, No. 294; Establishment of a Museum of the Revolution of the Peoples of Yugoslavia, December 8, 1960, No. 655; Commission for Cultural Relations with Foreign Countries, February 16, 1960, No. 147.

16.   Elections

Voters' Lists, August 10, 1945, No. 558; amended, July 5, 1946, No. 405; February 28, 1951, No. 120; Elections of Representatives to the Constituent Assembly, August 22, 1945, No. 595; amended, October 26, 1945, No. 794; November 9, 1946, No. 647; Election of Representatives to the National Assembly of the F.P.R.Y. [Federal Council and Council of Nationality], January 26, 1950, No. 54; Recall of Representatives of the National Assembly of Yugoslavia [Federal Council and Council of Nationality], July 5, 1950, No. 392; amended, February 28, 1951, No. 120; Election of the President of the Republic and the Federal Executive Council, January 13, 1953, No. 21; Rights and Duties, Election and Procedure for Recall of Federal Representatives, September 10, 1953; No. 293; amended, October 23, 1957, No. 555; December 9, 1957, No. 632; Election of Representatives to the Federal National Assembly for the Administrative Districts of Buje and Koper, December 31, 1954, No. 670.

17 Finance and Taxation

Disposal of Government Assets, September 2, 1945, No. 629; Financial Adjustments of Corporation Assets [Revaluation], October 27, 1945, No. 812; amended, August 14, 1946, No. 480; January 5, 1949, No. 9; October 8, 1951, No. 429; Budget of the DFY, October 26, 1945, No. 864; December 26, 1946, No. 737; superseded, Budgets, December 29, 1951, No. 570; superseded, March 24, 1954, No. 147; amended, December 31, 1954, No. 669; superseded, March 26, 1956, No. 126; amended, July 4, 1956, No. 358; Budgets and Financing Independent Institutions, December 30, 1959, No. 847; amended, June 14, 1961, No. 388; December 30, 1961, No. 767; Financing of Housing, November 23, 1959, No. 752; Establishment of Taxes, February 6, 1945, No. 91; amended, May 2, 1945, No. 267; affirmed, November 9, 1946, No. 647; Stamp Tax, September 2, 1945, No. 664; amended, August 19, 1946, No. 485; December 3, 1947, No. 759; February 28, 1951, No. 120; October 8, 1951, No. 429; superseded by Administrative Taxes, July 15, 1959, No. 513; amended, June 14, 1961, No. 389; Income, Estate and Gift Tax, October 26, 1945, No. 854; amended, August 11, 1946, No. 479; Taxation (General), December 26, 1946, No. 736; amended, January 5, 1949, No. 9; December 14, 1949, No. 802; January 17, 1951, No. 53; February 28, 1951, No. 120; superseded by Social Contribution and Taxation (General), January 1, 1952, No. 5; Compulsory Payment of Taxes and Other Budgetary Incomes, August 26, 1953, No. 283; amended, July 14, 1957, No. 316; Income Tax, March 18, 1947, No. 175; superseded, August 14, 1948,

No. 596; amended, October 15, 1948, No. 769; November 17, 1949, No. 754; January 21, 1950, No. 60; superseded, December 23, 1953, No. 482; amended, July 19, 1954, No. 387; November 10, 1954, No. 586; December 28, 1954, No. 661; January 4, 1956, No. 8; February 8, 1956, No. 37; superseded, Unified Text, April 10, 1956, No. 171; amended, April 16, 1958, No. 300; January 31, 1959, No. 90; November 24, 1959, No. 777; December 23, 1959, No. 862; March 15, 1960, No. 149; March 28, 1961, No. 193; superseded, Unified Text, May 12, 1961, No. 378; amended, December 26, 1961, No. 794; Tax on Individual Earnings of Citizens, December 31, 1958, No. 893; amended, December 30, 1959, No. 852; April 13, 1960, No. 195; June 8, 1960, No. 298; superseded, Unified Text, June 15, 1960, No. 311; Taxing Income from Copyright, July 28, 1954, No. 384; amended, December 31, 1958, No. 894; December 2, 1959, No. 771; June 15, 1960, No. 310; Unified Text, June 15, 1960, No. 312; amended, April 20, 1961, No. 270; Contribution to Socialist Society and Surtaxes, January 1, 1952, No. 5; Compulsory Payment of Taxes and Other Budgetary Incomes, August 23, 1953, No. 283; amended, June 19, 1957, No. 316; Gift and Inheritance Tax, May 4, 1955, No. 191; Enforcement of the Gift and Inheritance Tax, July 4, 1956, No. 360; Tax on Realty and Property Rights, January 26, 1954, No. 41; amended, August 18, 1954, No. 457; August 3, 1960, No. 449; Unified Text, November 16, 1960, No. 597; Municipal Taxes, January 20, 1960, No. 23; amended, February 15, 1961, No. 36; December 6, 1961, No. 699; Local Taxes, April 21, 1955, No. 194; amended, May 8, 1957, No. 241; December 31, 1957, No. 710; December 31, 1958, No. 892; December 30, 1959, No. 853; Court Fees, April 20, 1960, No. 220; Customs Duties, October 12, 1948, No. 773; amended, October 2, 1951, No. 409; October 8, 1951, No. 429; Fund for the Improvement of Customs Control Service, July 14, 1954, No. 341; amended, December 31, 1957, No. 712; Customs Tariff on Imported Goods and Merchandise, May 13, 1959, No. 340; superseded, Temporary General Customs Tariff, March 8, 1961, No. 94; amended, June 21, 1961, No. 415; October 25, 1961, No. 631.

18 Fishing

Deep-Sea Fishing, January 23, 1950, No. 114; amended, January

17, 1951, No. 53; February 28, 1951, No. 120; October 8, 1951, No. 429.

19 Government, Federal and Local

Temporary Jurisdiction of Boards and Commissions of the Federal Executive Council and Its Organization, May 14, 1953, No. 147; April 28, 1954, No. 203; affirmed, June 15, 1954, No. 307; amended, October 11, 1955, No. 492; affirmed, November 11, 1955, No. 532; amended, June 11, 1956, No. 323; amended, April 14, 1957, No. 182; July 19, 1957, No. 430; July 31, 1958, No. 430; May 27, 1959, No. 380; Government Administration, March 28, 1956, No. 127; amended, October 23, 1957, No. 556; Federal Administrative Agencies, March 28, 1956, No. 128; amended, November 2, 1960, No. 573; Agencies of Internal Affairs, July 18, 1956, No. 396 [including the militia]; People's Committees, May 21, 1946, No. 288; amended, June 6, 1949, No. 410; April 1, 1952, No. 244; September 8, 1953, No. 323; Jurisdiction of People's Committees of Municipalities and Counties, July 27, 1955, No. 371; amended, December 12, 1957, No. 644; December 16, 1957, No. 650; Organization of Municipalities and Counties, June 22, 1955, No. 269; amended, July 10, 1957, No. 366; June 17, 1959, No. 420; November 25, 1959, No. 755. Registration of Residence, June 26, 1948, No. 449; amended, June 7, 1950, No. 322; December 12, 1951, No. 534; May 29, 1952, No. 325; Registration of Residence and Place of Abode, March 4, 1959, No. 148.

20 Inheritance

Inheritance, April 29, 1955, No. 210.

21 Judicial System

(a) The Bar

Appointment of Delegates to Lawyers Chambers, November 17, 1944, No. 19; amended, March 18, 1946, No. 155; Representation of Agencies, Institutions, Enterprises and Organizations before Courts and other Government Agencies, August 3, 1945, No. 530; amended, October 30, 1946, No. 622; superseded, Government Solicitors, April 10, 1952, No. 258; The Bar, December 12, 1946, No. 716; amended, February 28, 1951, No. 120; superseded, March 29, 1957, No. 162.

(b)   Courts and Judges

Creation of the Supreme Court of the DFY, February 3, 1945, No. 53; Organization of People's Courts, August 26, 1945, No. 622; amended, June 17, 1946, No. 349; December 23, 1946, No. 746; May 4, 1948, No. 282; June 6, 1949, No. 417; April 10, 1952, No. 260; superseded, Judiciary Act, July 21, 1954, No. 376; amended, April 10, 1957, No. 163; June 17, 1959, No. 422; December 30, 1961, No. 758; Settlement of Controveries by Government Arbitration, December 12, 1946, No. 721; superseded, Government Arbitration, December 3, 1947; No. 790; amended, June 6, 1949, No. 419; superseded, Economic Courts, July 28, 1954, No. 383; amended, July 13, 1955, No. 350; June 17, 1959, No. 422, December 30, 1961, No. 759; Organization of Prize Courts, April 1, 1946, No. 177; Organization of Military Courts in the Yugoslav Army, August 31, 1945, No. 613; amended, July 17, 1946, No. 403; superseded, December 2, 1947, No. 770; amended, January 23, 1050, No. 97, February 28, 1951, No. 120; superseded, November 26, 1954, No. 622; Military Disciplinary Tribunals, May 4, 1948, No. 281; amended, April 10, 1952, No. 261; superseded, Jugoslav National Army, July 5, 1955, No. 302.

(c)   Government Solicitors

Government Solicitors, April 10, 1952, No. 258; superseded, Government Solicitors, November 14, 1955, No. 538.

(d)   Notaries Public

Abolition of Notaries Public and Notaries Public Associations, November 17, 1944, No. 11; affirmed, November 9, 1946, No. 647.

(e)   Public Prosecutors, Military Prosecutors

Jurisdiction of the Public Prosecutor of the DFY, February 3, 1945, No. 52; amended, July 22, 1946, No. 426; superseded, November 26, 1954, No. 612; amended, April 10, 1957, No. 164; amended, December 30, 1961, No. 757 Military Prosecutors, December 12, 1946, No. 711; superseded, Military Prosecutors, March 16, 1955, No. 82.

22 Labor Law

Workers' Delegates, July 23, 1945, No. 499; amended, October 26, 1945, No. 814; September 9, 1946, No. 404; superseded, Labor Inspectors, December 12, 1946, No. 705; amended, December 1, 1948, No. 884; December 14, 1949, No. 802; January 17, 1951, No. 53; October 8, 1951, No. 429; Settlement of Labor Disputes, July 5, 1945, No. 423; amended, September 9, 1946, No. 384; Establishment and Termination of Labor Relations, September 27, 1948, No. 711; affirmed, November 28, 1948, No. 885; amended, December 12, 1951, No. 534; superseded, Labor Relations, December 25, 1957, No. 663; amended, July 2, 1958, No. 491; January 7, 1959, No. 4; March 2, 1961, No. 60; Unified Text, May 3, 1961, No. 298; Election of Workers' Collectives in Economic Enterprises, January 1, 1952, No. 8; Extending the Functions of the Office of Workers' Collectives, January 7, 1959, No. 3; July 6, 1960, No. 376; March 15, 1961, No. 123; National Holidays, April 27, 1955, No. 183; amended, October 21, 1959, No. 695; October 27, 1956, No. 339; April 15, 1959, No. 254; Institute for the Study of Labor Movements, September 26, 1961, No. 602.

23 Land Reform

Land Reform, August 23, 1945, No. 605; amended, March 18, 1946, No. 152; November 26, 1947, No. 745; December 1, 1948, No. 870; January 17, 1951, No. 53; May 15, 1956, No. 241; December 23, 1957, No. 711; Cancellation of Mortgages on Real Estate Transferred to Government Ownership According to Law on Land Reform, December 13, 1947, No. 781.

24 Landlord and Tenant

Management of Dwelling Houses, December 23, 1953, No. 432; affirmed, January 29, 1954, No. 96; amended, June 30, 1954, No. 344; affirmed, December 30, 1954, No. 676; March 9, 1956, No. 96;

October 7, 1957, No. 534; November 23, 1957, No. 600; April 16, 1958, No. 241; superseded, Dwelling Relations, April 22, 1959, No. 279; amended, November 25, 1959, No. 753; July 6, 1960, No. 377; Appropriations to Housing Councils for the Maintenance of Dwelling Houses, October 28, 1954, No. 562; amended, July 22, 1955, No. 434; Lease of Business Premises, March 12, 1953, No. 69; amended, January 26, 1954, No. 42; affirmed, January 29, 1954, No. 96; on Dwelling Communities, April 16, 1959, No. 278; Business Buildings and Premises, April 22, 1959, No. 280; amended, December 2, 1959, No. 765; Dwelling Cooperatives, April 22, 1959, No. 282; amended, December 2, 1959, No. 763; April 26, 1961, No. 268; Ownership of Individual Units in Houses, April 22, 1959, No. 281; amended, December 2, 1959, No. 764; Basic Housing Principles, February 28, 1957, No. 118.

25 Maritime Law

Maritime Arbitration Boards under the Chamber of Commerce of the F.P.R.Y., March 26, 1947, No. 184; Use of Harbors and Ports, June 21, 1961, No. 406.

26 Nationality Law (Citizenship)

Yugoslav Citizenship, August 23, 1945, No. 606; amended, July 1, 1946, No. 370; December 2, 1947, No. 757; October 12, 1948, No. 757; December 1, 1948, No. 871; Deprivation of Citizenship of Commissioned and Non-Commissioned Officers of the Former Yugoslav Army Who Are Not Willing to Return to Their Country, and Those Belonging to Military Units Who Served with the Occupation Forces and Fled Abroad, August 23, 1945, No. 607; amended, October 23, 1946, No. 602; Citizenship of Individuals [Living] in the Territory Annexed to the F.P.R.Y. Pursuant to the Peace Treaty with Italy, December 2, 1947, No. 756.

27 Nationalization, Expropriation, Confiscation

Transfer of Enemy Property to Government Ownership, Government Administration of Property of Absentees, and Sequestration of Property Seized by the Enemy, November 21, 1944, No. 25; amended, July 31, 1946, No. 450; December 23, 1946, No. 745;

Handling of Property Which Owners Were Forced To Abandon During the Occupation and of Property Seized by the Enemy and Those Assisting the Enemy, May 24, 1945, No. 319; amended, August 2, 1946, No. 454; December 23, 1946, No. 740; February 28, 1951; No. 120; Nationalization of Private Economic Enterprises, December 5, 1946, No. 677; amended, April 28, 1948, No. 269; Procedure for Appraising and Determining Compensation for Nationalized Property, November 17, 1947, No. 716; Transfer of Ownership of Nationalized Property of Foreign Citizens, Foreign Institutions, and Foreign Private or Public Corporations, June 12, 1948, No. 421; Taking Over of Private Pharmacies by Eminent Domain, May 27, 1949, No. 416; Expropriation, April 1, 1947, No. 209; August 3, 1948, No. 732; superseded, February 28, 1957, No. 140; Compensation for Expropriated Real Estate, May 4, 1955, No. 197; superseded, February 28, 1957, No. 140; Payment of Bonds to Compensate for Property Taken by Expropriation, October 23, 1957, No. 562. Seizure of War Profits, May 24, 1945, No. 320; amended, June 24, 1946, No. 355; Confiscation of Property, June 1945, No. 359, amended, September 11, 1945, No. 654; July 5, 1946, No. 432; December 23, 1946, No. 747; February 28, 1951, No. 120; October 8, 1951, No. 436; Determination of Relations Created by the Confiscation of Property of Private Credit Enterprises, March 1, 1949, No. 172; Determination of Relations Created by the Confiscation of Property, March 15, 1949, No. 196; Law on the Nationalization of Dwelling Houses and Building Lots, December 28, 1958, No. 890; Decree Providing for the Procedure for the Nationalization of Apartment Houses and Building Lots, January 23, 1959, No. 52; amended December 31, 1960, No. 692.

28 Negotiable Instruments

Promissory Notes, December 12, 1946, No. 728; Checks, December 26, 1946, No. 735; Legal Holidays Pursuant to the Laws on Promissory Notes and Checks, January 22, 1947, No. 71.

29 Nuclear Energy

Creation of a Federal Commission for Nuclear Energy, March 19, 1955, No. 95; February 26, 1959, No. 143; amended, July 21,

1960, No. 451; Institute for Research Nuclear Raw Material, June 5, 1958, No. 431; June 15, 1960, No. 355; superseded, February 22, 1961, No. 129; Federal Management for Protection Against Ionizing Radiations, February 16, 1960, No. 86.

30 Pardon and Amnesty

Pardon and Amnesty, July 5, 1945, No. 422; amended, August 31, 1945, No. 620; November 2, 1946, No. 636; December 26, 1946, No. 748; February 28, 1951, No. 120; March 28, 1953, No. 87.

31 Patents, Trade Marks and Copyright

Copyright, May 25, 1946, No. 303; amended, January 17, 1951, No. 53; February 28, 1951, No. 120; superseded, August 28, 1957, No. 36; Inventions and Technical Improvements [Patent Law], December 1, 1948, No. 883; amended, February 28, 1951, No. 120; superseded, Patents and Technical Improvements, November 2, 1960, No. 569; Trade Marks and Models, November 15, 1961, No. 668; Weights and Measures, November 15, 1961, No. 670.

32 Police

People's Militia, December 12, 1946, No. 710; amended, December 14, 1949, No. 802; superseded, Agencies of Internal Affairs, June 27, 1956, No. 396.

33 The Press

The Press, August 24, 1945, No. 611; amended, July 8, 1946, No. 381; December 1, 1948, No. 872; March 1, 1951, No. 120; superseded, Press and Other Means of Information, November 9, 1960, No. 586; Publishing Enterprises and Institutions, March 16, 1955, No. 85; October 15, 1959, No. 719; Newspaper Publishing, July 11, 1956, No. 373; superseded, November 9, 1960, No. 586; Export and Import of Books, Newspapers, Periodicals and Publications, January 23, 1957, No. 27; Registration and Work of Foreign Correspondence Bureaus and Foreign Correspondents, February 11, 1961, No. 49.

34 Property Law

Acquisition of Real Property by Aliens, July 16, 1946, No. 487; affirmed, April 1, 1947, No. 269; repealed, Supervision of Transactions Involving Real Property, March 20, 1948, No. 163; repealed, Transactions of Real Property and Buildings, June 23, 1954, No. 290; Transfer of Italian Property in the Territory of Yugoslavia to Government Ownership by Yugoslavia Pursuant to the Peace Treaty with Italy, May 4, 1948, No. 280; Execution Proceedings on Property of Foreign States in the F.P.R.Y., July 11, 1952, No. 474; Settlement of Property Relations Arising from the Loss of Rights and the Duties of Yugoslav Citizens Due to International Agreements, December 31, 1957, No. 713.

35 Radio, Theaters, Motion Pictures

Radiobroadcasting Stations, November 28, 1955, No. 550; Establishment of Radiobroadcasting Stations and their Work, December 23, 1957, No. 681; Theaters, April 11, 1956, No. 151; Motion Pictures, April 18, 1956, No. 158.

36 Social Security and War Veterans

Social Security, May 2, 1945, No. 265; superseded, July 26, 1946, No. 467; Social Security of Workers and Employees, January 21, 1950, No. 72; amended, January 17, 1951, No. 53; February 28, 1951, No. 120; October 8, 1951, No. 429; Health Insurance for Laborers and Employees, December 8, 1954, No. 613; Retirement Pensions, December 11, 1957, No. 629; amended, November 5, 1958, No. 749; July 8, 1959, No. 490; December 2, 1959, No. 768; March 15, 1961, No. 120; Disabled War Veterans, May 25, 1946, No. 295; amended, December 2, 1947, No. 779; January 24, 1950, No. 138 and 139; January 17, 1951, No. 53; October 8, 1951, No. 429, July 10, 1957, No. 449; November 5, 1958, No. 750; October 21, 1959, No. 693; December 2, 1959, No. 767; March 15, 1961, No. 121; December 30, 1961, No. 761; Professional Rehabilitation of War Veterans, September 30, 1960, No. 533; amended, March 15, 1961, No. 133; Veterans Disabled in Peacetime, December 21, 1946, No. 727; amended, December 2, 1947, No. 779; October 19, 1959, No. 694; Unified Text, November 11, 1959, No. 738.

37 Statute of Limitations

Statute of Limitations of Claims, September 30, 1953, No. 324; amended, December 31, 1954, No. 673.

38 Territorial Waters

Territorial Waters, December 1, 1948, No. 876.

39 Trade, Domestic and Foreign

Specification of Goods Subject to Planned Distribution and Consumption, May 12, 1945, No. 282; Private Retail Stores, May 5, 1948, No. 288; repealed, November 16, 1954, No. 615; Creation of Commercial Enterprises, January 23, 1952, No. 49; superseded, Commercial Enterprises and Stores, December 23, 1953, No. 483; Commercial Activities and Commercial Enterprises and [Retail] Stores, July 30, 1955, No. 430; amended, January 3, 1957, No. 6; June 8, 1957, No. 302; July 19, 1957, No. 402; December 23, 1957, No. 680; March 26, 1958, No. 192; April 23, 1958, No. 303; August 5, 1959, No. 579; Unified Text, December 9, 1959, No. 801; amended, March 2, 1960, No. 117; May 11, 1960, No. 245; April 5, 1961, No. 197; July 12, 1961, No. 465; Government Supervision of Imports and Exports, March 20, 1945, No. 162; superseded, Supervision of Exports and Imports, January 22, 1948, No. 53; Export and Import Transactions Made for One's Own Benefit, March 31, 1954, No. 159; Corrections on Applications for Import and Export of Goods, September 20, 1961, No. 592; Foreign Trade Arbitration Under the Chamber of Commerce of the F.P.R.Y., March 28, 1947, No. 185; June 26, 1958, No. 558; Procedure for the Settlement [of Claims] by Foreign Trade Arbitration Under the Chamber of Commerce of the F.P.R.Y., October 16, 1948, No. 860; Procedure for Expert Tests Under the Chamber of Commerce of the F.P.R.Y., October 16, 1948, No. 861; Foreign Trade Transactions, December 23, 1953, No. 469; affirmed, January 29, 1954, No. 96; amended, April 6, 1954, No. 184; May 6, 1954, No. 217; both affirmed, December 30, 1954, No. 676; amended, June 7, 1955, No. 264; affirmed, November 10, 1955, No. 531; November 18, 1959, No. 756; December 30, 1959, No. 865; June 29, 1960, No. 358; December 27, 1961, No. 731; Yugoslav Bank for Foreign Trade, June 29, 1955, No. 288; amended, March 24, 1956, No. 131; August 2, 1961, No. 530.

AUTHOR INDEX

Arabic numerals following a reference indicate the consecutive numbers of works in this bibliography; numerals in italics refer to pages.

TITLE INDEX

Arabic numerals following a reference indicate the consecutive numbers of works in this bibliography; numerals in italics refer to pages. Only those titles are entered here for which no author is indicated.

SUBJECT INDEX

Arabic numerals following a reference indicate the consecutive numbers of works in this bibliography; those in italics refer to pages. For material dealing with Bosnia and Herzegovina, Croatia, Slavonia and Dalmatia, Macedonia, Montenegro, Serbia, Slovenia and Voyvodina, see under these headings.

St, Naum. *See* Church and State.
Stagno. *See* Ston.
State, Protection of
287, 288, 2409f
Stateless Persons. *See* Nationality.
Statute of Limitations. *See* Civil
Law; Contracts and Torts.
Ston. *See* Government, Local.
Supreme Administrative Tribunal.
See Administrative Tribunals.

Tapija. *See* Land Title Register;
Serbia, land title register.
Taxation. *See also* Financial Law
and Budget, fiscal execution, fiscal fees.
copyright, 298
corporate tax, 1600
direct, 1592–1593, 1598b, 1599,
1601, 1602a, 1604, 2390
excise tax, 1594, 1602b
general, 297, 298, 1587, 1588a,
1603, 1607a, 1608, 1610–1611,
1615–1619, 2333, 2402
income tax, 297, 298, 1590
inheritance and gift taxes, 297,
298, 1588b, 1606
land tax, 297, 298
local taxes and fees, 298, 1607b
payroll tax, 298, 1597
property, 298
sales tax, 1591, 1605
Teachers. *See* Education, general.
Territorial Waters. *See* International Law, Public.
Theaters and Motion Pictures
305
Torts. *See* Contracts and Torts.
Tourism. *See* Education; Physical
Culture and Tourism, general.
Trade. *See* Domestic Trade; Foreign
Trade.
Trade Unions. *See* Labor.
Trademarks. *See* Patents and Trade-
marks.
Transportation and Traffic. *See also*
Contracts and Torts, torts; In-
surance Law; International Law,
Public; Labor, wages and salaries;
Maritime Law.

aviation, 289, 1126–1128, 1128[1],
1129, 1129[1], 2302, 2335. *See also*
Airspace; International Law,
Public.
general, 2075, 2078, 2079a, 2080–
2081
motor vehicles, 2074
railways, 2067–2073, 2079b
roads, 2076–2077
traffic violations, 997a
Treaties, International. *See also*
Bosnia and Herzegovina, annexa-
tion of; History of Law, international law, public; Letters Roga-
tory; Occupation, Foreign.
agreements and treaties, 9, 292,
302, 305, 216–218, 1079, 1093b
arbitration and conciliation,
2244b
collections of, 203–209, 215, 219–
223, 225–226, 2278b, 2345b
concordat, 1072, 1269, 1270a,
1271, 1273, 1279–1280, 2319c,
2334
concordats, collection of, 1102
copyright, 1903b
emigration and immigration,
1077
fishery, 2301
labor, 2283
nationality, 2397
negotiable instruments, 1869,
1886a
Trials
general, 900, 919, 2089, 2091,
2097
political, 2082–2088, 2090, 2092–
2096, 2098–2100, 2237–2241,
2241[1], 2242, 2258, 2273, 2326,
2354, 2416, 2450
Trieste. *See* International Law, Public, frontier problems.
Trogir. *See* Government, Local.
Turopolje. *See* Government, Local.

Underground Army
četniks, 6
partisans, 7
Unfair Competition
287, 2101–2106